Homo Mimeticus III
PLASTICITY, MIMESIS AND METAMORPHOSIS
WITH CATHERINE MALABOU

Homo Mimeticus III

PLASTICITY, MIMESIS AND METAMORPHOSIS
WITH CATHERINE MALABOU

Edited by
Nidesh Lawtoo
and
Willow Verkerk

Leuven University Press

This project has received funding from the European Research Council (ERC) under the European Union's Horizon 2020 research and innovation programme (grant agreement n°716181: Homo Mimeticus, www.homomimeticus.eu)

The publication of this book was supported by the KU Leuven Fund for Fair Open Access.

This book is published in Open Access thanks to support by the Open Book Collective. For details on the supporting institutions participating in the Open Book Collective, see www.lup.be/obc.

Published in 2025 by Leuven University Press / Presses Universitaires de Louvain / Universitaire Pers Leuven. Minderbroedersstraat 4, B-3000 Leuven (Belgium).

Selection and editorial matter © 2025, Nidesh Lawtoo and Willow Verkerk
Individual chapters © 2025, the respective authors

All TDM (Text and Data Mining) rights reserved.

This book is published under a Creative Commons Attribution Non-Commercial Non-Derivative 4.0 License. For more information, please visit https://creativecommons.org/share-your-work/cclicenses/

Attribution should include the following information:
Nidesh Lawtoo and Willow Verkerk (eds), *Homo Mimeticus III: Plasticity, Mimesis and Metamorphosis with Catherine Malabou*. Leuven: Leuven University Press, 2025. (CC BY-NC-ND 4.0)

All images are expressly excluded from the CC BY-NC-ND 4.0 license covering the rest of this publication. Permission for reuse should be sought from the rightsholders.

ISBN 978 94 6270 500 5 (Paperback)
ISBN 978 94 6166 724 3 (ePDF)
ISBN 978 94 6166 725 0 (ePUB)
https://doi.org/10.11116/9789461667250
D/2025/1869/46
NUR: 736

Layout: Crius Group
Cover design: Anton Lecock
Cover illustration: *Transfigurations IV: Self-Fashioning Figura*, aquarelle on paper, 2025 © Michaela Lawtoo.

The clay is soft and malleable.
Quick! hurry to fashion it on that potter's wheel
which is forever spinning.

Aulus Persius Flaccus in Montaigne, *Essays*

CONTENTS

Introduction: Morphing Mimetic Studies   9
Nidesh Lawtoo and Willow Verkerk

Prologue: The Four Metamorphoses of Plasticity: Proteus to Figura, Self-Care to the Overhuman   43
Nidesh Lawtoo

PART I — GENEALOGIES OF MIMETIC PLASTICITY   75

Chapter 1: Epigenetic Mimesis: Natural Brains and Synaptic Chips   77
Catherine Malabou

Chapter 2: Plasticity, Mimesis, Transformativity: A Genealogy of Theories of Change   87
Tom Boland

Chapter 3: Material Mimetism: On Plastics, Plasticity and Mimesis   109
Alice Iacobone

Chapter 4: Negative Plasticity and the Indifference of the Body   129
Kristian Schaeferling

PART II — PLASTIC ENCOUNTERS AND MIMETIC STUDIES   151

Chapter 5: Benjamin's Great Criminal, a Plastic Mime   153
Gabriel Wartinger

Chapter 6: To Double Mimesis Bound: Mortal Plasticity between Malabou and Lacoue-Labarthe   171
Alex Obrigewitsch

Chapter 7: Eroticism, Gender and the Possibility For Transformation: With and Beyond Merleau-Ponty   187
Ida Djursaa

Chapter 8: Mimesis, Resonance and the Subject: A Critical Comparison   209
Mathijs Peters

PART III — FROM NEUROLITERATURE TO THE MIMETIC SUBCONSCIOUS   235

Chapter 9: Semiosis and Mimesis   237
Sergey Zenkin

Chapter 10: Neuroliterature and the Example   251
Tyler M. Williams

Chapter 11: Proust, Realism and the Plasticity of Natural Signs   273
Ian James

Chapter 12: Conflicting Subliminalities: The Other Ancestors of Mimesis   293
Catherine Malabou

Coda: The Three Metamorphoses of Mimesis: Thinking with Catherine Malabou   305
Catherine Malabou and Nidesh Lawtoo

Notes on Contributors   327

INTRODUCTION

MORPHING MIMETIC STUDIES

Nidesh Lawtoo and Willow Verkerk

This is the third volume of a trilogy on *Homo Mimeticus*, but it does not aim to bring mimetic studies to an end. On the contrary, the overarching ambition of this series of books is to mark a new beginning. Going beyond previous mimetic theories structured around triangular forms with universal aspirations still dominant in the past century, the *Homo Mimeticus* trilogy sets in motion the pluralist field of mimetic studies, the goal of which is to track the plastic metamorphoses of mimesis already underway in the present century. Despite these transformations, or rather because of them, one point seems clear: never have studies on *Homo sapiens*' tendency to imitate others—be they human or nonhuman, embodied or digital, consciously or unconsciously, actively or passively, for good or ill—been more urgent than now. From viral contagion to emotional contagion, crowd behavior to (new) fascist identifications, algorithmic bubbles to conspiracy theories, CG images to deepfakes, online influencers to AI simulations, among other forms of digital phantoms, what the ancients called, enigmatically, *mimēsis* continues to cast—from behind new metamorphic masks—a long material shadow on the present and future.

Mimetic studies provides new theoretical foundations to account for the protean, innovative, but also troubling metamorphoses of mimesis that take possession of contemporary subjects. Revitalizing the ancient practice of the agon, or contest, already central to influential accounts of *homo ludens*, the first two volumes of *Homo Mimeticus* aimed high: they picked up a massive concept (*mimēsis*) that traverses the entire history of western civilization—from antiquity to modernity—to propel it further into the future. If mimesis generated an "ancient quarrel" (Plato 1963, 607b) between philosophy and literature at the dawn of aesthetics, our hypothesis is that to be properly theorized this literary-philosophical concept benefits from both the *logos* of philosophy and the *pathos* of art—and, conversely, it needs both the *logos* of art and what Friedrich Nietzsche called "the pathos of philosophy," to go beyond ancient quarrels and face the hypermimetic challenges of the present and future. It is thus from this dynamic, sometimes agonistic, but always productive interplay between reason and affect, *logos* and *pathos*, that we propose a contemporary reevaluation of mimesis understood as a troubling patho(-)logy—that is, both as a contagious sickness (or pathology) and as a diagnostic account (*logos*) of the power of affect (*pathos*).

What was true for previous volumes remains true for the present one. We continue to join forces with influential philosophical-literary figures that played a pivotal role in the theoretical turns that dominated the past half-century—from the linguistic turn to the ethical turn, the affective turn to the cognitive turn, the new materialist turn to the neuro turn. And we do so by *re-*turning to the ancient, modern and still contemporary realization that humans are imitative creatures, for good and ill. In this process, the trilogy provides new conceptual and theoretical foundations to account for the birth, development and ongoing transformations of a subject matter that cannot be contained within a stabilizing unitary form, static figure or transcendental theory. Instead, it adopts different patho-*logical* perspectives to track the metamorphoses of homo mimeticus now under the lens of a transdisciplinary field of study we call mimetic studies.

The three volumes propose three steps for an open-ended and fast-growing field of exploration. In the process, they adopt a flexible, dynamic and perspectival approach adequate to outline the twists and turns of the moving subject at hand. For this and other reasons, then, the *Homo Mimeticus* trilogy does not propose a unitary mimetic theory structured within a singular triangular form; rather, each volume proposes a series of dynamic and interconnected steps forward for new mimetic studies that are already on their way.

Three Steps for Mimetic Studies

For the reader who joins *in medias res,* let us briefly retrace the general trajectory of these steps. Volume 1 of *Homo Mimeticus* sailed by, on the one side, the Scylla of theories of mimesis that, since Plato and Aristotle, have tended to restrict this concept to the logic of visual representation, and on the other, the Charybdis of mimetic theories that have framed mimesis in a triangular structure of mimetic desires and rivalries. As the subtitle indicates, its goal was to develop a "new theory of imitation" that joins philosophy, aesthetics and politics to provide theoretical foundations for the transdisciplinary field of mimetic studies. *Homo Mimeticus II* is an edited collection of essays that furthers contemporary "*re*-turns to mimesis" in the company of influential theorists and emerging scholars working across disciplines, such as philosophy, literary theory, media studies, environmental studies, new materialism and political theory; together, they broaden and deepen the genealogy of homo mimeticus from antiquity to modernity, reaching into the present. These two main steps were accompanied by several special issues in mimetic studies that further broadened the reach of this fast-expanding field. They included contributions by some of the most influential thinkers in the humanities writing today in areas as diverse as philosophy (Jean-Luc Nancy, Gunter Gebauer), sociology (Edgar Morin), feminism (Adriana Cavarero), literary studies (J. Hillis Miller), anthropology (Christoph Wulf), political theory (William E. Connolly), gender studies (Judith Butler), the history of psychology (Mikkel Borch-Jacobsen), and posthuman studies (N. Katherine Hayles), among others who joined forces to promote the mimetic turn or, as we also called it, *re*-turn.[1]

Homo Mimeticus III builds on these emerging developments in mimetic studies and extends the field towards unexplored territories. It does so via a plurality of diverse essays—ranging from philosophy to literary theory, aesthetics to sociology, psychology to the neurosciences—whose shared goal, as the subtitle says, is to account for the genealogical relations connecting "plasticity, mimesis and metamorphosis." A repetition with a difference should thus be apparent to the reader who has been following the previous steps in this mini-series: volume 1 ended with the eminent centennial sociologist and theorist of complexity Edgar Morin, who joined hands by adding homo mimeticus to a long list of all-too-human designations that—from *homo economicus* to *homo ludens*, *homo faber* to *homo demens*, *homo religiosus* to *homo digitalis*—add complexity to the rationalist ideal of *Homo sapiens*; volume 2 ended with a dialogue with neuroscientist Vittorio Gallese, one of the discoverers of mirror neurons in the 1990s, who recognized the importance of philosophical physicians such as Nietzsche in paving the way for this revolutionary scientific finding. In the process, Gallese joined mimetic studies, calling for more transdisciplinary collaborations to move beyond dualistic binaries that too often simply contrast the brain with the mind, the body with the soul and, by extension, the neurosciences with the humanities. As an extension of this collaborative gesture, we now *re*-turn to a contemporary philosopher who, over the past decades, has gone beyond ossified "two-culture" oppositions to promote dialogues between philosophy and the neurosciences. She did so by explicitly developing the concept of "plasticity" in relation to its neurological counterpart, "neuroplasticity," to account for the brain's "capacity to *receive form* [...] and to *give form*" (Malabou 2008, 5).[2] In the process, she also implicitly lent support to the fundamental hypothesis of homo mimeticus: namely, that we are embodied, relational and metamorphic creatures who are both vulnerable to passive forms of imitation and capable of active, innovative, but still mimetic transformations of the brain, and thus also of the body. Furthering an account of the "plasticity of mimesis" (Lawtoo 2022, 129–155) initiated in volume 1, we are thus delighted to pursue our inquiry into the plastic metamorphoses of mimesis in the company of the French philosopher Catherine Malabou.

The genealogical continuities between the concept of mimesis as defined by mimetic studies and the concept of plasticity as defined by Malabou are striking, manifold and productive. They are already constitutive of a *homo plasticus-mimeticus* configuration that must now be rethought as part of a longer and complex genealogical relation, rather than in autonomous isolation. In fact, there seems to be a disconcerting specular, if not speculative, relation between the concept of plasticity as Malabou theorizes it and that of mimesis as we understand it. This mirroring relation can be schematically outlined as follows: both concepts traditionally originate in aesthetics, yet in recent years they have turned out to play a central role in subject formation and transformation; both are old concepts that have been relegated to the margins of philosophy and the humanities for a long time, yet they have been receiving renewed attention thanks to recent developments in other fields, such as the neurosciences, molecular biology and artificial intelligence; both tend to be restricted to their devalued, passive and adaptable sides that lead plastic-mimetic subjects to simply reproduce, adapt to or be impressed by a pre-existing form or model. Yet, at a closer look, they turn out to be Janus-faced concepts also endowed with an active, productive and creative side generative of new formations, transformations or—to use a concept dear to both Malabou and mimetic studies—metamorphoses. Finally, both have pathological and disruptive consequences on a multiplicity of levels: individually and collectively, psychically and ethically, politically and ontologically. And yet, at the same time, and without contradiction, the plasticity of mimesis also generates critical and therapeutic thoughts that cut across obsolete nature/culture divides to account for a plurality of emerging phenomena: from passive adaptation to active imitation, from epigenetic subject formation to neoliberal exploitations, from crowd behavior to erased feminine pleasures, from (new) fascist phantoms to AI simulations, among other metamorphic subjects that speak to present and future generations.

If we are correct in our genealogical observation that mimesis is a plastic concept and plasticity is a mimetic concept—and this volume suggests this is the case—then there is no one better placed than Malabou to help us further the metamorphic transformations of homo mimeticus in the twenty-first century. It is in fact well known that Malabou's work is, as Ian James puts it, "consistently organized around the elaboration of a single guiding concept: that of *plasticity*" (2012, 83). It is in-*formed,* or given form, by perspectives as diverse as Hegelian phenomenology, Heideggerian ontology, Derridean deconstruction, new materialism, psychoanalysis and its precursors, feminism, and, last but not least, the neurosciences and molecular biology. The concept of plasticity has already received significant attention in recent years, propelling Malabou to the forefront of the philosophical scene as "a multifaceted philosophical personality" (2012, 4).[3] It also led Malabou to "reread certain texts from the past" so as to revitalize, and reveal that not only is it "loaded with a literary promise," it is also endowed with performative properties entailing the "exemplification of itself" (2022a, 313, 310). Malabou is speaking of plasticity of course, but exactly the same could be said about mimesis: that is, an old literary-philosophical concept that led us to reread ancient texts to reveal the performative properties, or rather improprieties, of a chameleon concept exemplifying mimetism itself, be they at play in literary, philosophical or post-literary (cinematic, digital, computer-generated) texts. It is thus perhaps not surprising that, in recent years, Malabou's philosophical personality (from Latin *persona*, mask worn in the theater) has turned to mimetic subjects as well. Either under the rubric of "identification" (2015), "AI simulation" (2017), "mirroring" and "phantom limbs" (2022b), or, more recently, in a chapter also included in this volume, with the title "epigenetic mimesis" (2023), mimetic subject matters turn out to inform Malabou's work via genealogies internal to mimetic studies.

The mirroring continuities that started an inquiry into the plasticity *of* mimesis (genitive reading in both senses) now call for furthering the bridge between Malabou's new materialist turn to plasticity and the mimetic turn, or *re*-turn to homo mimeticus. As Malabou herself recognizes, the question of "*return* in general" and "repetition" in particular "has become our topic" (Malabou 2015, 69), perhaps because the phantom of mimesis now haunts both human and nonhuman life. Thus, she gratefully acknowledges in the Coda to this volume that mimetic studies contributed to "making her aware of this concept" beyond its usual definition of copy or representation. Addressing both the question of "biomimicry" that concluded *Homo Mimeticus II* and the question of "posthuman mimesis" mimetic studies explored elsewhere,[4] Malabou goes on to extend the reaches of mimesis beyond the human, as she recognizes: "Even computers today try to imitate brain functioning" (70). This is certainly true at the level of what used to be considered a distinguishing human capacity, namely the generation of language, via AI chatbots like GPT-5—the latest iteration as we write—that, for Malabou, can no longer be dismissed as a passive or restricted imitation deprived of intelligence. If computers' hypermimetic simulations cannot approximate embodied, sensorial and above all self-conscious forms of imitations characteristic of humans, they certainly are already updating posthuman biotechnological supplements central to what Malabou also calls "epigenetic mimesis."

As the concept of metamorphosis suggests, this book takes an immanent and embodied approach inspired by the biological world of animal mimicry already explored in volume 1 to think about human, posthuman and technological mimesis. Linking both the mimetic and the anti-mimetic tendencies that set mimetic studies in motion to the problematic of metamorphosis, Malabou specifies: "Metamorphosis is at once mimicry of the other identifying with the other, the creation of a gap, of a limit to identification and to contact" (2022a, 121). At the most general, but also most fundamental level, metamorphosis is thus both mimetic and anti-mimetic; it inclines the subject toward the other while at the same time setting up a limiting distance generating a paradoxical double movement that sets mimetic studies in motion. Hence the need to recognize both the *pathos* of mimetic identification that unconsciously pulls the metamorphic self toward the other, be it human or nonhuman, and the conscious *distance* of critique and resistance that sets up a limit to the powers of mimesis to transform the self or subject.[5] In many ways, then, what Malabou says of cloning equally applies to the way we think of mimesis more generally: "The question [...] is no longer one of knowing how to differentiate between two individuals who resemble each other but of knowing how to interrogate the way in which the same transfers itself to remain the same in the other" (2022a, 38). A classical name for this transfer of the same into the other is, of course, mimesis, a contagious affect that is not based on auto-affection; rather, it opens the self or ego to the pathos of the other, generating what we called in volume 2, echoing Bataille, "mimetic heterology."[6] Malabou, echoing Derrida, calls it "hetero-affection" (2022a, 245).

The diagnostic effects of mimetic hetero-affections are at least double depending on whether the emphasis is on the homology or heterology of mimetic affects. On the one hand, this transfer of an identity that is not one risks turning the self, or ego, into a phantom of the ego without proper qualities. It does so via a passive logic of imitation that is not deprived of pathological dangers, as indicated since the dawn of mimetic studies. Such a pathology is also explained via the logic of mimetic rivalry and violence, which now plays a key role in the rise of (new) fascist pathologies.[7] On the other hand, this mimetic transfer is not necessarily passive and reproductive; it can also rest on a paradoxical metamorphic logic that is central to the paradox of mimesis animating homo mimeticus. As Malabou puts it: "Between the one and the other, the space of metamorphosis unfolds. Paradoxically, distance only results from the shifting identification with others, from the possibility of being everyone without being anyone in particular" (2022a, 119). As we already saw in volume 1, a lack of proper identity that leads the subject to be "no one in particular" is not always disabling and pathological. As Philippe Lacoue-Labarthe, the French philosopher and precursor of mimetic studies, indicated, a turn from a passive reproductive mimesis to an active productive mimesis is also at the heart of a paradoxical logic, or "hyperbologic," that leads the subject who is no one to "become everyone" (Lacoue-Labarthe 1989, 258–266). Malabou now relies on the same paradoxical logic to account for AI simulations that are almost the same as natural originals, but not quite. As she puts it in *Morphing Intelligence*: "The more the artificial imitates the biological, the more it reveals their incommensurability" (Malabou 2019, 159)—the more it imitates, the more it differs. This is, indeed, the paradoxical logic of mimetic agonism, which is also the patho-*logic* mimetic studies has been furthering all along.

Be it human or nonhuman, neurological or biological, pathological or patho-*logical*, mimetic repetition is indeed our topic in the pages that follow. It re-emerges in a different form if we address metamorphoses of homo mimeticus in an age of fast transformations that do not simply require the pathos of passive, unconscious adaptation but also the conscious distance of critical resistance. As Edgar Morin also recognizes, metamorphoses "are for the most part the product of unconscious processes" but they also require "the rescue of human consciousness" (2008, 2400; our trans.). As the contributions in the volume will show, their mirroring interplay is already subjecting the concepts of mimesis and of plasticity to a metamorphosis that furthers the heterogeneous field of mimetic studies.

Plastic Metamorphoses of Mimesis

Even a cursory look at the table of contents should make clear from the subject matter at hand that this genealogical mirror between plasticity and mimesis does not aim to reproduce a static image, or *imago*, which would passively copy, or represent, the so-called original. The hierarchy in-*forming* the original/copy metaphysical binary and their numerous avatars—truth/falsity, universal/particular, reality/appearance, mind/body, conscious/nonconscious, but also masculine/feminine, white/Black, colonizer/colonized, heterosexual/homosexual, natural/artificial among others—is what both the new materialist turn and the mimetic *re*-turn aim to displace. As Malabou rightly stresses in her chapter on "Epigenetic Mimesis"[8] reprinted in this volume: "The old, Platonic notion of 'mimesis' is not relevant any longer to characterize such a relationship [between the natural and the artificial], as it limits imitation or simulation to the simple act of copying" (2023, 180). The phantom of imitation qua false representation is of course still in circulation, yet it does not tell the complete truth about Plato's diagnostic of mimesis.

It is thus important to qualify Malabou's critique of Plato to push the plasticity-mimesis connection further in this volume. What the French philosopher objects to is the old dominant model of mimesis understood as a realistic, purely visual and transparent "mirror" (Plato 1963, 596d) or representation of nature qua phenomenal world. As is well known, for Plato this type of visual mimesis generates an "imitation of a phantasm" (598b), which, as we showed in volume 2, is far from transparent in the first place.[9] This is, indeed, the same dominant representational model the mimetic turn pushes against, if only because it casts a long shadow on the history of western aesthetics and thought more generally—stretching to include the neurosciences as well. Even some of the thinkers that directly inspire Malabou's thought on plasticity—most notably Hegel and Jean-Pierre Changeux—reproduce this old Platonic definition we are aiming to overcome. No wonder it is still in circulation. Since this bias goes beyond two-culture divides and applies to both philosophical and scientific influences, let us consider both sides.

On the philosophical side, in his *Introductory Lectures of Aesthetics* (1835), Hegel resurrects the ancient Platonic notion of mimesis qua "imitation of nature [*Nachahmung der Natur*]" and redoubles the critique for the moderns. Thus, he argues that according to this mimetic principle, "the essential purpose of art consists in imitation [*Nachahmung*], in the sense of a facility in copying [*nachzubilden*] natural forms as they exist" (Hegel 2004, 47). Even in the case of famous classical painters like Zeuxis, whose painting of grapes was so realistic as to deceive birds, copying nature generates what Hegel calls "*superfluous* labor [überflüssige *Bemuhung*]" (47) for mimetic art simply dubs a reality that is already there, and imperfectly so. In classical Platonic fashion, the German philosopher then proceeds to dismiss mimetic art as producing "*one-sided* deceptions," generating a "semblance of reality" (47) that he considers inferior to nature leading to a "failure of imitation [*Misslingen des Nachbildens*] [...] when contrasted with the original in nature" (48). Much better, for Hegel, would be for humans to "be prouder of having invented the hammer, the nail, and so forth, than of achieving feats of mimicry" (49). Realistic art is thus considered inferior to the original, whatever and wherever the original may be. Hence he severely and figuratively concludes: "In general, we may sum up by saying that, as a matter of mere imitation [*blößer Nachahmung*], art cannot maintain a rivalry [*Wettstreit*] with nature and, if it tries, must look like a worm trying to crawl after an elephant" (48).

Granted. This is after all, the repetition of an old quarrel, or rather, agon. And yet, as the example of the hammer also pinpoints, this does not mean that mimesis might not be a play in different, more inventive and productive, but still imitative forms. After all, the hammer is now considered a classic example of what philosophers of technology group under the rubric of "biomimicry." As Henry Dicks reminds us, according to Ernst Kapp "the basic function of technological artifacts [...] is to extend the reach and power of the human body" (2023, 85). How? By mimesis, or better, biomimicry. Thus, Dicks continues: "the hammer replicates the form of the forearm and fist, the spade the arm and outstretched palm" (85). This is a type of mimicry that may not be conscious of imitating in the technological act of creation itself, but it is still mimetic while not being narrowly realistic. Even from the example Hegel convokes, then, beyond the ideal of genial originality may always lurk the phantom of a different, more unconscious, embodied and immanent mimesis that cannot be simply restricted to realistic imitation—which leads to the second, and this time more scientific, perspective.

On the side of neurosciences, Jean-Pierre Changeux is mostly known for his bestselling *Neuronal Man* (1983), a book that sparked interest in the brain well beyond the confines of the neurosciences and directly informs Malabou's account of plasticity and epigenetics. For the moment, suffice it to note that on his side, Changeux has also been engaging with the humanities on topics such as ethics, epistemology and aesthetics. Thus, in a more recent book titled *The Good, the True, and the Beautiful* (2008), Changeux devotes a few illuminating pages that summarize the role of mimesis in western definitions of the beautiful. Innovative in his genealogical bridge between the neurosciences and aesthetics, he remains nonetheless trapped within the old Platonic/Hegelian definition of mimesis qua representation, as he writes, for instance, that, "for the neurobiologist, this question of *mimesis* is bound to visual perception [*perception visuelle*]" (2008, 109; our trans.). Changeux then recapitulates the Platonic account of mimesis as an "imitation—copy—of external reality" that restricts the "artist's production to a copy of a copy, a simulacrum," specifying that, for Hegel, mimetic art is simply a "caricature of life" (106). We are thus back, once again, to the old Platonic definition both Malabou and the mimetic turn aim to move beyond.

And yet, while adopting the definition of mimesis as representation, Changeux does not support its negative Platonic/Hegelian ontological evaluation. Thus, this time drawing on Aristotle, he inverts their devaluation by specifying that mimesis can also play an active role in bridging the binary dividing nature and culture. He does so by implicitly drawing on a passage in Aristotle's *Physics* where mimesis is not only defined as representation of nature but also as its completion. As Aristotle puts it in book 2: "generally art [*technē*] in some cases completes what nature cannot bring to a finish, and in others imitates nature [*technē mimeitai ten phusin*]" (1991, 199a 15–18). As we saw in volume 1, this is the paradox that sets Philippe Lacoue-Labarthe's mimetology in motion via a hyperbologic that turns passivity into activity, receiving form to giving form.[10] Changeux, however, is interested in deconstructing another binary as he mentions that, for Aristotle, "imitation prolongs nature and deserves our praise" (107). If *technē* prolongs *phusis,* the binary dividing art and nature, the symbolic and the biological, no longer holds, paving the way for a less hierarchical and collaborative relation between mimesis and nature that, contra the old Platonic notion, can be put to rational use. This is what Changeux also suggests as he turns to Aristotle's *Poetics* to specify: "Artistic activity is a natural tendency, source of pleasure, instrument of knowledge, so the profession deserves our praise. Mimesis does not deceive us [*la mimèsis ne nous trompe pas*]" (107). Thus, a mimetic pathology that operates on the irrational side of the soul generating *pathos* turns into a patho-*logy* that can be put to rational and logical use.

Valuable in countering the Platonic/Hegelian condemnation of mimesis as false visual appearance and in praising its active cognitive role central to understanding, Changeux may thus still explicitly rely on the old notion of mimesis understood as representation. Yet, between the lines, he also implicitly encourages more active and productive conceptions of mimesis developed by the theory of homo mimeticus. For instance, in his account of the role of "empathy" in art, he draws on Theodor Lipps's famous definition of *"Einfühlung"* or empathy understood as an "'inner imitation' [*inner Nachahmung*],"[11] and sets out to defines art as an "'intersubjective symbolic communication with multiple and variable emotional contents' in which *empathy* intervenes as an 'intersubjective dialogue between figures'" (Changeux 2008, 135). True, the link between empathy and mimesis is made by Lipps, not by Changeux; and as we saw in volume 2, neuroscientists like Vittorio Gallese revitalize interest in Lipps by acknowledging him as a pioneer of the discovery of mirror neurons.[12] Summarizing Giacomo Rizzolatti (the head of the Parma group of which Gallese was part), Changeux also addresses mirror neurons, as he later specifies: "there is thus reciprocity in the recognition of the gestures of others, 'resonance' between partners who are engaged in a mutual dialogue, endowed with the capacity for imitation, and thus communication, of intentions" (247). Although Changeux deems the role mirror neurons play in the "imitation and communication of intentions" to be "very modest" (247)—an evaluation Malabou echoes in this volume—his account of empathy revitalizes *aísthēsis* (perception but also sensation) as "the science of sensation or feelings" (Hegel 2004, 3). Thus understood, mimetic studies is far from opposed to aesthetics. On the contrary, it reorients the science of feelings to account for plastic processes of becoming that go beyond conventional oppositions between art and life.[13] This science, we should also add, is animated by what Plato called *mimesis*, Nietzsche called Dionysian imitation, Lipps called inner imitation, Gallese calls mirror neurons, and, drawing on ancient, modern and contemporary insights that go beyond two-culture divides, we call mimetic pathos: that is, an intersubjective, embodied and relational affect that, as we shall see, remains at play in the patho(-)logical sides of homo mimeticus we pursue while thinking with Malabou.

In order to do so, a last genealogical reminder is in order. If the affective definition of aesthetics is still operative in Hegel and Changeux, it was explicitly tied to mimetic affects, or *pathē*, by that very old figure who initially tried to define mimesis in the first place. As we have stressed in previous volumes,[14] already for Plato mimesis is far from being restricted to representation alone. It is also, as we argued, above all a dramatic concept genealogically rooted in Dionysian, theatrical and quite protean impersonations (mimesis, from *mîmos*, actor and performance) with the power to affect and infect the very nature of spectators. As Plato makes clear in books 2 and 3 of the *Republic*, mimesis has the performative power to impress the plastic souls of spectators in such a fundamental way that it turns nature into what he already calls, prefiguring epigenetics, "second nature" (Plato 1963, 395d). Thus, in a passage discussed in detail in volume 1, he writes, behind the mask of Socrates: "Do you not know, then, that the beginning in every task is the chief thing, especially for any creature that is young and tender? For it is then that it is best molded and takes the impression that one wishes to stamp upon it?" (377ab). Indeed, we not only know it; we now also have empirical confirmations from neurobiology that cultural experiences can turn first (genetic) nature into a second (epigenetic) nature—for both good and ill. Lastly, we also know that this plasticity is not restricted to youth; rather, it continues—albeit less intensely—well into adulthood, morphing the plasticity of a homo mimeticus on the move.

Many have tried to pin mimesis down to a unifying logic of the same, be it an organic structure, a stable *imago*, a narrative plot or a familial triangle. Yet this metamorphic concept continues, to this day, to twist and turn, assuming different forms at will. Unsurprisingly so, since its primary characteristic has always been to transgress unitary identifications—generating plastic and quite protean metamorphoses. It is thus no accident that the philosopher who, in this volume, will join forces to keep up with the plastic transformations of mimesis is sensitive to a notion of "form" that is not stable, unitary or ideal. Instead, Malabou specifies that this form "comes to light like an a posteriori metamorphosis" (2022a, 29) requiring an act of plastic reading in the strong sense to be outlined, figured out or sculpted.

If the chapters that follow further mimetic studies via a plurality of conceptual masks that, thanks to Malabou's inspiring work, now include "plasticity" as well, our goal is not to stabilize, frame or unmask mimesis, let alone give a unitary form to plasticity. Rather, it is to keep up with the twists and turns of a mimetic/plastic subject endowed with paradoxical (im)properties. Homo mimeticus receives new forms via external impressions (or passive mimesis) and, at the same time, and without contradiction, gives form to itself as it puts imitation to transformative use (active mimesis). This *re*-turn, as we shall repeatedly confirm, is vital not only in reevaluating the forms that shaped humans in the past; it also helps us figure out what forms (post)humans can possibly assume via plastic metamorphoses oriented toward the future.

Mimesis, not unlike plasticity, is a performative concept in the sense that it is "itself" endowed with both mimetic and plastic properties. Appearing behind different masks and conceptual personae that change historically and are fashioned by different *technai*, mimesis is a concept on the move that adapts, chameleon-like, to different disciplinary backgrounds, remaining open to transformations that escape unitary definitions. And yet, as it keeps morphing into new forms and figures, it generates performative effects that go beyond good and evil; they can be just as damaging, life-negating and pathological as they can be vitalizing, life-affirmative and, as we call them, patho-*logical*. Critical of passive forms of mimetic adaptation that lead docile subjects to conform to dominant models, ideologies or technologies, mimetic studies also aims to promote life-affirmative transformations with patho-*logical* potential. In fact, these patho-logies focus on both the affective (*pathos*) and logical (*logos*) drives animating a relational, embodied and plastic species that is not only *sapiens* but also *mimeticus-plasticus* and, we should now add, *metamorphicus* as well.

These introductory reflections should make at least one point clear: there are many reasons for re-turning to uncover a different, non-representational and metamorphic notion of mimesis that has been forgotten in the past century but is currently contributing to rethinking numerous problems that haunt the twenty-first century. Malabou's critique of the dominant metaphysical notion of mimesis qua imitation of nature is apt and in line with the mimetic turn. What was true for mimesis, then, remains true for plasticity as well: a break with traditional metaphysics and the violent hierarchies it entails is the first necessary step to affirming these concepts' theoretical vitality for the future. This also means that the mirroring relation between plasticity and mimesis is not trapped within the stabilizing logic of visual representation; rather, it includes the troubling problematic of the formation and transformation of subjects—stretching to include new hypermimetic technological subjects like synaptic chips that transgress the subject/object, original/copy, natural/artificial, *phusis/technē* metaphysical binaries. It is this different, decentered, embodied and metamorphic mimesis that we foreground in *Homo Mimeticus III*. Within the variety of perspectives at play, there is an immanent, embodied and materialist philosophical perspective that—via new discoveries in the neurosciences, molecular biology and artificial intelligence—reaches into the present.

Epigenesis and Metamorphoses

The contemporary masks of mimesis have the power to form and transform the plastic figure of *homo mimeticus*, just as they transfigure the mimetic form of *homo plasticus*. As Joseph LeDoux puts it: "most systems of the brain are plastic, that is, modifiable by experience, which means that the synapses involved are changed by experience" (2002, 8). True, LeDoux may have gone too far in controversially claiming that "You are your synapses,"[15] for human brains only function in connection with a whole human body: without a body and all it entails (heart, lungs, limbic system, liver, etc.), our synapses could not exist. Yet we can readily agree with LeDoux's point that "learning involves the nurturing of nature" (9) if we consider that neuroplasticity includes the shaping of synaptic connections through learning and experience more generally. Note that this insight was already internal to key precursors of mimetic studies we encountered in previous volumes. Nietzsche, for instance speaks of an "*innate talent*" seemingly rooted in nature and immediately specifies: "but only a few are born with and trained to a sufficient degree of tenacity, persistence, and energy that any one of them really becomes a talent, that is, becomes what he [*sic*] *is*" (1995, 180). The much-misunderstood Nietzschean imperative to "become who you are" is thus not simply based on the nature of what one *is*; rather, it is based on a cultural training to *become* what one is via a formative principle that goes beyond nature and culture, as Malabou and Lawtoo will show in the Coda that concludes the volume.

Since the 1990s, we are better able to understand the power of culture to shape nature. As Changeux puts it, "there is no opposition between the natural and the cultural" (2008, 105; our trans.). Developments in molecular biology have shown that the "genetic envelop proper to the human brain—what we sometimes call 'human nature'—includes an 'epigenetic opening' [*ouverture épigénétique*] to the environment and thus to the genesis of cultures" (105). Humans turn out to be less determined by genetic programming than previously thought; the human brain is not a passive mirror of our genotype, so to speak. Rather, the synaptic connections that compose it remain open to what Changeux—using a term the biologist Conrad Waddington borrows from Aristotle—calls "epigenetic" transformations that are influenced by life experiences, including education, habits and our relation to the environment more generally.

Far from being a mere cultural garment, the subjects at the center of what were once called the humanities have far-reaching consequences for the formation and transformation of our species. Drawing on the etymology of the term epigenesis, Malabou specifies that "the prefix '*epi*' signifies above. 'Epigenesis' thus literally signifies 'above genesis,'" a "second genesis" (2014, 59). Plato would have said "second nature." And Malabou later specifies: "An important part of epigenetic factors comes from the environment, from the outside [...] from learning, milieu, habit, in a word, from experience" (140). This explains the classical example of mimetic subjects with the same genotype: namely, identical twins, who show a variability in phenotype due to different life experiences. As

Changeux puts it: "considerable variability, as in identical twins, remains, despite the genes' power," providing evidence that "culture makes its impression progressively" (1985, 247, 248).

Note that Changeux does not say that genes have no power whatsoever. As any parent with more than one child can readily attest, significant variations of character occur even if children bathe in the same cultural environment. Sometimes the genome is hard to bend; several generations went into making it. Moreover, as Moheb Costandi puts it: "individual brains may differ in their capacity for plastic changes, so that the same experiences could induce different extents of neuroplasticity, and different types of plastic changes, in different people" (2016, 154). Yet if genes continue to have the power to shape the brain, learning experiences have the power to sculpt the synapses forming the brain as well. This also means that if our hypothesis is correct and mimesis plays a key role not only in aesthetic representations of nature to be evaluated from a visual distance but also, and above all, in intersubjective human experiences driven by mimetic pathos such as learning, then epigenetics and the brain plasticity it generates find in mimesis a key metamorphic principle that deserves more consideration than it has received so far.

But, we might still wonder, what kind of mimesis continues to form and transform the plasticity of epigenetic brains open to a plurality of environmental influences? Are we dealing with a passive imitation that subjects the brain to external and potentially pathological impressions, as a long tradition from Plato to Lacoue-Labarthe warns us? Or are we confronted with active mimetic processes that are creative, re-productive and generative of affirmative and perhaps revolutionary transformations, as a tradition that goes from Aristotle to Malabou indicates? Or perhaps an intermixture of both? Jean-Pierre Changeux, in one of the most important chapters of *Neuronal Man*, titled "Epigenesis," writes: "Most of the synapses of the cerebral cortex are formed *after* birth. The fact that synapses continue to proliferate postnatally permits a progressive 'impregnation' of the cerebral tissue by the physical and social environment" (1985, 242). Opening up a question central to the humanities in general, he then adds, in a language familiar to mimetic studies in particular:

> How is this cultural imprint acquired? Does the environment "instruct" the brain by leaving its imprint, as a bronze seal does in a piece of wax? Or, on the contrary, does it simply selectively stabilize successive combinations of neurons and synapses as they appear spontaneously during development? (242)

Reformulated in the scientific language of contemporary neurobiology, this is indeed a key question that convokes a metaphoric language we have encountered before and runs, like an undercurrent, throughout the *Homo Mimeticus* trilogy. We saw in volume 1 that a philosophical tradition going back to Plato relies on the trope of the seal impressed on the malleable wax, which the ancient philosopher compares to the plasticity of the soul, turning nature into second nature. The metaphor is well chosen, for it emphasizes the plasticity of the brain and its receptivity to external impressions in terms now confirmed by both epigenetics and neuroplasticity. At the same time, like all metaphorical transfers, it is limited. In fact, the stamp of the "bronze seal" implies the impression of a unitary figure, or form, that once stamped on a wax-like subject matter has the potential to solidify and remain unchangeable over time. This is indeed a danger internal to neuroplasticity rendered progressively rigid due to habit and repetition. Still, the plasticity of the brain is not only passively subjected to repeating the same pattern impressed on a wax-like subject matter; it is also engaged in an active process of transformation via education and other cultural practices that keep generating differences. The ethologist and neurologist Boris Cyrulnik speaks thus of the "fabulous plasticity of humans," by which he means "the plasticity of the brain, which continues until advanced age, and the plasticity of the person, who remains changeable," and he adds: "when it comes to culture, its plasticity is so great that we could say that its only permanent trait is that it changes!" (1989, 198; our trans.). The same could be said of mimesis: its only permanent trait is that it changes.

That mimesis is part of this educative process of change is made clear via an example that goes beyond the human/nonhuman binary and draws inspiration from birds. Giving the example of sparrows' songs, Changeux reports: "Sparrow fledglings produce a great variety of syllables spontaneously, but they are also capable of imitating 'model' songs synthesized by a computer. They invent and improvise but also imitate." Since imitation constitutes almost half of the sparrow's repertoire, the conclusion is that, even for birds, a mimetic "education can lead to a considerable diversification of the song" (1985, 243). If we return to Changeux's question about cultural imprinting, then, the second option based on the brain's "selective" process of stabilization of "combinations of neurons and synapses" epigenetically shaped by experience sounds more realistic. Further, it is based on mimetic processes that, over time, do not lead to a repetition of sameness but to a progressive possibility of diversification. If we then recall Morin's hypothesis that "the birth of language and poetry" might have emerged from an "imitation of bird songs" (Lawtoo 2022, 309), then the interplay between nonhuman and human mimesis is bound to generate a proliferation of differences. In fact, if education already plays a role in sparrow songs, it is certainly central in the formation of human songs that imitate them among other nonhuman animals. In sum, on both side of the nature/culture divide, mimesis and plasticity both give form and receive form in a spiraling move that blurs the line between subject and object, activity and passivity, first nature and a second epigenetic nature.

In light of these plastic considerations, an attempt at self-critique is in order: we shall have to both revisit and go beyond the too linear, or rather vertical, image of the active seal impressed on passive wax. It would also be important for mimetic studies to find alternative images that capture the dynamic process of stabilization and differentiation. In the Prologue, for instance, we begin by reviewing a number of classical thinkers and writers who anticipate Hegel's linkage between plasticity and subjectivity by relying on the metaphor of the seal and wax to sculpt a plastic figure of homo mimeticus from antiquity to the Middle Ages. As we move via the Renaissance into modernity, a more dynamic and interactive metaphor begins to emerge. For instance, essayists like Michel de Montaigne retain the trope of clay from antiquity. Yet in a characteristic experimental and artistic move (as on the cover of this book) the clay is transferred onto a potter's wheel whose figurative movement is future oriented. Paradoxically, then, the movement of the spinning wheel both forms and transforms the plastic subject matter at hand giving form to a "self-fashioning figura," while also progressively stabilizing it, as the wheel of experience turns and returns, reaching, via the mimetic turn, into the present.

In her opening contribution, "Epigenetic Mimesis," Malabou adds that epigenesis now stretches, via a productive mimesis, to include the genesis of AI where synaptic chips find in the plasticity of the brain a model to imitate or creatively re-produce. She also agrees with mimetic studies that the performative powers of mimesis-plasticity operate in subliminal ways that are not under the full agentic control of consciousness and are, in this sense, *un*-conscious, or *sub*-conscious.[16] Pre-Freudian thinkers like Friedrich Nietzsche, the French philosopher-psychologist Pierre Janet, the psychologist Hippolyte Bernheim and the sociologist Gabriel Tarde, among other philosophical physicians,[17] deserve to be *re*-discovered in light of recent developments in the neurosciences as well, as Vittorio Gallese indicated in volume 2, and Malabou confirms in the present volume. In the process, plastic-mimetic subjects trouble foundational concepts in western thought like the subject, freedom, intelligence, consciousness, anarchism, automatism, pleasure, the unconscious—including, in a self-reflective move, both plasticity and mimesis. For these and other genealogical connections discussed in detail in the chapters that follow, there are ample reasons to explore the productive continuities between plasticity, mimesis and the protean metamorphoses they generate as they face each other—without simply mirroring one another.

In sum, given that the productive patho(-)logical interplay between plasticity and mimesis have been accumulating, there are now considerable reasons to thicken the genealogical connection between *homo mimeticus* and *homo plasticus* in view of morphing mimetic studies in the double sense of giving/receiving new forms. In her work, Malabou already prefigures a decisive "shift from plasticity to *metamorphosis*" (2010, 24) on the shoulders of Hegel, while also supplementing deconstruction and psychoanalysis. The contributions that follow set out to further this paradigmatic shift from the heterogeneous perspective of mimetic studies. From the interstices of philosophy and literature, media studies and cultural studies, phenomenology and deconstruction, sociology and semiology, among other perspectives, contributors broaden the genealogy of plastic figures from antiquity to modernity to reach into the present metamorphoses of intelligence Malabou urges us to consider.

Finally, if the concept of metamorphosis takes its inspiration from non-human animals, it is also because both plasticity and mimesis challenge the binary that once divided nature from culture, the biological from the symbolic and artificial from human intelligence. It troubles a set of reified dualisms such as mind/body, brain/body, self/others, stretching to include sexual pluralities via a gendered theory of mimesis that goes beyond man and woman in view of "changing difference" (Malabou 2014) as well.

The Plasticity of Gendered Mimesis

Malabou's *Changing Difference*, first published in English in 2011 (in French in 2009), questions the nature/culture debate of feminism, positing that both essentialist and anti-essentialist positions are crude and ineffective tools for conceptualizing "woman." If anything, Malabou writes, it is violence which "confers her being" (2011, 98). However, since gender theory and deconstruction together have claimed an absence of "woman," the shared violence that women experience can arguably be seen as violence against a non-being and thus may even be considered impossible. If woman, then, is a caesura or an absence of being, what does it mean to live as a woman? This is a question that the gendered supplement to homo mimeticus invites us to consider. As Malabou notes, the struggle for emancipation is not at all over and real living women still seek to liberate themselves from violence. Yet neither the notions of biology, as a metaphysics of substance, nor culture, as discourse, are adequate for defining the essence of "woman."

Malabou argues in *Changing Difference* and more recently in *Pleasure Erased* (2022) that we need not abandon the notion of essence but can instead return to its real philosophical meaning, which has been misconstrued, inadequately understood as a "presence" and "substance." Citing Heidegger and Hegel in the earlier text, more recently she has referenced the Greeks on this, writing:

> for the Greeks an essence (*eidos*) is movement, the dynamic of coming into presence or appearing. An essence, then, is anything but a nature or fixed instance. The fact that, through a subsequent metaphysical contraction, essence has become just that does not alter its originary plasticity. (Malabou 2022c, 70)

Malabou can be seen to rehabilitate the notion of essence through her account of plasticity, which thinks not only about the brain, and more recently AI, as malleable and metamorphic, but also about gender and sex as such. In *Changing Difference*, she writes about "an original biological malleability," also stating: "If sex were not plastic, there would be no gender" (2011, 138). In both this text and the more recent *Pleasure Erased*, Malabou explores the plasticity of sex and gender in dialogue with feminist and queer pioneers, mimetic thinkers such as Luce Irigaray and Judith Butler, who employ notions of a sexed "mimicry [*mimétisme*]" (Irigaray 1977, 147) or "mimetism," "psychic mimesis," or gender "imitation" (Butler 1993, 316) to rethink identity, becoming and resistance.[18] Building on these and other feminist figures like Adriana Cavarero,[19] we propose the term "gendered mimesis" to further this feminist genealogy from the angle of mimetic studies.

Irigaray's focus on feminine pleasure and writing (which employs a mimetic strategy and style to undermine psychoanalysis and the history of philosophy more broadly) provided the foundation, Malabou notes, for rethinking the body (2022c, 73–74) in terms we consider both mimetic and plastic. As Lawtoo points out, "mimesis is plastic in the sense that it gives form" via figures, symbols or models to "material plasticity" (2017, 1210). But not only this: in questioning the dualistic cultural models of man/subject/active and woman/object/passive, and attacking the phallocentric for erasure of the feminine and her pleasure, Irigaray opened the door for others to challenge the symbolic order by playing with mimetic critique. Her thinking is continuous with the supposition that mimesis has the potential to expose the transformability of symbolic expressions of power (being themselves mimetically formed). Irigaray's claim that the feminine does not exist within the phallocentric economy means that women constitute themselves through mimesis, behavioral forms of imitation that enact but also undermine masculine desire.[20] The notion that femininity as a gendered form of mimicry can reify and liberate was further developed by Judith Butler's notion of the performative, and they give Irigaray a special place in their account of gender in their seminal book *Gender Trouble*.

Malabou and Butler have been, and continue to be, in dialogue with one another about human subjectivity, with Malabou critiquing the notion of performativity for being insufficient. Interesting enough, the notion that gender is something that "has us" as a phantom or *pathos* to which we are pulled towards, and is something that we conceive to "have" as an active and rational self-expression, is explored by Butler in their account of gender as performative. In *Gender Trouble*, Butler follows the tradition of deconstruction, claiming that gender is something that we "do," and not something that we "are" (1999, 33). Their early writings on gender here are also distinctly Foucauldian, focusing on how gender norms shape identity through surveillance and control. Butler's writings on gender put forward a "disciplinary mimesis" in which "bodies are compelled through disciplinary measures to represent and incorporate the norms that oblige them as if they are an essential feature of their body" (Verkerk 2023, 5). This is a kind of "repetition-response" in which one interpolates the given gestures, values, adornments, habits, etc. of culture with the potential to create fissures that reveal new possibilities for identity and relationality. In this text, Butler's notion of gender is a form of mimetic play without an origin; what is conceived as a stable self is "performatively constituted by the very "expressions" that are said to be its results" (1999, 33). This performative is distinctively mimetic in the troubling, dramatic and protean sense we attribute to the term.

While Malabou acknowledges the importance of the Foucauldian discursive model adopted in Butler's writings on performativity, she aligns herself more closely with Paul Preciado, stating that performativity alone cannot explain gender. Malabou agrees that "gender has the subject," that there is fragility of the body to variant disciplinary logistics (2022c, 92–94), but in *Pleasure Erased* she focuses on the metamorphic potential of this rather than its oppressive contours. She suggests that there is an automatic unconscious quality to gender subjectivation, in which one is "had" by gender, initiated into a mechanical response—but Malabou focuses on the materiality of this response, referencing not only norms but pharmacological and prosthetic enhancements via Preciado (2022c, 93–94). For her the subject is more than their performativity; their being involves a "carnal plasticity" (a term she borrows from Preciado), in which the material realities of the body contribute to the "genesis of gender" (2022c, 94). Here Malabou has something new to say about sex. "Sex is precisely that interchange that enables traffic between the symbolic and material dimensions of the body" (2022c, 94). While the discursive impact of the technologies of gender is considerable, according to Malabou, they work together with the visceral and empirical dimension of the body to become, in plastic terms, sex.

In conversation with Malabou, and others, then, the expression "gendered mimesis" points to the task of rethinking the notions of not only gender and gendered subjectivation, but also sex and sexuality via mimetic studies. While transformation of these concepts has occurred, notions of sex, sexuality and gender are still haunted by the prioritization of hetero- and repro-normative concepts of the subject which, in the European lineage of philosophy, center rationalistic and masculine Kantian ideals of the Enlightenment. This androcentric version of the subject fails to account for our relational vulnerability, which is "mimetically inclined," as Adriana Cavarero would say, towards others—whether it be people, values, ideas, aesthetic forms, machines or AI—as well as the experiences of embodiment and the material conditions that inform, support and limit human life. Further, while Butler's groundbreaking work on gender performativity in *Gender Trouble* did important work to challenge the functionalist logic of sex, gender and desire, their deprioritization of the materiality of the body, of our shared plastic "essence," in Malabou's terms, has proven incomplete.

The seeming tension between Butler and Malabou, between their notions of performativity and plasticity, can now be explored through the prism of "mimesis," where performativity lies closer to the deconstructionist tradition, and to the thinking of Lacoue-Labarthe, in which the ground of being is a *scene* of masks rather than something of essence or form. This comparison shares the concerns of many of the contributions to this volume, and the *Homo Mimeticus* series more broadly. In the process, it fosters the productive and metamorphic possibilities of staging a dialogue between Malabou's concept of plasticity and mimetic studies.

Metamorphic Program

In the Prologue titled, "The Four Metamorphoses of Plasticity," Nidesh Lawtoo furthers the "plasticity of mimesis" connection first developed in volume 1 of *Homo Mimeticus* by tracing four metamorphic figures from antiquity to modernity, reaching into the present. From the Homeric sea-god Proteus dramatized in book 4 of the *Odyssey* as having the ability to morph into nonhuman animals and natural elements, to the Latin concept of *figura* that—from Ovid to Montaigne—already calls attention to the plastic power of artistic figurations that make lasting impressions on what Dante, in *The Divine Comedy*, calls the "brain [*cervello*]," from the plasticity at play in what Michel Foucault, following Pierre Hadot, calls "care of the self," to Nietzsche's dramatization of the "three metamorphoses of the spirit" in *Thus Spoke Zarathustra* that rest on both mimetic and anti-mimetic drives, there is a long materialist tradition that ties both plasticity to mimesis and vice versa. Once joined, they further the metamorphoses of subjectivity this volume sets out to outline in the company of Catherine Malabou.

Part I: Genealogies of Mimetic Plasticity

We commence this collection of essays with Malabou's essay titled "Epigenetic Mimesis: Natural Brains and Synaptic Chips." In this contribution, Malabou contends that neither Platonic nor Kantian conceptions of mimesis can account for the recent developments of AI which show that machines, like humans, have the capacity to engage in a mimetic behavior that is creative and not reducible to the imitation or copying of some original model. Acknowledging the need for a mimetic turn beyond representation, she opens this chapter by asking how the notions of imitation and simulation are to be understood today taking into consideration new achievements where technology appears to be acting like the biological brain and specifically simulating its epigenetic abilities. As Malabou notes, her book *What Should We Do with Our Brain?* presumed that the epigenetic and plastic character of the brain distinguished it from machines. While epigenetic research has shown that the brain can no longer be understood as genetically determined, she thought that machines were built to follow a program and, as such, could not be conceptualized in epigenetic terms. Malabou now takes a self-critical stance. Taking stock of recent developments in AI that trouble her earlier distinction between the human brain and the machine, she proposes that the innovations of neuromorphic chips, which are self-learning, attest to the growing plastic qualities of AI. How can we understand the mimetic behavior of machines now, seeing that they imitate or simulate the activities of the human brain? Malabou states that a new account must be detailed, one which considers "the epigenesis of auto-affection of technique by itself" (84) via a creative mimesis whose metamorphoses are already in progress and to which she returns in the Coda to the volume.

In Chapter 2, "Plasticity, Mimesis, Transformativity: A Genealogy of Theories of Change," Tom Boland provides a genealogical account of change through a proposed notion of "transformativity," which is conceptualized in both mimetic and plastic terms. He proposes that while it is indisputable that things change, how this occurs is open to interpretation. Boland suggests that modern society thinks change in terms of "transformativity," a notion less drastic than complete metamorphosis, yet more dramatic than mere reconfiguration, insisting on continuity through change. He examines a series of historical examples of theories of change, moving from Renaissance humanism through revolutionary socialism, to liberal managerialism. Commencing with Pico della Mirandola's *On the Dignity of Man,* Boland explores how transformativist thinking is proposed through notions of mimesis and plasticity: while Pico urges his readers to emulate angels, which are divine models, this very possibility for change cannot occur unless human nature is itself considered plastic, which means it can also become bestial. Moving on to Vladimir Lenin, Boland considers a Marxist notion of transformativity in which society is deemed plastic and open to dialectical change. Yet, at the same time, he proposes that Lenin's version of communism after the "state withers away" is presented as the imposition of the model of a well-functioning factory. Finally, in Abraham Maslow's account of self-actualization, the subject is encouraged to view themselves as plastic and transformable yet also encouraged to enact mimetic play and take part in mimetic rivalry as a way into one's individuality. According to Boland, these three accounts of transformativity are significant because they are representative of dominant threads of modern thinking about change which put notions of plasticity "to work," in dialogue with imitative modeling. In conclusion, Boland argues that the potency of transformativist visions of change must be acknowledged, yet also noted for their limitations, especially considering the climate crisis and the urgency to rethink change beyond humanistic models.

In Chapter 3, "Material Mimetism: On Plasticity, Plastics and Mimesis," Alice Iacobone asks: what happens when plastics imitate ivory or when wax imitates the human flesh to the point of deceiving us? By framing such cases of inorganic matters as instances of material mimetism, Iacobone draws on Catherine

Malabou's concept of plasticity and Nidesh Lawtoo's affective, relational and embodied understanding of mimesis. She proposes that both Malabou's and Lawtoo's accounts display nonreductive materialist overtones and foundations; their materialisms, however, are concerned with human subjectivity and end up not focusing on inorganic materials. Filling this gap in mimetic studies, this chapter studies how the interplay between plasticity and mimesis is embodied by nonhuman materials by drawing on the method of "material complicity" outlined by German *Materialästhetik*, new materialisms and the assemblage theory of Deleuzean descent, and to an analogy with Roger Caillois's theorization of animal mimicry already driving the mimetic turn. In doing so, the case of plastics is made a subject of closer analysis in ways that entangle the mimetic turn with what Ranjan Ghosh calls the "plastic turn" (2022). By arguing that materials imitate each other, display mimetic behaviors and engage in plastic and transformative relationships, this contribution aims to outline a materialist supplement to plasticity and mimetic studies.

In Chapter 4, "Negative Plasticity and the Indifference of the Body" Kristian Schaeferling discusses the category of indifference in Hegel and Malabou through the lens of Malabou's notion of negative plasticity. He outlines the coordinates of a pathological dysfunctionality predicated on the split plastic unity of being and thought on the one hand, and on a mimetic non-relation between pathos and logos on the other, which cause mimesis to coincide with a fundamental drive geared towards bringing about disaffected indifference. Schaeferling thus explains how the ontologically constitutive embodiment of indifference can be understood as the real that underlies the modulation and remodulation of mimetic form. This is accomplished in three sections. First, Hegel's incorporation of indifferent being into the logic of the absolute, as shown primarily in the *Phenomenology of Spirit* and the *Science of Logic*, is considered. He then establishes a link to Malabou's reinterpretation of the Hegelian dialectic in *The Future of Hegel*. Finally, based on this ground, a reading of Malabou's notion of negative plasticity is shown to present embodied indifference as a deadlock within the mimetic process of subjectivation. In doing so, Schaeferling supplements the affirmative Nietzschean tradition of the studies of mimetic processes with a model based on the negative-driven Hegelian tradition of the dialectic.

Part II: Plastic Encounters and Mimetic Studies

In Chapter 5, "Benjamin's Great Criminal, A Plastic Mime," Gabriel Wartinger interrogates the law's fragility through Walter Benjamin's *Critique of Violence*, focusing on the figure of the "great criminal" and its implications for mimetic studies. He proposes that Benjamin's great criminal can be conceptualized as a plastic mime—a figure central to the *Homo Mimeticus* trilogy. According to Wartinger, the great criminal not only embodies the aspiration to create new legal norms, but, as a plastic mime, they also disrupt the relation between model and copy and expose the mimetic structure of the law itself. Criminal mimesis thus does not merely duplicate the violence of the law, but rather reveals the distance between imitation in terms of a copy and the action of a creative and violent force. It is argued that legal frameworks falter in addressing transgressions, a vulnerability starkly exposed by the great criminal's act of plastic mimesis. This act challenges the law's violent monopoly by employing a transformative violence that resists centralization; it also underscores the elasticity of legal responses and introduces plasticity through the figure of the great criminal and the transformative capacity that retains change. This analysis extends Benjamin's insights into the mimetic faculty via a criminal mimesis that exposes the law's inherent elasticity, thereby stressing the tension between creation, repetition and the law's foundational instability.

In Chapter 6, "To Double Mimesis Bound: Mortal Plasticity Between Malabou and Lacoue-Labarthe," Alex Obrigewitsch brings Lacoue-Labarthe's analysis of the mimetic primal scene into dialogue with Malabou's account of plasticity to argue for the abyssal origins of being itself. Furthering a connection between the two French philosophers started in volume 1, he contends that the relationship between mimesis and plasticity is that of "doubling and displacement" in which there is no fixed primordial beginning. Instead, Obrigewitsch argues that, when conceptualized as "mimetic plasticity," being is revealed as a form that occurs without any model. In doing so, he challenges the notion of a plastic foundation in Malabou's thinking, reading human existence through the lens of Lacoue-Larbarthe to claim that what appears to be a foundation is rather a *scene* which consist of masks, complicating the relation between origin and fiction. Whereas figures are produced from the mimetic articulations of the primal scene, Obrigewitsch argues that they rest on a void of our non-existence as finite creatures. As such, he poses "the tragic" as exemplary of the human condition, which, he claims, is suspended between the caesura of a foundation and the non-being of mortality.

In Chapter 7, "Eroticism, Gender and the Possibility for Transformation: With and Beyond Merleau-Ponty," Ida Djursaa develops a notion of sensible eroticism through an analysis of Merleau-Ponty's writings on sexuality, embodiment and sensation in his *Phenomenology of Perception*. In conversation with mimetic studies, critical phenomenology and feminist philosophy, she considers how "sensible eroticism" articulates the constitutive openness and binding of bodies to the world and others, making them vulnerable but also transformable, providing a new analysis of homo mimeticus in phenomenological terms. In addition to demonstrating the important role that eroticism holds in the existential structure of the mimetic subject/body, Djursaa also considers how patriarchy and heteronormativity impact the degree to which this sensible eroticism is experienced and enjoyed. Against the presumption that female desire is naturally low, she claims that the erotic life force of women (in both sexual and nonsexual domains) is limited by patriarchal heteronormativity. Drawing on Simone de Beauvoir's account of the sexual encounter, Merleau-Ponty's notion of the pre-reflective sexual schema, and research in social neuroendocrinology, Djursaa argues that to unlearn restrictive norms and habits, one must abandon oneself to simply being a body in the world. Through this return to sensible eroticism, one can dare "to *be* a body without judgment" (204) and, in doing so, reopen to oneself and others, and to new ways of desiring.

In Chapter 8, "Mimesis, Resonance and the Subject: A Critical Comparison," Mathijs Peters explores similarities between Nidesh Lawtoo's mimetic studies and Hartmut Rosa's resonance theory to propose an amalgamation, critique and transformation of the two. He explains that while both foreground processes of relationality that problematize the idea(l) of the autonomous, rational, free and individual subject, their accounts lack a normative dimension. As Peters explains, Lawtoo and Rosa share the contention that the discovery of mirror neurons proves that human beings are driven by relational processes over which there is limited control. However, this makes it difficult for them to discriminate between "good" or "healthy" forms of resonant/mimetic subjectivity and "bad" or "pathological" ones. Peters argues that a solution can be found by turning to Theodor W. Adorno, who outlines two kinds of mimesis: "primitive" (uncritical, passive, possibly pathological) and "aesthetic" (rational, self-reflective, physical, sensual, resonant). He builds on Adorno's account with Roland Barthes's writings on the middle voice, to argue that the middle voice makes it possible to conceptualize a form of resonant/mimetic subjectivity that is neither completely passive/determined nor completely active/free. Peters explains that this results in an account of a *semi-autonomous mimetic/resonant subject* that balances (self-)critical cognition with material embeddedness.

Part III From Neuroliterature to the Mimetic Subconscious

In Chapter 9, "Semiosis and Mimesis," Serge Zenkin provides a study of these concepts by way of pedagogical and literary examples to demonstrate their roles and interplays in teaching, communication and artistic representation. He commences with the example of teaching a gymnastic exercise to show how some modes of instruction employ the use of signs and others mimesis, providing preliminary definitions of how they differ. According to Zenkin, the one who receives the mimetic form of communication in being taught a physical exercise seeks to reproduce it literally, and have proximity to it, whereas a sign in the semiotic form of teaching (such as verbal instruction or visual representation) does not reproduce exactly what it denotes. However, he goes on to show that the two pedagogical forms are more closely interlinked than might be supposed and even permeate each other. When it comes to literary texts, he considers lyrical poetry, as well as epic and dramatic narrative forms. While Zenkin concludes that more examples need to be considered, he proposes that semiotic and mimetic devices are employed simultaneously to deliver meaning and impact together. The mimetic element allows for excess and impact to emerge. The semiotic element, on the other hand, allows for information to be delivered and coherence to be maintained. In this explanation Zenkin shows that while these two forms of communication may appear opposed, they work together often invisibly by interweaving themselves in our culture, whether it be in pedagogical or artistic modes.

In Chapter 10, "Neuroliterature and the Example," Tyler M. Williams explains that while Malabou's theorization of the concept of plasticity is most known for awakening within continental philosophy a confrontation with neuroscience, considerably less attention has been given to that which is among the most radical contributions of her thought: plasticity's transformation of the concept of literature. Furthering the aesthetic orientation of the mimetic turn which originates in literary modernism, Williams shows that, rather than abandoning literature for science, Malabou's analysis of the brain and destructive plasticity brings "the literary" into accounts of neural experience and subjectivity. In the process, Williams returns to Malabou's mentor, Jacques Derrida, referencing his statement that literature has the democratic right to say anything and everything, that it holds an "in-between, a neutral and indifferent non-allegiance," (264) arguing for a continuity between this statement and Malabou's account of the a-teleological economy of plastic self-fashioning. Attending to Malabou's coinage of the term "neuroliterature," Williams argues that her plasticization of the frontier between philosophy and science ultimately theorizes a new formation of literary production. Rather than confine this sense of literary production to classical senses of mimesis as the belated copy of an authentic original, neuroliterature, consistent with recent advances in "new mimetic studies," describes mimesis as an originary process of fashioning over being that plasticizes philosophy's frontier with literature from the start.

In Chapter 11, "Proust, Realism and the Plasticity of Natural Signs," Ian James interrogates the Proustian thematization of nature in *À la recherche du temps perdu* in terms of what one might call the existence of "natural signs" in a reading of Proust alongside Malabou's thinking of plasticity, on the one hand, and the contemporary science of biosemiotics on the other. He does so by sketching out an understanding of Proust's *Recherche* as a form of realism and of naturalism, one which bypasses the traditional understanding of literary realism and mimesis as the re-presentation of an existing reality, exterior to the work. The relation of the work to the real is understood as an operation of mimetic transformation of lived forms and of the life of natural signs. This chapter is less a reading of Proust through the theoretical lens of Malabou's plasticity or of the biosemiotic theory of signs borrowed from the philosophy of C. S. Peirce. Rather, a shared genealogy of all three is indicated, one which can be traced back to German idealism and philosophies of nature, and which offers a resource for the rethinking of literary realism within the contemporary mimetic turn that is the concern of this volume.

In Chapter 12, "Conflicting Subliminalities: The Other Ancestors of Mimesis," Malabou resumes her contribution to the mimetic turn. She does so by troubling the distinction between mimesis as reproduction and the deconstructive approach, which she claims explodes the very idea of a model. In conversation with Homi Bhabha and Sylvia Wynters, as well as the surrealist poet André Breton, she considers Pierre Janet's subliminal or subconscious workings of mimesis—a neglected figure that directly informs what we also call the mimetic unconscious. Furthering this pre-Freudian genealogy that had suggestion as a via regia, Malabou points out that a "plasticity of subliminal mimesis" can be found at the borders between reproductive and creative mimesis, but, at least partially due to the dismissal of the subconscious and the subliminal by psychoanalysis, it had been not fully explored. This plasticity of subliminal mimesis is articulated by Malabou in several ways. Via Breton, she explains that poetry is viewed as an expression of an inner subconscious model which is enacted automatically with the words, allowing for the inner model to take form in the world. Turning to neurobiology and mathematics, she shows how that which is conceived of as subliminal, whether it be subliminal processing in the brain or the inspiration that allows for mathematical insight, as a kind of inner poetry, can give rise to a "creative conscious dynamism" or even mathematical invention. However, the universalization of these models is called into question in dialogue with Sylvia Wynters, Bhabha, W. E. B. Du Bois and others. Malabou proposes that the subliminal mimesis of the Black, colonized subject is a doubling in which white reproduction is instantiated, contributing to the cognitive dissonance of the split Black consciousness. While, citing Wynters, Malabou notes that the way to Black creative mimesis is said to be through the voices of ancestors, she also points out that no model remains due to dispossession. Malabou's conclusion is that we have moved from a form of sublime mimesis to subliminal mimesis and, with this, have taken departure from a conception of mimesis that actualizes freedom from authority.

Finally, in the Coda that concludes the volume, titled "The Three Metamorphoses of Mimesis: Thinking with Malabou," the *Homo Mimeticus* trilogy seems to come full circle. Nidesh Lawtoo and Catherine Malabou discuss the future metamorphoses of mimesis via the philosopher who served as the main source of inspiration for the mimetic turn. This re-turn to Nietzsche's "On the Three Metamorphoses" that opens *Thus Spoke Zarathustra* is not to be understood as a closing of the circle. Rather, this parable allows for a spiraling diagnostic of the mimetic and anti-mimetic drives that inform the processes of transformations that concern and move beyond the human, reaching what Malabou calls "the three metamorphoses of intelligence" (Malabou 2017, 27). Lawtoo and Malabou propose that the mimetic figure of the camel, the anti-mimetic figure of the lion, and the creative, life-affirmative child are all figures that—like plasticity and mimesis—move beyond nature and culture, symbolic influences and natural influences. Moreover, since *das Kind* in German is not linked to a gender, these metamorphoses go beyond male and female binaries as well. This leads to an Intermezzo in which Gendered Mimesis team members Isabelle Dahms and Giulia Rignano join the discussion to further the problematic of gender/sexual difference. While Malabou regrets that influential women philosophers such as Luce Irigaray and even Simone de Beauvoir are not taught in her country of origin, France, she also makes a strong case for the importance of engaging critically and creatively with Judith Butler's concept of performativity and Paul Preciado's notion of dysphoria to expand the reaches of gendered mimesis.

Philosophical thinking, for Malabou, is thus not simply abstract and disembodied. On the contrary, it is immanent and can "change bodies," including her own. While Hegel is certainly the main philosophical influence on Malabou's concept of plasticity, Nietzsche's parable also serves as a pretext to consider the metamorphoses internal to philosophical transformation, including Malabou's own plastic and mimetic transformations. Thus, as the dialogue unfolds, she addresses several topics close to home, including her agnostic relation to intellectual models (Derrida), her critical evaluation of affect and auto-affection (Deleuze), and finally her own style of philosophical expression. Distinctly relational, driven by the rigor of conceptual logos, Malabou's writings are not deprived of an experiential pathos. Thus, she admits: "It is always as if someone was asking me something."

We asked Malabou to engage with mimesis from the angle of plasticity to further the transformations at play in the plasticity of mimesis, and she offered us a generous and rich responses. Located at the productive junctures of philosophy and literature, nature and culture, the biological and the symbolic, ancient models and future transformations, the pages that follow explore, from a variety of perspectives, the productive and reproductive relationships between plasticity and mimesis. We hope that readers will continue to engage with the metamorphic potentials generated from the mirroring and dynamic interplay of these concepts and continue to find agonistic play with the impressions left by the plastic figures that follow.

Notes

1. For the first volumes of *Homo Mimeticus*, see Lawtoo 2022, and Lawtoo and Garcia-Granero 2024. For an agonistic confrontation between mimetic studies and mimetic theory on violence and the unconscious, see Lawtoo 2023a and 2023b. For special issues on the mimetic turn see *CounterText* 8.1 (2022), *Journal of Posthumanism* 2.2 (2022), *Critical Horizons* 24.2 (2023), and *MLN* 138.5 (2023). For interviews on imitation with the figures mentioned and more see, HOM Videos, https://www.youtube.com/@homvideosercprojecthomomim971.
2. For an informed account of neuroplasticity showing that "far from being fixed, the brain is a highly dynamic structure, which undergoes significant changes not only as it develops but also throughout the entire lifespan" see Costandi 2016, 145–147.
3. See James 2012, 83–108. On Malabou's work on plasticity see also Bhandar and Goldberg-Hiller 2015 and Malabou's essays collected by Tyler Williams in Malabou 2022a.
4. On biomimicry see Henry Dicks in *Homo Mimeticus II*, ch. 14; on "posthuman mimesis" see Lawtoo 2024.
5. For a special issue that picks up both the "plasticity of mimesis" connection initiated in *MLN* 132.5 (2017) and the tradition of "dialogues on imitation" central to HOM Videos, see also "L'art de Malabou: discours, plasticité, mimèsis," *MLN* 137.4 (2022). In the dialogue that concludes this issue, Malabou confirms two fundamental hypotheses of mimetic studies: first, distinguishing between reproductive and creative mimesis—what we also

call active and passive mimesis—Malabou argues that in creative mimesis "we are dealing with a mimesis without a model" (Malabou and Opelz 2022, 812)—a genealogical point echoing a mimetology mimetic studies traced back to Lacoue-Labarthe (see Lawtoo 2017, 1207–1219); and, second, furthering the importance of transdisciplinary accounts of mimesis already internal to the aspiration of philosophy, Malabou adds: "it is clear that if there is no longer a model the concept of mimesis will transform itself" (813); and she specifies: "we are in the process of living, of experimenting, this transformation of mimesis" (813). If Malabou confirms insights already internal to mimetic studies, the present volume continues to further the transdisciplinary transformations of mimesis Malabou calls for.

6   See ch. 8, "Bataille on Mimetic Heterology," in Lawtoo and Garcia-Granero 2024, 183–205.
7   On mimetic pathologies see for instance the special issue on "The Mimetic Turn," *MLN* 138.5 (2023); on (new) fascist pathologies and their link with Girard's mimetic theory see Lawtoo 2019, ch. 1.
8   This chapter was first published in 2023 in a volume titled *Life in the Posthuman Condition*, eds. S. E. Wilmer and Audronė Žukauskaitė. The editors thank Edinburgh University Press for allowing us to reproduce it.
9   See Part 1 of *Homo Mimeticus II*, esp. ch. 2 by Henry Staten.
10 See Lawtoo 2022, 144–146; see also Lacoue-Labarthe 1989, 255–256.
11 On Lipps and empathy see also Carmen Bonasera's contribution to *Homo Mimeticus II*, ch. 11. For a study of *homo aestheticus* that goes beyond nature and culture by reevaluating "empathy theory" see Dissanayake 1992, 142–147.
12 See Gallese and Lawtoo 2024, 350. As part of this discussion, Gallese also clarified his critical position with respect to previous mimetic theories like Girard's (2024, 354–355). This critique is articulated in more detail in volume 1 of *Homo Mimeticus* and in Lawtoo 2023a, ch. 1. For a helpful first step connecting Girard's mimetic theory with imitation in neuroscience, see also Garrles 2013.
13 In its inception mimetic studies has paid particular attention to modernism, with Joseph Conrad as the first ally to promote both a "mimetic turn" and a turn to "neuroplasticity" (Lawtoo 2016a and 2016b), and Oscar Wilde as a precursor of the "imitation of life" (Lawtoo 2018). Since then, mimetic studies has quickly expanded to include film, theater, TV series, photography and video games, among other art forms.
14 See ch. 2 of *Homo Mimeticus* and Part 1 of *Homo Mimeticus II*.
15 LeDoux's claim that "the self, the essence of who you are reflects patterns of interconnectivity between neurons in your brain" (2002, 2) is adopted and supplemented by Malabou (2008, 55–77). LeDoux expands his conception of the self to include "*unconscious* cognitive processes" (2022, 23), which we group under the rubric of mimetic unconscious. Still, in our view, he relies too much on the representational model of mimesis as a mirroring reflection that the mimetic turn is up against. For his more nuanced account of plasticity, which is not intended as an "alternative" to approaches in the humanities and social sciences, see LeDoux 2002, 307–324.
16 For a pioneering materialist account of metamorphoses that recognizes the role of "unconscious identifications" at play in the "immanent encounter between subjects, entities, and forces," see Braidotti 2002, 40, 68.
17 For a reevaluation of this neglected mimetic tradition that is central to mimetic studies, see for instance Borch-Jacobsen 2009, Lawtoo 2013 and the essays assembled in Borch 2019.

18   Genealogically speaking, Irigaray's theory of mimicry rooted in mimetic behavior both recuperates the concept of *mimétisme* used by precursors of the mimetic turn like Roger Caillois discussed in volume 1 (see Lawtoo 2022, 157–190) and anticipates the "two mimesis," one active and "productive," the other passive and reproductive (Irigaray 1977, 131), that arguably paves the way for Lacoue-Labarthe's mimetology (see Hadikoesoemo 2024). Conversely, if Butler's mimetism furthers Irigaray from a deconstructive perspective, their use of the concept of "psychic mimesis" is directly borrowed from Mikkel Borch-Jacobsen, whose work is already internal to mimetic studies—see ch. 1 of *Homo Mimeticus II*. These genealogies are still little known but establish strong continuities between mimetic studies and feminist philosophy central to the gendered mimesis project. Some of them are discussed in dialogue with Judith Butler in Butler and Lawtoo 2025.

19   See Lawtoo and Verkerk 2023 and Cavarero and Lawtoo 2021.

20   In *This Sex Which Is Not One*, Irigaray writes: "To play with mimesis is thus, for a woman, to try to recover the place of her exploitation by discourse, without allowing herself to be simply reduced to it. It means to resubmit herself—inasmuch as she is on the side of the 'perceptible,' of 'matter'—to 'ideas,' in particular to ideas about herself, that are elaborated in/by a masculine logic, but so as to make 'visible,' by an effect of playful repetition, what was supposed to remain invisible: the cover-up of a possible operation of the feminine in language. It also means 'to unveil' the fact that, if women are such good mimics, it is because they are not simply resorbed in this function. *They also remain elsewhere*: another case of the persistence of 'matter,' but also of 'sexual pleasure'" (1985b, 76).

Bibliography

Aristotle (1984). *Physics*, in *The Complete Works of Aristotle*, ed. Jonathan Barnes. Princeton: Princeton University Press, 315–446.

Bhandar, Brenna, and Jonathan Goldberg-Hiller (eds.) (2015). *Plastic Materialities: Politics, Legality, and Metamorphosis in the Work of Catherine Malabou*. Durham, NC: Duke University Press.

Borch, Christian (ed.) (2019). *Imitation, Contagion, Suggestion: On Mimesis and Society*. London: Routledge.

Borch-Jacobsen, Mikkel (2009). *Making Madness: From Hysteria to Depression*. Cambridge: Cambridge University Press.

Braidotti, Rosi (2002). *Metamorphoses: Towards a Materialist Theory of Becoming*. Cambridge: Polity.

Butler, Judith (1993). "Imitation and Gender Insubordination," in *The Lesbian and Gay Studies Reader*, eds. Henry Abelove, Michèle Aina Barale and David M. Halperin. New York: Routledge, 307–320.

Butler, Judith (1999). *Gender Trouble: Feminism and the Subversion of Identity*. New York/London: Routledge.

Butler, Judith, and Nidesh Lawtoo (2025). *Mimetic Trouble with Judith Butler*, HOM Videos, ep. 10. https://www.youtube.com/watch?v=u38wLSRrg1Q&t=499s

Cavarero, Adriana, and Nidesh Lawtoo (2021). "Mimetic Inclinations: A Dialogue with Adriana Cavarero," in *Contemporary Italian Women Philosophers: Stretching the Art of Thinking*, eds. Silvia Benso and Elvira Roncalli. Albany: State University of New York Press.

Changeux, Jean-Pierre (1985). *Neuronal Man: The Biology of Mind*, trans. Laurence Garey. Oxford: Oxford University Press.
Changeux, Jean-Pierre (2008). *Du Vrai, du beau, du bien: une nouvelle approche neuronale*. Paris: Odile Jacob.
Costandi, Moheb (2016). *Neuroplasticity*. Cambridge, MA: MIT Press.
Cyrulnik, Boris (1989). *Sous le signe du lien: une histoire naturelle de l'attachement*. Paris: Hachette Littératures.
Dicks, Henry (2023). *The Biomimicry Revolution: Learning from Nature How to Inhabit the Earth*. New York: Columbia University Press.
Dissanayake, Ellen (1992). *Homo Aestheticus: Where Art Comes From and Why*. Toronto: The Free Press.
Gallese, Vittorio, and Nidesh Lawtoo (2024). "Beyond Brain and Body: A Dialogue with Vittorio Gallese and Nidesh Lawtoo," in *Homo Mimeticus II: Re-Turns to Mimesis*, eds. Nidesh Lawtoo and Marina Garcia-Granero. Leuven: Leuven University Press, 343–375.
Garrles, Scott (ed.) (2013). *Mimesis and Science: Empirical Research on Imitation and the Mimetic Theory of Culture and Religion*. East Lansing: Michigan State University Press.
Ghosh, Ranjan (2022). *The Plastic Turn*. Ithaca, NY: Cornell University Press.
Hadikoesoemo, Niki (2024). "Exhibition/Exposition: Irigaray and Lacoue-Labarthe on the Theater of Mimesis," in *Homo Mimeticus II: Re-Turns to Mimesis*, eds. Nidesh Lawtoo and Marina Garcia-Granero. Leuven: Leuven University Press, 225–243.
Hegel, George Wilhelm Friedrich (2004). *Introductory Lectures on Aesthetics*, trans. Bernard Bosanquet, ed. Michael Inwood. New York: Penguin Books.
Irigaray, Luce (1977). *Ce Sexe qui n'en est pas un*. Paris: Les Éditions de Minuit.
Irigaray, Luce (1985a). *Speculum of the Other Woman*, trans. Gillian Gill. New York: Cornell University Press.
Irigaray, Luce (1985b). *This Sex Which Is Not One*, trans. Catherine Porter with Carolyn Burke. New York: Cornell University Press.
Lacoue-Labarthe, Philippe (1989). *Typography: Mimesis, Philosophy, Politics*, ed. and trans. Christopher Fynsk. Stanford: Stanford University Press.
Lawtoo, Nidesh (2013). *The Phantom of the Ego: Modernism and the Mimetic Unconscious*. East Lansing: Michigan State University Press.
Lawtoo, Nidesh (2016a). "Conrad's Mimetic Turn." *Conradiana* 48.2/3, 129–142.
Lawtoo, Nidesh (2016b). "Conrad's Neuroplasticity." *Modernism/modernity* 23.4, 771–788.
Lawtoo, Nidesh (2017). "The Plasticity of Mimesis." *MLN* 132.5, 1201–1224.
Lawtoo, Nidesh (2018). "The Critic as Mime." *Symploke* 26.1–2, 307–328.
Lawtoo, Nidesh (2022). *Homo Mimeticus: A New Theory of Imitation*. Leuven: Leuven University Press.
Lawtoo, Nidesh (2023a). *Violence and the Oedipal Unconscious. Vol. 1: The Catharsis Hypothesis*. East Lansing: Michigan State University Press.
Lawtoo, Nidesh (2023b). *Violence and the Mimetic Unconscious. Vol. 2: The Affective Hypothesis*. East Lansing: Michigan State University Press.
Lawtoo, Nidesh (ed.) (2024). *Mimetic Posthumanism: Homo Mimeticus 2.0 in Art, Philosophy and Technics*. Leiden, Brill.
Lawtoo, Nidesh, and Willow Verkerk (eds.) (2023). *Mimetic Inclinations with Adriana Cavarero. Critical Horizons* 24.2.

Lawtoo, Nidesh, and Marina Garcia-Granero (eds.) (2024). *Homo Mimeticus II: Re-Turns to Mimesis*. Leuven: Leuven University Press.
LeDoux, Joseph (2002). *Synaptic Self: How Our Brains Become Who We Are*. New York: Viking.
James, Ian (2012). *The New French Philosophy*. New York: Polity.
Malabou, Catherine (2008). *What Should We Do with Our Brain?*, trans. Sebastian Rand. New York: Fordham University Press.
Malabou, Catherine (2010). *Plasticity at the Dusk of Writing: Dialectic, Destruction, Deconstruction*, trans. Carolyn Shread. New York: Columbia University Press.
Malabou, Catherine (2011). *Changing Difference: The Feminine and the Question of Philosophy*, trans. Carolyn Shread. Cambridge: Polity.
Malabou, Catherine (2014). *Avant demain: Épigenèse et rationalité*. Paris: Presses Universitaires de France.
Malabou, Catherine (2015). "From the Overman to the Posthuman: How Many Ends?," in *Plastic Materialities: Politics, Legality, and Metamorphosis in the works of Catherine Malabou*, eds. Brenna Bhandar and Jonathan Goldberg-Hiller. Durham, NC: Duke University Press, 61–72.
Malabou, Catherine (2017). *Métamorphoses de l'intelligence: Que faire de leur cerveau bleu*. Paris: Presses Universitaires de France.
Malabou, Catherine (2019). *Morphing Intelligence: From IQ Measurement to Artificial Brains*, trans. Carolyn Shread. New York: Columbia University Press.
Malabou, Catherine (2022a). *Plasticity: The Promise of Explosion*, ed. Tyler M. Williams. Edinburgh: Edinburgh University Press.
Malabou, Catherine (2022b). "Quand on n'a que le discours: Réflexions sur la forme." *MLN* 137.4, 637–645.
Malabou, Catherine (2022c). *Pleasure Erased: The Clitoris Unthought*, trans. Carolyn Shread. Cambridge: Polity.
Malabou, Catherine (2023). "Epigenetic Mimesis: Natural Brains and Synaptic Chips," in *Life in the Posthuman Condition: Critical Responses to the Anthropocene*, eds. S. E. Wilmer and Audronė Žukauskaitė. Edinburgh: Edinburgh University Press.
Malabou, Catherine (ed.) (2000). *Plasticité*. Paris: Editions Leo Scheer.
Malabou, Catherine, and Hannes Opelz (2022). "L'avenir de la mimèsis. Entretien avec Catherine Malabou." *MLN* 137.4, 801–813.
Morin, Edgar (2008). *La Méthode II: Les idées, l'humanité de l'humanité, éthique*. Paris: Seuil.
Nietzsche, Friedrich (1995). *Human, All Too Human I*, trans. Gary Handwerk. Stanford: Stanford University Press.
Plato (1963). *Republic*, in *The Collected Dialogues of Plato*, trans. Paul Shorey, 575–853.
Verkerk, Willow (2023). "A Re-evaluation of the Androcentric Subject of European Philosophy." *Critical Horizons* 24.2, 115–130.

PROLOGUE

THE FOUR METAMORPHOSES OF PLASTICITY

Proteus to Figura, Self-Care to the Overhuman

Nidesh Lawtoo

The field of mimetic studies is new, future-oriented and sensitive to transformations informing the paradoxical logic of imitation in the digital age. Yet the concept of mimesis and its multiple plastic masks (simulation, imitation, adequation, impersonation, dramatization, identification, influence, mirror neurons, epigenetic mimesis and, as should be clear by now, plasticity as well) are as old as the dawn of philosophy itself. If its protean forms triggered a quarrel between philosophers and poets, mimetic studies has shown that this quarrel was not as unilateral as it is often thought to be. It also generated productive entanglements between plastic and mimetic subjects whose genealogy is only now beginning to emerge. In the guise of a Prologue, I will outline, in broad and necessarily partial brushstrokes, the productive continuities between plastic and mimetic figures at play in a metamorphic conception of the subject that—from antiquity to modernity—continues to inform the "metamorphoses of intelligence" (Malabou 2017) that Catherine Malabou urges us to consider at the end of this volume.

It is true that dominant approaches to both mimesis and plasticity have tended to restrict these concepts to aesthetics; yet joining forces with Malabou allows us to confirm that both concepts transgress the binary that simply divides art from life. As Oscar Wilde said, "Life imitates Art more than Art imitates Life" (2007, 90), assuming plastic and thus metamorphic masks that go beyond mind–body dualisms as well. Just as mimesis originates in imitative subjects, and mimes can assume different theatrical forms, so plasticity originates in the malleable subject matter of the human soul, a materialist soul rooted in the brain, and thus in the body as well. Several ancient, (early) modern and contemporary precursors paved the way for mimetic/plastic insights into the formation and transformation of the subject now shared by mimetic studies and new materialism. Considering recent turns—from the performative turn to the affective turn, the ethical turn to the materialist turn to the neuro turn—these genealogical precursors deserve more attention than they have received. Hence the need for a step back in view of promoting plastic metamorphoses internal to the mimetic turn, or re-turn. Together, they deepen the genealogy of the process of "sculpting a determinate form" central to Malabou's account of a "plastic art of the brain" (2008, 19).

While the plasticity of the brain is a relatively new area of inquiry in the neurosciences, techniques of sculpting the self have a long history in the humanities and find in figures working at the juncture of philosophy and literature particularly sensitive configurations. Short of offering a complete overview of the metamorphoses *of* plasticity over the ages, the goal of this Prologue is more limited and selective in its theoretical focus: it aims to trace four metamorphoses of plasticity that—in their double power to both receive form and give form—continue to in-*form* and *trans*-form what we started calling, for lack of a more original term, the "plasticity of mimesis" (Lawtoo 2022, 129–155).

The origins of plastic and metamorphic subjects cannot be easily pinned down via a linear genealogy rooted in a single origin, though a plurality of precursors in mimetic studies have opened up paths to be explored further.[1] As is well known, Malabou traces this paradigmatic shift of perspective on discourses about plasticity from aesthetics to subject formation back to Hegel's idealist dialectical thought, which she reframes from an innovative (new) materialist perspective. Starting with her first book, *The Future of Hegel* (1996), and consistently in her work, Malabou argues that "for the first time […] [Hegel] snatches plasticity from its strictly aesthetic anchorage in order to attach it to a problematic space which, so far, had not been its own: subjectivity" (2000, 8–9; my trans.). While the centrality of Hegel for Malabou's revolutionary rethinking of plasticity is well attested, his restriction of mimesis to the old idea of imitation of nature might also have slowed down the plasticity of mimesis connection we now pursue. Either way, Hegel sets Malabou's thought in dialectical motion, opening up productive lines of inquiries that mark the "dusk of writing" and the "dawn of a new era" (Malabou 2010). In the process, she also puts the explosive logic of the negative to productive, revolutionary and "anarchic" theoretical and political use (2022b). Some chapters that follow will continue exploring this philosophical legacy from a variety of new materialist perspectives informed by Hegel, but also by Nietzsche, Heidegger, Merleau-Ponty, Proust, Lacoue-Labarthe and other genealogists of plasticity. These genealogists suggest that the binary dividing the "sculptural ties" of plasticity traditionally restricted to aesthetics and its contemporary focus on "subjectivity" might not always be as stable as it appears to be. Together, they also encourage us to look for more ancient, marginalized sources that both confirm and thicken the mimesis-plasticity-metamorphosis connection from the dual angle of both aesthetic and subject formation.

In the first volume of *Homo Mimeticus*, I already traced, somewhat paradoxically, a diagnostic of the plasticity of the soul back to Plato's idealistic critique of mimetic types and the impressions they make on a wax-like soul with agentic properties of its own.[2] As a Prologue for *Homo Mimeticus III*, let me now further the genealogy of plasticity by taking a few and necessarily partial additional steps back in order to leap further ahead. This entails reaching deeper into the past to revisit precursors of mimetic studies that—from Greek and Roman antiquity to the Middle Ages, through the Renaissance to modernity—were already sensitive to "protean" subjects, plastic "figures," "techniques of the self" and "metamorphoses of the spirit" that turn *homo mimeticus* into *homo plasticus*, and vice versa. Together, they comprise four metamorphoses of plasticity that allow us to keep thinking with Malabou in the present, while paving the way for future transformations in mimetic studies.

Protean Twists and Turns: Homer to Plato

First metamorphosis. The mimetic turn benefits from *re*-turning to influential predecessors who sensed early on, often to their dismay, that mimesis cannot be framed within a reassuring visual mirror reflecting a stabilizing *imago*, or visual representation. Mimesis is instead constitutive of a malleable, plastic and protean subject, or mime, which is not one, in the sense that it is "no one" in particular. And being no one, mimetic subjects can paradoxically assume a multiplicity of personalities (from Latin, *persona*, mask worn in the theater). Odysseus, as we saw in volumes 1 and 2, plays precisely such a mimetic role in the *Odyssey*; and so does his divine counterpart, Athena or Minerva, who, like the owl that bears her name, becomes imperceptible via an animal mimicry that informs human chameleons as well.[3] But these are not the only mythic figures to illustrate the paradox of a homo mimeticus who, being no one, can potentially assume a plastic mask to become everyone. As we turn to see, the poetic mime performing an identity that is not one on a theatrical stage is the paradigmatic example of a figure endowed with the plastic powers of metamorphosis.

Since the dawn of mimetic studies, philosophers have identified mimeticians as protean subjects, which also means that they have failed to identify them in a singular, unitary and above all stable form. Unsurprisingly so, for mimesis keeps morphing, or rather metamorphosing (from Greek *meta*, change, *morphē*, form), into someone or something other, thereby evading the universalizing grasp of idealist philosophers. This is what Plato was quick to recognize in a minor dialogue on poetic inspiration, *Ion*, which is central to mimetic studies. Since Ion is a rhapsode, or reciter of poetry, specializing in Homer, Plato's critique of the rhapsode targets, at one remove, the poet as well. He does so by speaking, as usual, from behind the mask of Socrates, via a direct mimetic speech that breaks the fourth wall—cinematically speaking—and, at two removes, addresses the reader as well. Thus, he says: "you are just like Proteus: you twist and turn this way and that, evading my [the philosopher's] grasp" (1963a, 541e–542a). In a paradox familiar to mimetic studies, Plato convokes a Homeric figure to fight contra Homer; and in a characteristic manifestation of mimetic agonism, he fights *contra* Homer *with* a Homeric myth. To understand the philosophical critique of the poet's mimetic metamorphoses it is thus crucial to remember the myth that is *both* the target of the critique *and*—according to the paradoxical logic of mimetic agonism—its source of inspiration.

Who, then, is Proteus, and wherein lie his metamorphic powers? The myth of Proteus was well known in ancient Greece as it is dramatized in a famous book towards the beginning of the *Odyssey*. Well before we encounter Odysseus "himself," his son, Telemachus, sets out to find some of the kings who fought at his father's side at Troy, including King Menelaus, whose wife's abduction, Helen, caused the war that launched a thousand ships in the first place. With Helen at his side, Menelaus then narrates to Telemachus how, stuck on an island near Egypt on their way home from Troy—mirroring and anticipating Odysseus' homeward journey (*nostos*)—"a spirit [was] blocking [him] from going home" (Homer 2020, 4.378). This spirit is none other than the sea-god Proteus, Poseidon's son, who is the same mythic figure Socrates convokes to account for the mimetic rhapsode's protean metamorphoses.

In the original Homeric text, the sea-god turns out to be both plastic and mimetic, for he twists and turns to elude Menelaus and his men's all-too-human grasp. He does so via a series of metamorphoses that are not limited to human animals but include nonhuman animals and natural elements as well. Thus Homer, speaking mimetically, in the name of Menelaus, tells Telemachus that Proteus

> first became a lion with a mane,
> then snake, then leopard, then a mighty boar,
> then flowing water,
> then a leafy tree. (Homer 2020, 4.456–458)

Who said that the masks of mimesis are limited to human figures? Certainly not Homer, who dramatized the world of becoming that Plato is up against. He did so via metamorphoses that go beyond human and nonhuman forms, anticipating the ontological view that a mimetic (will to) power, or, as Nietzsche will later say, pathos, streams through life in general, animating a metamorphic planet some call by the mythic name "Gaia."[4] Myth, then, comes before philosophy in the double sense that it both precedes it and in-forms it, often generating paradoxical effects. Note, in fact, that since Plato himself convokes precisely this Homeric god to depict the Homeric rhapsode's "twists and turns," in a mimetic agon *with* and *contra* Homer, he endows the poetic figure qua mime with metamorphic powers that go beyond the human as well. This is, indeed, a formidable threat for old idealist dreams of stabilization of Being and thus a strong ally for new materialist thinkers. Thus, in the *Republic*, Socrates asks in a critical mood, making clear that mimesis *is* the medium of these metamorphic transformations that go beyond the human: "Well, then, neighing horses, and lowing bulls, and the noise of the rivers and the roar of the sea and the thunder and everything of that kind—will they [poets] imitate these?" The predictable Platonic answer follows: "Nay, they have been forbidden, he said, to be mad or liken themselves to madmen" (1963b, 396b).

In the end, then, out of a maddening exasperation with poets' metamorphic powers of becoming different, Plato, in book 10 of the *Republic*, ultimately framed the active, embodied and plastic concept of *mimēsis* via a stabilizing, passive and reproductive visual trope: namely, a "mirror" (1963b, 596d). This move marked the metaphysical line dividing the original from the copy, the idea from the phenomenon, reality from appearance, the true world from the world of phantoms and simulations at three removes from the universal, ideal and thus intelligible Forms that both materialism and mimetic studies are up against. Plato's metaphysical fable that turns the material world into an illusory world is often told, mimetically repeated and thus remembered.[5] And yet, as any attentive reader of the Platonic dialogues cannot fail to notice, Plato's mimetic agon with Homer also leads him to steal narrative strategies and tropes from his opponent, such as mimetic dialogues, spellbinding myths and metamorphic gods.

We might wonder: why risk this aporia? For many reasons, or rather, affects, but also to try, and admittedly fail, to grasp a protean concept (mimesis) rooted in a plastic world of becoming (other) that, by definition, eludes idealist speculative Forms—as a chain of materialist figures will continue to confirm.

Plastic Figurations: Dante to Montaigne (via Auerbach)

Second metamorphosis. Already before the dawn of philosophy, plasticity and mimesis are entangled with the question of subject formation and protean transformations, generating a mimetic paradox that continues to inform the fundamental logic of plasticity as well in its double capacity to both give and receive form. What we must add now is that a few centuries after Plato, Latin and Roman authors introduced another concept deeply entangled with both plasticity and mimesis: namely, the concept of *figura*.

This is a concept that already makes some minor appearances in mimetic studies but has been largely restricted to its pathological political manifestations. For instance, for the French philosopher Philippe Lacoue-Labarthe who directly informs our account of the plasticity of mimesis in volume 1, "figure" (Latin, *figura*) has specific onto-political implications: it designates authoritarian leader figures who embody a racial type, or *tupos,* and have the will to power to impress the plastic materiality of the subject, both individually and collectively with a national/racial type. How? Via a form of passive or, in our language, pathological mimesis that turns "politics" into what Nazi politician and philologist Joseph Goebbels called "the plastic art of the State" (qtd. in Lacoue-Labarthe 1987, 94). Informing the onto-typology of what Lacoue-Labarthe and Jean-Luc Nancy call the "Nazi myth," this critique of authoritarian figures remains relevant for contemporary critiques of "(new) fascist" leaders that cast a shadow over the future of the twenty-first century and still deserves close attention.[6] And yet, at the same time, what Malabou says of deconstruction's critical stance toward form in general equally applies to Lacoue-Labarthe's critique of *figura* in particular. In her account of plasticity, Malabou argues, "form—formality and figurality" as she understands it "does not therefore open up the ideologically questionable space of 'ontotypology' as defined by Philippe Lacoue-Labarthe" (2010, 54).[7]

Furthering this line of inquiry, we add that *figura* has a long and complex genealogy that cannot easily be peeled off from a type of subject formation that is "living, and dynamic, incomplete and playful" (Auerbach 1984, 12), rendering it both metamorphic and patho-*logical* in orientation. This, at least, is what the philologist and literary critic Erich Auerbach helps us uncover.

To readers familiar with mimetic studies, this genealogical step back to the author of *Mimesis: The Representation of Reality in Western Literature* (1946) might initially surprise. So far, the mimetic turn has in fact been pushing *against* Auerbach's restriction of *mimesis* to the dominant definition of *representation* of reality, or realism, already indicated in the title of his famous book. This critique remains valid, but we are now in a position to complicate our opposition. What we said of the paradoxical logic of mimetic agonism in the past remains true in the present as well: critiques of influential precursors benefit from pushing both *with* and *against* them. If in volumes 1 and 2 we pushed against Auerbach's mimetic *realism* to promote a re-turn to mimetic *subjectivity*, we can now take a step further in volume 3: namely, push with Auerbach to deepen the genealogy of *plasticity* via the mimetic concept of *figura*.

Auerbach did not always restrict his analysis of mimesis to realism and the question of representation of reality it entailed, though that remained his main concern as a *literary critic*. As a *philologist*, he also linked mimesis to the question of plasticity along genealogical lines that are directly relevant for the mimetic turn. In an influential article titled "Figura" (1938), Auerbach takes this concept beyond mimetic realism toward plastic subject matters now central to both mimetic studies and new materialism. Thus, he explains that in its Latin origins, *figura* did not entail a copy, representation or realistic image of reality; rather, it indicated the "outline," "outward shape," or better, "mold" endowed with what he calls a certain "plasticity." As the German philologist puts it in the opening line of the essay: "Originally *figura*, from the same stem as *fingere, figulus, factor*, and *effigies*, meant 'plastic form'" (Auerbach 1984, 11). Not unlike mimesis, then, which is always central to the making of fictions, *figura* is from the very beginning already entangled with *plastic form*. The link with representational mimesis is direct,[8] but we could also not be closer to the mimetic turn now informing Malabou's theoretical preoccupations.

What, then, is the link between *figura*, plastic form and the mimetic metamorphoses that concern us in this volume? Auerbach shows that a genealogy of the concept of *figura* quickly troubles pathological associations with fascist political figures and unitary ontological forms that will later preoccupy deconstruction. In its Latin origins, *figura* positively in-*forms*, in the act of forming itself, the problematic of plastic formations and mimetic transformations now central to mimetic studies. Originally designating the "activity of forming" (Auerbach 1984, 11), rather than the formed object itself, Auerbach specifies that "*figura* is more concrete and dynamic than *forma*" (16). Relying on a plastic terminology, he adds: "Strictly speaking, *forma* meant 'mold,' French '*moule*' and was related to *figura* as the hollow form to the plastic shape that issues from it" (13). This allows Auerbach to take a further genealogical step, as he adds in a language familiar to mimetic studies:

> The original plastic sense [of *figura*] was not entirely lost, for *typos*, "imprint," and *plasis, plasma*, "plastic form," were often rendered by *figura* as the radical *fig-* suggested. From the meaning of *typos* developed the use of *figura* as "imprint of the seal," a metaphor with a venerable history running from Aristotle [...] through Augustine [...] to Dante. (1984, 15)

From figure to plasticity, type to mold, the meaning of *figura* is plastic and changes over time; yet its genealogy remains deeply rooted in the question that directly concerns us: namely, the formation and transformation of a plastic subject matter that mimetically assumes the impression of a type.[9] Following the genealogical traces of *figura*, then, has led us very quickly back to the chameleon subject that serves as a connecting thread for the *Homo Mimeticus* trilogy, allowing us to extend it toward new directions.[10]

The reader familiar with volumes 1 and 2 of *Homo Mimeticus* might in fact wonder: why have we not noted this foundational genealogical link before? After all, this is the very language Lacoue-Labarthe convokes to discuss the plasticity of a mimetic subject which, early in his career, he groups under the general rubric of "typography": as a philologically oriented philosopher invested in rethinking the concept of "figure" from the angle of the "plasticity" of a mimetic subject impressed by what he also calls a "type," he could not have failed to know Auerbach's classic text (Lacoue-Labarthe's philological learning was impressive). Yet, to my knowledge, he does not quote Auerbach in *Typography*, or elsewhere. In a modern form of agonism we call "*romantic* agonism" that is usually more characteristic of predecessors like René Girard,[11] Lacoue-Labarthe might not have quoted Auerbach's genealogy of *figura* because—like a mold out of which a plastic form emerges—it in-*forms* too directly his typographic theory of mimesis, or onto-typology, in general and his critique of the political pathologies of identifications with a rigid figure of authority in particular.

Following this genealogical trace puts us now in a position to confirm Malabou's point that *figura* cannot be restricted to a pathological totalitarian figure alone. On the contrary, it in-*forms* the plastic problematic of the mimetic subject via patho-*logical* formations that are creative, process-oriented and re-*productive*. What we add is that these genealogical traces reach from the Roman period into the late Middle Ages and the Renaissance, where, as we saw in volume 2, mimetic studies finds its "theoretical *élan*" in more dynamic, immanent and future-oriented images. Given that the problematic of plasticity as Malabou defines it, and of mimesis as defined by mimetic studies, have the question of plastic form—and the figurations, formations and transformations that ensue—in common, there is thus considerable interest in furthering a diagnostic of plastic/mimetic subjectivity via the longer genealogy Auerbach encourages us to consider.

Among Latin poets, Auerbach enlists Lucretius, Cicero and Virgil, who, from different perspectives, link *figura* with mimetic concepts such as the simulacra, ghosts and phantoms we are familiar with. But it is of course in Ovid that, as he puts it, "we find the richest source for *figura* in the sense of changing form" or "metamorphosis" (Auerbach 1984, 21). In the *Metamorphoses* (8 AD), in fact, Ovid reloads the plastic powers of mimesis by switching the focus from the sea-god Proteus to the god of dreams, Morpheus, out of which mimetic meta-*morphoses* are born. Thus, Ovid writes: "Morpheus, the skillful artificer and imitator of [man's] shape [*simulatoremque figuras*]; nature builds up forms from other forms" specifying in the process that "the soul [...] passes through various forms [*migrare figuras*]; water *gives and receives* new forms," (qtd. in Auerbach 1984, 22; my emphasis).[12] Far from being unitary and unchanging, thanks to a mimetic god, the soul goes through a plurality of *figuras* or metamorphoses via a plastic process of giving and receiving forms. After Homer and Plato, it is perhaps Ovid who delineates most clearly the plasticity of mimesis connection that, well before Hegel, in-forms both Malabou and mimetic studies.

What we must add is that the spiraling loop that goes from imitation to figura to plastic metamorphoses could not be more clearly outlined. Convoking the typographic language of impressing a seal, Auerbach adds that in Ovid there is also a "fine example of the imprint of the seal": "And as the soft wax is stamped with new *figurae* and does not remain as it was nor retain the same forms, though it remains itself the same" (1984, 22). This seals indeed the connection between plasticity and mimesis we first established via Plato. Moreover, Ovid—for whom, Auerbach specifies, "*figura* is mobile, changeable, multiform and deceptive" (23)—shows us that there is an interplay of sameness and difference that is constitutive of the genealogy of homo mimeticus as well. And it is this dynamic and changeable interplay that leads to metamorphoses of the spirit in which the subject matter keeps metamorphosing, while its plastic substance remains the same. In sum, the genealogy of plastic figures makes us see that one does not need to wait for Hegel or deconstruction, let alone contemporary neurosciences, to find confirmations that plasticity and mimetic subjectivity are constitutive of homo plasticus/mimeticus. Mimetic poets deeply concerned with giving new forms to ancient *figurae* already paved the way. As Auerbach recognized: "it is the poets who were most interested in the shades of meaning between model and copy, in changing form, and the deceptive likenesses that walk in dream" (1984, 21). There are thus ample reasons to keep thickening the literary-philosophical genealogy that give affective and theoretical substance to both plasticity and mimesis.[13]

In the wake of Roman authors, it is perhaps Dante who, in *The Divine Comedy* (c. 1321), goes furthest in shifting the concept of plasticity from aesthetics to subjectivity via the mimetic concept of *figura* as a medium of impression generating new forms via a new language. As Massimo Cacciari recognized in his essay on humanism, "Dante is not looking for another Latin but for the language capable of giving form to his experience of time, rendering it eternal without losing its intensity, its *pathos*" (2019, 20; my trans.). This pathos, it should be clear, is not simply mimetic in the sense of a passive imitation. Thus, Cacciari qualifies Dante's relation to his Latin model, Virgil, by saying that "no imitation or repetition would make sense" (2020). Wherein, then, lies the linguistic force of Dante's *pathos* of figuration? And if the intensity that drives this pathos is mimetic in a different, more material, immanent and artistic sense, which plastic forms does his *logos* take? Cacciari provides a clue to answer these questions as he notes: "this logos [...] is construed via an *interiorization* of the paradigms and models that are operating in the 'best ironsmiths' [*i migliori fabbri*]" (16). And thinking of Dante as the *"poet philosopher"* (21) who coined the phrase "*il miglior fabbro del parlar materno*"[14] in the first place, he adds: "It is the poet that, by hammering and rehammering the matrix language on the anvil, draws from it the illustrious vernacular" (20). Let us take a closer look at this patho-logical hammering of a plastic subject matter.

In Canto XII of *Purgatorio,* as Dante the protagonist ascends the mount in the company of his spiritual Roman guide, Virgil, he see sculptures of Christian figures cut in "white marble" that are so realistic he considers them superior to the ancient Greek sculptor, Polykleitos, whose technique of *contrapposto* introduced movement in Greek sculptures of human figures. Now, in order to delineate these figures sculpted in the plasticity of marble via the medium of his poetics, Dante convokes a familiar trope: he says that they are formed "as a figure is stamped in wax [*come figura in cera si suggella*]" (Dante 1991, X.28–45). This is a memorable vernacular phrase Auerbach also quotes. What we add is that it captures both sides of the plasticity of mimesis. On one side, we appear to be still within the traditional confines of mimetic realism. Dante, in fact, uses the plasticity of the wax metaphorically to account for the plasticity of the marble human figures formed by Giotto's chisel—at least if we consider that these figures are *already* formed. On the other side, a philological understanding of how *figura* operates as a dynamic, formative and transformative force qua "act of forming" reveals that Dante's focus is on the artistic process of impressing a plastic material figure, rather than on the static aesthetic product. Put differently, his double focus on both figure and wax delineates the double, paradoxical process of giving and receiving form, rather than the final form itself. We are thus back, via Dante's matrix language, to the matrix figure out of which the mimetic subject qua homo mimeticus is formed and transformed—out of a plastic subject matter.

Given Dante's focus on the language of impression, it is not surprising that he develops this sculptural analogy further in *Purgatorio* by taking it beyond aesthetics to the sphere of subjectivity. He does so in psychological—or should we say neurological—terms that anticipate the mimetic turn—if only because he later stretches the plasticity of wax impressed by a figure to the plasticity of the human "brain." Thus, Dante compares the effects of the words of his beloved muse, Beatrice, to an image that is now already impressed in the reader's imagination, informing mimetic studies as well:

> *Sì come cera da suggello,*
> *che la figura impressa non trasmuta,*
> *segnato è or da voi lo mio cervello.*

> As by a signet is the wax
> Which does not change the figure stamped upon it.
> My brain is now imprinted by yourself. (Dante, XXXIII:79–81, 216)

Just as the plasticity of wax is impressed by the figure on a seal, so the plastic brain is impressed by the beloved's voice. Even in its Christian conception of agape that was central to the Middle Ages, love not only informs the psychic life of a disembodied soul; rather, it delineates a figure that makes plastic impressions on the embodied "brain" of the mimetic subject. The rhyme between *suggello* and *cervello*, seal and brain, is unfortunately lost in translation. Its "original" aesthetic function is precisely to generate a lasting mnemonic impression in readers and listeners' brains as well, performing on the side of life what it appears to simply represent on the side of art. Thus, Dante's artistic seal doubles the impression of a memorable diagnostic phrase, proving his patho-logical point via performative linguistic practice.

No wonder that contemporary neuroscientists interested in going beyond narrow two-cultures divides do not hesitate to bring up Dante as a precursor of neuroscientific insights. As Vittorio Gallese puts it, commenting on different lines from *The Divine Comedy*:

> Both art and science are among the most distinctive expressions of human creativity. Both enable us to make visible the invisible. Art, however, does it in a much less prosaic way. This is also why it is perhaps more appealing than science. This example also clearly shows that almost always someone else in the past got it right before us. As scientists we should learn a little more humility. (Wojciehowski 2011, n.p.)

The example impressed in Gallese's memory is different, but the point is the same. In a mirroring genealogical reflection, we can only add that what is true for scientists remains true for philosophers and scholars in the humanities as well. This is a lesson contributors will keep in mind, or rather, in their "brain-bodies" (Gallese and Lawtoo 2024) in the chapters that follow as we keep tracing the metamorphoses of plastic figures that have made lasting impressions in the history of culture.

With humility, then, let us take a step further in our genealogy of plastic figures: a few centuries later, as the Renaissance rediscovered the classical period, it recuperated both medieval and ancient diagnostics of the plasticity of subjectivity. Although neither Lacoue-Labarthe nor Auerbach linger on the Renaissance, this genealogical connection is visible in literary-philosophical writers like Michel de Montaigne. A major influence on Nietzsche, Montaigne was also a careful reader of Plato and of the Roman authors just mentioned; he is thus a key ally for mimetic studies in general and for diagnosing plastic subject formations in particular.[15] In his famous concluding essay, "On Education," for instance, Montaigne draws directly from Plato's concern with the education of the plastic soul, with which we started in volume 1. He does so by reminding modern and, at one remove, contemporary readers that the soul is not unlike clay. And yet, he does not rely on the well-known trope of the seal and the wax. Instead, he develops an alternative metaphor that captures the dynamic process of plastic formation and stabilization via an experiential artistic movement. Thus, he quotes the Roman poet Aulus Persius Flaccus saying:

> *Udum et molle lutum est; nunc nunc properandus et acri*
> *Fingendus sine fine rota*

> The clay is soft and malleable [*humide et molle est l'argille*].
> Quick! hurry to fashion it [*le pétrir*] on that potter's wheel
> which is forever spinning [*la rue agile*] (Montaigne 2003, 1:26, 183).

Indeed, the soul has remained plastic over millennia; the potter's wheel of education is forever spinning, generating mimetic turns and re-turns that reach into the present, making lasting impressions on new generations as well. If epigenetics confirms the role of culture and experience in shaping human nature, Montaigne provides a metaphoric image to capture this artistic process of plastic formation. A new and stable form emerges paradoxically from the movement of a spinning wheel that puts a sensorial experience and a plastic material in creative touch, so to speak.

Figure 1. *Forming Hands*, drawing on paper, Nia Lawtoo 2025

Titled *Forming Hands,* figure 1 captures the plastic subject matter at hand by inscribing the plasticity of mimesis in time as well. The reader of this trilogy might recall that I started reflecting on the plasticity of mimesis in the company of my three-year-old daughter who sealed, via the hyperplasticity of her youth, the Play-Doh-Plato connection that started this investigation in the first place (see Lawtoo 2022, 140). A decade later, as a twelve-year-old, she now used her sensitive hands to give plastic form to the plasticity of clay on a spinning wheel that, via different turns and re-turns, is at play in the essays collected in this volume.

To give this wheel an additional spin, I include a series of haptic, porous and impressionistic figures, titled *Transfigurations,* which capture the dynamic interplay of hands fashioning clay while the wheel is in the process of spinning (figs. 2-5). What Gilles Deleuze says of Francis Bacon's artistic techniques that render palpable what he calls the logic of sensation equally applies to Michaela Lawtoo's artistic techne used in the following aquarelles: "The important thing is that they do not constrain the Figure to immobility; on the contrary, they must make tangible a sort of pathway [*rendre sensible une sorte de cheminement*], an exploration of the Figure within the space, or of itself" (Deleuze 2002, 11; my trans.).

As Horace used to say: *ut pictura poiesis,* poetry resembles painting. Or should we rather say: *ut poiesis pictura,* painting resembles poetry? Either way, both in poetic language and in artistic figurations, *Transfigurations* traces a dynamic pathway, or *cheminement,* that does not represent human hands forming clay from a visual distance; rather, the aquarelles aim to capture the dynamic sensation intimately felt by the material interplay of plastic clay (*argille*), on the one hand, and agile (*agile*) hands, on the other.[16] Again lost in translation, Montaigne's rhyme between *argille* and *agile* aims for the same effects, not via the medium of painting but of words: he does not simply represent plasticity within the text but, rather, performs it on plastic brains outside the text. Thus, this time drawing on Cicero, who was himself drawing on Plato, Montaigne quickly turns the wheel as he writes: "a belief is like an impression stamped on our soul: the softer and less resisting the soul, the easier it is to print anything on it" (1:27, 200).

The theoretical outline of *figura* is now becoming clearer: for a long genealogy that goes from Plato to Lucretius, Dante to Montaigne, beliefs, habits, models and culture more generally not only inform the mind; they also form and transform a "soul," a mimetic-metamorphic-plastic soul that a materialist tradition rooted in the brain—or, to use Gallese's term, in the "brain-body." If neuroscientists acknowledge this ancient tradition, mimetic studies reciprocates the gesture so as keep sculpting a plastic self whose genealogy we are still in the process of figuring out.

Figures 2, 3, 4. *Transfigurations I, II, III*, aquarelle on paper, 2025 Michaela Lawtoo

Sculpting the Self: Plotinus to Hadot (via Foucault)

Third metamorphosis. A genealogy of the Roman concept of *figura* unearths a materialist tradition that is sensitive to the power of art to give form to the self qua brain-body. Another way of framing this immanent process whereby the mimetic subject is transformed via the figural language of art in general and sculpture in particular is currently grouped under the rubric of "techniques of the self." Commonly associated with the last phase of Michel Foucault's career, as he turned to ethics to advocate for a "care of the self," or "*souci de soi*" (Foucault 1984) rooted in classical Greek and Roman authors, it has not been sufficiently stressed that this "care" presupposes the mimetic malleability of a metamorphic "self." The latter was already central to both Greek and Roman traditions and reaches, via aestheticism, into modernity.[17]

In the last decade of his life, Foucault's genealogical work on the history of sexuality led him back to the conception of the subject he had previously contributed to dissolving or erasing. His goal, however, was not to reinstate "man" as a figure of sovereign authority; rather, it was to reveal the aesthetic foundations of a relational, plastic, embodied and—we should now add—mimetic self.[18] His overturning genealogical move was deft and forceful: in characteristic Nietzschean fashion, Foucault shifted the focus from the dominant (transcendental) Platonic question of "self-*knowledge*" (*gnothi sauton*) restricted to *theoria* and the *vita contemplativa* to the marginalized (immanent) question of "*care* of the self" (*epimeleia heautou*) central to Socratic, Stoic, Epicurean, Cynic and early Christian ethical preoccupations with practices of self-transformation animating what we call a *vita mimetica*. On these immanent philosophical foundations, then, and in a modernist spirit close to the aestheticism of Baudelaire and Nietzsche—and, we should add, Wilde as well[19]—Foucault asked an untimely question: namely, whether "the life of each individual could not be a work of art"? (2017, 1436).

The question did not fail to generate accusations of aestheticism and capitulation to neoliberalism, but the telos of Foucault's arts of the self was not to restrict life within the self-enclosed confines of aestheticism, or *l'art pour l'art*. On the contrary, it was to open up the confines of aesthetics to plastic and metamorphic transformations of the self in the spirit of what mimetic studies also calls *l'art pour la vie*: that is, the power of art to form and transform human life. For Foucault, in fact, this shaping of the self qua work of art relies on what he calls a "*technê tou bio*," or "art of life" (*art de vie*) (2017, 1434) operating on a plastic material that is not simply passively subjected to power; it can also actively take hold of a plurality of "technologies of the self" whereby individuals "transform themselves" (1988, 18). How? Not in the solipsistic isolation of "auto-affection" Malabou is rightly critical of, but in relations of mimetic communication constitutive of "hetero-affection" instead.[20] This affection entails what Derrida calls "the other's existence in me" (qtd. in Malabou 2022a, 245); following Pierre Janet, I call this other a *socius* which finds in the experience of mimesis a principle to transgress the boundaries dividing self and other.[21] It is in fact important to recall that in addition to truth-telling (*parrhesia*), confessional practices, spiritual exercises and other *technai* of the self, Foucault adds the experience of following a teacher as a key instrument of self-care via an other qua *socius* already interior to the self. Foucault thus specifies that "for the Stoics, truth is not in oneself [as for Plato] but in the *logoi*, the teaching of the teachers" (1988, 35). And he adds: "one memorizes what one has heard, converting the statements one hears into rules of conduct" (35). Unsurprisingly given the emphasis on memory, this technical patho-*logy* is not deprived of mimetic principles. Foucault specifies for instance that its "*dessin* [plan but also drawing] was to give to their lives certain values, to *reproduce certain examples*, to leave behind an exceptional reputation" (2017, 1443; emphasis added). Again, the *dessin* of these figures is not based on a passive, representation or realistic mimesis; rather, it actively re-*produces* the "lives" of exemplary figures and the "values" they embody so as to become themselves worthy of active imitation for future generations. As Nietzsche had already put it, "those who are called artists are these heirs" (1974, 354: 298); and convoking the trope of the ring in a magnetic chain characteristic of the *vita mimetica*, he specifies that these figures "always come at the end of a long chain" (298).

Foucault's last turn to ethics, then, does not entail a return to the problematic of the subject that his early work had contributed to dissolving during the (post-)structuralist turn. Rather, philological lenses reveal that the care of the self, for him, is based on immanent techniques that operate on a plastic, relational and embodied self who is already other and is genealogically in line with the mimetic turn, or *re*-turn. He was not alone in thinking this. The classicist Pierre Hadot, whose definition of "philosophy as a way of life" (Hadot 1995) directly informs Foucault's account of "care of the self," confirms that imitation plays a key role in the formation of this self. Thus, Hadot writes that an ancient philosopher like Epicurus was considered a "model one had to imitate" (194). The same applies to other philosophers like the skeptic Pyrrhus who, Hadot tells us, "is satisfied with living and attracts thus disciples who imitate his way of life"

(174). Many more examples could be given, but the point remains the same: if imitation in-*forms* techniques of care of the self, it follows that the *souci de soi* does not entail a solipsistic concern with an autonomous, self-contained and sovereign self. On the contrary, as Hadot puts it: "the care of the self [*souci de soi*] is thus indissolubly a care of the city [*souci de la cité*] and care of others [*souci des autres*]" (68)—a relational mimetic insight that applies to Foucault's hermeneutics of the self as well.

Put in the language of mimetic studies, the relational dimension of the techne of imitation is re-productive, social and political in nature. It provides an instrument, or chisel, this *soi* can actively use to give form, or sculpt, a plastic subject matter that is both artist and artistic work at the same time. This also means that the self can paradoxically both give form to itself and receive form—while being in a relation of mimetic communication with privileged others. We are thus back to the paradox of mimesis, which mirrors the paradox of plasticity and reaches, via Malabou, into the present. But we are now in a position to see that the paradox is relational in orientation as the process of giving form to the self is entangled with the form of others with whom the self comes into being as a metamorphic subject.

Genealogy is the art of tracing surprising associations. This entails following the traces wherever they take us, provided they further our understanding of the mimetic qua plastic subject. Interestingly, and in another paradoxical turn, the focus on sculpting the materiality of the plastic self that is now central to new materialist thinkers finds another precursor in an idealist thinker close to the Platonic foundations with which we started. Hadot's ethics of the *souci de soi* that inspired the late Foucault is in fact genealogically in line with the founder of Neoplatonism: namely, the Greek-born Roman philosopher Plotinus.[22] Convoking the aesthetic language of the beautiful, which, as for Plato before him, rests on an idealist metaphysics, Plotinus relies—perhaps more explicitly than any other philosopher before him—on the metaphor of the sculptor giving material form to a plastic conception of the self qua statue. As he puts it in *Enneads* (c. 270 AD):

> Go back inside yourself and look: if you do not yet see yourself as beautiful, then do as the sculptor does with a statue, he wants to make it beautiful; he chisels away one part, and levels off another, makes one spot smooth and another clear, until he shows forth a beautiful face on the statue. Like him, remove what is superfluous, straighten what is crooked, clean up what is dark and make it bright, and *never stop sculpting your own statue*, until the godlike splendor of virtue shines forth to you. (I 6.9, in Hadot 1993, 21)

The metaphysical binary is by now familiar: model versus copy, ideal Form versus material form, transcendence versus immanence. At first sight, the genealogy of plasticity brings us back to the idealist metaphysics the mimetic turn is seeking to move beyond: namely, back to the old ideal of mimesis as a debased copy, shadow or phantom of reality. For Plotinus, as for Plato before him, the model the sculptor imitates remains fixated on an ideal, intelligible Form of the Beautiful far removed from this phenomenal world. And yet, the material language of sculpting a plastic self also balances this idealist metaphysics with what we could call an aesthetic physics sensitive to the process of formation, or figuration. The sculptor, in fact, puts the techne of mimesis to immanent work on the material subject matter that is the self, "chisel[ing] away," "level[ing] off," "mak[ing] one spot smooth," etc. It is only thanks to this materialist art of the self that mimesis brings a plastic form, or *figura*, into being—and perhaps Being as well.

What, then, has true Being in the end? The ideal ontological model mimesis reproduces, as an idealist tradition from Plato to Plotinus and beyond posits? Or rather, the plastic aesthetic figure the mimetic techne re-produces, as a materialist tradition from Socrates to Lucretius and beyond suggests? This agonistic confrontation between idealists and materialists entails what Plato, or rather Socrates, already called a "battle of the gods and giants" (1963c, 246ab);[23] its contest or agon traverses the entire history of metaphysics in general and in-forms the plastic foundations of the mimetic subject in particular. It also reminds us that Socrates's father was a sculptor. As Henry Staten noted in *Homo Mimeticus II*, this realization opens up a more down-to-earth materialist perspective: it reframes Plato's idealist metaphysics from the angle of a techne of mimesis that is already internal to mimetic studies.[24]

For our purpose, it suffices to say that, commenting directly on the lines by Plotinus, Hadot echoes Plato's idealist metaphysics, but he does so with a difference. He writes: "Art must not copy reality: in that case, it would only be an inferior copy which is the object perceived by our senses" (1993, 20). Sculpting the self cannot be reduced to a passive imitation of the phenomenal world restricted to the type of aesthetic realism Auerbach relies on in *Mimesis*, as we already saw.[25] But then, in a paradoxical phrase, Hadot adds: "The True function of art is 'heuristic': through the work of art, we discover, or 'invent' [*invente*] the eternal model, the Idea, of which the sensible reality is a mere image" (20). The idealist ontology is once again familiar, but the ambivalence Hadot introduces via the verb "*inventer*"[26] restages the agon between two antithetical ontological perspectives, redoubling the battle of the giants. At stake is not only materialism contra idealism but also a battle between modern and ancient interpretations.

On the side of the ancients, we could indeed follow etymology and translate "*inventer*" as "discover," thereby suggesting that the sculptor (or philosopher) working on the plastic material (or self) finds a pre-existing transcendental model (or Idea) that was already there all along and had implicitly served as the "original" model in the first place for the philosopher-artist to simply reproduce. Sculpting the self would thus reinstate the idealist metaphysics via a plastic material figure that is modeled on an ideal Form. Conversely, from a materialist but also modern perspective, we could be inclined to read *inventer* in its contemporary French meaning, "to invent." After all, Hadot writes in modern French—thereby opening up a more troubling interpretation. In fact, if the mimetic copy "invents" or *produces* the model "itself," it is the ideal model that turns out to be dependent on the plastic material for its proper "Being" to emerge. This second, more modern and forward-looking option would pave the way for deconstructions to come where the copy brings the original into being, while at the same time adding a materialist supplement in line with mimetic studies.

The entire history of western metaphysics hinges on this etymological hesitation and its overturning implications. While Hadot is eventually faithful to Plotinus's idealism, as he simply states that "the work of art is an attempt to imitate this idea" (1993, 20–21), both the mimetic turn and the new materialist turn would favor the second interpretation. Interestingly, in the end Plotinus himself, despite his undeniable idealist tendencies, uses the techne of writing to put mimesis to performative use on plastic subjects living in this world. Thus, he addresses the reader in direct mimetic (rather than diegetic) speech that reaches into the present, as he says: "never stop sculpting your own statute." What is rhetorically at play in this imperative is not simply a constative statement based on mimetic realism; nor is it only a "performative speech act" in which "the uttering of the sentence is, or is part of, the doing of the action" (Austin 1975, 5). I call a performative speech act that operates not only via linguistic actions but via bodily and affective actions a "mime-act" (Lawtoo 2023, 1454) to stress the performative properties at play in the concept of mimesis (from *mîmos*, actor or performance) and promoted by mimetic studies.

From plastic figures to the care of the self, from the aesthetic of existence to mime acts, a long chain of materialist thinkers that has been marginalized in the past is re-turning to inform new mimetic studies via plastic metamorphoses of a spirit, or soul, that is rooted in the body. This leads us to the last metamorphosis, which goes beyond mimetic and anti-mimetic principles.

(Anti-)Mimetic Metamorphoses: Nietzsche's Parable

Fourth metamorphosis. Given the previous, rather long, genealogical steps that go from antiquity to the present, it is perhaps not surprising that, in the modern period, the metamorphosis of a mimetic/plastic subject has been best dramatized in parabolic form by the philosopher-poet who provided the starting point for the mimetic turn, or *re*-turn, in the first place. In *Thus Spoke Zarathustra* (1883), Nietzsche dramatizes three metamorphoses of the spirit that served as the immanent, down-to-earth model for our four metamorphoses of plasticity—perhaps even stretching to inform the "three major metamorphoses of intelligence" (Malabou 2017, 28) that Malabou advocates for the digital age. As this genealogical connection will inform the Coda as well, a brief overview should suffice here.

Much has been said about "The Three Metamorphoses [*Verwandlungen*] of the Spirit" that open Friedrich Nietzsche's philosophical poem—a text that defines the human as something that needs to be overcome via the figure of the "Overhuman" (*Übermensch*). This concept, or rather figure, has caused much confusion in the past century as it was misappropriated by fascist and Nazi ideologues that erected it as a totalitarian figure. Yet a focus on mimesis quickly reveals the anti-fascist, creative and life-affirmative metamorphic drive that animates this philosophical parable. That a mimetic paradox is central to Nietzsche's conception of metamorphosis is already indicated by the book's subtitle: "A Book for Everyone and Nobody." In a paradoxical performative mime-act, this title addresses both mimetic (everyone) and anti-mimetic (no one) tendencies in readers, while also pointing to a (anti-)mimetic paradox we are by now familiar with. For Nietzsche, in fact, the metamorphic "spirit" oscillates, pendulum-like, between mimetic pathos and critical distance, as it is both vulnerable to mimetic infection and critical of it. This pathos of distance, as he also calls it, generates in turn what we called patho(-)logical effects with the power or, rather, will to power, to turn "no one" into every "everyone" and vice versa—for both good and ill.[27]

Reloading the paradox of mimesis, which as we know, mirrors the paradox of plasticity, the three metamorphoses Nietzsche outlines in *Zarathustra* also hinge on mimetic and anti-mimetic processes that go beyond the human. Thus, he dramatizes nonhuman animals that pave the way for that future-oriented figure of the "Overhuman." Contrary to grand teleological narratives of linear progress, Nietzsche makes clear at the outset that the human is "not a goal" but, rather, a "bridge" directing the Overhuman to what he calls, repeatedly, "a *going-over* and a *going-under*" (2005, 13). While "going-over" opens up a plurality of future-oriented metamorphic possibilities, the direction of "going-under" also restricts these possibilities to a material plane of immanence. Clearly, this Overhuman is not directed toward the sky of abstract ideal forms located in imaginary "worlds behind" [*Hinterwelten*]" (27) that oriented the *vita contemplativa* of figures like Plato or Plotinus. Instead, the Overhuman is of the earth, part of the material, embodied and finite existence of a mimetic life. That is, a *vita mimetica* characterized by protean metamorphoses of a spirit rooted in a body that, since birth, is tied to relations of affective communication with others.[28] It is from this immanent perspective that Nietzsche continues to inspire the metamorphoses of homo mimeticus via plastic animal figures that speak parabolically to contemporary transformations that go beyond nature–culture binaries. Thus, behind the mask of Zarathustra, Nietzsche tells the story of "how the spirit became a camel, and the camel a lion, and the lion at last a child" (23). Let us proceed in order.

The first metamorphic figure of the camel is thoroughly mimetic. It depicts the spirit as a herd animal that embodies a type of passive mimesis impressed on flexible and docile subjects. The camel is a figure that receives form from others and thus does not give form to itself—if only because it *con*-forms to other members of the herd, blending in with others by shadowing them, often unconsciously. Like other herd animals, it does so via a form of animal "mimicry" Nietzsche was among the first to theorize as constitutive of human mimicry in general and moral behavior in particular.[29] Being like everyone, the camel is no one; its ego is but a shadow or phantom of other egos. The metamorphosis into a camel represents thus a typical process of passive mimetic adaptation that, both in its animal and all-too-human manifestations, is herd-like, conforming and docile in nature, is representative of Christian moral values and is central to Nietzsche's critique of modernity, for he generally diagnoses it as a type of mimetic sickness, or pathology. Drawing on Nietzsche, Foucault would later qualify this camel-like figure as a "docile subject" subjected to a network of power-knowledge that turns "the soul" into what he calls, in a famous overturning of Plato, "the prison for the body" (1977, 30). Echoing Pascal (and thus Montaigne), Bourdieu will speak of a "habitus" passed down via "education" and generative of an "immediate adaptation" (1997, 201) to the social body. The language differs but the same mimetic point informs these diagnostics.[30]

And yet, for Nietzsche, as for the genealogical precursors from which he draws, mimesis is never unilateral. Rather, it goes beyond good and evil, generating both pathologies and patho-*logies*, or critical discourses on the logic of mimetic affect, or pathos. We are in fact told that "the heavy and the hardest are what its [the camel's] strength desires" (Nietzsche 2005, 23). There is thus a mirroring relation between the "heavy" mimetic burden on one side and the "strength" of the mimetic animal on the other, a strength reinforced by carrying cultural weights of the past which, with a good dose of endurance, creativity and life-affirmative pathos can be put to both critical and creative use for the future. Being no one, the spirit has the potential to actively imitate selective others in view of becoming, perhaps not everyone, but at least someone. Hence, passivity turns into activity, docile and automatic habits turn into re-*productive* habitus coinciding with the "birth of a passion" (Malabou 2008b, x). In many ways, what Malabou says in her preface to Félix Ravisson's *Of Habit* equally applies to Nietzsche's first metamorphosis of mimesis: far from being simply reduced to a "simulacrum of being, an imitation of virtue" based on "automatism" (2008b, vii), habit, just like mimesis, has the power to provoke "the transformation of receptivity (or passivity) into spontaneity (or activity)" (x).[31] In our language, the mimetic pathology of the spirit Nietzsche often excoriates as herd behavior can also be turned to affirmative, patho-*logical* use—which leads us to the second metamorphosis.

Contrary to the camel, the lion appears to be thoroughly *anti*-mimetic at first. Thus, it emerges from the "loneliest desert" (Nietzsche 2005, 23), where it is not inclined to conform to any moral or social types imposed from the outside. On the contrary, the lion is driven by an aggressive power, or pathos, that is down to earth in orientation. Let us not forget that, as a classical philologist, Nietzsche is likely to have remembered that the lion corresponds to Proteus' first metamorphosis in *The Odyssey*. He would certainly have known that it is the animal constantly associated with Homeric heroes. Of course, "lion-hearted Achilles" comes to mind, but we should not forget that Odysseus too, as he reveals himself to Nausicaa for instance, is compared to a "mountain lion trusting its strength" (Homer 2020, 6.130) and repeatedly so as his return home nears.[32] Force and power, or will to power, are needed to move beyond the chain of passive mimesis that burdens the soul with the moral values of the past.

At the more general ontological level, conjuring a Homeric world of becoming entails a modern re-enactment of the battle of the gods and giants generating an agon with another animal that dominated previous generations: namely, the "dragon" named "Thou Shalt" (2005, 24). This figure epitomizes moral imperatives of the past that, since the dawn of religions, pave the way for both Platonism and Christianity—i.e. the Persian prophet Zoroaster or Zarathustra Nietzsche aims to reconfigure *in primis,* had impressed a multiplicity of herd animals. Contrary to the camel, and contra the dragon, we are told that the lion finds in this agonistic confrontation its own "freedom," which Nietzsche considers necessary for "new creation" (24). Any theory of mimesis of Nietzschean inspiration, then, must be animated by *anti*-mimetic perspectives that reevaluate the value of mimetic values and theories of the past. This is, indeed, what the theory of homo mimeticus proposes by pushing against predecessors in order to go further—a strategy we shall see at play in Malabou's theory of plasticity as well.

But anti-mimesis is not the final drive, or pathos, that propels the human toward new metamorphic destinations. Going beyond pathos and distance, mimetic and anti-mimetic drives, Nietzsche adds that to move from critique to creativity and affirm a life of becoming, a last metamorphosis is still needed. As he puts it: "To create new values—that even the lion cannot yet do" (2005, 24). And pointing to a life-affirmative, innocent and future-oriented figure, Nietzsche proposes the child as a plastic subject to go beyond, or rather, over the human. As he puts it: "innocence the child is and forgetting, a beginning anew, a play, a self-propelling wheel [*ein aus sich rollendes Rad*], a first-movement, a sacred Yea-saying [*Ja-sagens*]" (24). We are far removed indeed from the caricatures of the *Übermensch* endowed with the will to power to impress docile subjects with the stamp of an authoritarian figure or type, not to speak about contemporary transhumanist fantasies of technological enhancement that aim to leave the body behind while the spirit is uploaded to cyberspace. Instead, Nietzsche roots the metamorphoses of the spirit back into a mimetic, all too mimetic, body that is not simply subject to what Montaigne—a major influence on Nietzsche—called the "wheel of education," but rather one that actively self-propels this wheel into motion, generating an interplay between cultural influences and the plastic subject matter at hand.

Children are, of course, mimetic-plastic figures par excellence. They can be impressed, camel-like, from the outside. But this does not mean that they cannot actively create, play or re-*produce* new beginnings that are self-propelling from the inside—for the distinction between the inside and the outside, passivity and activity, repetition and difference, is precisely what a mimetic metamorphosis blurs in the end. Although the brain remains plastic throughout our lives, it is indeed in childhood that what Malabou calls "the plastic art of the brain" (2008, 19) is most intense. Even prior to birth, "embryonic stem cells" discovered in the early 1990s have the (im)propriety to "differentiate into all the specialized cells" (Malabou 2015, 70). Also known as "pluripotent cells," they have the mimetic power, or will to power, to generate a re-production of cells based on biological processes of mimetic repetition. After birth, "the sculptor's chisel" is also fully at work, via a neurological phenomenon known as "apoptosis" or "cell death," which is intense in the first six months and is responsible for what Malabou calls "the progressive sculpting of the definitive form of the [neuronal] system" (2008, 19). Perhaps more than any other plastic figure encountered so far, children are thus endowed with the paradoxical powers of receiving form and giving form that seal the productive connection between the paradox of mimesis and the paradox of plasticity being traced in this Prologue. In the metamorphic processes that follow, contributors will continue to trouble dualist oppositions between activity and passivity, body and spirit, self and others, copy and model, art and life, and, increasingly, online and offline, digital influence and physical influencers, among other metaphysical binaries already rendered porous and precarious by the genealogy of figures we have been tracing so far—and figures yet to come.

As made clear in the introduction, these binaries now include gendered, sexed and sexual binaries as well. Despite his influence on feminist thinkers like Luce Irigaray, Nietzsche's gender politics were not without misogynist and patriarchal traces that must be examined, critiqued and supplemented by feminist philosophers and gender theorists who are already internal to the genealogy of mimetic studies.[33] It is important to note that, as a linguistic category, *das Kind* does not belong to any gendered or sexual identity. It does not prescribe any gendered type, leaving its sexual orientation open to what Malabou calls "the social plasticity of gender" (2020, 17). Thus, she speaks of an "original biological malleability, a first transformability. If sex were not plastic, there would be no gender" (2011, 138). And in Nietzschean fashion, she adds: "Transformability is at work from the start, it trumps all determination. Everything starts with metamorphosis" (139). A future-oriented figure par excellence, the child, not unlike the newborn's brain, remains ontologically open to plastic metamorphoses of the brain-body that cut across deep-seated patriarchal and phallocentric binaries in view of "changing difference" as well, as Malabou will confirm in the Coda.

A metamorphosis, in the end, does not simply replace previous stages, just as the butterfly does not simply replace the caterpillar. Rather, a metamorphosis (*meta*, after or change, *morphē*, form) goes through a *trans*-formation often mediated by subliminal alterations of consciousness akin to a hypnotic trance. It also entails an embodied, biological, physiological, but also, for Nietzsche, psychological, aesthetic, political and spiritual reorganization of the self that retains the critical powers internal to previous stages, including mimetic stages, while putting them to creative and life-affirmative use. If the child's innocence retains the anti-mimetic qualities of the lion to propose a "new beginning" (Nietzsche 2005, 24), the trope of the self-propelled wheel also points to an affirmative *re*-turn to a mimetic education that is not simply passive, docile and condemned to the repetition of the same. Rather, as the reference to play already suggests, this re-*turn* is active, joyful, metamorphic and creative of plastic figures that emerge from the dynamic interplay of both receiving form and giving form.

This paradoxical process of figuration is expressed artistically in the last aquarelle (fig. 5) that completes the *Transfigurations* series also reproduced on the cover of this book. It delineates the last step of a series of transformations that are not modelled on a static image or preexisting form. On the contrary, it is part of a metamorphic process of giving and receiving form generative of a self-fashioning figura emerging from that plastic subject matter that is life itself.

Figure 5. *Transfigurations IV: Self-Fashioning Figura*, aquarelle on paper, 2025, Michaela Lawtoo

The clay may be forever malleable, but artists of the self must nonetheless act quickly to give form to plastic figures on the spinning-wheel of an increasingly metamorphic life. It is thus in such a spirit of affirmation that the forming hands at play in this volume hasten to spin the wheel of a self-propelled homo mimeticus—generating repetitions with a difference that, from antiquity to modernity, form and transform the plastic clay of present and future generations to come.

Notes

1. As a precursor, I signal Edgar Morin whose insight that though "inconceivable in advance," "survival, progress, human development are bound to metamorphoisis" (2008, 2397-2400) in conjunction to our dialogic encounter reported in volume 1, provided the *coup d'envoi* for these reflections as well.
2. See Lawtoo 2022, 129–155.
3. See *Homo Mimeticus,* ch. 5, and *Homo Mimeticus II*, 36–51.
4. For a recent study that recuperates both Schopenhauer's and Nietzsche's view that there is but one metamorphic life generating what Bataille already called "continuity of Being," see Coccia 2022. As he puts it, "metamorphosis is the condition that obliges one to root the other in the self without being able to be completely oneself but without confusing oneself with others either" (Coccia 2022, 42; my trans.)—a pathos of distance, that, in our language, is central to both metamorphosis and mimesis. For a compelling retelling of Kafka's *Metamorphosis* in the context of pandemic lockdown and climate change, see Latour 2016; for a rich study that takes inspiration from Ovid's *Metamorphoses* to face climate wreckage in the Anthropocene, see Connolly 2024; for a courageous feminist account of the metamorphosis of one life born out of "hypermaternity," see Cavarero 2023. All these recent books entangle mimesis and metamorphosis to go beyond nature/culture binaries in ways that resonate with the genealogy presented here, opening up productive conversations with mimetic studies more generally.
5. For an informed critique of this metaphysical hierarchy informing book 10 of *Republic*, see Staten 2024.
6. See Lacoue-Labarthe 1989, 43–138; see also Lacoue-Labarthe and Nancy 1981, and Lawtoo 2019, 129–178.
7. In volume 1, I nuanced Malabou's critique by uncovering Lacoue-Labarthe's productive mimesis, see Lawtoo 2022, 144–155. In a mirroring inversion, I now further Malabou's critique by deepening the genealogy of *figura* beyond Lacoue-Labarthe's theory of fascist mimesis.
8. See Engelmeier and Balke 2018.
9. Commenting on Lucretius' use of *figura*, Auerbach also notes that it designates the "plastic figure shaped by man," including the "important transition from the form to its imitation, from the model to the copy, [which] may best be noted in the passage dealing with the resemblance of children to their parents" (1984, 16).
10. I signal here a forthcoming book by Ranjan Ghosh titled *Plastic Figures* that is not only likely to resonate with this Prologue, but also to entangle what he calls the "plastic turn" with the "mimetic turn" in productive configurations to be explored further.
11. On "mimetic" vs. "romantic agonism" see Lawtoo 2023a, 45–57.
12. For a rich account of Ovid's *Metamorphoses* sensitive to (non)human processes of becoming other directly in line with mimetic studies, see also Connolly 2024, 25–39.
13. Central to mimetic studies, Malabou also stresses the importance of literature in her account of plasticity in general and the emergence of plastic form in particular, stating: "I think that plasticity and literature share this common destiny: they invent the form that they are" (Malabou 2022a, 315).
14. A phrase Dante puts in the mouth of Guido Guinizzelli in *Purgatorio* xxvi to describe the Provençal poet Arnaud Daniel.

15 For a first connection between Montaigne and mimetic studies see *Homo Mimeticus II*, 13–14.
16 I would like to thank Michaela Lawtoo for a techne that played a central role in the birth of mimetic studies and whose plastic figures continue to enact, *à la lettre,* what Deleuze calls the visual logic of sensation.
17 As Malabou recognizes, "the epigenetic malleability of thought already expresses the auto-transformative imperative of modern humans Foucault sees at play in Baudelaire" (Malabou 2014, 179; my trans.). For Malabou's recuperation of Foucault's "fallback [*repli*] of the care of the self as an exclusive form of resistance," part of his genealogy of anarchism or "anarcheology," see Malabou 2022b, 205–265.
18 On Foucault as a precursor of mimetic studies see Verkerk 2023.
19 Foucault is here close to Oscar Wilde, another major precursor of mimetic studies. I offer a comparison of Foucault and Wilde via the focus of technologies of the self in Lawtoo (2025).
20 See Malabou 2022b, 243–246.
21 On the "psychology of the *socius*" that is central to Janet but also Nietzsche and Bataille, see Lawtoo 2013, 264–280; on Foucault's debt to Nietzsche and Bataille's conceptions of limit experiences whose aim was to "prevent one from being oneself," see Malabou 2022b, 263–264.
22 Not unlike Plato, Plotinus may appear an unlikely ally given the immanent foundations of mimetic studies, but as Malabou notices, Deleuze also recognized this genealogical continuity. Thus, she writes that, for Deleuze, "immanence is an ontological flow that connects [*relie*] Plotinus to Spinoza and Spinoza to Foucault" (Malabou 2022b, 243).
23 As the Stranger puts it in the *Sophist*: "One party is trying to drag everything down to earth out of heaven and the unseen [...] affirm[ing] that real existence belongs only to that which can be handled and offers resistance to the touch," the other "maintaining with all their force that true reality consists in certain intelligible and bodiless forms" (Plato 1963c, 246ab).
24 For a reframing of Platonic mimesis from the immanent perspective of Socrates see Staten 2024.
25 As Auerbach acknowledges: "The subject of this book, the interpretation of reality through literary representation or 'imitation,'" finds its "original starting point [in] Plato's discussion in book 10 of the *Republic*—mimesis ranking third after truth" (2003, 554).
26 As Hadot's translator notes, "the French word '*inventer*' derives from the Latin, *invenire*, 'to discover'" (qtd. in Hadot 1993, 20, n. 2). In modern French it simply means "to invent."
27 The foundations of this diagnostic reading of Nietzsche's patho(-)logies that inform mimetic studies more generally can be found in Lawtoo 2013, 3–83. For further developments see Verkerk 2021 and 2023, Lawtoo 2024a, and Garcia-Granero 2024.
28 On Nietzsche's theory of mimetic communication see *Homo Mimeticus*, ch. 1.
29 Already in *Daybreak*, Nietzsche had gone beyond nature/culture binaries in his diagnostic of homo mimeticus, arguing that "what English researchers designate [as] mimicry" also applies to humans insofar as "the individual hides himself in the general concept 'man'" for "security" out of "prudence" (1982, 20).
30 Foucault and Bourdieu have often been considered antagonists, but their agon is mimetic; both their perspectives on homo mimeticus also inform Malabou's critique of neoliberal pathological adaptations (Malabou 2017, 123–124), affecting what Bourdieu calls "*homo academicus*" (1984) as well.

31   Drawing on a Derridean pharmakology, Malabou specifies: "habit infects and cures, it is a poison that heals sickness" (2008, xx). On Malabou and habit, see also Wormald and Dahms 2018.
32   See Homer 2020, 17.128, 23.49. On the lion as a symbol of force, see also the Prelude to *Homo Mimeticus II*.
33   Verkerk's *Nietzsche and Gender*, forthcoming in 2026 with Cambridge University Press, will address this in detail.

Bibliography

Alighieri, Dante (1871). *The Divine Comedy*, trans. Henry Wadsworth Longfellow. Boston: Fields, Osgood & Co.
Alighieri, Dante (1991). *La Divina Commedia*, ed. Natalino Sapegno. Florence.
Auerbach, Erich (1984). "Figura," in *Scenes from the Drama of European Literature*. Minneapolis: University of Minnesota Press, 11–76.
Auerbach, Erich (2003). *Mimesis: The Representation of Reality in Western Literature*, trans. Willard R. Trask. Princeton: Princeton University Press.
Bourdieu, Pierre (1984). *Homo academicus* Paris: Les Éditions de Minuit.
Bourdieu, Pierre (1997). *Méditations pascaliennes*. Paris: Seuil.
Cacciari, Massimo (2019). *La mente inquieta: Saggio sull' Umanesimo*. Turin: Einaudi.
Cavarero, Adriana (2016). *Inclinations: A Critique of Rectitude*. Stanford: Stanford University Press.
Cavarero, Adriana (2023). *Donne che allattano cuccioli di lupo: Icone dell'ipermaterno*. Rome: Castelvecchi.
Coccia, Emanuele (2022). *Metamorfosi: Siamo un'unica, sola vita*, trans. Simona Mambrini. Milan: Einaudi.
Connolly, William E. (2024). *Stormy Weather: Pagan Cosmologies, Christian Times, Climate Wreckage*. New York: Fordham University Press.
Deleuze, Gilles (2002). *Francis Bacon: Logique de la sensation*. Paris: Seuil.
Engelmeier, Hanna, and Friedrich Balke (eds.) (2018). *Mimesis und Figura*. Leiden: Brill.
Foucault, Michel (1977). *Discipline and Punish: The Birth of the Prison*. New York: Vintage Books.
Foucault, Michel (1984). *Histoire de la sexualité III: Le souci de soi*. Paris: Gallimard.
Foucault, Michel (1988). *Technologies of the Self: A Seminar with Michel Foucault*, eds. Luther H. Martin, Huck Gutman and Patrick H. Hutton. Amherst: The University of Massachusetts Press.
Foucault, Michel (2017). "À propos de la généalogie de l'éthique: un aperçu du travail en cours," in *Dits et Écrits 1976–1988*, eds. Daniel Defet and François Ewald. Paris: Gallimard, 1428–1449.
Gallese, Vittorio, and Nidesh Lawtoo (2024). "Beyond Brain and Body: A Dialogue with Vittorio Gallese," in *Homo Mimeticus II: Re-Turns to Mimesis*, eds. Nidesh Lawtoo and Marina Garcia-Granero. Leuven: Leuven University Press, 343–375.
Garcia-Granero, Marina (2024). "Nietzsche's Legacy for Posthuman Mimesis: Metamorphoses, Embodiment and Immanence," in *Mimetic Posthumanism: Art, Philosophy and Technics*, ed. Nidesh Lawtoo. Leiden: Brill, 178–199.
Ghosh, Ranjan (forthcoming 2026). *Plastic Figures*. Ithaca, NY: Cornell University Press.

Hadot, Pierre (1993). *Plotinus or the Simplicity of Vision*, trans. Michael Chase. Chicago: The University of Chicago Press.
Hadot, Pierre (1995). *Qu'est-ce que la philosophie antique*. Paris: Gallimard.
Homer (2020). *The Odyssey*, trans. Emily Wilson. New York: W. W. Norton & Company.
Lacoue-Labarthe, Philippe (1987). *La Fiction du politique: Heidegger, l'art et la politique*. Paris: Christian Bourgois Éditeur.
Lacoue-Labarthe, Philippe, and Jean-Luc Nancy (1990). "The Nazi Myth," trans. Brian Holmes, *Critical Inquiry* 16.2, 291–312.
Latour, Bruno (2021). *After Lockdown: A Metamorphosis*, trans. Julie Rose. New York: Polity.
Lawtoo, Nidesh (2013). *The Phantom of the Ego: Modernism and the Mimetic Unconscious*. East Lansing: Michigan State University Press.
Lawtoo, Nidesh (2017). "The Plasticity of Mimesis." *MLN* 132.5, 1201–1224.
Lawtoo, Nidesh (2019). *(New) Fascism: Contagion, Community, Myth*. East Lansing: Michigan State University Press.
Lawtoo, Nidesh (2022). *Homo Mimeticus: A New Theory of Imitation*. Leuven: Leuven University Press.
Lawtoo, Nidesh (2023a). *Violence and the Oedipal Unconscious: vol. 1 The Catharsis Hypothesis*. East Lansing. Michigan State University Press.
Lawtoo, Nidesh (2023b). "Wilde's Mime Acts." *MLN* 138.5, 1438–1459.
Lawtoo, Nidesh (2024a). "Nietzsche contra Girard: Agonistic Steps for Mimetic Studies." *Contagion* 31, 145-176.
Lawtoo, Nidesh (ed.) (2024b). *Mimetic Posthumanism: Homo Mimeticus 2.0 in Art, Philosophy and Technics*. Leiden: Brill.
Lawtoo, Nidesh (2025). "Wilde *avec* Foucault: Technologies of the Self in *Epistola*." *Textual Practice* 39.8.
Lawtoo, Nidesh, and Marina Garcia-Granero (eds.) (2024). *Homo Mimeticus II: Re-Turns to Mimesis*. Leuven: Leuven University Press.
Malabou, Catherine (1996). *L'Avenir de Hegel: Plasticité, temporalité, dialectique*. Paris: Libraire Philosophique J. Vrin.
Malabou, Catherine (2008a). *What Should We Do with Our Brain?*, trans. Sebastian Rand. New York: Fordham University Press.
Malabou, Catherine (2008b). "Addiction and Grace: Preface to Félix Ravisson's *Of Habit*," in *Of Habit*, trans. Claire Carlisle and Mark Sinclair. London: Continuum, vii–xx.
Malabou, Catherine (2010). *Plasticity at the Dusk of Writing: Dialectic, Destruction, Deconstruction*, trans. Carolyn Shread. New York: Columbia University Press.
Malabou, Catherine (2011). *Changing Difference: The Feminine and the Question of Philosophy*, trans. Carolyn Shread. Cambridge: Polity.
Malabou, Catherine (2015). "From the Overman to the Posthuman: How Many Ends?," in *Plastic Materialities: Politics, Legality, and Metamorphosis in the Works of Catherine Malabou*, eds. Brenna Bhandar and Jonathan Goldberg-Hiller. Durham, NC: Duke University Press, 61–72.
Malabou, Catherine (2020). *Le Plaisir effacé: Clitoris et pensée*. Paris: Payot et Rivages.
Malabou, Catherine (2022a). *Plasticity: The Promise of an Explosion*, ed. Tyler M. Williams. Edinburgh: Edinburgh University Press.
Malabou, Catherine (2022b). *Au voleur! Anarchisme et philosophie*. Paris: Presses Universitaires de France.

Montaigne, Michel de (2003). *The Complete Essays*, trans. M. A. Screech. London: Penguin Books.
Morin, Edgar (2008). *La Méthode II: Les idées, l'humanité de l'humanité, éthique*. Paris: Seuil.
Nietzsche, Friedrich (1974). *The Gay Science*, trans. Walter Kaufman. New York: Vintage Books.
Nietzsche, Friedrich (1982). *Daybreak*, trans. R. J. Hollingdale. Cambridge: Cambridge University Press.
Nietzsche, Friedrich (2005). *Thus Spoke Zarathustra*, trans. Graham Parkes. Oxford: Oxford University Press.
Ovid (2010). *Metamorphoses*, trans. and ed. Charles Martin: New York: W. W. Norton & Company.
Plato (1963a). *Ion*, in *The Collected Dialogues of Plato*, trans. Lane Cooper, eds. E. Hamilton and H. Cairns. Princeton: Princeton University Press, 215–228.
Plato (1963b). *Republic*, in *The Collected Dialogues of Plato*, trans. Paul Shorey, eds. E. Hamilton and H. Cairns. Princeton: Princeton University Press, 575–844.
Plato (1963c). *Sophist*, in *The Collected Dialogues of Plato*, trans. F. M. Cornford, eds. E. Hamilton and H. Cairns. Princeton: Princeton University Press, 957–1017.
Staten, Henry (2024). "Techne vs. Mimesis in Plato's *Republic*: What Socrates Really Says about Homer," in *Homo Mimeticus II: Re-Turns to Mimesis*, eds. Nidesh Lawtoo and Marina Garcia-Granero. Leuven: Leuven University Press, 71–91.
Verkerk, Willow (2021). "A Feminist Genealogy of the Post-Enlightenment Subject with the Marquis de Sade's Juliette." *Graduate Faculty Philosophy Journal* 42.1, 27–51.
Verkerk (2023). "A Re-evaluation of the Androcentric Subject of European Philosophy." *Critical Horizons* 24.2, 115–130.
Verkerk (forthcoming 2026). *Nietzsche and Gender*. Cambridge: Cambridge University Press.
Wilde, Oscar (2007). "The Decay of Lying," in *The Complete Works of Oscar Wilde*, vol. 4, ed. Josephine M. Guy. Oxford: Oxford University Press, 73–103.
Wojciehowski, Hannah Chapelle (2011). "Interview with Vittorio Gallese," *California Italian Studies* 2.1.
Wormald, Thomas, and Isabelle Dahms (2018). *Thinking Catherine Malabou: Passionate Detachments*. New York: Rowman & Littlefield.

PART I
GENEALOGIES OF MIMETIC PLASTICITY

CHAPTER 1

EPIGENETIC MIMESIS

Natural Brains and Synaptic Chips[1]

Catherine Malabou

The purpose of this essay is twofold. First, it raises a specific issue: how are we to understand the verbs "imitate" or "simulate" when we are told that the most recent developments and achievements in cybernetics and Artificial Intelligence allow technology to "imitate" or "simulate" the biological brain, and more precisely its epigenetic capacities? Second, it situates this issue within the more general context of my own philosophical trajectory: that is, the part of this trajectory that started with my first book on the brain, *What Should We Do with Our Brain?* and continued with *Morphing Intelligence: From IQ Measurement to Artificial Brains*. Returning to the main steps of this trajectory does not respond to a narcissistic trend but aims to develop a continuous effort to find an accurate concept of "imitation" when it comes to the relationship between the natural and the artificial. As the theory of homo mimeticus makes clear, the old Platonic notion of "mimesis" restricted to a metaphysical copy, or representation of nature is no longer relevant to characterize such a relationship, as it limits imitation or simulation to the simple act of copying. AI does not "copy" the brain—which does not mean that the brain is *in*imitable. Getting out of this *aporia*, if such a thing is possible, has involved, and is involving, many efforts.[2]

Let me first expand on epigenetics and what current neurobiologists call the epigenetic turn in the history of neurology. Then, I will present some recent technological achievements that sustain the idea of an epigenetic turn in the history of cybernetics and AI. Lastly, I will propose a few philosophical reflections on the concept of imitation intended as future-oriented contributions to the plasticity and mimesis connection first explored in *Homo Mimeticus* (Lawtoo 2022, 129–155) and now pursued collectively in this volume.

On 15 February 2001, the American scientific journal *Nature* published the virtually complete sequence of the three billion bases of the human genome (International Human Genome Sequencing Consortium 2001). The result was surprising: the human genome is made up of only 30,000 genes, in other words, just 13,000 more than drosophila (commonly known as fruit flies). Furthermore, it appears that genes only make up 5% of the genome. Assembled in bunches and clusters, they are separated by vast expanses of so-called "gene deserts," made up of DNA called "junk" or "repetitive," that is, non-coding. According to studies, this "non-coding" DNA accounts for a quarter or a third of the totality of the genome. This means that within chromosomes there are long DNA sequences which, according to current understanding, do not appear to match the genes and cannot be given any particular function (Nau 2001; my trans.). The sequencing of the genome did not, therefore, offer the expected revelations. On the contrary, it indicated the weakening of genetic determinism. These discoveries marked the passage from the genetic to the epigenetic paradigm.

Epigenetics is a science that is dramatically transforming all previous (that is essentially genetic) conceptions of inheritance. This branch of molecular biology studies the relations between genes and the individual features they produce, in other terms, the relation between genotype and phenotype. Derived from "epigenesis," the term "epigenetics" is a neologism created in 1940 by British biologist Conrad Waddington. "Some years ago (e.g. 1947) I introduced the word 'epigenetics,' derived from the Aristotelian word 'epigenesis,' which had more or less passed into disuse, as a suitable name for the branch of biology which studies the causal interactions between genes and their products which bring the phenotype into being" (1968, 9–10).

Epigenetic mechanisms concern the expression, transcription, or translation of the genetic code into the phenotype, that is the biologically unique constitution and physical appearance of an individual. These mechanisms act essentially through the activation or silencing of certain genes, that is through a series of modifications. These changes in gene expression do not involve changes to the underlying DNA sequence. Epigenetic changes occur at the chemical internal level (DNA methylation, histone modification and non-coding RNA (ncRNA)) but can also be influenced by several factors including age, the environment, or lifestyle.

If the DNA is like a book, or a musical score, its readings are its epigenetic translations or interpretations. In the second half of the twentieth century, the concept of "program" dominated genetics. The idea of a program is exactly what is in question today with the acknowledgement of the importance of epigenetic mechanisms.

Now about the brain. The epigenetic turn in neurobiology is of course linked with this scientific revolution that also revealed that the brain, far from being made of fixed and rigid localizations, was undergoing continuous changes and wirings. The power of neuroplasticity has provoked a very important mutation in the definition of intelligence that still challenges all attempts at considering it as innate and genetically predetermined. We know now that the brain's development is for the most part epigenetic; it continues long after birth and depends, to a substantial extent, on environmental and cultural factors. In their book *The Mind and the Brain, Neuroplasticity and the Power of Mental Force*, Jeffrey M. Schwarz and Sharon Begley write:

> Although it would be perfectly reasonable to posit that genes determine the brain's connections, just as a wiring diagram determines the connections on a silicon computer chip, that is a mathematical impossibility. As the Human Genome Project drew to a close in the early years of the new millennium, it became clear that humans have something like 35,000 different genes. About half of them seem to be active in the brain, where they are responsible for such tasks as synthesizing a neurotransmitter or a receptor. The brain, remember, has billions of nerve cells that make, altogether, trillions of connections. [...] Call it the genetic shortfall: too many synapses, too few genes. Our DNA is simply too paltry to spell out the wiring diagram for the human brain (2002, 111–112).

This means that the brain has its own life and development, which does not depend entirely on genetic information. Neurobiologists agree that: "the brain is more than a reflection of our genes" (112). Synaptic development is never the mere implementation of a program or code. On the contrary, it "includes the spontaneous activity in the nervous system in addition to activity provoked by interaction with the environment" (7). Once again, this epigenetic view of the shaping of neural connections enables a break with strict determinism.

For a long time, I have been convinced that the epigenetic nature of brain development was what definitely proved its irreducibility to AI systems, or any cybernetic or robotic processes. Was not epigenetic cerebral plasticity the perfect intermingling of the biological and the symbolic, that marked its difference from technological functioning? By the intermingling of the biological and the symbolic, I mean the indiscernibility between biological development and personal history, materiality and sense, chemical mechanisms and the exposure of the brain to changes, education and the adventures of life. All of these developmental directions might be, I thought, summarized in one question: what should we do with our brain? If we can do something with our brain, it is precisely because the brain is not a machine and we are in part responsible for its plasticity.

However, the recent developments in Artificial Intelligence made me think differently. It was a shock to realize that I was wrong. That my book *What Should We Do with Our Brain?* should be revised, perhaps even entirely rewritten. This suspicion brutally came to me when I read an article about the most recent computational architectures, and particularly about IBM's design of a totally new type of chip, the *neuro-synaptic chip*. The title of the article was eloquent: "IBM's Neuro-Synaptic Chip Mimics Human Brain" (Murray 2013). IBM was releasing a neuro-synaptic computation chip that was able to simulate the neurons and synapses of the brain. Up until now, most computer chips have employed a von Neumann-type architecture, the mathematics-based system at the core of almost every computer built since 1948 that executes instructions in series. By comparison, the synaptic chip is made of different neurosynaptic-cores or, "corelets," that function autonomously, in a non-synchronic way, so that those which are not solicited remain inactive, thus resulting in a lower energy use. If it is said to mimic the brain, it is because this chip allows interactions between neurons (elements of calculus), synapses (memory) and axons (communications with other parts of the chip). The second reason is that the electronic synaptic components are capable of varying connection strength between two neurons in a manner analogous to that seen in biological systems. In a certain sense, the system develops what we might call its own "experience."

In 2011, Dharmendra S. Modha, founder of IBM's Cognitive Computing group at IBM Research, developed with his team the first cognitive chip, thus concretizing the SyNAPSE project (SyNAPSE for "Systems of Neuromorphic Adaptive Plastic Scalable Electronics"). The ambition was right from the start to develop low-power electronic neuromorphic computers that could scale to biological levels. More recently, a still improved chip came to light, called True North, made of 4,096 neuro-synaptic cores and able to simulate around 1 million neurons. On this Modha explains: "If we think of today's von Neumann computers as akin to the 'left-brain'—fast, symbolic, number-crunching calculators, then TrueNorth can be likened to the 'right-brain'—slow, sensory, pattern recognizing machines" (2016). TrueNorth's corelets are designed for sensory applications that include things like artificial noses, ears and eyes, are adaptable and can rewire synapses based on their inputs.

These chips and processors have undergone exponential growth since then. In a more recent report on the global neuromorphic chip market, "Self-Learning Neuromorphic Chip Market to Witness Astonishing Growth," devoted to an even more efficient IBM chip, the author explains:

> Neuromorphic chips come with artificial neurons and artificial synapses that mimic the activity spike that occurs in the human brain. The chip has the ability to learn continuously due to its synaptic plasticity. This results in smarter, far more energy efficient computing systems. Self-learning neuromorphic chips perform on chip processing asynchronously. It uses event driven processing models to address complex computing problems. Further, by combining improved learning, reduced latency, and improved energy efficiency, the self-learning neuromorphic chip can push the image recognition and speech processing to new levels of speed and accuracy (Craig 2021).

Thus, we can consider that cybernetics and AI have also had their epigenetic revolution, to the extent that the concept of program is not entirely adequate any longer here either. The new systems, like the IBM ones mentioned above, are able to change or adapt their programs. We can also think of recurrent neural networks. Deep learning is more akin to epigenetic than genetic development. In his book *The Singularity Is Near*, Kurzweil insists on the exponential growth of computing capacities and speed. He speaks of a "paradigm shift" in terms of quantity: "the rate of the paradigm shift (technical innovation) is accelerating, now doubling every decade" (2005, 25).

The shift is also qualitative. The singularity will also be that of the plasticity of machines. So, yes, it is plasticity that is at stake, and not only a metaphor or a way of speaking. "Human intelligence," says Kurzweil, "has a certain amount of plasticity," that is "ability to change its structure, more so than had been understood." Machines to come will also be plastic, more and more plastic. They will be capable of changing themselves: "once machines achieve the ability to design and engineer technology as humans do, only at far higher speeds and capacities, they will have access to their own designs (source code) and the ability to manipulate them, just as we manipulate genetics" (Kurzweil 2005, 27). Further, "machines will be able to reformulate their own designs" (ibid.). We can see how quantity and quality are intimately tied together.

Let's now turn to the issue of imitation, which, in its mirroring relation to plasticity, provides the guiding double thread for this volume. In the aforementioned article about synaptic chips Craig writes: "Neuromorphic chips come with artificial neurons and artificial synapses that mimic the activity spike that occurs in the human brain. The chip has the ability to learn continuously due to its synaptic plasticity" (2021). How are we to understand "mimic" here? Should we refer to the Greek mimesis, from which it derives etymologically?

We know well the usual questions: "Will AI systems replace us?" Or "Can a computer be intelligent?"; "Can it simulate a brain?"; "Can it do better than us?"; "Can it do better without us?" I share some of Hawking's fears, expressed on the BBC a few years ago: "The development of full artificial intelligence could spell the end of the human race." At the same time, I think that such predictions are not well grounded. And, in order avert them, many people are trying to comfort themselves by affirming that "machines" (I use this generic term) are only poor, faulty copies of human brain capacities. Machines, they say, do not *feel*, they cannot be affected. In other terms, machines, AI devices, robots, synaptic computers do not have a self (I will come back to this notion of self later). These discourses are commonly held while we constantly hear at the same time about new explorations in brain simulation, artificial imagination, artificial creativity, artificial capacity to improvise, artificial sexuality even.[3]

Are we just witnessing the emergence of new forms of copies? New forms of imitation, analogies, a new epoch of mimicry? Or do we have to bring to light a new concept of simulation? Is philosophy able to help us answer these questions now central to mimetic studies? It is clear that currently philosophers are not answering the challenge and are not proposing a concept of simulation that can substitute for the traditional ones, all revolving around the act of copying. Prior to the mimetic turn, or re-turn, we lacked an updated notion of mimesis that would adequately characterize the imitating power of artificial epigenetic systems. If we consider the most recent achievements in robotics, for example, like those accomplished in Japan by Hirochi Ichiguro, we cannot say that these robots are just "copies."

Even if the concept of *mimesis* has evolved through time and is now being reframed, within the dominant philosophical tradition it has nevertheless remained attached to its ancient definition, which involves a determinate relationship between nature and art. There are at least two decisive moments in the history, or genealogy, of *mimesis*. The Platonic moment, and the Kantian one. Plato's notion of *mimesis* means copy and reproduction. It entirely concerns the status of art—art being a specific branch of *tekhnē*. We have to distinguish, within *tekhnē*, between craft and art. The craftworker who is making a bed, for example, does not exactly imitate or copy a model, because the idea that serves as the model for such a making is directly imprinted in the craftsman's mind, without any possibility for them to interpret it, or play or cheat with it. The artist on the contrary intentionally uses deceptive means in their production, and this to blur the frontiers between the actual reality and its image, thus turning the idea, the *eidos*, into a treacherous copy. *Eidos* then becomes an *eidolon*, a simulacrum.

I think that many critiques of AI today unconsciously retain something from this Platonic conception. They see technological imitation as something voluntary, a delusionary production of replicas, and claim that the original, the natural, is necessarily superior, because of its authenticity, to its technological mimicry. The presumption here is that cerebral epigenetic development, for example, remains absolutely incomparable with—and irreducible to—synaptic chips, neural networks or intelligent robots.

Kant's concept of imitation is certainly more complex, but still insufficient for settling our problem. In the first part of the *Critique of Judgement*, Kant interestingly affirms that fine arts must find their topics in nature but should not "copy it" (2008, 188). Art undoubtedly finds its inspiration in nature, but it interprets it and reinvents it. This is the reason why Kant defines art as a creation of "genius" (188). Contrarily to a mechanical, purely technological process, art is understood as a production of freedom. A work of art is then no servile copy, plagiarism, or counterfeit but a "free imitation," he says in § 47. Later, this is followed by a puzzling declaration: "nature must serve as a model not for copying (*nachmachen*) but for imitation (*nachmachen*)." "Nachmachung" and "Nachahmung" should then be strictly distinguished (2000, 188). *Nachahmung* designates a reproduction that is inassimilable to a mere copy. However, as we know, genius, Kant writes in § 46, is a gift from nature: "Genius is the talent (natural endowment) which gives the rule to art" (2000, 176). Through the artistic invention, it is nature that interprets itself.

We can conclude from this that art, for Kant, expresses nature's relation to itself. The word "self" is important there. Art helps the creation of a self of nature. To the extent that artistic mimesis is a gift from nature, it exhibits the identity of nature. Art is the subject of nature. A natural artefact. An artificial naturality. We find, once again, a concept of imitation that is by no means reducible to a copy or a simulacrum.

We can now ask if what Kant says about art can be extended to contemporary technology, and if there is such a thing as a technological *Nachahmung*. We cannot find the answer in Kant, unfortunately. Kant comes to technique in the second part of the *Critique of Judgement*. But he precisely opposes technique to fine arts and to life. A living being, because of the harmony, the plasticity of its structure and organization, seems to be a work of art. It is "as if" nature were an artist. A mechanism, on the contrary, is never plastic. It does not have an epigenetic development. In § 65, Kant contrasts the functioning of a watch to that of a natural organism. Well assembled as they are, the different pieces of a watch do not have the power to repair themselves, contrary to an organism. Technical objects are just *Nachmachungen*, copies of life.

Kant would therefore have considered synaptic chips and plastic computing processes as similar to watches, as mechanical *Nachmachungen* of the biological cerebral organization. The problem is that if the internal regulation of the different parts of the watch is not the work of the watch itself, the internal regulation of current cybernetic processes is precisely self-induced and maintained, as visible in recurrent neural networks. We can then ask whether these new processes do not prove the existence of a relationship of technique or technology to itself? The emergence not only of a technical self, but of a *self of technique*? AI would then be said to exhibit the relationship of technique to itself through the *Nachahmung* of nature. An artificial self would be susceptible to emerge from such a relationship. A technological authentic mimetic self.

If it is true that AI systems, deep learning processes, and intelligent robots are "imitating" the human, or the natural biological functions, like epigenesis for example, we cannot return to Plato's concept of mimetic representation to understand the meaning of this imitation. Neither can we consider that these artefacts are new versions of artistic genius, or the relationship of nature to itself. We have to keep going deeper into the plastic nature of homo mimeticus and wonder whether there exists a new form of epigenesis, the epigenesis of an auto-affection of technique by itself. Just like nature mimics itself through art—for Kant—technology today mimics itself through nature, producing new mirrors for our brains.

Notes

1. This chapter first appeared in *Life in the Posthuman Condition: Critical Responses to the Anthropocene*, eds. S. E. Wilmer and Audronė Žukauskaitė (Edinburgh: Edinburgh University Press, 2023). The author is grateful for allowing its reproduction here. [The citation style was harmonised to fit the style used in this volume (editors' note)].
2. On imitation and AI, see for instance the essays collected in *Mimetic Posthumanism: Arts, Philosophy, Technics*, ed. Nidesh Lawtoo (Leiden: Brill, 2024).

3   The Human Brain Project is a large 10-year scientific research project, established in 2013, coordinated by Henry Markram (from the École polytechnique in Lausanne), and largely funded by the European Union. It is the European version of the American BRAIN Initiative (Brain Research through Advancing Innovative Neurotechnologies, also referred to as the Brain Activity Map Project), announced by President Obama in 2013, with the goal of mapping the activity of every neuron in the human brain using Big Data. The program develops information and communications technology platforms in six main areas: neuroinformatics, brain simulation, high-performance computing, medical informatics, neuromorphic computing, and neuro-robotics. Again, the goal is to propose in the end a complete and detailed cartography of the human brain. The Human Brain project develops the results of another project, the Blue Brain Project, also founded by Markram at Lausanne in 2005. The simulations are carried out on a Blue Gene supercomputer built by IBM, hence the name "Blue Brain."

Bibliography

Craig, Francis (2021). "Self-Learning Neuromorphic Chip Market to Witness Astonishing Growth." *Material Handlings*, October 5.
International Human Genome Sequencing Consortium (2001). "Initial sequencing and analysis of the human genome." *Nature* 409, 860–921. https://doi.org/10.1038/35057062
Kant, Immanuel (2000). *Critique of the Power of Judgment*, trans. Paul Guyer and Eric Mathews. Cambridge/New York: Cambridge University Press.
Kurzweil, Ray (2005). *The Singularity is Near: When Humans Transcend Biology*. New York: Penguin.
Malabou, Catherine (2008). *What Should We Do with Our Brain?*, trans. Sebastian Rand. New York: Fordham University Press.
Malabou, Catherine (2019). *Morphing Intelligence: From IQ Measurements to Artificial Brains*, trans. Carolyn Shread. New York: Columbia University Press.
Modha, Dharmendra S. (2016). "Introducing a Brain-inspired Computer," IBM TrueNorth, November 11. https://www.radiolocman.com/review/article.html?di=162687
Murray, William (2013). "IBM's Neuro-Synaptic Chip Mimics Human Brain." *EE Times*, September 18. https://www.eetimes.com/ibms-neuro-synaptic-chip-mimics-human-brain/
Nau, Jean-Yves (2001). "Les bouleversantes révélations de l'exploration du génome humain." *Le Monde*, February 13. https://www.lemonde.fr/archives/article/2001/02/13/les-bouleversantes-revelations-de-l-exploration-du-genome-humain_4182801_1819218.html
Schwartz, Jeffrey M., and Sharon Begley (2002). *The Mind & The Brain: Neuroplasticity and the Power of Mental Force*. New York: Harper Collins Publishers.
Waddington, Conrad Hal (1968). "The Basic Ideas of Biology," in *Towards a Theoretical Biology. Vol. 1: Prolegomena*. Edinburgh: International Union of Biological Sciences/Edinburgh University Press, 1–32.

CHAPTER 2

PLASTICITY, MIMESIS, TRANSFORMATIVITY
A Genealogy of Theories of Change

Tom Boland

"The times they are a-changing" is perhaps the motto of modernity, yet this perennially fresh protest song imitates tropes that are millennia old: "The first one now, will later be last"—echoing the Sermon on the Mount. On the one hand, this resonance across millennia indicates that thinkers have long recognized that things change. On the other, it suggests that ideas about change are imitated. The fact that something is imitated does not mean that it is necessarily fake, artificial or ephemeral—love, hate, belonging and much more are imitative. However, taking mimesis as the source of behavior or ideas along the creative lines suggested by mimetic studies in the *Homo Mimeticus* trilogy[1] means that alternatives are possible, that change is possible. How we think about change matters; this is investigated herein.

This chapter offers a genealogy of ideas about change by interrogating three influential thinkers: the Renaissance man Giovanni Pico della Mirandola (1463–1494), the socialist leader Wladimir Iljitsch Lenin (1870–1924) and the popular psychologist Abraham Maslow (1908–1970). Following Keohane and Kuhling in volume 2 of *Homo Mimeticus,* a methodological approach is taken up in which single figures are employed to shed light on historical ideas. While these figures span Renaissance humanism, revolutionary socialism and liberal management, and might seem to have very different spheres of influence, they are chosen for the different ways in which they deploy ideas of imitation and plasticity to explain change. As we shall see, each thinker resonates with

Catherine Malabou's idea of plasticity, wherein the self is both formed and forming (as is society as a whole). Each has mimetic qualities: Pico's mankind imitates God, Lenin's proletarian society imitates a factory and Maslow's self-actualization (which seems to involve original self-creation), is presented as a mimetic rival for individual distinction. This genealogy is less a contribution to the "return to mimesis" by reconstructing the thought of influential historical thinkers; instead, it questions present modes of thinking about change. This genealogy is not oriented towards establishing a lineage or pedigree, but to disassembling present ideas, treating them as historical hybrids.

The approach here draws on Michel Foucault's (1977) genealogy, with a resolutely post-structural approach (Bachi 2015), which employs a strict nominalism (Hansen and Triantafillou 2022). The discussion suspends any truth claims about "mimesis" or "plasticity" or anything else for that matter. These are strategically useful words for describing situations Foucault generally terms "discourses." There are no special terms outside discourse and especially not the term introduced here—"transformativity." Indeed, the term "imitation" is not a neutral or transparent concept, even when used in common-sensical explanations of consumption or bullying, whether in crowds or on social media. Plasticity has been a highly successful counter-explanation to "hard-wired" theories of the brain and is widely taken up in childrearing and educational settings. But within academia, the provisional status of these concepts as particular discourses must be acknowledged.

That things change is generally undisputed today. However, quite how this change is modeled is under-theorized. Rather than offering a model for how things actually change, genealogy is concerned with tracing how change is modeled discursively.[2] Summed up here in a deliberately jargonistic term, namely "transformativity," our contemporary culture imagines that things—selves, institutions, societies—are transformed, meaning that there is not only continuity through change but also aspects which are jettisoned or added, but most importantly, that some sort of transformation is also wrought. In "transformativist" thinking, which is very widespread, something is somehow changed, yet retains some sort of identity to itself through time.

The encounter between mimetic studies and ideas of plasticity challenges us to think through change in detail. Plasticity is explicitly a model of change, which can be mimetic but can involve radical discontinuity. Mimesis also involves change, but with the possibility of imitating others, and therefore creating continuity of form. The tension between continuity and change, between mimetic models and plastic variations, is a recurrent tension within "transformativist" thinking. Whereas ideas of complete, sudden, drastic metamorphosis existed in more mythic cultures, and models of additive and accretive change prevailed in medieval Christianity, modernity distinctly combines these—perhaps with some ancient precursors (Bynum 2000). As genealogy unpicks promiscuous crossings, this chapter seeks to unpack the hybrid mingling of imitation and plasticity in modern thought, taking up pathways from Nietzsche and Marx to Lawtoo and Malabou.

This matters because how we imagine change shapes how we pursue change. The need for dramatic, radical, even revolutionary change has never been clearer in the face of global warming, tipping points and ecological collapse, yet thinking through these challenges in terms of transformativity may restrict us to ideas of society slowly developing. Simply changing "hearts and minds" or "changing social attitudes" is not enough. Rapid rearrangements of institutions—for instance around the welfare state, private property and borders—will be needed sooner rather than later (Murphy 2023). So, the genealogical aim here is to disrupt present thought, and thereby to make alternatives possible (Lorenzini 2020).

Plasticity and Mimesis as Modes of Transformation

Any genealogical investigation will reveal different ways of thinking about change. That things change is assumed here. But how we think that change matters. Rather than sudden and complete metamorphosis, or gradual or incremental reconfiguration, I suggest that in modernity we tend to think change in a transformativist key. This metaphor insists on both change and continuity, and the persistence of identity across time, whether concerning the self or society. This "transformativity" is considered not as a reality to be uncovered, but as a description, an account, a model. Within this model there is a tension, not just between change and continuity, but between imitation and plasticity, the two key themes of this volume.

The pervasiveness and persuasiveness of transformativist models of change are clearly in evidence in contemporary discussions of "brain plasticity." Rather than considering the brain on the model of a computer or telephone exchange, as the relatively static and rigid center from which messages are relayed back and forth from nerves via synapses, brain plasticity refers to the continuous development, usage, die-off and repair of neural pathways. Against the idea of the brain as a fixed organ with definitive characteristics, your brain is what you make it: "you are your synapses" (Malabou 2008, 55–58). This has become common knowledge, reflected in health advice around keeping the brain active through mental activities, for instance in cognitive-behavioral therapy, a way of changing your brain which, curiously, works so long as we believe in it (Johnsen and Friborg 2015). This means that attempts at self-transformation depend on the credibility or novelty of specific techniques, or something like a "self-fulfilling prophecy," in order to be efficacious.

Of course, this apparently scientifically proven "plasticity" provokes philosophical and sociological questions, not least of which is the problem of the self as both the agent and the target of interventions, which troubles the question of agency (Butler 1997). While following cutting-edge neurological science, Malabou argues that the relationship between the brain and the self, or neurons and subjectivity, is still unfathomable, ineffable even. Importantly, she identifies how certain ideas about brain plasticity may well reflect neoliberal conceptions of flexibility, the demand for project-oriented, synergistic workers who need to be almost protean chameleons in the social and economic conditions of the "new spirit of capitalism" (Boltanski and Chiapello 2005). Against this flexibility, which acquiesces with economic or even governmental demands, Malabou insists on plasticity being not just the capacity to receive form, but also the capacity to give form (2008, 15–19).

Some commentators draw determinist conclusions from neurological studies, insisting that impulses within the brain are detectable before consciousness becomes aware of them (Paley 2016). By contrast, Malabou is not a voluntarist, but thinks in a dialectical mode, introducing her *What Should We Do with Our Brains?* via a Marxian allusion: we make our brains, but not in the situation of our own choosing. Her thought draws on a deconstructionist reading of Hegel, wherein the dialectic emerges as a diagnosis of the process of plasticity (2000). The brain, the subject, we ourselves, are formed by the continuous open-ended process of creation and destruction of neural pathways.

While acknowledging contemporary neurological research, Malabou's account of plasticity resumes longstanding philosophical or even theological ideas about will, choice and consciousness. "Plasticity designates generally the ability to change one's destiny to inflect one's trajectory, to navigate differently, to reform one's form" (2008, 17). This resonates with Christian notions of the will whereby the subject is a malleable yet choosing agent (Foucault 2021). Theologically this opens the subject to moral judgments about their character, which continue into contemporary politicized judgments (Boland and Griffin

2021). Implicit here is the idea of a subject who is capable of choosing and thereby shaping themselves, and furthermore persists through change, a self who accounts for their own emergence.

Perhaps it is simply language or even syntax which inserts a self behind or distinct to the brain: "our brain is in part essentially what we do with it" (Malabou 2008, 30). Thus, the existence, if not the undisturbed persistence, of an agency which can choose to undertake particular activities and thereby reshape itself is central to Malabou's account. Without recourse to any form of essentialism, this offers a transformativist model of change and continuity of the self or brain: "It is a contradictory continuity not a rupture" (2000, 139). Just as the flexitarian model of subjectivity might reflect neoliberal ideas, the idea of plasticity in Malabou, and many others, reflects a cultural idea of change. While foregrounding resistance, autonomy and critique, what also emerges in her account is a self or identity—or even more minimally than that, a substance—that undergoes change yet persists.

By comparison to plasticity, mimesis initially appears to provide a less transformativist account of change. In conversation with Malabou on plasticity, Lawtoo (2022, 129–155) recognizes that repeated mimesis leads to the transformation of the plastic neural pathways, and bodily shape might change through regular, repeated imitation. However, imitation also has the capacity for fleeting, dramatic but non-transformative change. Joining in the cheers of a crowd or the animosity of a mob might well transform individuals, but when the event passes and the group disperses, the mimetic emotions and actions pass away (Thomassen 2014). Importantly, Lawtoo locates his theory of imitation within a longer genealogy of thinkers who recognized the role that mimesis plays in culture and society, from Plato through Nietzsche to Girard and beyond. Interestingly, Lawtoo avoids the overly negative evaluation of mimesis that prevails in these thinkers, theorizing the possibility of positive mimesis.

For the purposes of this chapter, Lawtoo's key contribution is how he integrates imitative actions and desires with mimesis in art and other forms of representation. Thought thus, mimesis is not merely the replication of others' actions or desires, but potentially a creative variation on cultural forms. Indeed, reflexively *Homo Mimeticus* positions itself within a consciously imitative tradition of thinking about mimesis that is far from static, but rather dynamic, evolving, creative, perhaps plastic—or even transformativist. For Lawtoo, the self is "a wax-like plastic matter that is formed by exemplary models" (2022, 141). Thus, the process of imitation—both conscious and unconscious, directly through proximate actions or through artistic and creative activity—forms the plastic self. Unlike Girard's almost wholly negative vision of imitation, Lawtoo's mimetic studies allow for the possibility of conscious imitation, the deliberate and positive following of a model.

Like Malabou, Lawtoo is aware of the dangers of plasticity and imitation, pointing to the problematic circuits of imitation in contemporary politics, particularly the far right, and the acceleration of imitation through the circuitry of digital media. Lawtoo explores "[t]ransformations of personality that can be truly horrifying" (2022, 193). The plastic subject can be overcome by imitative urges, or be a mime without character, even a "human chameleon" which can transform itself for any purpose, as the cases of Woody Allen's *Zelig* or of Adolf Eichmann show (191–254). The flexible entrepreneur of capitalism, the populist demagogue, the technological whizz, all these figures are empty, imitative, infinitely flexible, comparable to the anthropological notion of tricksters (Szakolczai and Horvath 2019). They take advantage of our propensity to imitate without knowing it, or our reticence to adopt positive forms of mimesis, since all ideals are now critiqued and deconstructed (Boland 2019). The double-edged sword of mimesis in art and action, as unthinking imitation or deliberate artifice, offers a transformative model of social change.

Evidently, plasticity and imitation proffer distinct yet compatible models of transformation. Both Lawtoo and Malabou recognize the historicity of their thinking, acknowledging lineages through Plato and Nietzsche on the one hand, and Hegel and Derrida on the other. Of course, in any genealogy there are many more threads of intersection and influence than can be reconstructed. Thinking about change and continuity clearly involves a tension, one which we can explore through a longer genealogy of modern thinkers to keep expanding mimetic studies.

Giovanni Pico della Mirandola (1463–1494), Wladimir Iljitsch Lenin (1870–1924) and Abraham Maslow (1908–1970) are marginal compared to canonical philosophers, but they are nonetheless very widely read: a "Renaissance man," a socialist leader and a popular psychologist respectively. These thinkers are chosen to further the plasticity of homo mimeticus because they are consequential and culturally influential, and because of the presence of—and tension between—change and continuity, imitation and transformation in their accounts. How the notion of imitation is deployed to explain change rather than continuity emerges from this genealogical investigation. Furthermore, examining multiple accounts of change emphasizes that these, and all other texts, are merely accounts, discourses, consequential but also contingent and—ironically—open to change.

The Dignity of Man

Pico's *Oration* subtitled "On the Dignity of Man" has been variously hailed as the manifesto of the Renaissance and a precursor to Protestantism. His fame was resurgent in post-WWII America as he was popularized in college-level history books (Copenhaver 2022). His work is not only influential on subsequent modern thought, but also a sample of what is "thinkable" within a combination of rediscovered Greek philosophy and Christian theology, mixed with elements of gnostic thinking, Zoroastrianism and suchlike (Cohn 1993). Most centrally, he asserts the transformability of mankind, principally through imitating divine models and creation—what Henry Dicks, in his contribution to *Homo Mimeticus II* addressing the medieval tradition of *imitatio*, calls "theomimicry" (2024, 311). Here, while mankind is implicitly special amid all creation as "God's image," Pico imagines transcending nature, mentally at least, risking heresy perhaps or simply falling into idiocy according to conventional theology.

As a work of Renaissance humanism, Pico's *Oration* begins by declaring "Man" astonishing and a miracle (the unsurprisingly androcentric language is retained here for brevity). This partly rearticulates the theological idea that man is midway between the divine and the earthly, not the same as the other beasts of the world but supplied with conscience and the possibility of faith and salvation. This position of man as "liminal" is emphasized by Pico, as a sort of undefined character; obviously plants and beasts have their station, but so too do angels, as dictated by God. In the order of creation, man comes last on the sixth day according to Genesis. Pico claims: "Therefore, he took man as a work with *no distinct image*" (Copenhaver 2022, 6). This contrasts with the claim that God made man in his own image (Genesis 1.27) or implies that God has no distinct image. Aside from the theological complexity, this renders man as implicitly malleable clay, but also a self-forming, plastic consciousness.

Reflecting a more anthropocentric perspective, Pico places man "in the mid-region of the world" for a specific reason: "The *Artificer* wanted someone to assess the reason for so great an undertaking, to love its beauty, to be astonished by its immensity" (Copenhaver 2022, 4). Here, man appears as a judge over all of creation, taking up something of the supervisory and overseeing position which was typically reserved for God. This is a strident view of man as quasi-divine, or more precisely, as imitating the divinity of God, which may approach heresy, but certainly puts plastic self-transformation within reach. More intriguing still is Pico's speech that he puts in God's mouth; it is worth quoting and analyzing at length:

> According to your desires and judgment, you will have and possess whatever place to live, whatever form, and whatever functions you yourself choose. All other things have a limited and fixed nature prescribed and bounded by our laws. You, with no limit or no bound, may choose for yourself the limits and bounds of your nature. [...] [W]ith free choice and dignity, you may fashion yourself into whatever form you choose. (2022, 6)

The unfixity, malleability, plasticity of mankind is made clear, and followed by an account of the capacity for something closely akin to positive mimesis.

> To you is granted the power of degrading yourself into the lower forms of life, the beasts, and to you is granted the power, contained in your intellect and judgment, to be reborn into the higher forms, the divine. (2022, 6)

Pico insists that man has no fixed place, form or function, having no specific image or place within creation—neither plant, beast nor angel, all of whom are predetermined. This sets up the possibility of mankind, addressed as Adam, being able to follow his desires, use his own judgment and make free choices. In this spatial but also ontological position of indeterminacy, mankind can develop knowledge about the world, surveying creation but also acting freely. Through this, mankind might fashion itself, even unto being "reborn," in effect, man is malleable and can transform himself. Here Pico declares that he follows the Chaldeans, *"a man is a living thing whose nature is variable, manifold and inconstant"* (2022, 10).

How is this transformation to be effectuated? For Pico there are ways of purifying the self, by becoming like angels: "Let us be their rivals for rank and glory...Once we will it, in nothing shall we be their inferiors" (Copenhaver 2022, 11). How this can actually be achieved is described rather indirectly in terms of mysticism and secret rites. Certainly, Pico departs from the classical Renaissance *"imitatio Christi"* into an ambitious reaching for divine status (Szakolczai 2007). Implicitly, this is a deliberate positive mimesis whereby homo mimeticus chooses its own models.

Among the heavenly, Pico identifies Seraphim, Cherubim and Thrones, associated with love, intelligence and judgment or power respectively. To become angelic, he proposes imitating the Cherubim, developing great intelligence and wisdom, taking on their form mimetically, but also shaping oneself as plastic. This process involves philosophy and theology, but also great enthusiasm, even frenzy—highly mimetic emotional states, so that people can become "transported beyond ourselves [...] we shall be ourselves no longer but shall be him, the very one who made us" (Copenhaver 2022, 29). This pretension to divinity verges on gnostic heresy, but what is of interest here is how Pico conceptualizes malleability and change. He invokes wisdom from Zoroaster: "*The soul has wings [...] Drench your wings* he said *in the waters of life*" (29). This leads to a highly opaque discussion of magic—good and bad—the kabbalah, secret knowledge and so forth, but overall the sense is of a sort of purification of the self as a route to transformation in a divine key.

Paradoxically, the defining character of mankind for Pico is its characterlessness. The first discursive step is to insist that mankind has no fixed form, nature or place. This is akin to the *khora* in Plato's *Timaeus*, which Pico invokes, a liminal womb or winnowing through which things come to be but which has no definite form of its own (Horvath 2013). Yet, within this formlessness, mankind is defined by its capacity to desire, judge and choose, an intelligence not commensurate with, but similar to, the divine active creator, whose works it surveys. The capacity to choose, from Zoroaster to Milton Friedman's *Free to Choose*, is positioned as the central ontological feature of humanity. Such choices serve to shape the self, not just incrementally or incidentally, but through deliberate transformations, which fundamentally alter the self, yet maintain continuity.

Notably, Pico's model of transformation is also imitative—for instance, the deliberate imitation of the Cherubim, or following the good models of ancient philosophical and theological wisdom. But more importantly, Pico's text positions mankind as imitating God, becoming like God, rather than being contented with the prime position in divine creation. The divine power to create is imitated in the power of the self for self-transformation. Within this scenario, mankind is also posited as having the freedom and power to choose, to act independently, or at least to choose between imitating bestial and lower creatures, the way of sin, and heavenly examples such as the angels. Yet it is in unfixity and possibility that Pico locates the astonishing miracle of mankind's character. Following René Girard's mimetic theory of unconscious mimetic desire, it is precisely the moment in which one appears to oneself to be acting autonomously that one is most imitative (1965; 1987). By contrast, positive imitation, modeling oneself on ideals and others, is conscious and social, reinscribing positive imitation at the heart of self-formation, as described in Lawtoo's account of mimetic studies

(2022). What matters most for our genealogy is the Renaissance humanist positioning of the self as plastic, incompletely formed yet capable of self-formation, primarily through deliberate imitation, historically hybridizing the two into a model of transformativity.

Lenin: The Withering of the State

Marxist thought is unequivocally a theory of change, perhaps most famously conceptualizing transformation through the notion of the historical dialectic, which offers a materialist conception of change. Economic relations give rise to political conflict, which transforms not only social systems but also the character of individuals. This is rendered poetically in the *Communist Manifesto*:

> Constant revolutionising of production, uninterrupted disturbance of all social conditions, everlasting uncertainty and agitation [...] All fixed, fast-frozen relations, with their train of ancient and venerable prejudices and opinions, are swept away, all new-formed ones become antiquated before they can ossify. All that is solid. (Marx and Engels 2018, 27)

Marxism recognizes the transformations wrought by capitalism, critically re-describing historical changes since feudalism, particularly industrialization, liberal market economies and democratization. In this transformativist model, elements of the past are retained in each new synthesis of the dialectic, but the process of history also reveals the truth or essence of the economic reality.

There is no dispute that modernity has wrought great changes. However, Marxist thought also projects change into the future, not through utopian planning but in predicting future transformations. Particularly, Marxism anticipates revolution, state socialism and the eventual development of full communism. This blueprint for change has been consequential, inspiring the Russian Revolution and many other subsequent instantiations. Central to this model of transformation is the notion that the state will "wither away," discussed at length in Lenin's *State and Revolution*, wherein the state largely appears as a system of oppression, parasitic on the workers, operated by the bourgeoisie.

Composed in the interregnum between the February and October revolutions in 1917, Lenin writes against bourgeois economists, anarchists, utopians and socialist chauvinists, that is, Parliamentary Labor and advocates of a welfare state. He draws heavily on Marx and Engels, citing at length and equating their historical science with natural science like biology—with attendant metaphors of "birth pangs" and so forth. Lenin describes the glimpse of communism in the Paris Commune as "a thoroughly flexible political form" (1992, 50). Rather than planning an ideal state or instantly dispensing with the state, Lenin outlines a process of transformation tracing change, continuity and imitation as proletarians move from capitalist individualism to communist sensibilities.

Firstly, the proletarians become armed and overthrow the repressive state forces, taking control of the means of production. After this violent uprising, a strong state is still considered necessary to administer equality of pay, to ensure that all commit to work and to run the complex apparatus of state services: an interim period known as state socialism. Here, society becomes classless, in that the bourgeois owners of the means of production are expropriated, and the various experts who worked for them must now labor on behalf of the proletariat, perhaps under very different conditions. Remnants of the past persist, for instance the idea of "bourgeois right," the pursuit of larger rewards from the economic system (1992, 83–84). Only gradually can the workers learn to adopt and put into practice the motto "From each according to his ability, to each according to his needs." Incrementally, new models of producing and consuming emerge, the need for the control by the state disappears; it is not wholly "smashed" by revolution, but rather withers away. Arguably, the actual results of this mimetic transformation are cycles of violence and scapegoating, rather than a classless society (Girard 1987; Horvath 2013).

Notably, Lenin's account promises communism as a certainty but makes no precise predictions, discussing a "lengthy and undefined process," using words like "transition," "transformation," "forthcoming" and so on to describe a future situation without specification. But he definitively declares that "historically there must undoubtedly be a special stage or special phase of *transition* from capitalism to communism" (77). Essentially, proletarians are socialized into specific attitudes under capitalism, and only gradually do they become accustomed to the new situation and develop new habits. Here the sociological elements of Marxism emerge, in the broad thesis that workers have been socialized into "bourgeois right," which effectively means competitive individualism.

Evidently, the model Lenin advances envisages not just change but a transformativist logic of continuity through change: "Life shows us remnants of the old surviving in the new at every step, both in nature & society" (89). There are other interesting elements, for instance the idea of a revolution which instantly generates a classless society through the seizing of the means of production. Broadly, this means a sharp crisis which generates an undefined and undifferentiated situation, a flux from which the future can emerge. The possibility of violence and sacrifice of the few by the many resembles Girard's notion of the sacrificial crisis whereby crises are resolved by collective scapegoating (1987). Lenin was not coy about this "need for utmost ferocity and savagery in this process of suppression" (Lenin 1992, 81). Yet, rather than a single conflagration, the change is incremental or transformativist. Indeed, Lenin anticipates less a sudden change than the "Gradualness of the process and its spontaneous nature" (80). Rather than a mechanical re-engineering of society, what emerges is a plastic process of transformation, of individuals and a whole people.

Despite communism being considered in Marxist dialectics as the antithesis to capitalism, there are curious replications: rivalry, doubling, imitation even. The state of capitalism is reconceived within communism: "Until such time as the higher phase of communism arrives, the socialists demand the strictest control by society and by the state," exercised by armed workers (Lenin 1992, 87). For Lenin, the socialist state mirrors the capitalist state, which he conceived as expressing wholly capitalist interests, but now, under the plastic conditions of revolution, extends to everyone, so that each member of society takes on the role of administering the state, via a sort of socialist governmentality which "creates the prerequisite for everyone really to be able to take part in the administration of the state" (90). The state withers away but society takes on its functions in a sort of mimetic mirroring, implying a positive form of mimesis, which does not just replicate the state but surpasses it.

Thus, this is not the reproduction of the same, but a plastic imitation: "the whole of society will have become a single office and a single factory with equality of labor and equality of pay" (91). Thus, there is a plastic transformation here whereby full communism is posited as replicating the form of the state and the factory, precisely the inventions of capitalism, incorporated and idealized, now without exploitation, oppression or inequality, dispersed throughout the body politic. Marxist conceptions of revolution might seem a decisive break, and yet they are transformativist, emerging through a dialectic which ensures continuity and proceeds via imitation, howsoever occluded.

Maslow's Theory of Change: Self-Actualization

While Pico captured Renaissance ideas of change and Lenin provided the recipe for communist revolution, Maslow's idea of self-actualization is widely influential today, moving from psychology to the realm of management and organization (Boland and Griffin 2021). Writing in the shadow of the critique of capitalism articulated and embodied in Lenin's legacy, Maslow suggests that human existence is characterized by desires and needs, which must be fulfilled for the individual to flourish. These range from basic survival needs through desires for esteem to "self-actualization" in a "hierarchy of needs." While the need for shelter, safety, food and security is more basic, for Maslow the subsequent needs are "higher," culminating in "self-actualisation"—not just success in the eyes of others, but becoming, self-developing, unfolding what one can become.

Furthermore, the fulfilment of these desires approximates personal transformation: "Man has his future within him, dynamically active in this present moment" (Maslow 1968, 15). Only through personal efforts, work, action, struggle, giving vent to desires for becoming can these potentials be "actualized." Strikingly, this self-actualization assumes both a plastic self and an agency within, capable of transforming and shaping the self. Rather than purifying the self, as per Christian confession, self-actualization involves inventing the self, akin to Pico's Renaissance self-fashioning (Greenblatt 1980). Yet the models imitated in self-actualization are rarely acknowledged, which we should understand through Girard's (1965) explanation of the claim of originality as especially imitative.

For Maslow, self-actualization means that a person employs their innate potential within the world, thereby becoming the person they are capable of becoming: "What a man can be, he must be. This need we may call self-actualisation" (1998, 261). The continuity of this "man" (Maslow employs androcentric language) across change is not merely grammatical but expresses the model of transformativity. For Maslow, every person self-actualizes to a greater or lesser extent, and those who are "highly self-actualising" tend to become leaders or otherwise highly successful. "One's deepest nature cannot be altogether denied" (315). Obviously, this conception of the self employs a "metaphor of depth," whereby the person we see is described as the result of inner potentialities rather than socially situated.

Interestingly, there is no definite end to this quest for self-actualization because Maslow's hierarchy of needs defines man as a "perpetually wanting animal

[...] A want that is satisfied is no longer a want" (256). For Maslow, such desires emerge from within. Yet, for mimetic studies, they should be recognized as imitative, reflecting social models which can generate endless desires (Lawtoo 2022). Following Lawtoo, Maslow's hierarchy of needs corresponds to various sorts of imitation, ranging from biological desires like hunger to social imitation of status through outside validation. Self-actualization could be a positive version of imitation, which deliberately chooses a model, but very often Maslow follows a highly individualistic notion of self-forming. There is implicitly no model whatsoever here, only unlimited plasticity, which might seem to hold the potential for revolutionary change. Yet all that Maslow imagines is an ideal personal development, within existing structures.

Strikingly, this mode of self-formation also positions the world—physical, social and cultural—as a testing ground for the person. This person's life becomes something of an experiment: the idea of the person as plastic has been commonplace since Renaissance humanists like Pico.[3] Such experiments and trials reflect the modern orientation towards "tests" wherein everything is not just tested, but subject to transformation (Marres and Stark 2020). For Maslow, work is not mere labor or drudgery, but an exciting arena of challenges and projects: "Life is a continual series of choices" (2000, 35). So, self-actualization happens through the exercise of choice, autonomy, self-expression and other higher virtues in any scenario, but most especially work, wherein "work and play" and even life itself becomes almost indistinguishable. This emphasis on choice as self-forming was equally found in Pico but now it is also socially situated. Just as brain plasticity reacts to the entire ecology or environment around it (Malabou 2008), so too self-actualization is performed upon a social terrain, but by a choosing and self-developing personality in accordance with the entrepreneurial subjectivity of neoliberalism (Boltanski and Chiapello 2005).

Strikingly, Maslow positions life as a series of challenges and trials, as though ordained by a divine overseer, where "[o]ne must permit oneself to be chosen" (1998, 14). Finding a fitting line of work, or a vocation, is the key to self-actualization, which requires self-scrutiny, careful choices and dedicated work. Life in work, or anywhere else for that matter, is not random according to Maslow, but a sorting system for finding our destiny: "we are all called to a particular task for which our nature fits us" (2000, 316). As an individual increasingly identifies with their work, the more they subsume their being in that task, the greater their self-actualization. Yet, as noted earlier, this is an interminable pursuit; no "vocational" accreditation can complete the "career." This plastic selfhood is formed by such challenges, but equally gives form to that self, yet within Maslow's model, this actualization of the self is considered pre-existent, essential, unchanging. Thus, Maslow's ideal of self-actualization is not only non-mimetic, but also insists on a non-plastic personhood within.

Plastic Mimetic Transformations

What can we draw from this brief genealogy of transformativist ideas of change? The initial insight of any genealogy is that ideas within the present do not represent an essential truth or an immutable state of affairs, a point which also makes it clear that genealogy itself proceeds according to a transformativist ontology: things change (Lorenzini 2020). But how do they change? Metamorphosis? Reconfiguration? Transformation? Effectively these are descriptions of change; what change is and how it can be understood and described is historically contingent and changeable, thus we can begin to recognize here the "social construction" of change (Hacking 1999).

Importantly, genealogy is not a quest for the source of a singular idea, as though something would be invented once, de novo, and crystallized forever. The historical conditions through which ideas emerge matter, and traces of the past "conditions of emergence" persist, but they are not decisive forever (Foucault 1977). From the three chosen examples, Pico's Renaissance humanism, Lenin's revolutionary communism and Maslow's individualistic self-actualizing, we derive a relatively distinctive modern account of change, not so dramatic as metamorphosis, nor so modest as mere addition or reconfiguration, but one of transformation. Specifying this as "transformativity" becomes possible through historical distance. Thus, while any genealogy could be expanded almost indefinitely, even this brief examination of three historically distinctive notions of change can serve to pluralize our models of change. That is, transformativity as described here is to be understood not as a singular model of change, but one which has multiple forms with different emphases and innumerable sources— the three chosen above are illustrative not exhaustive.

Each of the figures examined above describes a certain kind of change, wrought upon a subject, whether "mankind," the proletariat or the self-actualizing individual. There is continuity despite this change, and the subject of change knows and experiences this change directly and maintains identity through it over time, even if this identity is utterly plastic. The subject of transformativity is akin to the proverbial "Ship of Theseus," and moreover, often the author of its own transformation. Indeed, this "transformativity" has something of the character of an experiment, which makes sense within modernity, given the suffusion of empiricist ideas into culture in general (Wierzbicka 2010). The subject of change is considered as one who is shaped by their circumstances but is also agentic and capable of change, one who both receives and gives form to transformations (Lawtoo 2022, 127–129).

There are different emphases in these three accounts of change. For Pico, choice is central to mankind's self-making and this can even lead to divine transformations. For Lenin, circumstances shape the proletariat, and their initial revolutionary choice to take arms and seize the means of production does not recondition them; only persistent work reshapes them into communists. For Maslow, choice is central, but this occurs within circumstances which appear as the testing ground for self-actualization, so rather than simple choice in the sense of volition, transformation involves the unfolding of inner qualities, which are discovered incrementally, episodically, through challenges in the world. What emerges from all three is a model of change which is "transformativist"— not a sudden drastic metamorphosis, not a mere reconfiguration, but involving change and continuity with identity over time. This model of change is very familiar, adopted almost automatically by many thinkers but comprises a tension, which the concepts of plasticity and imitation can help us explore.

To be clear, "transformativity" was not always the dominant mode of thinking about change, with metamorphosis prevailing in ancient times. Transubstantiation is a well-known model of change from medieval times, but the insistence on full bodily resurrection meant that nothing could change or pass away (Bynum 2001). Yet there are credible precursors for transformative thinking in how Judeo-Christian thought modeled individual change: conversion, confession, pilgrimage, enlightenment and so forth. By contrast, political theory often considered the orders of society—rank and status—to be static, or in a perpetual but non-generative cycle between monarchy, democracy and oligarchy. Whether ideas about self-transformation have been translated into models of social or political change cannot be explored in this chapter, which mainly seeks to investigate the tension between imitation and plasticity within transformativity, that is, how modernity thinks through change.

What then is the tension between plasticity and imitation? Within the thinkers we have examined, it emerges in different and complex ways. Pico builds beyond the Renaissance theme of the *imitatio Christi* to urge his readers to emulate angels so that the human becomes divine. For this to be possible, "mankind" is interpreted as plastic, not a limited, embodied being, not constrained by biology, in contemporary anachronistic parlance. Yet the transformation of mankind only appears possible through imitating models which were in the first instance created by divine agency. While choice seems possible—man can become bestial instead—transformations are limited to the range of models which can be imitated. And while quasi-heretical, Pico is not alone in this: from the early Renaissance, dichotomous thinking was increasingly joined by processual notions, even adopted into official Catholic theology and practice (Le Goff 1986). For instance, heaven and hell are supplemented by the invention of purgatory, a place where sinners can be purified, another transformative imaginary.

Consistently, Marx refused to provide predictions about the communist future, avoiding utopian blueprints and seemingly avoiding the imitation of any example. Yet both Marxist and utopian thought partakes of the modern sense that society is plastic, open to revision and transformation, an idea reflected in bourgeois revolutions and reformist governmentality (Foucault 2005). Nonetheless, imitation emerges in this mode of thought: from Hegel's master–slave dialectic to the conflict of capital and labor, we can see imitative rivalry distinctly. Lenin's presentation of communism after the "state withers away" is an efficient factory writ large upon the whole society, where all are coordinated and in harmony. Revolution appears here not as a complete break, but the re-inscription of a model which can scarcely be acknowledged. Change and continuity, identity over time.

Maslow's self-actualization is sometimes critiqued as a form of individualistic fantasy, whereby a person somehow creates themselves from within, giving scant attention to the cultural scripts and intersubjective interactions which generate selfhood. Furthermore, Maslow's conception of "self-transcendence" included the transformations through dedication to a cause or altruism (1969). Yet, as management advice or psychology spilling over into the genre of self-help, imitation is a core principle in this way of thinking. Confronted with texts which insist that being an idiosyncratic and unique individual is a form of self-fulfillment beyond any social goods, like esteem or status, readers are encouraged to not only view themselves as plastic, transformable selves, but also partake in an imitative play for individuality. Strikingly, Maslow associated greater levels of success within organizations with a higher level of self-actualization. So, while occluded by the emphasis on individual uniqueness, clearly these are mimetic desires, where self-actualization is not the mere unfolding of inner personhood, but the implicitly limitless pursuit of wants and needs.

In gathering these three figures, this genealogy does not argue that they are special or unique, but that they are representative of significant strands of modern thinking. In each, a version of plasticity is put to work, insisting that change is possible, but also, perhaps less obviously, that some sort of imitative modeling or even imitative rivalry is notable. Arguably, this tension, whatever terms are used to describe it, makes it possible to describe change in a specific way, what I conceptualize as transformativity. But such a genealogy makes no claims about the reality of any of these key terms nor does it reveal special lineages of thought: the contribution here is much more modest, simply illustrating the contours of how we think change in dialogue with recent developments on the plasticity of homo mimeticus, recognizing that this is a hybrid which emerges from history and can be thought otherwise.

Conclusion

While discussed herein primarily as a discourse, as a somewhat dry philosophical concept, historicized and relativized, transformativity also gives expression to desires for change. From the Renaissance through socialism to contemporary liberalism, change emerges as a project, and the model of transformativity gives shape to the oftentimes bewildering changes that occur, establishing continuity, giving meaning to alteration and asserting identity and agency. Indeed, the social significance and political valency of transformativist ideas is unmissable, yet ambivalent.

Compare, for instance, Obama's "Change We Can Believe In" and Trump's "Make America Great Again." Both slogans promise positive change of very different sorts, but both also react to change, to the supposed dissipation of the American way. Each promises transformation of the polity, which changes yet maintains identity over time, and this transformation is to be achieved by deliberate choices of political agents. Each assumes the plasticity of the polity, but also positive imitation of ideals, even imaginary nostalgic versions of the past. Surprisingly, the inspiration for Trump is perhaps more Leninist, via right-wing adaptations of Gramscian thinking, whereas Obama's failure to move beyond neoliberal individualism perhaps represents the widespread tendency of becoming confined in self-actualization without altruistic self-transcendence. From these grandstanding world-famous politics of transformation, a myriad of examples proliferates, as almost any social or cultural issue might well be addressed through transformation.

As a genealogical exploration of how we think change through plasticity and imitation, this chapter is mainly concerned with unpacking the quotidian but complex discursive model of transformativity. However, genealogy is not mere historical curiosity and never politically sterile. Recognizing transformativist discourses also serves to relativize them, opening up the possibility of thinking change differently. While great transformations in history are often to be celebrated, we should equally recognize the limits of transformativity.

One of the greatest challenges of our contemporary era, as the concluding essay in *Homo Mimeticus II* indicated (Dicks 2024), is the climate crisis, from global warming to ecological destruction, prompting tipping points that will precipitate changes imperiling populations and peace. How will we respond to these limits of transformativity? Perhaps more radical responses are needed, not just "transformations" of society, economy and politics which maintain continuity and identity over time. Indeed, given that this challenge is unprecedented, what sorts of models can we imitate now? Is homo mimeticus really plastic enough to react and adapt?

The task of genealogy is to specify how we think today as an artefact of the past, to enable us to think differently. Rather than pursue transformation, which implicitly involves maintaining something of the past, the time is fast approaching for drastic and dramatic changes. Today our situation requires rapid radical institutional change, around institutions such as private property, borders, resource allocation, debt, land use and much more. Of course, such changes are usually thought as revolution, a political project with a theological genealogy, which assumes that people are malleable clay and imitates the image of apocalyptic conflict leading to heaven on Earth.

Yet genealogical thinking reveals that there are other modes of change. The myth of a golden age is properly about universal peace, not the domination of one nation, and more importantly involves a human society dedicated to a philosophical way of life. Leviticus ordained periodic jubilees which canceled all debts every fifty years and freed indentured workers, which served to stabilize ancient Judaism against the growth of inequality. Fabled islands of delight and the medieval land of Cockaigne slowed work to a minimum, reveling in relaxation, a vision of a post-work future (Stypinska 2023). Such utopian dreams do not involve an acceleration into the future, a dialectical clash or the transformation or perfection of humans. The revolution here is to slow down and accept our limits and the environment, without the ambition to turn back the clock, to desist from transformations.

Making such forms of change thinkable is a key task for theory today. This vision of mimetic studies incorporates positive imitation, envisaging the possibility of a virtuous circle of deliberately cultivating ideals. Such possibilities depend on the assumption of plasticity. The dynamic tension between these two, mimesis and plasticity, can generate something more than transformation, perhaps a transformation of transformation even, or a transformation away from transformation to the acceptance of ecological limits and new models of society.

Notes

1. See Lawtoo 2022 and Lawtoo and Garcia-Granero 2023, in addition to the essays in this volume.
2. Genealogy plays a major role in mimetic studies. See for instance *Homo Mimeticus*, ch. 1.
3. On Renaissance plasticity see also the Prologue to this volume.

Bibliography

Boland, Tom (2019). *The Spectacle of Critique: From Philosophy to Cacophony*. London: Routledge.
Boland, Tom, and Ray Griffin (2021). *The Reformation of Welfare: The New Faith of the Labour Market*. Bristol: Bristol University Press.
Boltanski, Luc, and Eve Chiapello (2005). *The New Spirit of Capitalism*. London: Verso.
Butler, Judith (1997). *The Psychic Life of Power*. Stanford: Stanford University Press.
Bynum, Carol Walker (2001). *Metamorphosis and Identity*. Princeton: Princeton University Press.
Cohn, Norman (1993). *Cosmos, Chaos, and the World to Come: The Ancient Roots of Apocalyptic Faith*. New Haven: Yale University Press.
Copenhaver, Brian (ed.) (2022). *Life of Giovanni Pico della Mirandola / Gianfrancesco Pico della Mirandola. Oration / Giovanni Pico della Mirandola*. Cambridge, MA: Harvard University Press.
Dicks, Henry (2024). "The Biomimicry Revolution: Contributions to Mimetic Studies," in *Homo Mimeticus II: Re-Turns to Mimesis*, eds. Nidesh Lawtoo and Marina Garcia-Granero. Leuven: Leuven University Press, 305–322.
Foucault, Michel (1977). "Nietzsche, Genealogy, History," in *Language, Counter-Memory, Practice*. Ithaca, NY: Cornell University Press, 139–164.
Foucault, Michel (2005). *The Hermeneutics of the Subject: Lectures at the Collège de France, 1981–1982*. London: Palgrave MacMillan.
Foucault, Michel (2021). *Confessions of the Flesh: The History of Sexuality (Vol. 4)*. London: Vintage Books.
Girard, René (1965). *Deceit, Desire and the Novel: Self and Other in Literary Structures*. Baltimore: The Johns Hopkins University Press.
Girard, René (1987). *Things Hidden Since the Foundation of the World*. Stanford: Stanford University Press.
Greenblatt, Stephen (1980). *Renaissance Self-Fashioning*. Chicago: The University of Chicago Press.
Hacking, Ian (1999). *The Social Construction of What?* Boston: Harvard University Press.
Hansen, Magnus, and Peter Triantafillou (2022). "Methodological reflections on Foucauldian analyses: Adopting the pointers of curiosity, nominalism, conceptual grounding and exemplarity." *European Journal of Social Theory* 25.4, 559–577.

Horvath, Agnes (2013). *Modernism and Charisma*. Basingstoke: Palgrave Macmillan.
Horvath, Agnes, and Arpad Szakolczai (2019). *The Political Sociology and Anthropology of Evil: Tricksterology*. London: Routledge.
Johnsen, Tom, and Friborg Oddgeir (2015). "The Effects of Cognitive Behavioral Therapy as an Anti-Depressive Treatment Is Falling: A Meta-analysis." *Psychological Bulletin* 141.4, 747–768.
Keohane, Kieran, and Kuhling, Carmen (2023). "Fernando Pessoa and the ([P]Re)-Birth of Homo Mimeticus," in *Homo Mimeticus II: Re-Turns to Mimesis*, eds. Nidesh Lawtoo and Marina Garcia-Granero. Leuven: Leuven University Press, 263–285.
Koselleck, Reinhardt (2002). *The Practice of Conceptual History*. Stanford: Stanford University Press.
Lawtoo, Nidesh (2022). *Homo Mimeticus: A New Theory of Imitation*. Leuven: Leuven University Press.
Lawtoo, Nidesh, and Marina Garcia-Granero (eds.) (2023). *Homo Mimeticus II: Re-Turns to Mimesis*. Leuven: Leuven University Press.
Le Goff, Jacques (1984). *The Birth of Purgatory*. London: Scholar Press.
Lenin, Wladimir (1992 [1918]). *The State and Revolution*. London: Penguin.
Lorenzini, Daniele (2020). "On Possibilising Genealogy." *Inquiry*, 67.7, 2175-2196.
Malabou, Catherine (2000). "Deconstructive and/or 'Plastic' Readings of Hegel." *Bulletin of the Hegel Society of Great Britain* 21.1-2, 132–141.
Malabou, Catherine (2008). *What Should We Do with Our Brain?* New York: Fordham University Press.
Marres, Noortje, and David Stark (2020). "Put to the Test: For a New Sociology of Testing." *British Journal of Sociology* 71, 423–443.
Marx, Karl, and Frederick Engels (2018). *The Communist Manifesto*. London: Verso.
Maslow, Abraham (1968). *Toward a Psychology of Being*. Princeton: Van Nostrand.
Maslow, Abraham (1969). "Various Meanings of Transcendence." *Journal of Transpersonal Psychology* 1.1, 56–66.
Maslow, Abraham (1998). *Maslow on Management*. Oxford: Wiley-Blackwell.
Maslow, Abraham (2000). *The Maslow Business Reader*. Oxford: Wiley-Blackwell.
Paley, Chris (2014). *Unthink: And how to harness the power of your unconscious*. London: Hachette.
Stypinska, Diana (2023). "Confronting Time out of Joint... – On Economic Rationality and Imagination." *Journal of Classical Sociology* 23.2, 181–194.
Szakolczai, Arpad (2007). *Sociology, Religion and Grace: A Quest for the Renaissance*. London: Routledge.
Thomassen, Bjorn (2016). *Liminality and the Modern: Living through the In-Between*. London: Routledge.
Wierzbicka, Anna (2010). *Experience, Evidence & Sense: The Hidden Cultural Legacy of English*. Oxford: Oxford University Press.

CHAPTER 3

MATERIAL MIMETISM

On Plastics, Plasticity and Mimesis

Alice Iacobone

Introduction

This chapter discusses the relationship between plasticity and mimesis by examining a phenomenon that I call *material mimetism*. To grasp it intuitively, we can look at the spaces in which we live: for example, the many surfaces that appear to be wooden floors or marble countertops but that are actually made from plastic. The same phenomenon can be observed in more specific cases, from the arts to the natural sciences. An example is provided by wax, a material notoriously capable of imitating human flesh, which for this very reason has been widely exploited for both medical and artistic purposes.

Materials are seemingly capable of imitating each other: plastics can look like marble and wood, wax can simulate the human *incarnato*, and so on. The concept of material mimetism aims at addressing these kinds of phenomena without leading them back to the activity of a human observer, whose perception would provide grounds for the relationship between the two otherwise unrelated materials. The notion of material mimetism offers the possibility to conceive of mimetism as an ability (or, better, a *behavior*) enacted by plastic materials themselves, endowed with agency and capable of entering meaningful, transformative relationships with one another.

Plasticity and mimesis are at the core of the argument developed in these pages. The concept of plasticity, to which French philosopher Catherine Malabou has devoted considerable research, proves to be very much in line with the concept of mimesis as understood in the context of mimetic studies, which aims to counter the traditional conceptualization of mimesis as a deceitful, illusory and ontologically depleted copy of nature. The profound solidarity of the two concepts has been highlighted and explored by Nidesh Lawtoo within the field of mimetic studies (Lawtoo 2017; 2022, 129–155). Both Malabou and Lawtoo develop their respective accounts by deepening their concepts with particular reference to human subjectivity. Malabou's philosophy of plasticity as well as Lawtoo's mimetic studies have nonreductive materialist foundations and scopes (Lawtoo 2022, 157–189, 255–276; Malabou 2009, 9). Both accounts, however, tend to explore materialism by privileging the connection with human life and by paying less attention to inorganic materials, with regard to their plasticity and their mimetic abilities.[1]

The present chapter interrogates these dimensions that are still in need of further developments; it does so by turning to the methods and conceptual tools of German *Materialästhetik*, outlined since the turn of the century by scholars such as Monika Wagner (2001b), Dietmar Rübel (2012) and Petra Lange-Berndt (2015a), and by engaging with new materialist accounts, such as Manuel DeLanda's (2005; 2016), that can be traced back to the influence of Gilles Deleuze and Félix Guattari (1994). A more specific analysis of the case of plastics, then, will give us the opportunity to explore the relationship between the plasticity of nonhuman materials, on one hand, and their inclination for performative mimesis, mimicry and mimetism, on the other.

Despite the increasing attention around "material mimesis" in recent years (see Bol and Spary 2023), the problematic anthropocentrism inherent to this perspective is not really addressed. Therefore, this chapter asks: what happens if one moves away from human subjectivity and considers the plasticity and mimesis of materials themselves? In doing so, it contributes to mimetic studies and to studies on plasticity and aspires to broaden them by deepening the nonreductive materialism already active in Malabou's and Lawtoo's accounts.

The argument for a nonhuman understanding of material mimetism is structured as follows. First, I provide an analysis of the concept of plasticity. Going back to its etymological roots shows that three different meanings and semantic areas have been associated with plasticity: (1) formation of inorganic materials; (2) formation of human subjectivity; and (3) imitation. While Malabou has worked at the intersection of the first and second semantic areas, and Lawtoo has investigated the relationships between the second and third meanings, this chapter devotes attention to the intertwining of the first and the third. Admittedly, phenomena of material mimetism display cases of imitation enacted by inorganic materials that ask to be examined by materialist means. After rejecting representational theories that lean on human perception as a means for elucidating these cases, I outline a material aesthetics based on a method of "material complicity" that, in a new materialist fashion of Deleuzean descent, focuses on sensation and the behaviors of materials themselves.

This method proves to be particularly valuable when considering the specific case of plastics. Invented precisely for mimetic purposes, plastics indeed offer several examples of material mimetism—so much so as to be described as a "chameleon material" (Bensaude-Vincent 2013, 19). Drawing on this expression, I propose to understand material mimetism in comparison with animal mimicry as it has been conceptualized by Roger Caillois (a thinker of paramount importance for mimetic studies), i.e. as a phenomenon based on affects without an observer, rather than on external appearances that must be perceived. This chapter is thus meant to open a speculative path concerning plasticity and mimesis from the point of view of nonhuman materiality, therefore broadening the debate on these concepts while remaining profoundly sympathetic to the perspectives of the authors who have shaped this debate.

At the Roots of Plasticity

Plasticity and mimesis are linguistically entangled, as the etymology of the former term shows. The noun "plasticity" comes from the Greek word *plássein*, a verb that means "to model," "to mold," "to shape," "to form." Malabou has pointed out this linguistic reference to form and formation by describing plasticity as the ability to both *give* and *receive* form (2010, 87; 2011a, 487). Plasticity thus refers concurrently to the *activity* of formation and to the *passivity* of acquiring a form: it brings together what is *gestaltend* ("forming") and what is *gestaltet* ("formed") (2005, 8). Reference to the form—or, better, to the dynamics at stake in the process of formation (*Gestaltung*)—is therefore a paramount feature of plasticity, which can be conveniently regarded as a morphological concept.[2] However, the morphological overtones of this concept remain far from the ideality of form: plasticity is a concept that asks to be framed within a materialist philosophy. Such materialism should not be mistaken for reductionism, as is the case with other concepts: the concept of flexibility, for example, displays exclusively the passive side of plasticity (Malabou 2008, 12–14) and inspires poorer materialist accounts that easily comply with the social and political status quo (46–54).

Furthering our examination of the linguistic roots of plasticity, the reference to materials and materiality becomes more and more radical. In its very first meaning, *plássein* did not mean "to form" in general; it rather meant "to form out of a malleable material (especially wax and clay)" (Dongowski 2002, 815; my trans.). French philosopher Dominique Chateau, among others, has stressed such entanglement of forms and materials within the early concept of plasticity and its ancient vocabulary: "The word *plastikós* is first of all a category relating to matter and its relationship to the form. It designates the specificity of being modeled, what is proper to the malleable matter, and its force of formation (in the sense that formation is the action of the form)" (Chateau 1999, 11; my trans.). He adds: "The idea of plasticity attests of features belonging strictly to modeling and to the specific category of a material that is soft enough to be kneaded and compact enough to take on permanent forms" (1999, 13; my trans.). If reference to form represents a paramount feature of plasticity, the reference to inorganic materials (most notably clay) is equally important in the very first occurrences of the term.[3] Plastic materials are endowed with physical ambiguity: they disturb the dichotomy that divides flexibility from rigidity, suppleness from resistance, liquidity from solidity, metamorphosis from morphological stability. By bringing together opposite behaviors and features, plastic materials display what art historian Georges Didi-Huberman has called a "paradox of consistency," which points to the fact that materials such as waxes "discard the contradiction of material qualities" (Didi-Huberman 2000, 217). In a sense closely tied to nonliving materials, Malabou similarly specifies that "plasticity designates solidity as much as suppleness" (Malabou 2008, 15).

It is thus possible to outline the first meaning of plasticity as (1) material formation occurring both in an active and a passive sense. However, focusing on the Greek and Latin occurrences of this vocabulary (*plássein*, *plastikós*, *plásma*) also reveals interesting shifts in meaning that had broadened the domain already in ancient times.[4] Let us examine them closely.

First semantic shift: the concept of plasticity as material formation was soon transposed from physical bodies to human souls. Plasticity then started referring to (2) education—what in the *Goethezeit* would be called, not by chance, *Bildung*, that is, a "formation" capable of fashioning a young person's character, a training through which it is possible to shape young people and their personality. This shift in meaning is already visible in Plato's different uses of *pláttein* (Attic for *plássein*). In the *Republic*, for instance, he claims that mothers and nurses should "spend far more time shaping [the children's] souls [πλάττειν τὰς ψυχὰς] with [...] stories than [...] shaping their bodies [τὰ σώματα] by their hands"

(1963a, 624, 377c). According to Plato, it is at a young age that a soul is "best moulded [πλάττεται]" and therefore "best tak[es] on the impression [τύπος] that one wishes to stamp [ἐνσημήνασθαι] upon it" (624, 377b);[5] adults too, however, can be modeled by means of theatre (830, 604e)—a fact that notoriously takes on a negative connotation in Plato's thought, but that nonetheless accounts for the plasticity of human beings. The idea of a certain malleability of the immaterial soul can also be found in the *Theaetetus*, in which the image of a wax tablet in the mind allows for an explanation of memory: things that have been thought or perceived are not forgotten so long as their imprints last on the tablet (1963b, 897, 191d).[6] Thanks to this semantic change in focus, the human being is now ranked among the "plastic materials" that bring together suppleness and rigidity, malleability and resistance. By taking on this second meaning, plasticity comes to concern the soul in antiquity and the subject in modernity.

Malabou's entire reflection can be seen as an articulated variation on the theme of plastic subjectivity. From her initial engagement with Hegel, which not by chance begins with an analysis of the role of habits in the "Anthropology" (2005, 28–38), to her dialogue with neurosciences (2005; 2012a) and the epigenetic paradigm (2014), Malabou is constantly grappling with the problem of subjectivity in the light of plasticity.[7] Interestingly enough, the French philosopher post-dates the semantic shift of plasticity referring to the human being.[8] "For the first time with Hegel, plasticity reaches the essential," she claims, and continues: "The philosopher snatches plasticity from its strictly aesthetic anchorage in order to attach it to a problematic space which, so far, had not been its own: *subjectivity*. It is now that the *subject* is called *plastic*" (2000, 8–9; my trans., emphasis added). Of course, Malabou is no longer considering "souls" as "immaterial": quite the contrary, she devotes a great deal of attention to the body, from the brain (2008; 2012a) to the clitoris (2020). Broadly speaking, Malabou's account of the human subject is developed from the perspective of a nonreductive new materialism.[9]

Malabou's new materialism—which is also described as dialectic, deconstructive and nonreductive (2009, 9)—ultimately consists in a profound entanglement of the philosophy of the spirit with neurosciences, or, better, in a philosophy of the spirit (and therefore of the subject) that results from, and is coherent with, the evidence offered by up-to-date neurobiology (2012a, 212). Malabou's materialism is therefore a "materialism of the flesh," as it is inherently tied to the living matter, if not to humanity all together. A materialism interested in inorganic materials is not at stake in her thought.[10] If we circle back to the reference to clay made by Malabou, it is possible to notice that she tends to place nonliving materials on the passive side of plasticity: clay is regarded as inert unless human agency activates it; it is used as an example of being "susceptible to changes of form" (2005, 8) or of the "capacity to *receive form*" (2008, 5). In Malabou's account, the power to bestow form never pertains to such an inorganic material, which can be regarded as plastic only in a reductive, passive sense. Proper plasticity, characterized by the never-ending oscillation between activity and passivity, seems to belong exclusively to the human body and more specifically to the brain, which is what best brings together spirit and matter, production and reception of form. This is why, while being a new materialism in its own right, Malabou's thought can be fully inscribed in the second field opened up by the concept of plasticity: that of plastic human subjectivity.

Let us now turn to the second semantic shift experienced by the vocabulary of plasticity in its early uses. This further change bent plasticity in the direction of (3) mimesis and simulation, as the verb *plássein* gradually took up various meanings ranging from "to invent," to "to fake," "to simulate," "to counterfeit." Baldine Saint-Girons (2000, 33–34) has devoted relevant pages to this change in meaning, pointing out that this connotation was further consolidated in the Latin translation of *plássein* as *fingere*, from which both the words "figure" and "fiction" come.[11] Despite coming from a different linguistic root, *fingere* too maintained the first meaning of "modeling in clay," as the noun *figulus* ("potter") attests. Here, by digging in the different semantic layers of the term and in its remote history, we witness an unexpected encounter between plasticity and mimesis. Of course, this is not the only space in which these concepts can meet—the present volume represents a collection of the possible, multifaceted encounters that can occur between plasticity and mimesis well beyond any lexicographic consideration. Moreover, mimetic studies has already acknowledged the fruitful entanglement between mimesis and plasticity, specifically in Nidesh Lawtoo's article on "The Plasticity of Mimesis" (2017), which later became part of *Homo Mimeticus* (2022, 129–155). However, focusing on this rich etymology could help us shed light on yet another possible way in which plasticity and mimesis can meet, opening up to a materialist supplement that broadens mimetic studies while maintaining a continuity with it.

Let us briefly examine the strategy adopted by mimetic studies so far. In his 2017 paper, Lawtoo does not mention the fictional meaning associated with the vocabulary of plasticity in ancient times; he rather retraces a theoretical genealogy up to the point where the philosophical joint adventure of the two concepts begins. Drawing on Philippe Lacoue-Labarthe's mimetology, Lawtoo argues for plasticity and mimesis to be, in fact, two sides of one and the same concept—a concept whose origins are to be found in Plato's thought. Plasticity thus loses its autonomous conceptual history and reveals itself as "one of the most recent [...] manifestations of what the Greek called, enigmatically, mimesis" (2017, 1201).[12] What are the elements underpinning this claim? Interestingly, Lawtoo (via Lacoue-Labarthe) folds the discourse on mimesis-plasticity from ontology back to "physio-psychology": the problem of fictionality is brought back to the problem of subjectivity (2017, 1208–1209). Avowedly, Lawtoo makes mimesis and plasticity converge on human subjectivity regarded of course in plastic, even posthuman terms; this move is in solidarity with Malabou in turning to physio-psychology and the subject. We are thus sent back to the understanding of plasticity as subject formation: subjects are shaped plastically, that is, by means of stories and myths—but the spotlight is now on the theatrical actor or mime, rather than on the *pièce* performed on stage. Theatrical *fictioning* is, at the same time, *fashioning* of subjects: mimesis and plasticity overlap, and they do so specifically on the problematic of the formation of subjectivity. This is Lawtoo's first argument. The second one regards the very structure of the concepts of mimesis and plasticity: just like plasticity, mimesis is said to possess a passive, receptive side (i.e. uncritical, blind imitation, that on a mass scale becomes disconcerting for political reasons, as it renders the subjects docile and easy to subjugate) as well as an active, creative side (i.e. the virtuosity of the actor, who is capable of (re-)producing any character). In this sense, "the double structure of plasticity shadows the double structure of mimesis" (2017, 1213). Plasticity maintains intimate relations with mimesis for their common duplicity, and they both still engage with subjectivity.

If we were to consider Malabou's and Lawtoo's accounts by referring to our scheme (Table 1), we could understand Malabou's thought as a rich exploration of the interplay between the first and the second meaning taken up by *plássein*: (1) material formation encountering (2) the fashioning of the plastic human subject. Lawtoo's account, on the other hand, could be understood as a theoretical intertwining of *plássein*'s third and second meaning: (2) the formative process of education (subjectivation, or formation of psychological and physical subjectivity) encountering (3) the domain of imitation, invention and fictionality.

I would like to explore the possibility of a third option: the connection between the first and the third meaning of *plássein*; that is to say, the relationship between (1) the formation of nonhuman materials and (3) imitation, mimicry, fictionality and simulation. By steering away from (2) human subjectivity, I do not intend to mount a criticism of those accounts that have focused on plastic and mimetic subjectivity. On the contrary, this chapter aims to broaden the debate while remaining strongly sympathetic to such accounts. In other words, the purpose here is not to go against those who have conceived plasticity and mimesis in relation to subjectivity. This contribution rather takes a different path, a side step we might say, by considering the fortunes of plasticity and mimesis when embodied by something that is not a human subject. By exploring the entanglements of material and nonliving plasticity, on the one hand, and mimesis on the other, this chapter points to a new direction to further mimetic studies.[13]

Table 1. Ancient vocabulary of plasticity

	1. Morphological and material meaning	= to form inorganic matter
First semantic shift:	2. Subject-related meaning	= to form human subjects
Second semantic shift:	3. Mimetic meaning	= to simulate, to counterfeit

Material Complicities

The sheer materiality of mimetic objects and mimetic practices has not often been examined from a theoretical standpoint, remaining the prerogative of engineers and material scientists, who usually work with material resemblances without calling them into question on a speculative level. However, some recent, meaningful exceptions show that scholarship has started taking this issue into account from a theoretical point of view. In 2023, the editors of a collected volume on *The Matter of Mimesis* gathered a number of scholars from the social sciences, the arts and the humanities (as well as some from the hard sciences) and asked them to elaborate on the topic of "material mimesis," i.e. on "the various roles played by materials in mimetic practices" (Bol and Spary 2023, 1). Before this book, philosophy had already been interested in the possibility of a material being able to reproduce the appearance of another substance. Such phenomena mainly drew the attention of phenomenologists, attracted, for instance, to the classic case of wax as capable of imitating flesh (Conte 2014).

The perspectives I have just mentioned share a decisive trait. The contributions collected in the 2023 volume tend to consider materials as embedded in social and cultural practices, taking on general anthropological overtones that loosely place the volume within the field of material culture studies. These essays do investigate phenomena of material mimetism by discussing "ways in which artisans and makers transformed wood into the appearance of bronze, made bronze or wax look like human flesh" (Bold and Spary 2023, 185). But they do so from the perspective of the human subject who interacts with these items in cultural terms and is deceived, or not, by their mimetic appearance. The same holds (although for different reasons and in different terms) for the phenomenological approach, which is centered on human perception and tellingly resorts to the vocabulary of illusion, delusion, deception and depiction—that is, the dominant ontological conception of mimesis that mimetic studies aims to overcome. In his book on a phenomenological aesthetics of waxworks, Pietro Conte significantly claims: "*In so far as it is perceived as a human being*, the statue is no longer made of wax, but flesh" (2014, 28; my trans., emphasis added). The transition from one material to the other is inextricably tied to the beholder's perception.

These approaches indeed have many merits; for instance, they contribute to the shift in focus from the concept of "matter" to a closer consideration of singular materials.[14] But, in contrast to these accounts, I would like to investigate material mimetism by considering this issue not as a problem of human perception—e.g. "*I perceive* wax as if it were flesh"—but rather as a problem of non-human aesthetics, i.e. from the perspective of an aesthetics of materials. With the specific and local purpose of steering away from human subjectivity, the perspective I adopt is not that of the relations of materials with human beings, but that of the relations that materials have with each other. The question, thus, would no longer be: "Why does wax look like flesh *to me*?" but rather: "What is happening *between wax and flesh*?" Within a phenomenological framework, the assumption is that nothing really occurs between the two materials: it is our (deceitful) perception that associates them. On the contrary, I would like to suggest that something actually happens between materials that imitate each other, and that it is the plastic material itself that actively displays mimetic behaviors and engages in mimetic relationships in the first place.

My strategy consists in bringing into play a "material aesthetics," in partial continuity with the German *Materialästhetik* (Wagner 2001b; Wagner, Rübel and Hackenschmidt 2002; Lange-Berndt 2015a). Although trained in art history, the scholars belonging to the *Materialästhetik* do not use traditional art historical methods: they do not focus on symbolic or iconographic contents, but rather "follow the materials" (2015b, 15) of the artworks they consider. The material aesthetics I outline aims at following the materials as well, while maintaining a contingent reference to artworks. A material aesthetics, or an aesthetics *of* materials, will still have to do with *aisthēsis* (sensation), as the Greek etymology of aesthetics suggests; this *aisthēsis*, however, will not be ascribed to a human observer—rather, it will be embodied by the materials themselves. In this sense, it is with a subjective genitive that one speaks of the sensation *of* wax, of the sensation *of* plastics—where such sensation is to be understood less as a subjective fact and more as a relationship between different objects that allow them to behave similarly.

This shift in perspective comes to the fore by adopting a "methodology of material complicity,"[15] which Petra Lange-Berndt describes as follows:

> To be complicit with the materials means, above all, to acknowledge the nonhuman. This is not about a block of throbbing bodily sensations a subject might carry around in joy or anger, but *sensation of this or that material*, sensation embodied as and in material forms. (2015b, 15; emphasis added)

While such a claim may sound outlandish at first, this argument can in fact be traced back to Gilles Deleuze and Félix Guattari's theory of affects and percepts. "Sensation," they write, "is not realized in the material without the material passing completely into the sensation, into the percept or affect. All the material becomes expressive. It is the affect that is metallic, crystalline, stony and so on; and the sensation is not colored but, as Cézanne said, coloring" (1994, 166–167). Such a material sensation, which sets the conceptual basis for a material aesthetics, is at the core of a resemblance grounded in materiality rather than in optical appearance. To quote again Deleuze and Guattari,

> sensations are not perceptions referring to an object (reference): if they resemble something it is with a resemblance produced with their own methods [...]. If resemblance haunts the work of art, it is because sensation refers only to its material: it is the percept or affect *of the material itself*, the smile of oil, the gesture of fired clay, the thrust of metal, the crouch of Romanesque stone, and the ascent of Gothic stone. (1994, 166; emphasis added)

The affective resemblance that the materials produce *with their own methods* lays the foundation for the phenomena of material mimetism. If more subjectivist accounts tend to consider the macroscopic level of exterior appearance and subjective perception (what Deleuze and Guattari would have called the "molar" plane) as primary, material aesthetics instead tries to put the focus on the microscopic level of affects (the "molecular" plane): it looks at the inapparent affective interactions occurring between different materials. Instead of considering the sensible properties of a given material (the ways in which it appears), material aesthetics focuses on the "complex dynamical *behavior*" of the material (DeLanda 2005)—a behavior that manifests itself by taking on certain phenomenal qualities, but that occurs at the molecular level.

If a macroscopic analysis deals with "material mimesis," a microscopic analysis regards the same phenomena as cases of "material mimetism": while the former implies a human subject who witnesses and/or performs the material-mimetic act (someone *to whom* wax appears like flesh), the latter dares to conceive of a mimesis *of* plastic materials themselves. Mimetism, in other words, is a "behavioral mimesis" (Lawtoo 2022, 165). At this level, plasticity is not a quality of materials but a material and processual *behavior*: the more a given material is available to enter relationships with other materials, the more it can be regarded as plastic. At the same time, plasticity should not be confused with flexibility (Malabou 2008, 12–13), i.e. with supple availability to any sort of encounter: despite being available for a variety of interactions, plastic materials have inherent tendencies that make them enter certain relationships and not others. For instance, wax can mimetically interact with flesh, while glass cannot; glass can, in turn, mimetically interact with gemstones, which is not an interaction available to wax. Becoming complicit with the materials thus means looking into the ways in which materials actively become complicit with one another at a microscopic and affective level.

Ventures of a Chameleon Material

Plastics represent the category of materials most suited to investigating cases of material mimetism: they are indeed "materials of mimesis" (Davis 2022, 22).[16] But how to be complicit with such a controversial material? Plastics have a very bad reputation, which stems from the political implications of their production and circulation: they are an agent and a result of petrocapitalism, they endorse forms of contemporary colonialism, they represent an ecological threat for the planet, they create unseen violence, harm, inequality—to name just a few of the issues they raise.[17] All these problematic aspects should definitely be kept in mind; but this does not prevent us from critically investigating the mimetic plasticity of plastic materials, especially since plastics inherently produce a "material and psychological dissonance" (Abrahms-Kavunenko and Brox 2022, 6) that makes them eschew any simplistic, dichotomic categorization as either "good" or "bad," thus opening up a zone of complexity.

Here, adopting the method of material complicity means, first of all, following plastics through their history and pinpointing some of the moments in which they have engaged in complicity with other substances: moments in which they have behaved mimetically. The history of plastics begins in the 1860s when celluloid was invented by John Wesley Hyatt[18] in response to a specific need: billiards was very popular at the time, but billiard balls were made out of ivory, the scarcity of which resulted in high prices for the game. This is why the American firm Phelan & Collender offered a monetary reward for anyone capable of inventing effective substitute, a material capable of imitating tusk ivory (Miodownik 2014, 124–153; Freinkel 2011). Celluloid was invented for this very specific purpose. Soon, its mimetic abilities were put at work in other contexts too: for instance, celluloid was widely used for producing toiletry items—the so-called "vanity set" that was so important for female identity in Victorian society (Beaujot 2012, 139–177). The mimetic association between this early plastic and tusk ivory was so tight that in 1917 a new kind of celluloid was put in the market with the name of "Ivory Pyralin."[19] However, this material and its mimetic ability elicited mixed feelings: on the one hand, celluloid democratized some goods (and, somewhat paradoxically, it curbed the ivory trade, thus contributing to sparing elephants' lives); on the other hand, it was seen as a cheap, light, superficial and fake material. As philosopher and historian of science Bernadette Bensaude-Vincent recalls, "far from being praised as a quality, plasticity was the hallmark of cheap substitutes, forever doomed to imitate more authentic, natural materials" (2013, 19). Plastics' proneness to imitation, understood in the Platonic sense of a deceptive copy, led to them taking on a negative connotation that associated them with inauthenticity—a connotation that, to a certain extent, persists to this day. At the beginning of their history, plastics therefore represented a material space where plasticity and mimesis met—but with negative, reductive overtones that are far from both Malabou's philosophy of plasticity and the complex understanding of mimesis offered by mimetic studies.

It is true that nowadays plastics have become more and more autonomous, and yet they have continued to replace a wide variety of materials, ranging from wood to metals to marble. Celluloid was born out of complicity with ivory, and, in general, "the systematic development of plastics (*Kunststoffen*) began by looking for a substitute substance (*Ersatzstoff*) imitating the characteristics of other materials" (Mextorf 2002, 161–162; my trans.). Subsequently invented polymers deepened the complicity of plastics with natural or organic materials by exploring further mimetic relationships to them. Starting in the 1990s, plastics with built-in intelligence were developed: smart materials whose properties change according to changes in their environment (Bensaude-Vincent 2013, 23).

How to conceive of the plastic imitation performed *by* these materials? Bensaude-Vincent recalled that "celluloid was described as a 'chameleon material' that could imitate tortoise-shell, amber, coral, marble, jade, onyx, and other natural materials" (2013, 19). This expression, "a chameleon material," a material with chameleon-like behaviors, can provide us with a crucial hint—the chameleon also being the symbol of mimetic studies, to which we can now circle back in search for a nonreductive solution to the puzzle of plastic imitation.[20] Admittedly, to talk about a "chameleon material" suggests a continuity, or better, a plane of analogy, between the domain of living organisms and the domain of inorganic matter. Celluloid *behaves* like a chameleon: this allows us to point out a continuity between biology and material science. By focusing on behaviors more than on properties, it becomes possible to draw an analogy between material mimetism and animal mimicry. This analogical operation provides us with an explanation of material mimetism from a nonhuman perspective.

The thinking of Roger Caillois can be of assistance here. An otherwise marginalized and overlooked author, Caillois has been regarded as an important ally and even a precursor to mimetic studies and new materialisms (especially in Jane Bennett's version) (Lawtoo 2022, 160–165). The work of Caillois is relevant for two different yet interconnected reasons: first of all, the French essayist outlined a theory of animal mimicry which stresses how these phenomena push life towards inorganic matter (instead of understanding them, as most theories do, as strategies for survival); secondly, Caillois's theory of mimetism (*mimétisme*) is, to use his word, "diagonal": not only does it cut across different disciplinary fields,[21] but it also crosses different domains of reality, establishing a strong continuity between human and nonhuman entities.

In the essay *Mimétisme et psychasthénie légendaire*, first published in 1935, Caillois diagonally correlates insect mimicry with anthropological accounts of magical thinking in so-called primitive societies, on the one hand, and with cases of psychasthenia analyzed from the point of view of modern scientific epistemology on the other. All three kinds of phenomena, Caillois argues, can be brought back to an "appeal" or "lure of space" (2003a, 102, 99), an "instinct of letting go" ("*instinct d'abandon*," 102) which attracts life toward inanimate matter. Mimicry, magical thinking and psychasthenia can all be regarded as forms of "pathology" (91) of the distinction that demarcates the organism from its *milieu*, the subject from the surrounding space. The correlation between these very different domains does not account for a projection of human categories onto nonhuman entities—far from it. As Caillois will claim in a later essay (*Nouveau plaidoyer pour les sciences diagonales*), anticipating and rejecting all accusation of anthropomorphism, "the point is not to explain certain puzzling facts observed in nature in terms of man [*sic*]. On the contrary, it is to explain man [...] in terms of the more general behavioral forms found widespread in nature" (2003b, 345–346). Caillois, and Lawtoo (2022, 157–189) as a reader of Caillois's texts, start from animal mimicry to observe the human subject. This diagonal, non-hierarchical method, allows for a transposition of the same theses to the domain of materials too, i.e. to see behavioral correspondences between the realm of animality and that of inorganic materials. The method and the object of investigation overlap here: "Slicing obliquely through our common world, [diagonal sciences] decipher latent complicities and reveal neglected correlations" (Caillois 2003b, 347). There are unseen complicities, unforeseeable relationships not only between the insect and the inorganic material, but also between, say, plastic and marble—meaning that, for instance, plastic can be attracted toward marble just as the organism can be attracted toward its background.

Observing animals' behaviors, Lawtoo explains that Caillois argues for mimetism to be "not only a visual but also [a] physiological phenomenon" (Lawtoo 2022, 174), "not simply a visual exterior phenomenon, [...] [but] rather an affective, interior, inner experience" (176). As Lawtoo writes:

> It is [...] from the inside out rather than from the outside in that [Caillois] approaches the riddle of mimetism. [...] In fact, he notices that the immobile animal nested against inorganic matter is not simply invisible to the observer's eye—*a question of exterior representation*. Rather, it enters in what he calls a state of "catalepsy" whereby "life," as he says, "steps back a degree" as in a sort of "trance"—*a question of inner experience*. (174–175; emphasis added)

According to Lawtoo, Caillois thus shifts the focus from the optical appearance, which is a macroscopic resulting property, to the microscopic field of processes and experiences. "Mimetism [...] is not only something seen, or a mimetic representation; it is above all something *felt*," Lawtoo points out (178; emphasis added). By transposing this argument from the animal world to the domain of materials, we are confronted once again with a feeling, or sensation, experienced by materials themselves—thus circling back to our material aesthetics.

Still, one may ask: how can plastic imitate ivory, if it cannot see it? Following Caillois, an approach centered on vision cannot explain this phenomenon by acknowledging an agency of plastics: it needs to postulate an observer, to which all the agency is ultimately ascribed. From this perspective, "the resemblance exists solely in the eye of the beholder" (Caillois 2003a, 93). The explanation I outline goes in a different direction, claiming that material mimetism can be understood as the behavior of a given material that undergoes an affective correlation with a different one. Of course, from many philosophical perspectives it may appear problematic to talk about affects or experience without subjects. If we adopt the lens of a new materialism of post-structuralist descent, however, the possibility of a transmission of affects through materials starts appearing sounder: what matters is to acknowledge meaningful relations between materials, relations that are capable of transforming the materials that enter them—relations to be regarded on the model of *agencement* or assemblage (DeLanda 2016). From this perspective, the point is not that plastic may or may not superficially resemble ivory or marble, but rather that between plastic and marble or between plastic and ivory there is a plane of analogy that allows for a material to experience a mimetic contagion. Coherently with mimetic studies but broadening the field in a material-oriented direction, my perspective rejects vision as the main sense to frame mimesis (a position still assumed by the dominant ontological view), turning the attention towards contagion, which is to be conceived of on the model of *touch*.

What is, then, material mimetism? What happens when materials enter imitative relationships with one another? The provisional answer is: material mimetism is a phenomenon of behavioral synchronization between different materials, occurring as the emergence of a common plane of non-organic affects. Non-organic affects can be conceived of as possibilities of elaborating non-automatic responses to external stimuli in the absence of biological organisms. The possibility of a "material intensity" goes beyond the scope of this chapter and can dictate the way for future research. What is important to hold firm is that these affective events occur as relationships between different materials; and that these relationships support phenomenal properties that the observer describes as mutually similar. Plastic resembles ivory not so much in the sense that the former *looks like* the latter according to visual and deceitful standards. Rather, plastic and ivory engage in a meaningful, transformative encounter that unfolds in material and mimetic terms.

Final Remarks

Material mimetism can be defined as the affective becoming *of* materials imitating each other. They can do so by means of their plasticity, which is, at the same time, a (1) material plasticity and a (3) mimetic plasticity, but not a (2) human plasticity (see Table 1), as it does not present traits such as consciousness, cognition and—more broadly—organic life. The investigation of material mimetism makes us circle back to the concept we started with, that of plasticity, which we can now consider in a new light. Material mimetism, intended as a phenomenon in which no human subject is implied, forces us to take seriously material plasticity: if plasticity, in general, defines the coalescence of activity and passivity, often it is only the latter which is ascribed to inorganic, inert materials. Through the analysis of material mimetism, it is possible, instead, to conceive of plasticity as also representing a form of material agency. Plasticity thus comes to describe not a property of materials, but a behavior they enact. Engaging in mutual complicities, materials affectively resonate with each other: by acknowledging this point, we extend the concept of mimetic plasticity beyond the domain of human subjects to witness the ways in which mimetism, as a behavior, can be performed by inorganic materials too.

Notes

1. Within mimetic studies, the first steps to consider mimesis beyond human behavior have been taken via animal mimicry, see the discussion of Roger Caillois and Jane Bennett in chs. 5 and 8 of *Homo Mimeticus*, and via biomimicry, see ch. 14 of *Homo Mimeticus II*. Malabou's focus on AI equally takes mimesis beyond humans. See Malabou 2019 and the Coda to this volume (editors' note).
2. Malabou stretches the concept to include destruction as well as formation (2011a; 2012a; 2012b). However, for Malabou, even destructive plasticity ultimately remains an "adventure of the form" (Malabou 2012a, 17).
3. This aspect is indeed mentioned by Malabou (e.g. 2005, 8; 2008, 5).
4. These shifts in meaning have not gone unnoticed: relevant literature does touch upon the subsequent meanings taken on by the vocabulary of plasticity (e.g. Dongowski 2002, 815; Saint-Girons 1999, 33–34; Chateau 1999, 15–18). These authors record such semantic shifts, but do not fully explore their theoretical potential.
5. This passage from Plato's *Republic* (1963a, 624, 377b) is also quoted by Lawtoo to seal not only the connection between plasticity and Plato, but also the connection between plasticity and mimesis. In Lawtoo's analysis, plasticity and mimesis meet on the topic of the formation of subjectivity, which is explored by bringing into play a peculiar plastic material, Play-Doh, used by "those mimetic subjects par excellence who are children" (Lawtoo 2017, 1208–1211; 2022, 140–141).

6   It is worth noting that, despite adopting an apparently empiricist metaphor, Plato most certainly does not give ground to either materialism or empiricism because of the ontological distinction he makes between the wax tablet and the entities that get impressed on it (Chiurazzi 2017, 42).

7   Some of Malabou's recent endeavors may seem to represent important exceptions: let us think, for instance, of her interest in AI and artificial brains (2019; 2023a), of her engagement with ecology and the Anthropocene debate (2017; Malabou and Majewska 2019), and her political works on feminism and anarchism (2022; 2023b; but see already 2011b for a reflection on femininity and philosophy). However, it seems to me that in exploring these topics Malabou is still guided by an underlying, profound question that functions as a general theoretical lens, and which could be labeled "the question on plastic subjectivity" broadly intended. This is, to my view, the *fil rouge* and philosophical sensibility that orient Malabou's work and make it so significant.

8   Lawtoo has critically analyzed this peculiar aspect of Malabou's theory and has offered a convincing explanation for it (2017, 1206).

9   Already in the introduction to the proceedings of the 1999 Colloquia at Le Fresnoy, Malabou called for "another materialism" (2000, 10), a materialism that should have been able to think anew the relations between matter and spirit.

10 Malabou's work on AI confirms the centrality of life for her materialism, since the difference between the biological and the technological tends to be obliterated in the direction of the development of "plastic machines" (2023a, 90), "electronic subjectivity" (88) and the hypothesis that "the future of AI [will be] biological" (87). Inorganic materials are not at stake in their own nonhuman and "non-intelligent" terms, and their functioning is framed on the model of the living.

11 For a careful and broad philological analysis of the transposition of this Greek vocabulary into Latin, see Auerbach 1939.

12 This is not to say that plasticity and mimesis end up being conflated with one another. In his text, Lawtoo explores the genealogical links between the two concepts in order to deconstruct the binary that divides them, but he also theorizes the plasticity of mimesis to preserve an interplay between the two concepts. The focus on a Janus-faced plastic-mimetic figure captures this connection (plasticity as one of the masks of mimesis) while maintaining the duplicity of the "faces" to preserve their respective differences.

13 Some steps in a similar direction have already been taken, see for instance Varga and Adams 2022.

14 On the differences between "matter" and "material" see Wagner 2001a, as well as Smith 1968.

15 The method of material complicity is also mentioned and applied by Dietmar Rübel (2012, 15), yet another exponent of German *Materialästhetik*, in his book devoted to plasticity as an art historical category. Ranjan Ghosh (2022) also develops a material-aesthetic approach that examines the conjunction of plastics and the arts from a perspective that resonates with mine.

16 In an often-quoted (but not very specific) short essay, Roland Barthes too underlined how plastic can be regarded first and foremost as an imitation material (2014 [1957]).

17 The ecological and political concerns raised by the human use of plastic materials are of the greatest importance, and they have been examined widely in the existing literature (among the many writings that could be mentioned, see for instance Gabrys, Hawkins and Michael 2013; Harvey 2014; Davis 2022; Abrahms-Kavunenko 2023). The politics of plastics being a rapidly growing field of inquiry, it would be necessary to examine phenomena of materi-

al mimetism from this perspective too, critically addressing them in the framework of the pathological materialism of capitalism. However, outlining a political critique of material mimetism goes beyond the scope of this chapter, while representing the most relevant direction for further research on this topic.

18 A few caveats are in order. Celluloid is a semi-synthetic polymer obtained by combining nitric and sulfuric acid with vegetable oils and camphor, which is why it cannot be said to be the first completely synthetic plastic. The very first polymer derived exclusively from fossil fuels was instead Bakelite, which was invented in 1907 and patented in 1909 by Leo Hendrik Baekeland. Moreover, slightly before Hyatt's experiments, Alexander Parkes had already presented his Parkesine (a celluloid with a different name) at the London International Exhibition in 1862.

19 From yet another perspective internal to mimetic studies (the one offered by Henry Dicks in the second volume of this series), it would be possible to frame the invention of Ivory Pyralin as an example of the biomimicry revolution, whose defining trait consists in human systems and productions being organized on the model of nature (Dicks 2024, 308).

20 Moreover, Lawtoo explicitly refers to mimesis as a "chameleon concept" (2022, 14).

21 In Caillois's approach we find the same transdisciplinary spirit that animates Lawtoo's research, and mimetic studies in general, which confirms the soundness of applying his analyses in this context; moreover, connecting plasticity and mimesis by observing their material, nonhuman encounter can be regarded as a diagonal theoretical gesture too, making the argument of this chapter methodologically consistent with mimetic studies at large.

Bibliography

Abrahms-Kavunenko, Saskia (2023). "Toward an Anthropology of Plastics." *Journal of Material Culture* 28.1, 3–23.

Abrahms-Kavunenko, Saskia, and Trine Brox (2022). "Plastic Asia. Material Ambiguities and Cultural Imaginaries." *The Copenhagen Journal of Asian Studies* 40.1, 5–22.

Auerbach, Erich (1939). "Figura." *Archivum Romanicum. Nuova Rivista di Filologia Romanza* 22, 436–489.

Barthes, Roland (2014 [1957]). "Le plastique," in *Mythologies*. Paris: Éditions du Seuil, 159–161.

Beaujot, Ariel (2012). *Victorian Fashion Accessories*. London/New York: Berg.

Bensaude-Vincent, Bernadette (2013). "Plastics, Materials and Dreams of Dematerialization," in *Accumulation. The Material Politics of Plastics*, eds. Jennifer Gabrys, Gay Hawkins and Mike Michael. London/New York: Routledge, 17–29.

Bol, Marjolin, and Emma C. Spary (eds.) (2023). *The Matter of Mimesis. Studies of Mimesis and Materials in Nature, Art and Science*. Leiden/Boston: Brill.

Caillois, Roger (2003a [1935]). "Mimicry and Legendary Psychasthenia," in *The Edge of Surrealism: A Roger Caillois Reader*, ed. Claudine Frank, trans. Claudine Frank and Camille Naish. Durham, NC/London: Duke University Press, 87–103.

Caillois, Roger (2003b [1970]). "A New Plea for Diagonal Science," in *The Edge of Surrealism: A Roger Caillois Reader*, ed. Claudine Frank, trans. Claudine Frank and Camille Naish. Durham, NC/London: Duke University Press, 343–347.

Chateau, Dominique (1999). *Arts plastiques. Archéologie d'une notion*. Nîmes: Chambon.

Chiurazzi, Gaetano (2017). *Dynamis. Ontologia dell'incommensurabile*. Milan: Guerini e Associati.

Conte, Pietro (2014). *In carne e cera. Estetica e fenomenologia dell'iperrealismo*. Macerata: Quodlibet.
Davis, Heather (2022). *Plastic Matter*. Durham, NC/London: Duke University Press.
DeLanda, Manuel (2005). "Uniformity and Variability: An Essay in the Philosophy of Matter." http://www.t0.or.at/delanda/matterdl.htm
DeLanda, Manuel (2016). *Assemblage Theory*. Edinburgh: Edinburgh University Press.
Deleuze, Gilles, and Félix Guattari (1994 [1991]). *What Is Philosophy?*, trans. Hugh Tomlinson and Graham Burchell. New York/Chichester: Columbia University Press.
Dicks, Henry (2024). "The Biomimicry Revolution: Contributions to Mimetic Studies," in *Homo Mimeticus II: Re-Turns to Mimesis*, eds. Nidesh Lawtoo and Marina García Granero. Leuven: Leuven University Press, 305–322.
Didi-Huberman, Georges (2000). "La matière inquiète (Plasticité, viscosité, étrangeté)." *Lignes* 1, 206–223.
Dongowski, Christina (2002). "Plastisch," in *Ästhetische Grundbegriffe. Historisches Wörterbuch in sieben Bänden*, vol. 4, eds. Karlheinz Barck, Martin Fontius, Dieter Schlenstedt, Burkhart Steinwachs and Friedrich Wolfzettel. Stuttgart/Weimar: Metzler, 814–832.
Freinkel, Susan (2011). "A Brief History of Plastic's Conquest of the World." *Scientific American*. https://www.scientificamerican.com/article/a-brief-history-of-plastic-world-conquest/
Gabrys, Jennifer, Gay Hawkins and Mike Michael (eds.) (2013). *Accumulation. The Material Politics of Plastics*. London/New York: Routledge.
Ghosh, Ranjan (2022). *The Plastic Turn*. Ithaca, NY: Cornell University Press.
Harvey, Penny (2014). "The Material Politics of Solid Waste. Decentralization and Integrated Systems," in *Objects and Materials. A Routledge Companion*, eds. Penny Harvey, Eleanor Conlin Casella, Gillian Evans, Hannah Knox, Christine McLean, Elizabeth Silva, Nicholas Thoburn and Kath Woodward. London/New York: Routledge, 61–71.
Lange-Berndt, Petra (ed.) (2015a). *Materiality*. London/Cambridge, MA: Whitechapel Gallery/MIT Press.
Lange-Berndt, Petra (2015b). "Introduction. How to Be Complicit with Materials," in *Materiality*, ed. Petra Lange-Berndt. London/Cambridge, MA: Whitechapel Gallery/MIT Press, 12–23.
Lawtoo, Nidesh (2017). "The Plasticity of Mimesis." *MLN* 132.5, 1201–1224.
Lawtoo, Nidesh (2022). *Homo Mimeticus. A New Theory of Imitation*. Leuven: Leuven University Press.
Malabou, Catherine (2000). "Ouverture: Le vœu de la plasticité," in *Plasticité*, ed. Catherine Malabou. Paris: Léo Scheer, 6–25.
Malabou, Catherine (2005 [1996]). *The Future of Hegel. Plasticity, Temporality and Dialectic*, trans. Lisabeth During. London/New York: Routledge.
Malabou, Catherine (2008 [2004]). *What Should We Do with Our Brain?*, trans. Sebastian Rand. New York: Fordham University Press.
Malabou, Catherine (2009). *La Chambre du milieu: De Hegel aux neurosciences*. Paris: Hermann.
Malabou, Catherine (2010 [2005]). *Plasticity at the Dusk of Writing. Dialectic, Destruction, Deconstruction*, trans. Carolyn Shread. New York: Columbia University Press.
Malabou, Catherine (2011a). "Souffrance cérébrale, souffrance psychique et plasticité." *Études* 4144, 487–498.
Malabou, Catherine (2011b [2009]). *Changing Difference. The Feminine and the Question of Philosophy*, trans. Carolyn Shread. Cambridge: Polity Press.

Malabou, Catherine (2012a [2007]). *The New Wounded. From Neurosis to Brain Damage*, trans. Steven Miller. New York: Fordham University Press.
Malabou, Catherine (2012b [2009]). *Ontology of the Accident. An Essay on Destructive Plasticity*, trans. Carolyn Shread. Cambridge: Polity Press.
Malabou, Catherine (2014). *Avant demain. Épigenèse et rationalité*. Paris: Presses Universitaires de France.
Malabou, Catherine (2017). "The Brain of History, or, the Mentality of the Anthropocene." *The South Atlantic Quarterly* 116.1, 39–53.
Malabou, Catherine (2019). *Morphing Intelligence. From IQ Measurement to Artificial Brains*, trans. Carolyn Shread. New York: Columbia University Press.
Malabou, Catherine (2022 [2020]). *Pleasure Erased. The Clitoris and Thought*, trans. Carolyn Shread. Cambridge/Hoboken, NJ: Polity Press.
Malabou, Catherine (2023a). "Epigenetic Mimesis: Natural Brains and Synaptic Chips," in *Life in the Posthuman Condition. Critical Responses to the Anthropocene*, eds. S. E. Wilmer and Audronė Žukauskaitė. Edinburgh: Edinburgh University Press, 280–288.
Malabou, Catherine (2023b [2023]). *Stop Thief! Anarchism and Philosophy*, trans. Carolyn Shread. Cambridge: Polity Press.
Malabou, Catherine, and Ewa Majewska (2019). "The Plasticity of the World: Philosophy, Neuroscience, and Feminism for the Future," in *Plasticity of the Planet: On Environmental Challenge for Art and Its Institutions*, ed. M. Ziółkowska. Milan: Mousse, 147–166.
Mextorf, Lars (2002). "Kunststoff," in *Lexikon des künstlerischen Materials. Werkstoffe der modernen Kunst von Abfall bis Zinn*, eds. Monika Wagner, Dietmar Rübel and Sebastian Hackenschmidt. Munich: C.H. Beck, 161–165.
Miodownik, Mark (2014). *Stuff Matters. Exploring the Marvelous Materials that Shape our Man-Made World*. Boston/New York: Houghton Mifflin Harcourt.
Plato (1963a). "Republic," in *The Collected Dialogues of Plato Including the Letters*, trans. Paul Shorey, eds. Edith Hamilton and Huntington Cairns. Princeton: Princeton University Press, 575–844.
Plato (1963b). "Theaetetus," in *The Collected Dialogues of Plato Including the Letters*, trans. Paul Shorey, eds. Edith Hamilton and Huntington Cairns. Princeton: Princeton University Press, 845–919.
Rübel, Dietmar (2012). *Plastizität. Eine Kunstgeschichte des Veränderlichen*. Munich: Silke Schreiber Verlag.
Saint-Girons, Baldine (2000). "Plasticité et *Paragone*," in *Plasticité*, ed. Catherine Malabou. Paris: Léo Scheer, 28–57.
Smith, Cyril Stanley (1968). "Matter versus Materials: A Historical View." *Science* 162.3854, 637–644.
Varga, Bretton A., and Erin C. Adams (2022). "Metallurgic Matter(ing)s: Mirrored Mandalorian Metal-Scapes, Mining(s), and Mimesis." *Journal of Posthumanism* 2.2, 167–179.
Wagner, Monika (2001a). "Material," in *Ästhetische Grundbegriffe. Historisches Wörterbuch in sieben Bänden*, vol. 3, eds. Karlheinz Barck, Martin Fontius, Dieter Schlenstedt, Burkhart Steinwachs and Friedrich Wolfzettel. Stuttgart/Weimar: Metzler, 866–870.
Wagner, Monika (2001b). *Das Material der Kunst. Eine andere Geschichte der Moderne*. Munich: C.H. Beck.
Wagner, Monika, Dietmar Rübel and Sebastian Hackenschmidt (eds.) (2002). *Lexikon des künstlerischen Materials. Werkstoffe der modernen Kunst von Abfall bis Zinn*. Munich: C.H. Beck.

CHAPTER 4

NEGATIVE PLASTICITY AND THE INDIFFERENCE OF THE BODY

Kristian Schaeferling

Introduction

This chapter discusses how Catherine Malabou's notion of "destructive" or "negative" plasticity allows for thinking indifference as an ontological category tied closely to the body. Malabou first developed the concept of plasticity in her seminal reading of Hegel in *The Future of Hegel* and has since explored numerous facets of what one might call its "positive" side—an infinite process of giving and receiving, of shaping and reshaping form. But from the outset she has also pointed out that plasticity can equally refer to the force of plastic explosives, which brings about the abrupt annihilation of such a process of continuous modulation and remodulation. Malabou develops this destructive "negative" dimension of plasticity in *The New Wounded* and in *Ontology of the Accident*. It marks a break in the differential, biological-symbolic continuity of plasticity. The effects of this break are drastic and far-reaching. One could speak here of a truly ontological difference—a difference so radical it is impossible for it to be reintegrated into identity. Negative plasticity puts in place a fundamentally indifferent, material, bodily layer outside of difference. It allows for the conception of an ontology where the accidental does not just modulate but entirely reshapes the essential, distorts it even. As Malabou writes, this opens an "unexpected, unpredictable, dark [pathway]" (2012a, 6) where the differential coordinates upon which the symbolic is predicated are irretrievably lost. But we are also told, somewhat enigmatically, that the event giving rise to this fundamental indifference "results as much from the contingency of its occurrence as from the internal work of the drive" (2012b, 212).

In other words, Malabou seems to suggest that we must think the possibility of a disastrous metamorphosis that (1) leaves the individual in a state of disaffected indifference; (2) blocks all paths towards any further change; and (3), perhaps the most shocking of all, shows that this state of things was not only harbored within an absolute but abstract potential, as one possible occurrence among all possible others, but that it was somehow there all along, carrying the subject in a very real way. We thus appear to be dealing with the possibility of a metamorphosis that exits its own paradigm of life, change and plastic suppleness once and for all, only for it to then be revealed that this very paradigm was resting on an undercurrent of rigidity and death all along.

How can we conceive of this strange tension between immanence, contingency, necessity and indifference—a tension that envelops not only bodies but the subject itself in a trancelike state? And of what relevance is a discussion of these matters for the project the editors of the *Homo Mimeticus* trilogy propose to call "mimetic studies"? If the issue of mimesis still warrants continued examination today, even after having vexed philosophical thought for almost two and a half millennia, this is because it remains a problem that is still far from being "resolved" in a simple sense.[1] Perhaps this difficulty is due to a fundamental characteristic of mimesis itself: one might say that the mimetic configuration is objectively indeterminate. Surely this is why Plato, one of the first and harshest critics of mimesis, was so adamantly opposed to it. In mimesis the copy somehow retroacts on the original, so that origins become unclear, thereby confusing the order of representation. In this sense, mimesis should not be understood as referring to a copy of a stable "same," as it traditionally has been.[2] Once the mimetic process is set in motion, there is no telling where it will end up. Certainly, there is no guarantee that the result will comply with the boundaries pure reason would like to establish for it. "Rather," as Lawtoo and Garcia-Granero put it, "mimesis turns out to be constitutive of the birth of a protean, embodied, relational and eminently innovative species caught in an ongoing process of becoming other" (2024, 2).

Mimesis is not only an old problem *for* thought but also an "old" means *of* thought, an early, primitive way in which the subject begins establishing itself before reason has fully developed. Adorno and Horkheimer, for example, described mimesis as a sort of phylogenetic atavism, a residue of magical thinking through which the subject aims to gain control over that which it approximates through the image.[3] However, mimesis would hardly constitute a problem spanning millennia if it were situated only on such a phylogenetic and not also on an ontogenetic level. It seems that mimesis is part of human nature, in the sense that it provides the hole in nature through which nature flees itself, in a process that repeats itself in every individual human being. Mimesis is what we do with the idea of our body before we are truly able to use our body the way we would like to. Here one will perhaps think of Lacan's theory of the mirror stage where the child, in a "jubilant assumption" (2006a, 76), takes on the image of its body reflected to it as a totality for the first time in the looking glass. Henceforth this image of a body—which, as the infant perhaps does not yet know, must die—will lay the phantasmagorical ground for the ideal ego of the subject. Together, the phylogenetic and ontogenetic levels account for a reversal in which the quasi-magical practice of gaining control over objects through mimesis ultimately amounts to remaining caught in what Lacan calls the gaze (*le regard*),[4] a continuous modulation of images that imply the subject in every object.

In this sense one could say that what Adorno and Horkheimer described as a dialectic of enlightenment (through reason) is entwined with a dialectic of control (through mimesis), predicated on the body. The following discussion of indifference and negative plasticity attempts to shed further light on this logic of mimetic processes. These processes provide the rocky ground on which reason stumbles, thus causing a reversal of reason into unreason, or of mastery not just into the powerlessness of slavery, but even into the complete and utter symbolic disconnect of bodily indifference.

The following essay cannot claim to give answers to how we might exit such a dialectic. It merely aims to contribute towards further clarifying some of the logical operations, and hence the stakes, that are at play within this dialectic. As one of the editors writes elsewhere: "Mimesis [...] constantly transgresses disciplinary boundaries, all too easily coming to mean different things to everyone who approaches it through different theoretical lenses" (Lawtoo 2013, 10). The multidisciplinary backgrounds of the contributors and readers of this volume speak to this reality. Nonetheless, "mimetic studies" is based on clearly stated theoretical assumptions: its philosophical genealogy is rooted in the legacy of the critique of idealist thought, as it has been traditionally understood. Following a Nietzschean approach of affirmation, as opposed to negation, Lawtoo has proposed the notion of "patho-logy" to account for a mimetic configuration of sensual, affective, embodied being (*pathos*) that interacts with the word, speech or reason (*logos*) and as such can give rise to disease or sickness (pathology) (Lawtoo 2013, 6; 2022, 21). The "patho-logical" process involves a contagious retroaction of the (sym)pathetic object on the subject of reason—a process said to be both "disabling and [...] enabling" (Lawtoo 2013, 7–8).[5] Yes, on the one hand there is a contagion, a pathological effect of the affects that are being studied on the critical observer who deems himself beyond this sphere of unreason; but, on the other hand, it is only through imbuing knowledge (*savoir*) with such affective experience (*connaissance*) that it can truly become real knowing. According to such an approach, then, the affirmation, not the negation, of affective, sensuous being is what might allow for knowing the real, insofar as real knowing can only be conceived as *logos* satiated with affect.

While fully endorsing the necessity to tie thought to its bodily and affective ground and ramifications, this chapter aims to complement the affirmative foundations of "mimetic studies" with an account rooted in the tradition centered around the driving force of the negative. Thereby it will perhaps help to pose a precise albeit precarious and difficult question in a more comprehensive way: how might we think the logic of pathologies engendered by "patho-logy"? Or, put differently, why is it so important for theories that call for viewing reason as interlaced with affects to remain tied to a critical discourse?

A difficulty for any critique of idealism consists in accounting for the complex and insidious ways in which idealist thought attempts to ensure the primacy of the idea over matter. A particularly striking example of this is provided by the work of Hegel, alongside Plato certainly the arch-idealist philosopher par excellence. Let us simply recall here the speculative coincidence of divergent meanings in Hegel's master-signifier *Aufhebung*. *Aufhebung*, typically translated into English as "sublation," is "picking up to a higher level," "preserving," and "canceling" or "annulling" all in one. Hegel was very happy about such strokes of luck of language. Perhaps one can understand this in the following way: there is a part of being that simply cannot be accounted for in thought. So thought accounts for what it cannot account for by canceling this part out. *But this itself is accounted for in thought.* Thus, engaging with the tradition of the negative based on this structure can help give us further insight into the troubling problematic that the pathologies of subjectivation occur not only when thought is not functioning in a proper mimetic fashion, but precisely *despite* and even *through* thought's mimetic qualities themselves.

Malabou's notion of negative plasticity as well as her characterization of the subjective indifference resulting therefrom seem particularly well suited to unravelling this paradoxical mimetic constellation of *pathos* and *logos,* or of reason and the body. If mimesis is constitutive of an embodied, not pure, form of subjectivation, and if indifference marks the *limit* of the symbolic, i.e. the point from whereon identity dissolves and differences become indifferent, this begs the question of how indifference acts *within* living mimetic form as the internal stumbling block of subjectivation. The following discussion of this question is divided into two parts. The first section of part one tries to logically and conceptually ground what I take to be the role of the category of indifference in a negative-driven account of subjectivation, by considering indifference in Hegel's logic of being. Based on this foundation, the second section then consists in an analysis of how Malabou's rereading of absolute knowing in *The Future of Hegel* allows for establishing the fundamental logical connection between indifferent being and (positive) plasticity. Part two then explicitly, if briefly, examines Malabou's notion of negative plasticity. This notion presents the category of indifference as the real presence of death in life, forming a dead branch in the dialectic, as a pathology that cannot be taken back up into a "patho-logical" form despite having been caused by it.

The chapter aims to reopen the question of how to conceptually deal with this fundamental negativity. It hopes to supplement an affirmative approach to studying mimetic processes with a negative-driven account of mimetic plasticity. It thereby attempts to show how the real of anti-logicist, embodied, relational subjectivity—i.e. a form of subjectivity mediated by the imaginary—can reveal itself precisely in the entire loss of all relations, without therefore being any less embodied.

Indifference in Hegel

To enter our discussion of the category of indifference in relation to Malabou's account of negative plasticity, let us first consider the conceptual groundwork in Hegel, who lays out the logical and ontological matrix within which it becomes possible to think an absolute negativity of plasticity. In order to gain insight into how even the positivity of living, mimetic form rests on a fundamental drive towards the negative, it is crucial to consider how the absolute indifference of being in Hegel is both that which grounds and sustains his entire logical apparatus, as well as that which is radically annulled within the system of absolute spirit. This section will therefore focus on a reading of the first part of *The Science of Logic*, the logic of being. Next, I will examine Malabou's exploration of positive plasticity in absolute knowing, linked to her interpretation of the logic of essence from the second part of the *Logic*.

Indifferent Being

We can begin with the first chapter of the *Phenomenology of Spirit*, the section on sensuous-certainty, where Hegel discusses the universalization of the deictic particle "now" in relation to night and day, both of which it can refer to equally. Indifference is produced here by negation of immediate substantial reality and functions as a central ontological operator.

> This self-maintaining Now [*Dieses sich erhaltende Jetzt*] is thus not an immediate Now but a mediated Now, for it is determined as an enduring and self-maintaining Now as a result of an other not existing, namely, the day or the night. Thereby it is just as simply as what it was before, Now, and in this simplicity, it is indifferent to what is still in play alongside it. As little as night and day are its being, it is just as much night and day. It is not affected at all by this, its otherness. Such a simple is through negation; it is neither this nor that, it is both a *not-this* and is just as indifferent to being this or that, and such a simple is what we call a *universal*. The universal is thus in fact the truth of sensuous-certainty. (Hegel 2018, 62; 1986a, 84f.)[6]

It is worth noting here that already what our senses capture as immediate is registered as a determinate difference. Our senses can register light or darkness. There is a determinate difference between the quality of being dark and being light, between night and day. It seems as if difference were always already there. In this sense, not only will the certainty provided by the senses lose itself in the further progress of consciousness' unfolding and immediate content thereby prove to be semblance, but the immediate as such in Hegel is always already lost. For everything that might seem immediate will prove to have actually resulted from mediation. This is why immediacy in Hegel is not mere sensuality, but sensuous-*certainty*. The progressive process of *Aufhebung* is constantly at work, annulling any leftovers. Simultaneously, empty form must be filled with material content, sensuality must be tied to historical forms of presentation. What this means is that all that we see, all that we experience, is to be understood as knowledge getting to know itself. This is what Hegel is referring to when he speaks of the *Phenomenology* as the "exposition of knowing as it appears" (*Darstellung des erscheinenden Wissens*) (2018, 52; 1986a, 72).

The plastic operation at play here rests on a fundamental negativity. What is non-identical to identity is treated through the self-modulation of identity.

Difference gets introduced in the context of the qualities of sensuous-certainty as the immediate union of sensual matter and universal form that is always already present in order for the subject to be able to come into being. The universal, as such, on the other hand, which can come forth only through the reflection of the immediate unity between itself and its sensual other, and by means of an explicit *negation of immediacy*, is characterized as indifference. Whenever we say "this," we mean something sensuous which we might be able to point at, but what we say is: "this." As Hegel puts it, that amounts to saying "*it is*, i.e. *being as such*" (2018, 62; 1986a, 85). The indifference of the universal to "what is still in play alongside it" has to do with abstracting from immediate sensual qualities. This is to say that the *immediate* affect registered by the senses is annulled, while *immediacy* counts for nothing. Thought, for Hegel, arises through canceling out affect, which is not the same as saying that it is without affect.

We clearly see this logical structure at play at the beginning of the *Science of Logic,* where immediate being, whose only quality is to have no qualities, immediately passes over into nothing. In the *Science of Logic* what follows from the abstraction of quality is quantity. Justifying his decision to begin the *Logic of Being,* unlike Kant, with the category of quality and not with quantity, Hegel states that quantity is "quality which has already become negative; magnitude is the determinateness which, no longer one with being but already distinguished from it, is the sublated quality that has become indifferent" (2010, 56; 1986b, 80). From now on, the being of what is being determined can be changed without affecting what is being determined—that is, being (56; 80). Thought can fully account for all being by canceling out in being what cannot be made to adhere to the order of reason. Whether this canceling out is effected through force to make conform or by leaving-be as irredeemable, the result is the same: from its outset, the subject rests on a negativity that is irreconcilable within the "patho-logical" unity through which this negativity was brought about in the first place.

If the *Phenomenology* is about the recollection of self-consciousness from its dismemberment in the external world into the inner self of absolute knowledge, and in this sense about consciousness recognizing that it already knows (ultimately: that it does not know in advance, but only retroactively), then the *Logic* is about the unknown in the sense of the logical forms that first enable such retroactive knowledge, i.e. the opening of the subject onto nature.[7] This difference is important because it means that for Hegel it is not just the consciousness of individuals with its natural ties to sensuality that is mimetic. Rather, the same goes for the subject itself. The logic of the absolute concept, or the entirety of ontological laws under which being can disclose itself, is fundamentally "mimetic" in as far as these laws are open to plastic impression by the real of nature or spirit, which make up the domains of Hegel's *Realphilosophie*.

By including from the outset a radically asubjective component into the subject, Hegel aims to overcome skepticism. The skeptical position is referred to as the state of "unhappy consciousness" because its knowing remains trapped within the coordinates of the belief that all knowledge is ultimately determined by contingent subjective interest. Against such a claim Hegel therefore shows that any true experience of the absolute must be grounded beyond interest, in disinterested indifference. So, what Hegel points out against the skeptic is that the movement of the logical process must take into account even what appears to be absolutely indifferent so as to not simply give up when the individual's interest might have been satisfied.

Indifference then circumscribes a void, an empty space that surpasses the ego and an empty time that is waiting to be filled. It is clear that in order to achieve such indifference, the mimetic unity of thought is predicated on a fundamental drive towards the negative: negation does not stop with negating objects but can also negate itself. Thereby, negation is supposedly able to return to affirmation, which now becomes conceivable in its truth as what Hegel famously speaks of as the negation of negation: if the first negation is a negation of difference and produces indifference, the negation of negation brings indifference back to difference and it then nonetheless becomes possible to know the absolute. For negation is then directed not by contingent individual interest, but rather, as one might say, by the interest of the system of absolute self-consciousness.

In order to account for this absolute drive towards the negative, Hegel's ontology rests on the immanent inclusion of nothing into logic. In all truth, nothing and indifference are not directly related. But Hegel nonetheless makes this claim. What is indifferent counts for nothing, consistent with the speculative identity of *Aufhebung*'s opposite meanings. Hegel thus states that "whether a beginning is made with the [doing] of nothing or with nothing is [...] indifferent, for the doing of nothing, that is, the mere abstracting, is neither more nor less true than the mere nothing" (2010, 76; trans. modified; 1986b, 105). But this indifference is not as innocent as Hegel claims: it is because there can be no reflection of nothing that this nothing, as that which is entirely *indeterminate*, or *not determined*, must become abstracted into *indeterminateness*. The negation of the negation allows for introducing direction, normativity into being. If even nothing, entire annulment, can be included in the concreteness of ontological determinateness, then it is certain that all possible content can be included.

If being and nothing for Hegel can be regarded as the same, this is due to the fact that both are similarly related to indifference. Being is just as indifferent to abstraction as nothing (cf. 2010, 76; 1986b, 105). As the final step of the *Logic of Being*, we accordingly find a chapter that characterizes being as "absolute indifference."[8] In contrast to "quantity," the aspect of being Hegel has discussed in the sections leading up to absolute indifference, where being is described as "abstract indifference" because it is open to any determination without being internally tied to these differences, absolute indifference is indifference mediated with itself through negation "to form a simple unity" (326; 446). Hegel here aims to set in motion a self-mediating unity which contains no point of rupture, able to take up, preserve and annul, i.e. to sublate, everything that was originally there. It is supposed to be able to include every otherness, hence also everything that would allow for it to become radically other itself, despite resting on an absolute drive towards the negative. By including even a form of nothing, unity will always be possible.

Hegel further explains that any determinateness of qualitative difference in this indifferent unity of being is merely a state, something external which has indifference as its substrate. As such an externality to being, the qualitative difference disappears, sublates itself, insofar as it is only empty, abstract differentiation. "But it is precisely this empty differentiation which is the indifference itself as result" (2010, 326; 1986b, 446). The logical operation here consists in taking up all conditions of thought that have not been self-produced but simply are there. Although abstraction and concretion, indifference and difference are always already mediated and none can claim logical priority over the other, indifference nonetheless precedes difference insofar as it marks the non-produced conditions of thought, which one might call real. These are not necessary preconditions but rather both contingent and necessary insofar as they did not have to be, but it now becomes necessary to account for them so as to complete the mediation of absolute self-consciousness.[9] Indifference is concrete, that is, mediated in itself, as "the negation of all determinations of being" (326; 446). What first presented itself as an external state now instead shows itself as immanent self-differentiation of an indifferent void. Inside and outside disorient themselves—"It is precisely this externality and its vanishing which make the unity of being into an indifference: consequently, externality is inside indifference, which thereby ceases to be only a substrate and, within [*an ihr selbst*], only abstract" (326; 446).

In Hegelian indifference we thus find a sort of non-orientable exchange happening between quality and quantity, grounding speculative logic as a mimetic enterprise.[10] This step of the *Logic* constitutes the passage of being into essence and prepares Hegel's replacement of Spinozian substance with the identity of the subject. Hegel contrasts the external reflection of substance in thought with the self-determining universality of the absolute subject. Through the logical indifference of being and nothing it becomes possible to think the permeation of things in themselves by thought.

Synthesis without an I: Necessity and Contingency in Absolute Knowing

We can now perhaps better understand the relevance of Malabou's critical interpretation of plasticity in Hegel. In *The Future of Hegel*, Malabou pushes Hegel's *Logic* beyond itself and develops what it might mean that, amidst the supposed self-enclosure of the absolute, the innermost essence of substance cannot be thought separately from contingent accidentality. As we have seen, for Hegel, sensuous material and universal determination go hand in hand from the very outset. In the final step to absolute knowing in the *Phenomenology*, Hegel writes that living self-consciousness is the identical unity which makes the difference between a negative externality and itself. Absolute knowing is the moment when this fact of internal scission becomes explicit self-knowledge.

> This letting-go [of independent determinateness] is the same renunciation of the one-sidedness of the concept that in itself constituted the beginning; but it is now its own act of renunciation, just as the concept which it renounces is its own concept. (Hegel 2004, 484; trans. modified; 1986a, 581)

As emphasized in this quotation, for Hegel the letting-go of the one-sidedness of the concept by consciousness in itself is already there at the beginning. The moment in which the absolute now truly comes to itself, comes into (the self as) its own, consists in the fact that the letting-go of this one-sidedness of the concept by consciousness becomes recognized by consciousness as *its* own renunciation. This also means giving *itself* up. Malabou speaks of absolute knowing as surpassing the unity of apperception so as to form "a synthesis without an I," open for future determinations:

> Absolute Knowledge, confirming the identity of substance and subject, introduces a relation between knowing and the known unlike any that has gone before. For this knowledge does not emerge from a new

formation of this subject–object gap; instead it arrives in the suspension of that gap. Hence that gap, emerging when the subject separates itself from all its determinations in order to 'see them coming' *(les voir venir)*, is neither definitive nor fundamental. Consequently, the end of the gap obviously does not mean the closure of all perspective. On the contrary: this end reveals, in the process of becoming-fluid, a more fundamental mode of occurrence *(structure de l'advenir plus originaire)* than the rigid and fixed way in which the subject distanced itself from its own determinations, its own accidents. The 'I think'—the pure certainty of self—is simply one moment, lasting only for a certain period of time in the deployment of subjectivity itself. In the third syllogism, the very sequence followed makes this clear. The originary synthetic unity, or the a priori concordance of opposites, was not always a unity of apperception, nor will it always be so, if by 'apperception' we mean exclusively that absolute identity of a subject, a subject defined as an 'I = I'. From now on, there will be a synthesis but without an I. (2005, 157–158)

Malabou draws attention here to the crucial importance of the entwinement of necessity and contingency in Hegel, the relation of substance and accidents. In absolute knowing, consciousness renounces a difference (grounded on self-identity) which would supposedly enable it to externally reflect a reality opposite to it. Instead, it recognizes this difference as immanent to a more fundamental indifference of identity and difference. Absolute knowing is not an external reflection of a reality faced by a consciousness that is closed off in itself. As absolute, consciousness is self-consciousness. This entails an indifference between inner and outer, in the double sense of a phenomenological state of "feeling" indifferent and of an ontological non-differentiation. In this respect, at the end of the process of the unfolding of stages of absolute consciousness, the renunciation of a separateness between consciousness and a world externally opposed to it is explicitly consummated. Therefore, although one might imagine the identity of indifference and difference as initially arising from an external relation, what we actually find is mimetic entwinement:

> Everything begins in the same moment, where the becoming essential of the accident and the becoming accidental of essence mutually imply one another. There is nothing beforehand [...] The dialectic of the origin is inscribed within the very origin of dialectic as a concept. (Malabou 2005, 164).

There is thus a mechanism at work here which one cannot help but marvel at as extremely strange. This mechanism appears to unfold as a hypertrophy of the subject, which is raised all the way up to an absolute identity with substance, only for the I to disappear from the subject. There is now absolute knowledge, but no longer any knowing or, for that matter, any feeling I. Something beyond lived experience appears to be the real even of functioning "patho-logy," where there is mimetic alignment of reason and affective substantial reality, thereby subjecting the I to absolute negativity. Does this not show the constitutive presence of death underlying even absolute knowing, i.e. the pinnacle of positive plasticity? But what has brought about this pathology? Malabou's reading simultaneously corroborates and undermines Hegel's attempt to seal that absolute knowing does not simply produce an arbitrary knowledge about the world but rather constitutes the inner logic of things themselves from the very outset.

Hegel writes that the immediate object "is an indifferent being" (2018, 455; 1986a, 577). However, the essence of the immediate thing itself is nothing else: "the being of the I is a thing.—namely, [...] a sensuous immediate thing" (455; 577). "The thing is I" (456; 577). This eerie identity of the ego and the thing is the real which cannot be conceived of in the imaginary. For imagination, the relation between the essential being of substance and the accidents can only appear as an external opposition between a "simple identity of being" and "the flux of accidents within it" (Hegel 2010, 491; 1986c, 220). Yet such a representation is merely what Hegel calls a "*formell*" (i.e. bad formal) understanding of the freedom of what is supposedly the pure, self-identical, absolute negativity of the concept. It is possible for spirit to think pure, abstract, self-contained universality, by abstracting from its existence under the "infinite pain" which the "negation of its immediate individuality" brings with it (Hegel 2012, § 382).[11] But whence comes this possibility if not precisely from the understanding that abstracts and that Hegel refers to as "the absolute power" (2004, 18; 1986a, 36)? Hegel describes substance as a kind of circle that is closed off in itself, sustaining its moments. This is the "immediate relationship [...] which has nothing astonishing about it" (18; 36). The power of analytical understanding lies in its ability to dissect this relationship, to chop up and reconfigure the indifferent continuity of the immediate real that precedes its symbolization through thought.

> [T]hat an accident as such, detached from what circumscribes it, what is bound and is actual only in its context with others, should attain an existence of its own and a separate freedom—this is the tremendous power of the negative; it is the energy of thought, of the pure 'I'. (19; 36).[12]

In this quote, Hegel emphasizes as astonishing the causal effectiveness of the accidental taken for itself. It can detach itself from the substantial unity that carries it and retroact on the conditions that sustain it, resulting in the inner contingency of the necessity of original substance. For what is necessity? Simply being that cannot be other than it is. "Necessity is being, *because* being is; it is the unity of being with itself that has itself as *ground*," writes Hegel; "but, conversely, because this being has a ground, it is not being; it is simply and solely *reflective shining, reference* or *mediation*" (2010, 504; 1986c, 239). Being is necessary, causa sui. It is so because it is so, period. There is nothing further beyond this (except for nothing). This is being that is entirely enclosed in itself and indifferent towards external influences. But, *causally grounded* in itself, the necessity of being destabilizes itself. Within necessity there is contingency because the real of the totality of being consists in its split into a plastic self-relation of an I to its conditions—which vastly surpass it. The concept, i.e. that which according to Hegel is the logic of things in themselves, is precisely this "reciprocity of action" (*Wechselwirkung*) of substance and accident. And this self-referential reciprocity is initially grounded in "the relation of causality" which Hegel calls "real" (489; 218). If absolute knowing then is "real knowing" (Hegel 2018, 52; 1986a, 72), this is not because it knows *another object*, i.e. not because it knows *something else* than cognizing understanding does, but rather because it *thinks more*. In the midst of the process of knowing, it thinks how thought works: "A point of sheer randomness dwells within essential being, within the 'original substance'" (Malabou 2005, 162).

Can we now give a first answer to the question raised above about the agent of pathology in the plastic process of "patho-logy"? There is pathology because there is I. But rest assured, the pathological disturbance of substance caused by the I will ultimately be "resolved" by the disappearance of I.[13] Malabou's account of the plasticity of the Hegelian subject enables us to detect the logical structure of this uncanny to-and-fro where the result retroactively configures its ground, up to such an extent that both ground and result are wiped out in an absolute forgetting that haunts absolute knowing as its shadow.

Negative Plasticity and Indifference

Malabou's reinterpretation of indifference as constitutively embodied can now be retraced within the established coordinates. As just discussed, Malabou's reading of Hegel in *The Future of Hegel* argues for thinking absolute knowing as a synthesis without an I. Against this background, the reader will now be able to better appreciate the conceptual implications of Malabou's notion of "destructive" or "negative" plasticity, extensively developed in *Ontology of the Accident* and *The New Wounded*. Negative plasticity is the most drastic form of Malabou's Hegelian, negative-driven account of plasticity. The idea of a "synthesis without an I" enables Malabou to think *Aufhebung* being folded back on itself in absolute knowing, as a renunciation of itself, letting itself go. But this does not put an end to the dialectic as such, as we find beautifully expressed in the following passage:

> But to renounce intervening as a 'knowing I' does not by any means suggest that all subjectivity is to be renounced. The letting-go of the Self in the act of reading does not suspend all power of decision; on the contrary, it produces the condition of the possibility of decision. The speculative proposition checks our confidence in 'knowing how to read', thus training the reader in an illiteracy of the second power which will make the reader write what he or she reads. (Malabou 2005, 182)

I would argue that throughout the entire development of her work, Malabou's fundamental position remains tied to the interest of using the concept of plasticity to rethink the dialectic. Thus, although Malabou develops the notion of negative plasticity primarily in a discussion of affect theory and the neurosciences, I read the category of indifference, which goes hand in hand with her discussion of negative plasticity, through the question of whether the findings regarding this category can be reintroduced back into the dialectic. However, it should be pointed out in advance that the destruction wrought by negative plasticity necessitates an additional turn of the screw regarding the quotation above: if the plastic, speculative proposition implies an illiteracy of the *second* power, making the reader write what they read, one might say that negative plasticity instead unfurls an illiteracy of the *third* power where the reader can no longer read what has been written by their reading. We find here a terrifying reversal of absolute knowing into not knowing anything and no longer being able to know.

As already mentioned, for Malabou this post-Hegelian embodied but absolute indifference is made visible through the neurosciences and, in particular, through the pathologies which the neurosciences address. The realm of neurological accidents points to the theoretical desideratum of a radical negativity: a non-presence of the subject to itself. Here Malabou finds what she claims allows for conceiving of a form of negation no longer tied to any form of positivity or affirmation. Negative plasticity consists not in the potential of giving and receiving form within a continuous process of modifying identity. Rather, it has to be understood as a negative force that ruptures all ties to subjective identity, and yet somehow results in a strange new form of the subject. However, this new form can no longer be symbolically reintegrated. It is absolutely foreign to identity. It is so different that it is entirely indifferent to it.

As a means of clarifying what this destructive plasticity is *not*, Malabou refers us to the myths of Apollo and Daphne, or of Menelaus and Proteus (2012a, 7–9). While both present extreme forms of metamorphosis, they nonetheless do not suffice to explain the envisioned negative plasticity. In the case of Proteus, there is metamorphosis within a frame that, ultimately, is fixed—having passed through a finite number of changes, the demon-god must divulge his secrets. That is to say, these differences can still be domesticated by, quite literally, holding on to a fundamental identity carrying these differences. And Daphne succeeds in fleeing through metamorphosis. Both of these forms of metamorphosis are properly mimetic in that they topologically fuse original and differential image(s) into new forms of identity. By contrast, the change of form effected by destructive plasticity's rupture with difference is precisely due to the traumatic event of *not* being able to produce any further image, of not being able to flee.

Based on this, then, we find two different paradigms of the relation between death and life: one where *death serves the power of life*, such as in apoptosis (Malabou 2012a, 4–5), the process of cellular self-destruction that is a normal part of the development of the functional shape of life forms, human organs; the other in which there is *a form of death in life* that is entirely impossible to subjectivize. And yet Malabou appears to be claiming that it is necessary to begin thinking how it is possible for a body to be dead in life. To do so, we now find a differentiation between two levels: the level of *being affected*, but also the more fundamental level of *being able to be affected*. Destructive plasticity diagonally traverses both levels. It pertains to "an affection of the affects themselves that causes their ruin or their disappearance"—what Malabou, in contrast to subjective auto-affection, calls not just hetero-affection, but "hetero-hetero-affection" (2013, 11). Negative plasticity in Malabou thus seems to delineate a purely material dimension of the body that is severed from soul and spirit and, precisely as such, can influence, or even entirely derail, soul and spirit.

But one is left asking whether this non-relation does not run both ways. Is there nonetheless some strange causality of spirit at work here? Such a line of questioning can base itself on at least three points. Firstly, generally, negative plasticity is still plasticity; it is inherently tied to form. Secondly, it would be worthwhile to carefully consider the examples of negative plasticity Malabou discusses, which I am unfortunately unable to do within the scope of this chapter. Certainly, the most intuitive examples we find for negative plasticity stem from the field of neurological accidents and diseases, but we also read about sudden, life-changing decisions, terrorism, depression, addiction, general societal unhappiness or simply aging, and we are left to wonder about what may connect this seemingly disparate list. Thirdly, Malabou designates the form of accidentality that is able to bring forth the indifference of the subject to its accidents, this loss of auto-affection provoked by negative plasticity, as "material event." She claims that this notion of event is to serve as "the basis for a new philosophy of spirit" and that it "results as much from the contingency of its occurrence as from the internal work of the drive" (2012b, 212).

This "new materialism" (211) of the indifferent body and soul envisioned by Malabou thus in no way lends itself to the questionable spiritualization of matter itself, which we find in some of the adherents of the so-called "new materialisms." Rather, Malabou develops the idea of a "material event" within the context of her polemic against the psychoanalytical—i.e. the Freudian and Lacanian—understanding of causality of the unconscious specific to the psyche. Freud is very clear that his so-called "topography" of the unconscious is not to be confused with a physical localization of the unconscious in the brain. And Lacan's materialism of the signifier strictly follows Freud in this regard. It is this point that Malabou vehemently opposes: For her "the only valid philosophical path today lies in the elaboration of a new materialism that would precisely refuse to envisage the least separation, not only between the brain and thought but also between the brain and the unconscious" (211–212).[14] So, Malabou intends to discard neither spirit nor unconscious. She does however want to tie the symbolic to the brain, as its "elementary form [...] [i.e.] the emotional and logical core where the processes of auto-affection constitute all identity and all history" (212). The material event, Malabou claims, even goes beyond the Lacanian triad of the imaginary, the real and the symbolic (212).

One will of course agree that the destruction of the brain has disastrous implications as far as the individual is concerned. But how are we supposed to understand in this context what it means for the indifference of the subject itself to result "from the internal work of the drive"? Again, we are therefore lead to ask: in what sense does the mimetic interplay between pathos and logos produce subjective pathologies?

If Hegel allows for discussing the mediation of indifference and difference through negation, Malabou's insistence on the material reality of bodily organs points us towards an additional level of affective negativity that cannot be ignored in this process of mediation. Affects confront us with the *real of the imaginary* in a subject predicated on an existing, mortal body. Certainly, indifference as an affective state is not the same as a deliberate choice. If one is in it, one is in it. And yet one must wonder if one could have also chosen not to enter this state, not to stay in this state. There is a strange responsibility towards something that exceeds direct, or at least immediate subjective control.

It is of great importance that Malabou explicitly marks this missing difference within indifference as a moral problem: "Our inquiry revolves around the identification of evil" (2012b, 213). It seems that the phenomenon of indifference opens up the ethical duty of thought as such: the task of thinking the problem of an evil that is not yet adequately understood. The indifferent body, this form of subjective—or rather asubjective— indifference, is depicted as a "form of us without redemption or atonement, without last wishes, this damned form, outside of time" (2012a, 2). Such formulations should not just be read as rhetorical metaphors. Rather, they point to a certain type of spatiotemporal selection, or even a subjective decision. Malabou's account of negative plasticity unflinchingly throws us back on the reality that no matter how hard we may strive to get "beyond good and evil," it appears that the hope of reaching such a beyond by letting the "patho-logical" drive run its course is doomed to fail. One cannot not decide, let be.

What about negation and affirmation then? For Malabou, to think negative plasticity, it is necessary to think "a cut and dry 'no' that is inconvertible to a 'yes'" (2012a, 73). Only thereby, she claims, can it become possible to think "the vertigo of the wholly other origin," which is "excluded and rejected always, one way or another" (86). Malabou's notion of destructive plasticity has the great merit of having firmly tied indifference to the body. *As such*, it becomes active in the dialectic. Also, it is particularly important to have tied the question of indifference of the body to the field of the unconscious. However, precisely as far as the moral, or collective political, dimension of the subjective "evil" of indifference is concerned, it is impossible to do away with an internal split between negation and affirmation. *This state presupposes a "yes" that was rendered indifferent.* Is it not precisely this lost affirmation which makes thinking the "other" so vertiginous? Here we reach the *real as such*. In this respect the psychoanalytic notion of "negation" (*Verneinung*), this affective and intellectual operation Freud describes as standing at the outset of the birth of the concept and in which affirmation and negation coincide, gains great significance.[15] Negation is simultaneously a "no" that persists against all proffered affirmation and a "yes" that persists against all proffered negation. In *Ontology of the Accident*, Malabou dedicates an intensive close reading to Freud's short text on negation, only to ultimately reject what she perceives as psychoanalysis' "messianic" opening towards healing and redemption, since she claims it obstructs comprehension of the fundamental negativity (i.e. the "evil") of indifference.

Nonetheless, if not all ties to the dialectic are to be severed and if we are to make sense of what it means for "the history of being itself [to consist] perhaps of nothing but a series of accidents which, in every era and without hope of return, dangerously disfigure the meaning of essence" (Malabou 2012a, 91), I would claim it is precisely with the question of negation that we must further tarry. For a better understanding of the meaning of indifference I think it will prove particularly fruitful to conduct this renewed examination of negation (which Freud also refers to as "*Verneinungssymbol*") through the lens of the Lacanian real. The affective force of the real, Lacan tells us, has nothing to do with lived experience. It is there but is also produced through its intersection with the symbolic, without imaginary mediation. Thus, we read, it is mediated, but in a way that goes back on itself, by what was excluded when symbolization first took place.[16] So, if it is true that affect has a history, then it was not made by affect itself but by its negation. While, as Lacan also tells us, the inaugural affirmation can no longer recur as such, this does not mean that it does not seep into history through veiled forms; stupid, impure, dead—indifferent one way or another.

Conclusion

In this chapter I have examined the role that the category of indifference plays in the mimetic process of subjectivation. In reading together Hegel and Malabou, I have discussed how this category functions in a way that ties together ontological, logical, phenomenological and embodied levels. The section on Hegel revealed that the logical mediation of the categories of indifference and difference through negation functions as the production of an internal surplus of absolute negativity where the canceling-out of otherness coincides with canceling out the self. Against this background, the absolute affective negativity of bodily indifference, with which Malabou's notion of negative plasticity presents us, further underlines how negation and the body are constitutively bound up with each other in the subject.

Following Malabou, I have argued that negative plasticity means disclosing not just another difference, but rather a difference that is ontologically indifferent to all differences. Certainly, logically speaking this is then identical to the universal. Even if we are more precise, the indifference of the body is nothing less than the shadow of the universal. However, the reality of suffering warns us against foolishly glorifying such findings. Negative plasticity implies an internal connection between indifference, subjective identity and its own exteriority or loss. It can therefore be concluded that in the mimetic process of subjectivation, subjective indifference is situated on the very border between making difference compatible to thought and making difference altogether impossible as such. Thus, the category of indifference would imply a (counter-)activity of what should be pure passivity interacting, or even interfering, with subjectivation: the activity of producing yet another image. This is where pathology creeps into a mimetic process of subjectivation.

Although the analysis has focused on indifference, this is neither intended to suggest that difference should be disregarded, nor that one category could replace the other. Rather, these categories relate to each other as the two sides of one and the same surface of a Möbius strip. The same goes for affirmation and negation, which coincide while being simultaneously different and indifferent from (and to) each other. But if the category of difference is what allows for incorporating the bodily and the affective into thought, the category of indifference forces us to think the opposite as well: it compels us to come up with a form of how to think an influx of thought-as-affect into a plastic unity of body and thought that has run dry. If one can still hope to incorporate mimesis in such a task, it may have to take the strange form of miming itself in a radically different manner: through complete indifference towards itself. The utter indifference of the body that is revealed in negative plasticity, on the other hand, points us to the difficulty of how to read phenomena that seem purely immediate in as far as they were not intended to be mediated but that are nonetheless profoundly historical—and must be negated.

Notes

1. See also the first two volumes of *Homo Mimeticus,* Lawtoo 2022 and Lawtoo and Garcia-Granero 2024.
2. Was mimesis really ever understood in this way? Why would Plato have worried about mimesis at all if we could clearly differentiate between original and copy? Deleuze suggests that Plato himself was the first to point out the direction of a reversal of Platonism (Deleuze 1990, 256). For a recent rereading of aspects of mimesis in Plato that critically engages with a metaphysics of original model and copy, see Part 1 of Lawtoo and Garcia-Granero 2024.
3. See Horkheimer and Adorno 2002, especially in "The Concept of Enlightenment."
4. Lacan 1998.
5. Lawtoo additionally stresses links between the idea of "patho-logy" and Derrida's notion of the *pharmakon* as an instantiation of *différance* in the Platonic text. See Lawtoo 2022, esp. ch. 3.
6. If not noted otherwise, I refer to the translation by Pinkard.
7. For a discussion of the relation between the *Phenomenology of Spirit* and the *Science of Logic* see Heidegger 1993. For a recent account of these difficulties see Comay and Ruda 2018.
8. Hegel here explicitly refers to the difference between the two German words *Gleichgültigkeit* and *Indifferenz*, both of which mean "indifference." Hegel's dislike for *termini technici* and preference for the vernacular is well known. But here Hegel reserves *Indifferenz* for a purely ontological level: "when this trait is to be thought by itself as being [...] in which there is not supposed to be as yet any kind of determinateness" (Hegel 2010, 326; 1986b, 445). *Gleichgültigkeit*, on the other hand, thus perhaps carries a more phenomenological dimension of feeling indifferent. If I have chosen to render both using the English term "indifference," this is because I understand indifference not just as the totality of pure differences that constitute the void, but also as the exchangeability between phenomenological and ontological properties, characteristic of its own self-difference.
9. Karen Ng has focused on the constitutive role of life for the Hegelian concept (Ng 2020). This allows for grounding relations of difference as the production of thought, which enter into the life of spirit. By contrast, the category of indifference is where death, or the death drive, are incorporated into Hegelian logic.
10. Cinzia Ferrini, comparing the 1812 and the 1832 versions of the *Logic of Being*, has shown how subtle modifications in Hegel's exposition of the relation between quantity and quality in measure speak to how Hegel's thought successively moved further away from any type of formalism or external dualism and towards a self-mediation of being with itself (Ferrini 2020). In the ultimate version of the *Logic of Being*, being sublates its own externality. In 1812/13, Hegel speaks of quality being nothing apart from its determination through quantity, i.e. quantity passes into *its other*, quality (cf. Hegel 1978, 186f.), whereas in 1832 it is quality itself that reemerges insofar as it has shown itself as passing over into *its truth*, quantity (cf. 2010, 279; 1986b, 383f.).
11. Note that pure abstraction and infinitely strong feeling coincide, recalling the form of infinite judgment, which, as Kant states, points to the limitations of a predicate, calling for the placement of an object into the sphere of a concept that lies outside of the sphere of another concept. It is neither this nor that, something else. Infinite pain, because all sources of pain—one after the other? Or all of them abruptly at the same time, outside of time?—are torn off, subtracted, abstracted.

12 I rely here on Miller, as Pinkard's translation of this passage seems to me to entirely misconstrue the meaning in Hegel.
13 Lacan's analytical distinction between *moi* and *je* may be helpful to further understand this paradox. In a sense, the I is swallowed here by the ego. One has to marvel at how this 'patho-logical' mechanism—a mechanism where sickness and cure through elimination of the cause of sickness *fully coincide* and which precisely therefore must *repeat*—can be sustained not only for more than a mere logical moment, but can even unfold proper historical actuality without immediately unleashing destructive consequences of apocalyptic proportions.
14 See also Malabou's contribution to this volume titled "Conflicting Subliminalities." Lawtoo, drawing on Pierre Janet and Nietzsche, has proposed to discuss physiological dimensions of the unconscious within the framework of a pre-Freudian theory of a "mimetic unconscious" (Lawtoo 2013; 2022).
15 Freud 1955.
16 Lacan 2006b, 320.

Bibliography

Comay, Rebecca, and Frank Ruda (2018). *The Dash—The Other Side of Absolute Knowing*. Cambridge, MA: The MIT Press.

Deleuze, Gilles (1990). *Logic of Sense*, trans. Mark Lester. London: The Athlone Press.

Ferrini, Cinzia (2020). "Hegel's Revisions of the Logic of Being." *Rivista di storia della filosofia* 2, 199–221.

Freud, Sigmund (1955). "Die Verneinung," in *Gesammelte Werke XIV: Werke aus den Jahren 1925–1931*. London: Imago Publishing, 11–15.

Hegel, G. W. F. (1978). *Gesammelte Werke 11: Wissenschaft der Logik. Zweites Buch. Die Lehre vom Wesen*. Hamburg: Meiner.

Hegel, G. W. F. (1986a). *Werke 3: Phänomenologie des Geistes*. Frankfurt am Main: Suhrkamp.

Hegel, G. W. F. (1986b). *Werke 5: Wissenschaft der Logik I*. Frankfurt am Main: Suhrkamp.

Hegel, G. W. F. (1986c). *Werke 6: Wissenschaft der Logik II*. Frankfurt am Main: Suhrkamp.

Hegel, G. W. F. (1986d). *Werke 10: Enzyklopädie der philosophischen Wissenschaften im Grundrisse 1830. Dritter Teil. Die Philosophie des Geistes. Mit den mündlichen Zusätzen*. Frankfurt am Main: Suhrkamp.

Hegel, G. W. F. (2004). *Hegel's Phenomenology of Spirit*, trans. A. V. Miller. Oxford/New York: Oxford University Press.

Hegel, G. W. F. (2010). *The Science of Logic*, trans. George di Giovanni. Cambridge/New York: Cambridge University Press.

Hegel, G. W. F. (2012). *Philosophy of Mind. Translated From The Encyclopaedia of the Philosophical Sciences*, trans. W. Wallace and A. V. Miller, The Project Gutenberg E-Book of Hegel's Philosophy of Mind. Oxford.

Hegel, G. W. F. (2018). *The Phenomenology of Spirit*, trans. Terry Pinkard. Cambridge/New York: Cambridge University Press.

Heidegger, Martin (1993). "Erläuterung der Einleitung zu Hegels *Phänomenologie des Geistes*," in *Hegel*, GA 68. Frankfurt am Main: Vittorio Klostermann, 63–150.

Horkheimer, Max, and Theodor W. Adorno (2002). *Dialectic of Enlightenment. Philosophical Fragments*, trans. Edmund Jephcott. Stanford: Stanford University Press.

Lacan, Jacques (1998). *The Seminar of Jacques Lacan. Book XI. The Four Fundamental Concepts of Psychoanalysis*, trans. Alan Sheridan. New York: W. W. Norton & Company.

Lacan, Jacques (2006a). "The Mirror Stage as Formative of the *I* Function as Revealed in Psychoanalytic Experience," in *Écrits*, trans. Bruce Fink. New York: W. W. Norton & Company, 75–81.

Lacan, Jacques (2006b). "Response to Jean Hyppolite's Commentary on Freud's 'Verneinung,'" in *Écrits*, trans. Bruce Fink. New York: W. W. Norton & Company, 318–333.

Lawtoo, Nidesh (2013). *The Phantom of the Ego. Modernism and the Mimetic Unconscious*. East Lansing: Michigan State University Press.

Lawtoo, Nidesh (2022). *Homo Mimeticus. A New Theory of Imitation*. Leuven: Leuven University Press.

Lawtoo, Nidesh, and Marina Garcia-Granero (eds.) (2024). *Homo Mimeticus II: Re-Turns to Mimesis*. Leuven: Leuven University Press.

Malabou, Catherine (2005). *The Future of Hegel. Plasticity, Temporality and Dialectic*, trans. Lisbeth During. New York/London: Routledge.

Malabou, Catherine (2012a). *Ontology of The Accident*, trans. Carolyn Shread. Cambridge/Malden, MA: Polity.

Malabou, Catherine (2012b). *The New Wounded*, trans. Steven Miller. New York: Fordham University Press.

Malabou, Catherine (2013). *Self and Emotional Life: Philosophy, Psychoanalysis, and Neuroscience*, with Adrian Johnston. New York: Columbia University Press.

Ng, Karen (2020). *Hegel's Concept of Life. Self-Consciousness, Freedom, Logic*. Oxford: Oxford University Press.

PART II

PLASTIC ENCOUNTERS AND MIMETIC STUDIES

CHAPTER 5

BENJAMIN'S GREAT CRIMINAL, A PLASTIC MIME

Gabriel Wartinger

> The wisest thing—so the fairy tale taught mankind in olden times, and teaches children to this day—is to meet the forces of the mythical world with cunning and with high spirits [*mit List und mit Übermut*].
>
> —Walter Benjamin, "The Storyteller."

Introduction

Upon the establishment of new legislation, the law subtly reveals its fragmentation—by redistributing the violence at its disposal, legal continuity is to be ensured. To further the reach of the law, its subjects must remain deprived of their violent potential.[1] Yet, within such legal expansion, there are moments when the fragility of the law's violent monopoly becomes discernible. Among these instances, Walter Benjamin's great criminal stands out as a poignant example. Before turning toward this lesser-known figure of the Benjaminian text(s), it is important to recall Benjamin's seminal role in foreshadowing contemporary mimetic studies by way of what he terms the mimetic faculty (Lawtoo 2022b, 34). By foregrounding Walter Benjamin's reflections on law and violence, this chapter suggests an alternative to Girard's sacrificial model of mimetic violence, further positioning Benjamin—alongside Nietzsche and Bataille—as a foundational voice in the development of post-Girardian mimetic theory.

To do so, this chapter draws on Benjamin's 1921 *Kritik der Gewalt* (*Critique of Violence*), to probe the figure of the great criminal—an actor whose defiance, as Benjamin posits, elicits the admiration of the masses and thereby succinctly exposes the law's monopoly on violence. Aside from granting this *mimetic* significance, Benjamin's *Critique* subtly questions the efficacy of the great criminal's deed. Criminal transgression, at least upon first notice, paradoxically underscores the law's resilience or, rather, its *constitutive elasticity*. This elasticity is understood, following Catherine Malabou, as the capacity to undergo deformation and yet to inevitably return to an original form (2012a, 36). Transposed to Benjamin's essay, elasticity gains particular significance: despite an apparent susceptibility to morphological adaptation, the law's fundamental structure, grasped as a monopolistic concentration of violence, remains unperturbed.

Contrary to Benjamin's suggestion of interpreting the criminal as a mimetic apologist of the law, I focus on the *plasticity* of "great" criminal transgression. Contrasting the partial malleability of elastic matter, plastic form has the potential to retain (and metamorphose) its modified shape. *Plasticity*, involving both the creation of form (*Formbildung*) and the processivity of such creation (*Formtätigkeit*), contrasts with elastic stupor, which inevitably implies the return to an initial and initiating outline.[2] Hereby, Benjamin offers a crucial conceptual link between modernist critiques of law and the contemporary concern with mimesis as a malleable, affectively charged force. By introducing the notion of *plastic criminal transgression*, this chapter contributes to the volume's broader aim of tracing mimesis not as a fixed structure, but as a process of continuous metamorphosis—legal, aesthetic and affective. Against the *elasticity* of a legal and violent monopoly, the law's *plasticity*, exposed by the great criminal, thus gestures toward a disavowed dimension of the law: its fundamental and, perhaps, non-centralizing transformability.[3]

As already indicated, Benjamin's criminal, in reaching for the violence which has been monopolized, *mimes* judicial practice.[4] In his essay, the critical potential of such legal hubris is limited; it remains ensnared within the purview of what Benjamin interchangeably describes as mythical or positive law. This law, violently performing through retribution, marks the vanity of transgression. In analogy to the petrification of Niobe, the culprit's defiance remains a beacon of the law's monopoly. While Benjamin's delinquent shifts the boundaries of legal means, they are not integrally corrupted[5]—the transgression can but ensure the expansion of legal ends, corroborating the law's violence. Prometheus serves as another example for this limitation; the stolen flame solely heralds the emergence of new legal principles. The "great" criminal act is constrained: it can but challenge and thereby seize juridical violence from a preceding legal framework.

Beyond Benjamin's cautious stance, his great criminal implies more than an ambition to establish new legal norms. *Criminal mimesis,* supplemented by *plasticity,* reaches beyond the reappropriation of legal mechanisms. In disrupting the hierarchy between model and copy, the "great" criminal exposes what may be termed the law's mimetic modality—that is, the specific way that legal structures rely on forms of repetition, imitation and substitution to maintain their authority (Lawtoo 2022b, 103). This modality not only constitutes positive law's relation between means and ends—a relation where solely "legal" means can justify an end—but it simultaneously marks the vacuity or fragmentation at play in this relation. In this sense, *criminal mimesis* does not merely replicate the law's violent means; instead, it exposes the distinction between "mere" imitation and the enactment of a creative, violent force which acknowledges that the creation and the destruction of law are related to the same function. While the law is *elastic,* the criminal gestures toward its *plasticity.* In challenging a notion of *elastic* law that is never at risk of thorough transformation, the great *criminal mime* lays bare the common yet differentiating site of creation and repetition. This summons the possibility of another (or no other) law.

In short, this chapter's argument can be summarized thus: Benjamin's great criminal is a *plastic mime.* Positive law operates *elastically,* which implies that any modification of the law ultimately returns to its originating frame. Against such morphological return, which equates to a monopolization of violence, *criminal mimesis* sets itself apart. The law can never sever itself from its originating frame; otherwise it would solidify the fragmentation of violence, and thereby imperil its own monopoly.[6] Hence, unlike *elastic* mimesis, the potential of *plastic* mimesis, demonstrated by Benjamin's criminal—henceforth called *criminal mimesis*—exposes the law's dynamic. It illustrates that creative and reproductive acts, despite pertaining to the same site, are radically different. In the context of the law, creative acts potentially gesture beyond the law's monopoly on violence, while reproductive actions reinforce the legal framework, ensuring its perpetuation. The great criminal highlights the minimal distance between these mimetic modalities.

Benjamin has largely informed a deconstructive philosophical genealogy.[7] Likewise, mimetic studies iterates Benjamin's notion of a mimetic faculty, one that does not merely imitate "nature" but becomes historically constitutive of it (2011b, 445). This chapter will further the understanding of the *plasticity of mimesis,* interpreted through Benjamin's great criminal.

The *Critique of Violence*

Typically, the introduction of new law serves to reaffirm the concentration or centralization of power, which inherently involves the exercise of violence.[8] This consolidation, whether achieved through the expansion or mere enforcement of the law, centralizes violence by denying individual capacities for violent action.[9] To assure their functioning, legal systems constitutively rely on an uneven distribution of violent means. In the *Critique of Violence* Benjamin identifies a legal maxim where the potential for individual violence must be restrained through legal measures, stating: "From this maxim it follows that law sees violence in the hands of individuals as a danger undermining the legal system" (1978, 280). He theorizes the centralizing violence of legal economies and drafts a *Critique* to inform the analysis of both the law and its inherent violence. In developing his essay, he elliptically establishes three principal distinctions: first, the differentiation between natural and positive law; second, the divide between law-making and law-preserving power (or violence); and third, the difference between so-called divine violence and its mythical counterpart.

Both natural and positive law make a distinction between means and ends. Within the purview of the former, any means are acceptable if the end that follows from them can be deemed just. In other words, natural law, unlike its positive counterpart, ignores a more nuanced justification of means, as long as the end is considered justifiable. A prime example is private property, where the assumed legitimacy of a land-ownership title justifies the use of violence against those who challenge this claim. Whether this legitimacy is rooted in natural or theological principles, natural law lacks the analytical criteria for assessing the violent methods used to enforce these claims. Consequently, the use of violence to defend (or apprehend) what is considered "justifiable" remains unchecked. As Benjamin puts it:

> This thesis of natural law that regards violence as a natural datum is diametrically opposed to that of positive law, which sees violence as a product of history. If natural law can judge all existing law only in criticizing its ends, so positive law can judge all evolving law only in criticizing its means. (1978, 278)

Diametrically opposed to natural law, positive law assumes that if the means are just, then the ends they achieve should inherently be just as well. In search of a historical index, Benjamin situates his *Critique* within the realm of positive law.[10] Only positive law, he claims, can distinguish between different forms of violence, different violent forms.

The *Critique* thus provides a crucial appeal for the discourse on violence, asserting that any such critique must focus on positive law's distinct historicity. Unlike natural law, which regards violence as a "natural given," positive law sees it as an outcome of historical becoming (180). A critique of violence must therefore interrogate the historically concrete justifications for particular means in the pursuit of a just end.

This brings me to the second distinction in Benjamin's essay: lawmaking and law-preserving violence (*rechtssetzende/rechtserhaltende Gewalt*) (186). Typically—note the precarity of the "typical" in an analysis of violence—judicial systems attempt to separate the functions of law preservation and law creation. Yet, paradoxically, the fluidity of these boundaries renders these forms of violence particularly apparent. The police are a prime example of an agent that conflates these forms. As Benjamin writes: "in a kind of spectral mixture [*gespenstische Vermischung*], these two forms of violence are present in another institution of the modern state, the police" (1978, 286). According to Benjamin, police violence operates within the defined means of the law (right of disposition), yet it also possesses the power to reshape these limits via its right to decree (*Verordnungsrecht*) (1991, 189). Between the preservation and the creation of law, "law enforcement" thus occupies a liminal space. In instances where the judicial text lends no sufficient precedent,[11] or when the criminal idiosyncrasy of the police necessitates it, new law is created on the spot. In other words, if the law fails to provide a suitable response—a suitability that pertains solely to safeguarding the law's monopoly on violence—then new measures may be readily adopted. Hence, the police reveal that while alterations are feasible, they ultimately reinforce the law's uniformity. Modifications are absorbed back into the foundational framework: any change returns to its initiating outline.

The position of the police is ostensibly evident—it enforces the integrity of a violent monopoly through a shift in boundaries. As Benjamin puts it: "in this authority, the separation of lawmaking and law-preserving violence is suspended [*aufgehoben*]" (1978, 286). In policing the limits between the making and the preservation of the law, the police illustrate the fragility of these limits. This fragility, as previously signaled, is *elastic*, movable, yet partisan to its initiating frame. In this case, *Formtätigkeit*, the formational activity of the judicial apparatus remains constitutively indebted to its outset. It cannot permit a plastic proliferation of form without jeopardizing dominion over violence.

Third, and lastly, Benjamin borrows George Sorel's notion of the revolutionary general strike, aligning it with the notion of divine violence.[12] This violence derives its sanctity from the capacity to annihilate the violent traces of the state. Benjamin invokes the example of the rebellion of Korah, where those who defied Moses' guidance were consumed by a chasm that swallowed them, leaving no traces of their existence (199). Unlike mythical violence, for Benjamin, divine violence annihilates limits and traces. He writes: "If mythical violence is lawmaking, divine violence is law-destroying; if the former sets boundaries, the latter boundlessly destroys them; if mythical violence brings at once guilt and retribution, divine power only expiates" (1978, 297).

By contrasting this form of celestial obliteration with the mundane perpetuation of state power, Benjamin formulates his differentiation between divine and mythical violence. This distinction, he suggests, is mirrored in the contrast between the revolutionary potential of divine violence and the cyclical reinforcement of power found in mythological narratives:[13] "Niobe's arrogance [*Hochmut*] calls down fate upon itself not because her arrogance offends against the law but because it challenges fate" (1978, 294). The myth of Niobe illustrates Benjamin's interpretation of mythical violence and its relation to state violence. Niobe's hubris, manifested in her challenge to the divine order, culminates in the loss of her children. She, in turn, is transformed into stone. This petrification damns her to eternally grieve the loss of her children and serves as a trace for anyone seeking to mimic her deed. Both punitive and exemplary, mythical violence solidifies the authority of the state (and/or the divine) by marking the consequences of rebellion with indelible traces. According to the *Critique*, it is this hubristic dimension that prompts our admiration when we are confronted with the transgressive deed of the great criminal (*großer Missetäter*).

Benjamin's understanding of the (great) criminal's deed suggests that it does not fundamentally undermine the (mythical) law; instead, it describes how even the greatest transgression remains ensnared within a legal topology. He does not bestow these criminal practices with the potential to veritably challenge or complicate the state's violent monopoly. In his view, such transgressions are mythical specters that merely bespeak shifts in the dominion over state violence. Or even worse, these practices partake in the law's violence: "Lawmaking is power making, and, to that extent, an immediate manifestation of violence" (1978, 295). Benjamin suggests that criminality or delinquency, far from escaping the orbit of legal violence, participates in its very foundation. By foregrounding this complicity, he exposes the mimetic entanglement between law and transgression—a dynamic that corresponds with the figure of homo mimeticus as both an imitator and potential disruptor of dominant forms. Yet Benjamin's own framing tends to limit the great criminal's act to a tragic reiteration of violence. In contrast, this chapter questions whether *criminal mimesis* might gesture toward a plastic, transformative potential that is not wholly subsumed by the law's mythical repetition.

The vanity of mythic transgressions, their failure to move illegally beyond legality, finds another parallel in the Promethean myth, echoing Benjamin's interpretation of Niobe's defiance. He understands the Promethean endeavor to seize Zeus's fire not simply as an act of rebellion but as the deliberate effort to institute a new law, thereby replacing one rule of fate with another. As a result, such rebellious theft is but another example in the litany of failed attempts to contain, corrupt or reformulate violent authority.[14] None of these efforts seem to articulate themselves from a sufficient distance; they cannot but bespeak another, albeit different, law. Their absence of critical detachment prompts Benjamin to interpret criminal hubris as an alternative form of legalism. Nevertheless, he speaks of "secret admiration":

> Violence, when not in the hands of the law, threatens it not by the ends that it may pursue but by its mere existence outside the law. The same may be more drastically suggested if one reflects how often the figure of the "great" criminal, however repellent his [*sic*] ends may have been, has aroused the secret admiration of the public. This cannot result from his deed, but only from the violence to which it bears witness. (1978, 281)

Our (secret) admiration for the criminal is not a result of the mobilized means; it is not the crime itself which most succinctly summons our attention, but the exposure of the legal system's violence. Criminality, unlike the insipid sobriety of the law, is seemingly more honest in its exposure of the intimate bond between law and violence. Hence, in defying the law, as Derrida records in his discussion of Benjamin's *Critique*, the great criminal exposes the violent coordinates of the judicial order itself, accepting the stigma of a prophet or an originary lawmaker.[15] Benjamin puts it as follows:

> In the great criminal this violence confronts the law with the threat of declaring a new law, a threat that even today, despite its impotence [*Ohnmacht*], in important instances horrifies the public as it did in primeval times. The state, however, fears this violence simply for its lawmaking character. (1978, 283)

This figure, which I interpret as a conceptual modality, nevertheless occupies a marginal position in the essay. First and foremost, it proves that any kind of transgression, operating within the purview of positive or mythical law—that is, within its peculiar logic of means and ends—fails to destabilize the law's monopoly on violence. Against this reservation, I propose a notion of *criminal mimesis*.

Now, I move toward the conceptual importance of this occluded motive. This should assist in a conceptualization of the creative potential inherent in criminal mimesis. Furthermore, this development implies a comprehensive exposition of my understanding of *plastic mimesis*, contrasting the constitutive *elasticity* of the law. Such recalibration involves reading Benjamin's great criminal not solely as a profane mime, copying or reproducing the law's violence, but as an agent, or a performance that catalyzes a differentiated notion of mimesis. This differentiation complicates an understanding of mimesis as a mere rehearsal and submits, in its place, a notion of plastic iterability. This operates through the constitutive connection between imitation as both repetition and creation.[16]

From Elastic to Plastic Law

My understanding of the law's elastic mimesis results from the simple observation that judicial pronouncements often retroactively frame transgressions, casting post-factum verdicts onto actions that predate the legal interpretation.[17] In other words, the law's response to transgressions is not merely reactive but mimetic, violently mirroring the very acts it seeks to regulate. Consequently, akin to the great criminal, the law engages in a form of mimesis. This involves confronting the violence of a transgression with equivalent legal violence. The mimesis of legal violence seeks to neutralize or assimilate the disruptive force of transgression without endangering its hegemony. The law's mimesis thus emerges as inherently elastic, perpetually stretching to accommodate new challenges yet always snapping back.[18]

The suspensive dimension, revealed through the criminal performance, alludes to a larger instability within the law. Thus, it is not necessary to detach Benjamin's concept of the criminal from its mythological underpinnings to ascribe to it the transformative potential reserved for divine violence.[19] The criminal, already within the mythological criteria of positive law, complicates the law's mimesis.

The suspension, mobilized by the great criminal's transgression, exposes the law's paradox of demanding compliance while resisting foundational change.[20] Although the great criminal transgression might not paradigmatically exemplify modulation—Niobe or Prometheus, as Benjamin proposes, can be read as mere successors or heirs of the mythical rule—it nevertheless mimetically exposes the law's foundational vacuity. Strictly speaking, the law's sole content is the preservation of its monopolistic status. This invites a reassessment of Benjamin's swift dismissal of the great criminal's significance.

To do so, let me situate *criminal mimesis within* the *elastic frame* of the law. Elasticity, akin to flexibility, implies the inevitable return to an initial form. The elastic matter or the elastic concept thus ignores or consumes the deformation that has taken place. Elasticity is marked by a return without a definite formative change (Malabou 2012a, 36). The law, despite its alterations, returns to its violent monopoly. Here, elasticity corresponds to the merely repetitive polarity of imitation or mimesis versus its creative polarity. Malabou affirms that "these two mimetic trends, reproductive and creative, operate in the same site, i.e. the subliminal, the subliminal being both the site of influence and suggestion as well as the site of creation […] they are almost the same, but they remain radically different."[21]

Within Benjamin's analysis of mythical violence, it is noticeable how the transgression—no matter how significant its challenge to the rule of fate—remains ensnared within its own logic. Neither Niobe nor Prometheus, despite their substantial violations, transcend the profane or mythical violence associated with the law. Nevertheless, Benjamin emphasizes a particular inspirational, or awe-inspiring, tendency deriving from their deeds. The dialectic of the mythical rule, its interplay between law preservation and law creation, is complicated by the figures who occupy the margin between preservation and creation. The criminal is one of these figures. However, Benjamin rejects the idea of the criminal having the potential to transcend the law, as revisited in the context of the pure, non-violent means of divine violence. For Benjamin, the criminal is, at best, a reminder of the elastic rigidity of the law and, at worst, a reactionary figure mobilizing a law that has yet to be established. However, in both of these scenarios, Benjamin's criminal exposes the rigidity of the law, which ultimately remains elastically tethered to its initiating form.

While the law might quickly adapt, expand its dictum, or rather its legislature, it nevertheless remains ensnared within its monopoly. Any of its reformulations, or re-formations, are marked by a return.[22] Nevertheless, the law cannot be a wholly elastic medium. If that were the case, it would retain none of its changes. Certainly, regarding the monopolization of violence, such thorough elasticity is given—no change (i.e. no differing violence) is allowed to modify such a monopoly. However, constant alteration simultaneously shapes the legal system. While these alterations do solely reform the mythological apparatus (for Benjamin, they would otherwise be divine), they nevertheless mark and demarcate, inflate and deflate the boundaries of their applicability.

The body of the law can be understood as a rigid corpus, which is nevertheless marked by the movement of the trace (it is iterability that leaves the mark of difference). Malabou's notion of plasticity thus allows one to conceptualize the specific resistance or inertia encountered in differentiating forms. Her interpretation helps one understand that rigidity and resistance are the conditions of possibility for the ambivalent iteration of identity and difference, i.e. the condition of possibility for an inscribable medium.[23]

Now, with regard to these varying economies of differentiation, the police serve as an example. If the police abuse their violence (an abuse which is both common and deliberately equivocal), the elasticity of the law is quick to return to its initiating form: the rule of law. Hence, the relevant act is either relegated as criminal or inscribed within a yet-to-be-established law. Any monopoly of violence, if it seeks to retain its dominance, has to be *elastic*.

Transgression

The concept of mimesis, prior to the mimetic turn, implies a form of replication. Within such a notion of replication, Walter Benjamin introduces a transgressive dimension through the figure of the great criminal. This figure does not merely reproduce the law's dictates but uses the law's inherent violence to reveal its foundational contradictions, thereby preventing the law from seamlessly returning to its original state.

I have noted that the depths of crime remain occluded, outside the purview of Benjamin's *Critique* (it suffices to know that a deed hubristically challenges the law's monopoly). As developed above, the great criminal is but formally indicative of the law's mechanisms. These mechanisms are elastic.

How does the plasticity of criminal mimesis differ from the understanding of mimesis as the mere reproduction of a model? In this plastic scenario, the great criminal forms the law without reform, thereby confronting the paradox of the mythological impasse (this impasse concerns the dilemma of attempting to surpass the inherent violence of the state without stepping outside its legal framework). Evidently, such a move beyond the law's established syntax seems difficult. Nevertheless, Benjamin's criminal is more than an envoy of another law. The great criminal is a mime who mobilizes the law's violence against the law itself.

Through this mimetic moment, the law does not necessarily lose its elastic dimension; rather, for once, a return to its initiating frame seems to be stalled. Think of elastic matter that is forcibly prevented from settling into its initial state. In its elastic suspension, the law is *supplemented* by a plastic dimension, which was heretofore suppressed. The function of Benjamin's great criminal lies not only in the exposure of an elasticity that will eventually yield (to its dissolution, its supplementation, etc.), but it also leaves a mark that suggests possibilities beyond the confines of the law.

A plastic, unlike an elastic, transformation does not allow for the return to an initial form (Malabou 2012b, 177). Plasticity, destructive or not, describes *Formtätigkeit* that entails a more definite change. The plastic concept retains its form. Thus, the plastic alteration of the law implies a thorough modification of the legal coordinates, a practice which Benjamin solely reserves for divine violence (the pure means of a revolution or a divine act). Above, I proposed a way to read the presumed elasticity of the criminal as a plastic modality. The power of the great criminal's transgression is cultivated in a reconciliation of imitation, which manifests the difference between an elastic and a plastic transgression.

The distinction between the mimetic faculties mobilized by the criminal and the law itself is fragile. However, it might be precisely this difficulty that is decisive. I insist once more on the juxtaposition between the elastic law and the plastic criminal. This contrast exposes the absence of the law within the law. Unfortunately, I have to concede that Benjamin would no longer be interested in my perusal of the mythological register. For him, the criminal is a Promethean wretch who cannot but declare another law, and thereby another form of violence. As I decided to set aside, Benjamin privileges the theorization of a specific form of violence. This violence, located in the revolutionary rendition of a strike, annihilates the legislative apparatus without the appetite for another form of law. Said revolutionary means derive their "purity" from a complication of the relation between means and end.

The criminal, considered as a plastic force, exposes the suspension inherent to the law. This tendency, ignored by Benjamin, is already nascent in his *Critique*. It implies a complication of his harsh division between mythological and divine violence. In other words, the divinity of purificatory violence seeps into the mythology of the state and vice versa. Despite such mutual contamination, there is one decisive difference.

The violence of the law lies in its elastic rigor: nothing other than the law's violence can be tolerated. At times, the law might adapt, might prompt one to think of a more complex distribution of violent means. But no matter how complex the distribution of these means, they are ultimately tethered to an elastic frame. Benjamin reads the criminal as an agent who potentially makes new law. Any such practice, following Benjamin, remains ensnared in the rule of fate and thus cannot transcend a violent economy (1991, 186). Nevertheless, such an amendment must not merely be read as a reformist (elastic) attempt or, even more profane, as a demand for the redistribution of power. Rather, the plastic transgression mobilizes a decisive vacuity. Benjamin signals such vacuity but prefers to relegate the criminal to the mythical domain. My reading implicitly accepted this relegation but insisted on a divisive fracture. At times, the criminal might be but another contender who seeks to operate via the rule of law. But at other times, and this is what lies nascent in Benjamin's great criminal, a gesture toward the vacuity of the law,[24] toward its fracture or its immanent suspension, might suffice to summon the admiration of the masses and mobilize a mimetic dimension which the law heretofore suppressed: its plasticity (197).

Conclusion

Who is now the mime? Much like the great criminal, the law is mimetic. Legal responses are not merely reactive measures but acts of imitation and adaption. Both variants of mimesis (the criminal and the legal) rely on such imitation. However, they nevertheless differ. The elasticity of the legal frame relies on a fragmentary understanding of mimesis. It solely refers to a relatively vulgar understanding of imitation, where any modification is marked by a return. Both dimensions, while being radically different, pertain to the same formational process. Benjamin, owing to his pessimism regarding lasting change through malleability, suppresses the plastic dimension of his great criminal. However, paradoxically perhaps, it is the same Benjamin who, despite his pessimism, outlines a supplementary path: one that is plastic and transgressive.

The criminal's plastic mimesis does not allow for a return. One need only consider Niobe's petrification to understand that transgression leaves an indelible mark. While Benjamin's criminal might be read as a rival to the prevalent violent regime, the inherent plasticity of the transgression implies an understanding of the veritable malleability of the law. Such transformation cannot be anticipated, unlike its elastic counterpart; such a change will not prompt an automatic return to the previous state. Like Benjamin's tentative proposal, such a mark or imprint transforms not only the criminal but the law itself. Benjamin acknowledges the potential of such transformation but insists that it necessarily remains inscribed within the law's monopoly; it is but the envoy of another law, another rule of fate. Arguably, Benjamin is all too cautious regarding his own motive; criminal mimesis does not merely replicate the law's model. Rather, its plastic and mimetic dimensions seem to expose a fragile suspension, inherent to the law itself.[25]

As I insisted, it is the *plasticity* of *criminal mimesis* that does not only break the law but also increases the legibility of this fracture. Benjamin's great criminal provides a brief glimpse into the *law's lawlessness*. Such a glimpse exposes the profound expanses of malleability, of transformative processes, which are not predetermined by a prevalent rule. In this regard, the criminal mimesis catalyzes an understanding of the mimetic which accepts the simultaneity of repetition and creation. Despite their radical differences, creation and repetition pertain to the same site.

Legal mimesis only partially mobilizes such simultaneity. Its creative dimension remains elastically ensnared in a relatively narrow domain. Certainly, the law seems fluid. To an extent, it claims to read, and understand, that which has not yet been written (cf. Benjamin 2011b, 347). The law anticipates transgression, changes its dictum, its reach. Without such hermeneutical conjuration, the law's own violence would constantly expose itself. Thus, the law lacks its sediment (or continuously suspends sedimentation).

Integral to the institution of the law is denial. Neither its suspension nor its elastic stupor must be apparent. The loosening tie to natural law implies that positive law's "just means" must constantly be reformulated, iterated. In the repetition of these means, positive law is obliged to deny the absence of a foundation (apart from the elusive foundational categories of justice, humanity, the people). The law attempts to relinquish the violence of its own inauguration. Thereby, the law fluidifies the material foundation it always lacked.[26]

However, this fluidity is quick to congeal if a violent monopoly is to be eclipsed by another. Beyond the miming of the elasticity of the law, beyond elastic mimesis, I insist, finally, on the conceptual pertinence of Benjamin's plastic (and *criminal*) mimesis, transgressing the mere profanity of an elastic assertion of power. The torchlight of Prometheus does not necessarily mark the failed inauguration of a new judicial frame but might equally denounce the constitutive absence that invariably taints the law.

Notes

1. I provisionally set aside the question of subjectivation that the law instigates. Arguably, the law constitutively relies on the circumscription of the subjects it includes and rejects (Arendt 1970, 44; Mbembe 2017, 132).
2. Malabou initially developed the notion of plasticity through a reading of Hegel's *Phenomenology of Spirit*. In the introduction to the *Phenomenology*, Hegel schematizes substance's (self-)unfolding, eventually resulting in the subject. Hegel's dialectical development prompts Malabou to speak of the plasticity of substance (2009, 11), a plastic metabolism shaping both subject and substance (2010, 27).
3. I understand law, following Butler, as: "the implicit or explicit framework in which we consider whether or not violence is a justified means for achieving a given end, but also whether a given force should be called 'violent' or not" (2020, 124). Hence, discussing the law implies a discourse on the fragile status of *dikē*, justice.
4. Here, mimesis does not merely refer to aesthetic realism and the economy of reproduction that such realism summons. Rather, it is linked to its theatrical origins in mime and performance (Lawtoo 2022a, 6). The great criminal might be assessed as a homo mimeticus: a figure whose mimetic excesses expose both the law's affective contagion (*pathos*) and its normative containment (*logos*).
5. This corruption entails the exposure of the impossibility of a violent monopoly, prompting redistribution.
6. Nevertheless, as Derrida did not tire of insisting, the law is marked by an internal division or suspension (1992, 23). While I am yet to recapitulate how this suspension operates, one can foreshadow that new law is never insured by a rule; its introduction thus amends, destroys and founds anew. One could infer—and I will need to develop this more patiently—that the law is thus inherently lawless. Or, in Butler's assessment: "the law is broken prior to any possibility of having access to the law" (1997, 108).
7. See Lacoue-Labarthe's theorization of mimesis, particularly in relation to aesthetic and political formation, and his emphasis on Benjamin as a central figure in this trajectory (cf. Lawtoo 2022b, 130).
8. In German, the idiomatic link between power and violence is evident. *Die Gewalt des Gesetzes* (the violence of the law) is synonymous with its power. The foundational tautology (new law defends the legal apparatus, i.e. its monopoly) will become important in the pages to come (cf. Derrida 1992, 33).
9. Upon first sight, this may seem to fail in signaling the circumscription that the law enacts, imposes or performs. However, at present, it is not particularly significant that we presumably form the judicial body, delegate it and bring it into being through our volition, our voice or our signature.
10. Benjamin's *Critique* provisionally situates itself within the purview of positive law only to eclipse such a foundational choice. According to Benjamin, it is solely a historically informed philosophical assessment (*geschichtsphilosophische Rechtsbetrachtung*) that provides criteria which are removed from both positive and natural law (1991, 182).
11. When considering how certain judicial systems implement *stare decisis*, or precedent, the debate regarding the preservation and the creation of law becomes more complex. Nonetheless, this heightened complexity does little to alter the enduring significance of Benjamin's *Critique*. Precedent implies no alteration of the law's *elastic* frame.

12 Readings of Benjamin's *Critique* tend to emphasize, or abandon, the possibility of divine violence. The former follow Benjamin's reference to George Sorel, and accept Benjamin's cues to interpret divine violence as a revolutionary general strike, resetting the discursive coordinates of that which is to be deemed violent and just. The latter shift the emphasis and neglect the divine. Both interpretations warrant different treatments of mythical violence. A reading which focuses on the divine rejects mythical violence because it figures as the vulgar purview of state violence. A reading focusing on mythical violence potentially establishes instabilities within the mythical domain of the law (and indeed I provisionally ignore all the reactionary options). My reading treads somewhere between these poles as it seeks to analyze the fragile locus of positive law via an emphasis on Benjamin's great criminal. Such an intermediate position, I suggest, does not curtail the purview of thinking a profound alternative.

13 Positive law is then associated with mythical violence. Yet it is not all too surprising to theorize the violence of the law within a mythological register (cf. Benjamin 1991, 188). After all, the law's performance seems to echo many mythological criteria: one only needs to think of destiny, fate and guilt.

14 The criminal's specific violence speaks of a certain violent potential which has not yet been subsumed by the state (or any other monopolizing force). Contrary to the monopolization of violence qua positive law, the criminal transgression operates through a form of violence which resists such centralization.

15 Derrida's *Force of Law* ties an analysis of Benjamin's essay to the larger inquiry regarding the relation of deconstruction and justice. Derrida 1992, 33, 40.

16 See also Malabou's discussion of the dual polarities of imitation in ch. 12 of this volume.

17 In its most extreme manifestations, we are confronted with what Malabou characterizes as a text devoid of any trace (2022, 288f).

18 In its minimal form, mimesis here refers to the imitation of a violent force (Lawtoo 2022b, 145).

19 In a seemingly remote analogy, one can echo Hans Blumenberg's words: the work on myth (*die Arbeit am Mythos*) is what we have to dedicate ourselves to (2014, 39).

20 As developed by Butler's 1997 *Psychic Life of Power*, the law might be broken, even before we are granted access to it. My use of this passage is rather diachronic as Butler develops this in the context of her understanding of subjectivation, indicating that "a critical view of the law is […] limited […] by a prior desire for the law" (1997, 108). With Derrida, such a rupture would rather allude to a moment of non-law within law (1992, 36).

21 Malabou 2023, 28:42–29:05.

22 This would merit a discussion of Schmitt's conviction that the law cannot suspend itself, hence the need for a sovereign to introduce a state of exception when major legislative changes are mandated (2015, 13f).

23 The resistance to form is the condition of possibility for giving into, giving way to or facilitating form (cf. Malabou 2010, 13f.). I would like to extend my gratitude to my colleague I. A. Roland-Rodriguez for providing crucial insights into the specific aspects expounded upon in this paragraph.

24 One can think this vacuity with Derrida (an instance of non-law within the law) or with Butler, who complicates the law's subjectivizing mechanisms. According to Derrida, a "just" decision must be both regulated and unregulated: "it must conserve the law and also destroy it or suspend it" (1992, 23). Butler's *Force of Non-Violence* follows Benjamin in the attempt

to read the law beyond an "instrumentalist framework," beyond the perimeters that attempt to measure the justifiability of violence (2020, 15).

25 This results in a plethora of questions (which I will need to leave for another time): What conditions the possibility for a plastic inscription? How does the law, or the whole domain of legal utterance and address, turn from an elastic (non-)medium to a plastic medium? What is different, finally, from the suspension of the law here, suspending foundational moments that are sedimented, and the suspension of law by the law itself, when it either creates laws post facto to justify itself, or else when it puts the law into a state of exception altogether?

26 Such fluidity does not derive from itself but relies on a repetitive supplement. One understands the extent to which it forms that which it codifies, legislates, apprehends. What seems less obvious is the degree to which the judicial body itself is formed. Of course, the law's edifice is contingent, constantly re-modulated, bespeaks its historicity. However, apart from a Schmittian state of exception, the law cannot accomplish its own disintegration (cf. Schmitt 2015, 13). While it would be fruitful to interrogate the intricate interplay between procedural and material norms, I will, for now, have to set these questions aside.

Bibliography

Arendt, Hannah (1970). *On Violence*. Austin et al.: A Harvest Book, Harcourt.

Benjamin, Walter (1978). "Critique of Violence," in *Reflections: Essays, Aphorisms, Autobiographical Writings*. New York: Schocken Books, 277–300.

Benjamin, Walter (1991). "Zur Kritik der Gewalt," in *Gesammelte Schriften II. I*. Berlin/Frankfurt: Suhrkamp, 179–203.

Benjamin, Walter (2007). "The Storyteller. Reflections on the Works of Nikolai Leskov," in *Illuminations. Essays and Reflections,* trans. Harry Zohn, ed. Hannah Arendt. New York: Schocken Books, 83–111.

Benjamin, Walter (2011a). "Der Erzähler. Betrachtungen zum Werk Nikolai Leskows," in *Gesammelte Werke II*. Frankfurt: Zweitausendeins, 600–622.

Benjamin, Walter (2011b). "Über das mimetische Vermögen," in: *Gesammelte Werke II*. Frankfurt: Zweitausendeins, 445–448.

Blumenberg, Hans (2014). *Arbeit am Mythos*. Frankfurt: Suhrkamp.

Butler, Judith (1997). *The Psychic Life of Power. Theories in Subjection*. Stanford: Stanford University Press.

Butler, Judith (2020). *The Force of Non-Violence*. London/New York: Verso.

Derrida, Jacques (1992). "Force of Law: The Mythical Foundation of Authority," in *Deconstruction and the Possibility of Justice*, ed. Drucilla Cornell et al. New York/London: Routledge, 3–67.

Lawtoo, Nidesh (2022a). "The Mimetic Condition: Theory and Concepts." *CounterText* 8.1, 1–22.

Lawtoo, Nidesh (2022b). *Homo Mimeticus. A New Theory of Imitation*. Leuven: Leuven University Press.

Malabou, Catherine (2009). *The Future of Hegel. Plasticity, Temporality and Dialectic*. London/New York: Routledge.

Malabou, Catherine (2010). *Plasticity at the Dusk of Writing. Dialectic, Destruction, Deconstruction*. New York/Chichester/West Sussex: Columbia University Press.

Malabou, Catherine (2012a). *Ontology of the Accident. An Essay on Destructive Plasticity*. Cambridge/Malden: Polity Press.
Malabou, Catherine (2012b). *The New Wounded. From Neurosis to Brain Damage*. New York: Fordham University Press.
Malabou, Catherine (2022). "Are There Still Traces? Memory and the Obsolescence of the Paradigm of Inscription," in *Plasticity. The Promise of Explosion,* ed. Tyler M. Williams. Edinburgh: Edinburgh University Press, 287–296.
Malabou, Catherine (2023). *Mirroring and Conflicting Subliminalities.* https://www.youtube.com/watch?v=M9WtEN3NJHE
Mbembe, Achille (2017). *Critique of Black Reason*. Durham, NC/London: Duke University Press.
Schmitt, Carl (2015). *Politische Theologie*. Berlin: Duncker & Humblot.

CHAPTER 6

TO DOUBLE MIMESIS BOUND

Mortal Plasticity between Malabou
and Lacoue-Labarthe

Alex Obrigewitsch

> What these deathly forms, beings, entities were, this could only be said by a double-faced word; nevertheless, they ended, on the threshold of irremediable destruction, by revealing themselves as being these obscure laws called to disappear.
>
> —Maurice Blanchot, *Thomas l'obscur*

We begin with a doubling in questioning these two "concepts," plasticity and mimesis, and their relation to one another. Two, each a double in "itself," and doubling the other, displacing, in effect, the position, and positing, in and of the place of *origin*. As I shall show, both plasticity and mimesis posit the other—as *suppository*, in the sense of the Latin *supponere* or the French *suppôt*, "to place under"—even as each would itself be posited or would posit "itself."

I shall therefore address the question of the relationship between mimesis and plasticity by way of a suspension, by showing that this relation exposes an abyssal dynamic of doubling and displacement within which these "concepts" (as well as their identity as *concepts*) find themselves suspended. What suspends these "concepts" in their relation to one another is the force of mimesis "itself," as the force of doubling and displacement (displacing even mimesis "itself," and hence the abyss that shall be exposed). In order to further the mimetic turn initiated by the *Homo Mimeticus* trilogy, I shall take as support for (re)thinking mimesis the thought of Philippe Lacoue-Labarthe, and for plasticity that of Catherine Malabou. After describing these "concepts" by way of these thinkers, I shall explore the force of mimetic plasticity which binds the two together, via a form without form (without model). My intention is to further our appreciation of the convergences of these two thinkers, and what continuing to question their thoughts might reveal for mimetic studies, were Malabou to take seriously the problem of mimesis which Lacoue-Labarthe exposed.

I shall then link the double movement between mimesis and plasticity to the figure of mortal existence to begin to rethink the tragic as an avenue for the continued genealogical elaboration of homo mimeticus. This will entail a brief examination of the thought of the caesura, which provides a means for thinking the form without form behind mimesis and plasticity. This will be bound to the non-appearance of death, marking the existence of homo mimeticus by what I call "mortal plasticity"—the displacement of originary support in being suspended in an abyssal movement. Because death remains the absence of form in-forming our existence, we must mime a figuration of death in order to think the suspended explosion of mortal plasticity.

"As a Scene of Beginnings..."

Let us begin with these two words, then, already double even unto themselves, exposing us to the opening of this abyss and the displacement which it effectuates. As Malabou is fond of noting, "plasticity," derived from the Greek *plassein*, bears a double sense or double power—"it means at once the capacity to *receive form* [...] and the capacity to *give form*" (2008, 5). Plasticity would therefore be a double power (in the sense of the German *Vermögen*) oscillating between activity and passivity in terms of the question of formation or figuration. And what of mimesis? Part of the long history of problematic (mis)interpretations of mimesis derives from what Nidesh Lawtoo, following Lacoue-Labarthe, calls its "duplicity" and its "destabilizing double movement" (2022, 129).[1] Mimesis does not quite conform to being, or take the form of being, a concept which stabilizes and allows for grasping by thought.[2] Mimesis must not, all too simply, be translated as "imitation" or "copying." It is a complex process which entails, at once, the presentation of an appearance or semblance—in terms of the power or force behind such a presentation, the "formative force," "*die bildende Kraft*" (to employ a Kantian phrase),³ of *Darstellung* ((re)presentation)—and the state, status, or form of the appearance or semblance produced. Mimesis would therefore also bear the mark of a double power or double movement, between activity and passivity, much as plasticity does.

We can see, then, that mimesis and plasticity double one another in terms of their movements in the formation or figuration of appearance, in the broadest possible sense. This is the case from the very beginning, insofar as appearance and its conditioning or constitution configure something like a beginning. "It [*Ça*] begins," Lacoue-Labarthe claims, speaking to the question of the displacing relation between *origin* and *fiction*, "therefore—and this is the 'imitation'—with the 'plastic' [*le 'plastique'*] (the fashioning, the modeling, the fictioning), by the impression of the *type* and the imposition of the *sign*" (1975, 257; 1998a, 126; trans. modified). In the beginning, in the place of origin, of the shaping, forming, or fictioning, there are already two—the plastic and its mimetic production. Or should we say there is mimesis and its plastic figuration? As Lawtoo reminds us, citing the previous quotation from Lacoue-Labarthe, "this is as a scene of beginnings; yet no singular concept originates here" (2022, 138). We remain still, as it were, suspended between the double question moving between mimesis and plasticity, and the Janus-headed figure, that these two would appear to present to us: "Is mimesis a plastic concept? Or plasticity a mimetic concept?" (129).

But is this figure of Janus adequate for supporting the doubled play of dissimulation? Would this figure not suggest that plasticity and mimesis are but two faces, two masks, of one and the same power or movement? Are mimesis and plasticity one and the same (in their difference of expression)? For though mimesis may be the force of plastic presentation of the figure understood in the inscriptive marking or stamping of the type or *typos*, plasticity equally allows for the establishment of the figure, the taking-of-shape for the shaping force of mimesis. Neither the one nor the other can therefore be posited as primary, as originary, over and before the other. The one supports the other, even as it is supported by it—they are bound in a relation of suspension, each lapsing back into the other, infinitely. This is the destabilizing movement which Lacoue-Labarthe calls "hyperbological," where the activity of the one lapses into the passivity of the other, and this passivity then lapses back into its activity as it passes into the passivity of its other.⁴ We cannot therefore posit one "concept" over the other because their intricated movement refuses any stabilizing ossification that would be fundamentally graspable, allowing us to grasp some sort of foundation.⁵ In this "alternation of appropriation and disappropriation" (Lacoue-Labarthe

1986b, 64; 1998b, 231) —the hyperbological relation within which the more one of these "concepts" comes into its own, the more it relies upon or takes the figure of the other—the play of masks passes off its face for another (the face as the mask of another face, *ad infinitum*). And so the head of Janus explodes (as with Malabou's third sense bound to "plasticity," marked in the oscillation between the homophonic pair of *le plastique* and *le plastic*),[6] exposing an abyss of masks, of doubling faces *mise en abyme*, displacing the identity of Janus as a double-faced figure.

Yet this explosion of identity, explosion in the excess of form, would be anterior to the very establishment of a fixed giving and receiving of plasticity. The "third" sense of plasticity, the explosion of the form, would appear to have occurred prior to the proposed double movement of plasticity, of which Malabou speaks. But would this prior disruption, destabilizing the double movement of formation, not "itself" double the movement of mimesis once more? The explosive character of plasticity, marking "a refusal to submit to a model" (Malabou 2008, 6)—this appears to indicate nothing other than the movement of de-figuration entailed by mimesis, according to Lacoue-Labarthe; that is, the destabilizing of the figure marked in the same movement of establishing it mimetically *as* figure. The explosion of the form, to "break the spectacle" (Lacoue-Labarthe and Nancy 2013, 24)—these two movements of displacement turn around one another, turning hyperbologically into one another, once more.

This anterior explosion of plasticity and mimesis exposes the fragmentary as, or in, the place of the originary. As Maurice Blanchot has shown us, the fragmentary never refers to the fragments of an original One or unity, but is instead, from before the beginning, multiple and relational.[7] The fragmentary binds us to yet another doubling displacement, which Lacoue-Labarthe speaks of in terms of

> *the obligatory reversibility of the motifs of engenderment and of the figure, of conception and of the plastic*, or, if one prefers, in this sort of reciprocal and unsurpassable metaphorical (figural) exchange between the "concepts" of *origin* and *fiction* (1975, 258; 1998a, 128; trans. modified).[8]

The "origin" thus exposes itself as fictional—as figured and fashioned—and this is why Lacoue-Labarthe tells us that beginning with the plastic is "imitation" (1975, 257; 1998a, 126), revealing itself as derivative of an anterior figuration or formation: the mimetic force inscribing the plasticity of the plastic subject-object (given the duplicity of giving and receiving form). This anterior force remains absent from the form of the scene as origin or beginning, however—else it would not be originary and would not mark a beginning at all. We see herein the paradox upon which the relation between plasticity and mimesis remains suspended. It is for this reason, concerning the fictional status of the "origin" and the displacement and suspension that this unravels, that Lawtoo writes that "this is *as* a scene of beginnings" (2022, 138; emphasis added). What we have is not simply a scene of beginnings, but the presentation of something *as* a scene of beginnings—and it is this little "*as*" which bears all the weight of the suspended relation.

... That is To Say Also a Primal Scene?

In the beginning, in the place of origin, there is neither simply plasticity nor mimesis. Instead, what is at play is a *dédoublement*, the "origin" doubled and divided in and from "itself" in the abyssal doubling between mimesis and plasticity. The origin is thus displaced from its position or place, even as it is plastically formed *as* origin, in the form of a scene (even one without model).[9] The origin therefore only appears *as* origin insofar as it appears as originally suspended, in terms of being figurally (that is, mimetically) derived. There would thus be traced a double movement in the (re)presentation or formation—in Malabou's plastic, materialist sense—of the "origin," by which it is at once established or figured, while also bearing the mark of its own fault, default, or de-figuration. This "distance" internal to the doubling movement of figuration is marked by the "*as...*" structuring the schema of figuration. For to appear *as* something, as "thus and so" or "such and such," is the mark of semblance and dissemblance, of "appearance" in its manifold senses.

But the stamp of this mark or type, between semblance and dissemblance, is precisely the work of mimesis! In the opening of the fourth chapter of the *Poetics*, Aristotle claims that it is through mimesis that we, as children, first come to learn and see—and thus that *mathein* and *theōrein* are conditioned by mimesis.[10] Through the comparison of different appearances, we come to the understanding of similitude and the concept of the same—mimesis being the force behind the faculty or power of comparison, Aristotle's *metaphorikon einai*.[11] The form of the same, the concept of similitude, is thus produced (fictioned?) by the force of mimesis—differences discerned in a perceived plurality render apparent what is the same (as well as what is different, and the plurality *itself*, *as* plurality) by rendering it *as* apparent, letting it appear and be received in the *between* which is disclosed.[12]

But this derivation of similitude, grounded in mimesis, has a paradox. For if mimesis is to be taken as a form, as something identical to, or the same as, "itself," then this would entail the very working of mimesis to ground and constitute "itself." Mimesis cannot act *as* its own condition, for even this "as" repeats the mark of mimesis once more, ever redoubling "itself," dividing it in "itself" from "itself." In other words, mimesis "itself" cannot be established as an originary or primal ground or support, as it is "itself" already subject to mimetic force and its *dédoublement*. Suspended between the giving and receiving of form, in Malabou's terms, plasticity mimetically explodes the limits of conceptual ossification. Thus, Esa Kirkkopelto speaks of mimesis as "the very principle of *dédoublement*" (2008, 46; my trans.), insofar as it doubles and divides even as it brings together in a double movement of appearance. At the same instant, mimesis doubles and divides *itself*, *se dédouble*. There is thus an abyss (a groundlessness) exposed through "mimesis," through this force which divides and suspends "itself" beneath this name, demanding to be placed in inverted commas.

I claim, therefore, that in tracing the genealogical link between mimesis and plasticity, we must be careful not to simply posit mimesis as primary, even when the relation between plasticity and mimesis bears in itself the traces of an anterior mimetic effectuation. For mimesis ever divides and doubles "itself," unworking the identificatory establishment of a concept even as it bears out its work or effect, its *ergon*, in the figuration or formation of appearance. Once again, we do not have a beginning, but only a *scene* of beginnings, *as* a scene of beginnings. As Lacoue-Labarthe phrases it, "everything 'begins' *also* by representation" (1975, 247–248; 1998a, 117). No beginning, no origin, but *as* already lapsing back into an abyssal turning between plasticity and mimesis, suspended in a relation which is mimetically figured but which refuses to give its name, ultimately, to the ends of something like the figure of "mimesis." The ficticity of this relation that I am concerned with, sketched out between Lacoue-Labarthe and Malabou, is ineluctable and insuperable (like the relation between origin and fiction), as it lapses back into the abyss figured by mimesis (one as another as one as another, *ad infinitum*). In other words, the origin is always as if it were a *scene*—staged, framed, performed, and pre-formed.

"The scene is primal," wrote Lacoue-Labarthe in 1979, as the (revised) title of one of his essays dealing with the theatrics of psychoanalysis.[13] The scene (in the double sense of the French "*scène*" as both "stage" and the "scene" staged upon it), the theatrical doubling and dissimulation, as well as the formation and fashioning of something like a "scene of origin," is how "the first," "the beginning," appears. And yet, as we have seen already, mimesis has a double demand of a double movement, suspension between affirmation and negation. And so Lacoue-Labarthe, writing of Blanchot's late *récit* "(*Une Scène primitive?*)" ("(A Primal Scene?)")[14] in 2003, will claim the opposite: "the scene was thus not 'primal'" (2011, 148; 2015, 80).[15] And this by necessity, for its very status as *scene*, as fictional (dis)semblance, exposes the non-originality of this "origin," that it bears the mark or stamp of "imitation," the duplicity and duplexity of mimesis in its plasticity. Of course, this is the very nature of the *primal scene*—to be but a fictional origin, a fiction of origin, standing in the place of that which does not and cannot appear. The primal scene is essentially displaced and displacing—it is inherently *mimetic*. And therefore, it exposes (in dissimulation) the very absence in the place of the "prime," the "first," the originary ground. The mimesis *of* the primal scene thus marks a suspension, supported as though upon nothing, without ground, in the abyss (the *Abgrund*) which perpetually produces figures in the void of its displaced place or position.

In a recent interview on mimesis, Malabou makes what appears to be, on further reflection, a startling claim regarding the relation between mimesis and the primal scene. When Hannes Opelz, furthering the re-turn of plasticity to homo mimeticus, asks her about "the primal scene of mimesis in [her] own philosophical history or story [*histoire*]," Malabou says that "mimesis is a fundamental concept which is born at the same time as philosophy and will die with it, therefore I do not know if one can speak of a primal scene" (Malabou and Opelz 2022, 801; my trans.). But would the "birth" and "death" of mimesis be so strictly bound to those of philosophy? Is not mimesis at work already, anterior to the positing and positioning of philosophy and its origins?[16] Would the fictioning of philosophy not take its figure from the abyssal mimetic double movement which we have been at pains to grasp thus far? The abyssal reproduction of mimesis would appear to suspend the very positing of beginning, of birth, as well as infinitizing the end, death, as equally suspended. This would then entail that, in fact, one *must* speak of a primal scene in relation to mimesis (as well as plasticity). The ineluctable imperative, the *il faut*, would be the very mark of mimesis as the setting to work or setting into work of semblance and dissemblance (even as this work is doubly marked by its own unworking or *désœuvrement*, by a de-figuration). The origin is always already second—this is what mimesis demands of us. And this is what Lacoue-Labarthe has attempted to address or bring to appearance across the entirety of his work and his engagement with (re)thinking mimesis.

Yet this expression of the secondary of the origin, due to its fictive form, is also the very expression of the primal scene *as such*. The question of mimesis, opening onto the abyss, demands the presentation of a primal scene, even as it suspends it as *primal*, and emphasizes its status as *scene*. We might figure this mark of mimesis, a mark *dédoublé*, as a *schiz* (the split, division, or cleavage), demanding what Malabou calls a "schizology" (see, for example, Malabou 2010, 7). But can such a *logos* get behind the *schiz*, to grasp and mold it, when it is mimetically marked in a sort of explosion anterior to the "form" of plasticity "itself"? Even if, as Malabou writes, "plasticity refers to *the spontaneous organization of fragments*" (7), would this plastic figuration not take the form or figure of the production (or staging) of a primal scene—organizing the "originary" fragmentary based upon the mimetic figuration of a *bildlos Bild*, an image without image or formless form (the "pure schema" of Kant), of the void in the vacant place of origin?[17]

The abyss of mimesis, exposed even as it is covered over by the figuration of the primal scene, therefore marks our mortal existence as bound to the very question disclosed between mimesis and plasticity—the question of origin and ficticity, of form and (its) grounds. We are formed or fashioned as the finite figure suspended in the passage of the infinite. For we are not made or figured in the image of God, but, as Blanchot writes, in our own image, which is an absence of image, of proper figure, and thus demands that we also are "*undone or defeated* [défait] *according to* [*our*] *image*" (1955, 350; 1989, 260; trans. modified). "Our" image, our mortal figuration, would thus be the image of death, absence in the place of image, or suspended image—for death remains infinitely improper to "us," marking our proper (dis)appropriation. This is Lacoue-Labarthe's term for the hyperbological disturbance of an appropriation which expropriates "itself" in the same, doubled movement; the more it appropriates "itself," the less proper it is as or to "itself."[18]

We might figure this mortal form or "image," following Hölderlin, as that of the caesura—the "tragic transport" which is "properly empty and the most unbounded" (1952, 196; 2009, 318; trans. modified). The caesura figures as a cut, an interruption (a *schiz*, even)—a formal feature (of poetics) which exceeds mere form and inflects the expression of the fiction (the figure) in, or as, its expression. The caesura marks a suspension which is also in motion or transport, a movement in suspension, of a suspended (absence of) instant[19]—such as the (absent) instant of death—turning round its silence, its emptiness, its absence given form by the fictive double of an absence in presence (such as the fiction of a death which is never "there" or "here," which is ever coming but never comes or arrives). The passage of the infinite passes by the caesura, passes through it, even as it remains at an impasse, *as* an impasse, for those fated to finitude, for we mortals who remain suspended in this caesural passage. The caesura marks the silent turning between mimesis and plasticity, holding open, in suspension, the abyss of "mimesis" whose question demands further thought. I offer the caesura as the figure for this figuration-in-default of mortality[20] in that we are the finite beings bound to representation, refused immediacy or something like an "original" formation or plasticity, and so must bear the mark of mimesis even as it exposes us, as suspended, within an infinite abyss. Thus, the tragic figure of mortality (which Lacoue-Labarthe refers to as "the Law of finitude," and which he too relates to the tragic)[21]—we are bound to the finite, even as we are exposed to the passage of the infinite through this finitude, in infinite interdiction of this infinity. That is, as mortal, finite beings, we remain in relation to a death which remains absent, in excess of our experience, marking our dying as an infinite passage without end—the miming of a death without form, yet in-forming the existence of homo mimeticus.

The primal scene of mortal existence thus presents what Lacoue-Labarthe speaks of as an "originary theatre,"[22] an act of mimesis in the place of origin—in accordance with Aristotle's famous opening to Chapter Four of the *Poetics*. As the existent without proper essence (our "essence" displaced by the mark of mimesis in the place of essence; the plasticity of our existence, in Malabou's terms), our existence is "originally" bound up with abyssal mimesis, suspended from before the beginning upon a void or absence of proper figure. This *bildlos Bild* of our mortal schema binds us to a "pure" plasticity, the plasticity of nothing, the figuring or forming of the void, a pure fiction(ing) of nothing (in the subjective *and* objective genitive). Malabou claims that "plasticity never presents itself without form" (2010, 74), but what of the original instant (ever in default), the primal scene, where plasticity must give form to, and from out of, nothing? From whence would this form, the formation or fictioning of the mortal, take its figure, if not from the form (without form) of the void, of nothingness, in the explosion of an instant which can never be placed or marked within the limits of temporality? A "miming of nothing," then, to echo another titular phrase of Lacoue-Labarthe.[23]

However, the repetitional abyss of mimesis does not simply destine us to the infinite reproduction of (plastic) figurations, to what Lacoue-Labarthe terms "onto-typology."[24] Because nothing, the void of the abyss, impossible death, exposes itself in the double play of the abyss of mimesis—as the form without form of the absent origin, the anterior explosion of all plastic giving and receiving—every plastic act of formation also bears the mark of this double movement. This mark is that of mimetic *dédoublement*, of a suspension between the absence of origin and an unstable secondary status; support without support, in which the mimetic abyss retreats from the form of appearance and (re)presentation once more. It is this double movement of mimesis and plasticity which inscribes the demand of a de-figuration, which Malabou appears to misinterpret in the thought of Lacoue-Labarthe. Malabou figures Lacoue-Labarthe as "privilege[ing] the formless, the unpresentable, the 'de-figuration,' the scenic removal" (2010, 54).[25] But this is no capricious privileging from the outside. Rather, it is an exigency inscribed in the double movement of figuration, marked between mimesis and plasticity. For de-figuration is part of the very *form* of figuration (as double movement of *dédoublement*), the fault exposing the originary default of its form or *Bild* (being figured, "originally," upon nothing). And the "scenic removal"—that is, the removal or retreat from the scene, leaving its traces nonetheless in and upon the scene, demanding retreatment by way of de-figuration as the active unworking of appearance and (re)presentation, as the mark of the double movement of mimesis in its caesural suspension—is itself, duplicitously, figured as the demand of a retreat traced anterior to the "staging" of the scene, but traced nonetheless *in a scene, by the scene*, in the form of a transcendental figure of a *primal scene*.[26]

Retreating a Beginning, in the Retreat of the End

As already acknowledged, all of these questions that we have been exposing and exploring require further explication and critical tracing. This remains a provisional opening, an incitation to further thought and questioning in mimetic studies. To close this opening, then, I hope not to end, but rather to designate the mark of another beginning already underway, called for by this very retreat of, and into, the abyss of mimesis.

This retreat marks its exigency upon our mortal existence, in the demand of an infinite retreatment or retreating (in the double senses of *retrait* which Lacoue-Labarthe often employs). That is to say, the form of our mortal plasticity, bound to the abyss of mimesis, demands that we treat the question of the relation between mimesis and plasticity once more. And this "once more" is due to the abyssal character of the relation, to the fact that its explosion of the form of any stable relation ever retreats, leaving the persistent form of a question. By taking up once more the *question* of mimesis marking the figuration of plasticity with the doubled movement of a de-figuration—taking account of how the formation of plasticity always bears an explosive element of mimetic force which holds the form in suspension—this question places us back into the abyss, back in question, to rethink this question which mimesis marks out. The question, staged in terms of Malabou's thought, is of the duplicity of form, or the explosive third element interrupting the giving and receiving elements of plastic formation.

As mortals, suspended in the void of the abyss, the void of origins, what is demanded of us, marked in our very figure (our mortal plasticity), is the exigency of "another relation to death," affirming the radical negativity which suspends all dialectics, affirming the impossible in *miming* it, repeating its mark of suspension. "Playing at death and *to death*," as Lacoue-Labarthe puts it at the close of his 2006 paper—"*jouer à la mort et* à mort."[27] Would this not entail exposing death—the void displaced and displacing the origin and the end, equally suspended (appearing as the caesura of mortal existence)—in turning towards us the infinite passage of a turning-away already departed and distanced? A *détournement* of an originary *détournement*, traced in the abyss of mimesis, revealing in the place of origin a disappearing in appearing, always already disappearing, presented in an approach which never draws any nearer, yet which exposes the pure void of distance and passage to which we are exposed in our suspension as mortal. Our relation to the originary disappearance of death marks a passage back into the abyss of mimesis, under the explosive form of the displacement of origins. The figuration of this relation is that of our mortal existence in the form of the mortal plasticity of homo mimeticus. Mortal plasticity, without support, remains suspended in this question of death, the void, and the impasse which it marks upon us as from the beginning.

"There is nothing to do with death but theatricalize it," Lacoue-Labarthe writes (1979, 208; 1993, 112; trans. modified). We are bound, doubly, from beginning to end, to a mimesis and plasticity based upon nothing, supported by nothing, turned toward the catastrophe (the *katastrophē*, the down-turning) of an infinite retreat into the abyss figured duplicitously by mimesis. Bereft of beginning as of end, we are bound, tragically, to trace this retreat, to work through the unworking of figuration doubly marked in all plasticity—we must continue to think the *question* of mimesis, for it bears no stable answer. Mimesis is figured, abyssally, as nothing but the *question* which we must think, enact and repeat—the *question* binding mortal plasticity to the void from whence it comes and to which it tends, wandering as though in an infinitely finite suspension, tracing its anterior disappearance in the figuration of the question *as such*. This *question* of mimesis, which Lacoue-Labarthe proposes in the form of a problematic formlessness or explosion of form anterior to any plastic taking-and-giving of form, remains to be thought in the genealogy of homo mimeticus, as an ineluctable (though paradoxical) support which Malabou must engage with in the (re)turn of mimesis in her own thought.[28]

Notes

1. Lawtoo's text was originally published in the 2017 volume of *MLN* devoted to Lacoue-Labarthe. It was revised and republished as the fourth chapter of his book on mimesis and homo mimeticus in 2022: it elaborates upon the connection between plasticity and mimesis furthered in this chapter. References to Lawtoo's text give the pagination in the 2022 revised version.
2. Cf. Stephen Halliwell's remark that part of the difficulty in pinning down Aristotle's use of the term derives from the fact that "Aristotle nowhere offers a definition of it" (Aristotle 1987, 71). This gap in the Aristotelian text perhaps echoes and results from the gap or *écart* which mimesis marks within the history of metaphysics.
3. See Kant 2000, 246 (§ 65) and 293 (§ 81). For an elaboration of this phrase and its relation to mimesis, see Lacoue-Labarthe 1986a, 97–98; 1990a, 218. Lacoue-Labarthe here refers to this "*bildende Kraft*" as a "*plastische Kraft*" ("plastic force") as well.
4. Cf. Lawtoo 2022, 144, on the workings of hyperbologic and the hyperbological.
5. Lawtoo is aware of the duplicity of the double movement of mimesis, noting that it is a "destabilizing *movement*" rather than establishing a "stabilizing *structure*" in terms of form or (re)presentation (2022, 37). And yet the figure of Janus, seeking "to join rather than oppose these competing perspectives" (18) concerning mimesis, is also unbound by the mimetic agon which destabilizes even in its joining (as a sort of de-distancing, an *Ent-fernung* or *é-loignement*). Where the figure of the Janus head (re)presents a solidity in its figuration—like a stele, marking the death of the non-identity of mimesis in the form of a crypt—the figure of Escher's *Drawing Hands*, presenting the infinite movement of each hand being drawn even as it draws, which Lawtoo presents in the opening of his book (2022, 10–11), would perhaps act as a better figure for (re)presenting the abyssal double *movement* which mimesis entails. On the stele and its relation to figuration and establishment, see Lacoue-Labarthe 1975, 190–224; 1998a, 63–95.
6. See, for example, Malabou 2010, 87 n. 13. As the translator, Carolyn Shread, points out here, this sense of explosivity bears upon the French "*plastic*" rather than "*plastique*." Shread claims that the former "is more evidently derived from the two terms *plastiquage* and *plastiquer*" than from the Greek *plassein*, though it would seem, on the contrary, that these terms are derived from *le plastic*, and not the other way around. *Le plastic* is borrowed from the English "plastic," in the sense of "plastic explosives," so called for their malleability, their ability to be formed in the shape of a recess in what is to be destroyed (multiplying the recess, the absence in or of form, which mimetically gives it form).

7   On the fragmentary as explored and explicated by Blanchot, see Blanchot 1973, 61–63, 71; 1992, 42–43, 49; and 1980, 99–101; 1995, 60–61. Given the complexity of this thought, a further explication of the fragmentary greatly exceeds the scope of this chapter. For an extensive engagement, see Hill 2012.

8   The translator, Eduardo Cadava, strangely effaces Lacoue-Labarthe's guillemets around the word "concepts"—even though this is meant to designate the suspension of the establishment of either "origin" or "fiction" as a concept, because of the very reversibility and infinite exchange being spoken of in the passage, which is marked out between these two (or, rather, given their displacement and mimetic exchange of identity between one another, these *more, and yet less, than one*).

9   Recall Malabou 2008, 6, quoted above: that the explosive element of plasticity entails "a refusal to submit to a model." Cf. Lacoue-Labarthe 2008, 196, where he speaks of a "miming without model" in terms of marking a "distance from oneself" (my trans.).

10 See Aristotle 1987, 34 (Chapter IV, 1448b). Cf. Lacoue-Labarthe 2002, 85; 2019, 65, where, in the wake of Aristotle, Lacoue-Labarthe writes that mimesis "offers the condition for learning (*mathein*) and for seeing (*theōrein*), that is, for recognition of the same or of likeness [or 'appearance,' *semblable*] (the singular thing itself, *the same*)" (trans. modified). The final words, "the same," are in English in the original text.

11 On the metaphorical power or faculty which allows for comparison (through "the perception of similarities" distinguished amongst differences), see Aristotle 1987, 57 (Chapter XXII, 1459a). Cf. Lacoue-Labarthe 2002, 49; 2019, 33.

12 This conception of the same derived from difference, by means of metaphor (the carrying-over or -across of the *metaphora*), is strikingly similar to that proposed by Nietzsche in "On Truth and Lying in a Non-Moral Sense." Cf. Nietzsche 1999, 145 in particular. In Lacoue-Labarthe 1986a; 1990a, the figure of Nietzsche's understanding of mimesis and art are traced back to Aristotelian conceptions. See ch. 1 of Lawtoo 2022, 43–67, on the importance of Nietzsche for the genealogical project of homo mimeticus.

13 See Lacoue-Labarthe 1979; 1973. This essay was originally published under the title "Note sur Freud et la représentation," in *Digraphe* 3 (Autumn 1974).

14 This *récit* can be found in Blanchot 1980, 117; 1995, 72. For a precis of the complicated publication history of this *récit*, which binds Blanchot and Lacoue-Labarthe together, see Lacoue-Labarthe 2011, 133–138; 2015, 71–74.

15 This work was originally given as a conference paper in March 2003, and was published in *Maurice Blanchot: Récits critiques*, eds. Christophe Bident and Pierre Vilar (Tours: Farrago, 2003).

16 Lawtoo poses this question in terms of the mimetic agon between philosophy and poetry, antedating the Platonic institution of philosophy by way of a mimetism which counters poetry while also doubling it (in a repressed manner, establishing another "primal scene"). See, for example, Lawtoo 2022, 11–19, 80–85.

17 In his *Critique of Pure Reason*, Kant speaks of the pure schema as providing "the form of an experience in general" (A 125), through the operations of the "pure synthesis of the imagination" (A 118; cf. B 150–151) in its transcendental function, providing "the ground of the possibility of all cognition, especially that of experience" (A 118; cf. B 147–148). That is to say that the schema, as providing the pure form informing experience by synthesizing the manifold received by intuition, provides the form or image (*Bild*) by which representation, and thus experience, is possible as such. And yet this schema as formative force does not

itself appear in representation (Kant notes, in the "Transcendental Schematism," that "the schema [...] is something that can never be brought to an image [*Bild*] at all" [A 142; B 181]), and its "purity" is the mark of its absolute lack of appearance, as the void form which gives all form. These references refer to the established method of referencing the first *Critique*, with A referring to the page numbers in the first edition, and B referring to those in the revised second edition. Translations provide the page numbers for both editions in the margins. My citations are from Kant 2009.

18 On (dis)appropriation, see, for example, Lacoue-Labarthe 1986b, 67; 1998b, 233–234. Lacoue-Labarthe here relates (dis)appropriation to tragedy as well ("tragedy exposes (dis) appropriation")—tragedy being the (re)presentation of our mortal form or figure. The genealogy of homo mimeticus could benefit from a (re)thinking of the tragic, given its pathos and its relation to mimesis in Ancient Greece.

19 Malabou employs the term "caesura" to refer to the gaps or *écarts* between neurons, which the synapses join together in bridging a passage over. See Malabou 2008, 36. Malabou must certainly be aware of the importance of the term for Hölderlin, but one can but wonder whether she also knew its importance for Lacoue-Labarthe after him.

20 I am fully aware, of course, that this figuration demands further explication, exceeding the limits of this work. The provisional nature of this work, as an opening or a gesture, setting forth this figuration for further questioning regarding the relation between mimesis and plasticity in the genealogy of homo mimeticus is stressed here once more.

21 On "the Law of finitude," see Lacoue-Labarthe 1987, 67–71; 1990b, 43–45. Cf. Lacoue-Labarthe 1998c, 38–39, where Lacoue-Labarthe speaks of tragedy as "the very inscription of the Law" (my trans.), at once binding and exposing us, as mortals, to our finitude. This is a finitude which is ever fragmentary, opening upon the infinite ever refused to us (and thus the comparison which Lacoue-Labarthe makes here as well with what is disclosed in Kantian *critique*).

22 Because this is no "proper" name, and remains (necessarily) inadequate in its nomination, Lacoue-Labarthe will also speak of this as "arche-theatre" or "anterior theatre." See Lacoue-Labarthe 2002; 2019. See also Lacoue-Labarthe and Nancy 2013, 22–28.

23 "*Mime de rien*" being the title of Lacoue-Labarthe's presentation on January 28, 2006, at the conference "Déconstruction mimétique," which was devoted to his work and thought. This conference paper, "*Mime de rien*," remains unpublished. My thanks to Aristide Bianchi and Leonid Kharlamov for graciously providing me with the audio recording and transcription of Lacoue-Labarthe's presentation.

24 The determination, and critique, of onto-typology traverses the entirety of Lacoue-Labarthe's work. For some determinations and explorations of this concept, see Lacoue-Labarthe 1975, 180–190; 1998a, 54–63; and Lacoue-Labarthe and Nancy 2013, 24.

25 Cf. Malabou 2003, which is a response to Lacoue-Labarthe's *La Politique du poème* (2002) [*Heidegger and the Politics of Poetry* (2007)].

26 On the complexities of figuring a "scenic removal" in or *as* a scene, in the form of a primal scene in all its abyssal questionability, see Lacoue-Labarthe 2011; 2015.

27 "*Mime de rien*" (my trans.). Cf. Lacoue-Labarthe 2002, 130; 2019, 102, where Lacoue-Labarthe writes that "*Mimēsis* of *nothing* [...] is *play* [*le* jeu]."

28 In a recent article (Malabou 2023) reprinted in this volume, Malabou begins to formulate a genealogy of mimesis as thought otherwise than as "imitation," looking to Plato and Kant. She notes that this genealogy must be continued, but what she does not note is that La-

coue-Labarthe had been undertaking such a thought and work from at least the late 1970s onwards. Even should there be a mimetic agonism at work between the two thinkers, this *itself* remains something to be reflected upon and written about by Malabou in the pursuit of this genealogy.

Bibliography

Aristotle (1987). *The Poetics,* trans. Stephen Halliwell. London: Duckworth.
Bident, Christophe, and Pierre Vilar (eds.) (2003). *Maurice Blanchot: Récits critiques.* Tours: Farrago.
Blanchot, Maurice (1955). "Les Deux versions de l'imaginaire," in *L'Éspace litteraire.* Paris: Gallimard, 341–355.
Blanchot, Maurice (1973). *Le Pas au-delà.* Paris: Gallimard.
Blanchot, Maurice (1980). *L'Écriture du desastre.* Paris: Gallimard.
Blanchot, Maurice (1989). "The Two Versions of the Imaginary," in *The Space of Literature,* trans. Ann Smock. Lincoln, NE: University of Nebraska Press, 254–263.
Blanchot, Maurice (1992). *The Step Not Beyond,* trans. Lycette Nelson. Albany: State University of New York Press.
Blanchot, Maurice (1995). *The Writing of the Disaster,* trans. Ann Smock. Lincoln, NE: University of Nebraska Press.
Blanchot, Maurice (2005). *Thomas l'obscur: Première version, 1941.* Paris: Gallimard.
Hill, Leslie (2012). *Maurice Blanchot and Fragmentary Writing: A Change of Epoch.* London: Bloomsbury Continuum.
Hölderlin, Friedrich (1952). "Anmerkungen zum *Oedipus,*" in *Sämtliche Werke,* vol. 5, ed. Friedrich Beissner. Stuttgart: W. Kohlhammer Verlag, 195–202.
Hölderlin, Friedrich (2009). "Notes on the *Oedipus,*" in *Essays and Letters,* ed. and trans. Jeremy Adler and Charlie Louth. London: Penguin, 317–324.
Kant, Immanuel (2000). *Critique of the Power of Judgment,* trans. Paul Guyer and Eric Matthews, ed. Paul Guyer. Cambridge: Cambridge University Press.
Kant, Immanuel (2009). *Critique of Pure Reason,* trans. and eds. Paul Guyer and Allen W. Wood. Cambridge: Cambridge University Press.
Kirkkopelto, Esa (2008). *Le théâtre de l'expérience: Contributions à la théorie de la scène.* Paris: Presses de l'université Paris-Sorbonne.
Lacoue-Labarthe, Philippe (1975). "Typographie," in Sylviane Agacinski et al., *Mimesis: Des articulations.* Paris: Flammarion, 165–270.
Lacoue-Labarthe, Philippe (1979). "La scène est primative," in *Le Sujet de la philosophie: Typographies I.* Paris: Flammarion, 185–216.
Lacoue-Labarthe, Philippe (1986a). "Histoire et mimèsis," in *L'Imitation des modernes: Typographies II.* Paris: Galilée, 87–111.
Lacoue-Labarthe, Philippe (1986b). "La césure du spéculatif," in *L'Imitation des modernes: Typographies II.* Paris: Galilée, 39–69.
Lacoue-Labarthe, Philippe (1987). *La fiction du politique: Heidegger, l'art et la politique.* Paris: Christian Bourgois.
Lacoue-Labarthe, Philippe (1990a). "History and Mimesis," trans. Eduardo Cadava, in *Looking After Nietzsche,* ed. Lawrence A. Rickels. Albany: State University of New York Press, 209–231.

Lacoue-Labarthe, Philippe (1990b). *Heidegger, Art and Politics: The Fiction of the Political,* trans. Chris Turner. Oxford: Basil Blackwell.

Lacoue-Labarthe, Philippe (1993). "The Scene is Primal," trans. Karen McPherson, in *The Subject of Philosophy,* ed. Thomas Trezise. Minneapolis: University of Minnesota Press, 99–115.

Lacoue-Labarthe, Philippe (1998a). "Typography," in *Typography: Mimesis, Philosophy, Politics,* ed. Christopher Fynsk. Stanford: Stanford University Press, 43–138.

Lacoue-Labarthe, Philippe (1998b). "The Caesura of the Speculative," in *Typography: Mimesis, Philosophy, Politics,* ed. by Christopher Fynsk. Stanford: Stanford University Press, 208–235.

Lacoue-Labarthe, Philippe (1998c). "Métaphrasis," in *Métaphrasis, suivi de Le théâtre de Hölderlin.* Paris: Presses Universitaires de France, 7–42.

Lacoue-Labarthe, Philippe (2002). *Poétique de l'histoire.* Paris: Galilée.

Lacoue-Labarthe, Philippe (2006). *Mime de rien.* Unpublished conference paper. Originally presented on January 28, 2006, at the conference "Déconstruction mimétique."

Lacoue-Labarthe, Philippe (2008). "Bye bye farewell." *L'Animal* 19–20, 191–198.

Lacoue-Labarthe, Philippe (2011). "Agonie terminée, agonie interminable," in *Agonie terminée, agonie interminable: sur Maurice Blanchot,* eds. Aristide Bianchi and Leonid Kharlamov. Paris: Galilée, 131–151.

Lacoue-Labarthe, Philippe (2015). "Ending and Unending Agony," in *Ending and Unending Agony: On Maurice Blanchot,* trans. Hannes Opelz. New York: Fordham University Press, 71–82.

Lacoue-Labarthe, Philippe (2019). *Poetics of History: Rousseau and the Theatre of Originary Mimesis,* trans. Jeff Fort. New York: Fordham University Press.

Lacoue-Labarthe, Philippe and Jean-Luc Nancy (2013). "Scène," in *Scène, suivi de Dialogue sur le dialogue.* Paris: Christian Bourgois, 9–64.

Lawtoo, Nidesh (2017). "The Plasticity of Mimesis." *MLN* 132.5, 1201–1224.

Lawtoo, Nidesh (2022). *Homo Mimeticus: A New Theory of Imitation.* Leuven: Leuven University Press.

Malabou, Catherine (2003). "L'Insistance de la forme." *Poé&sie* 205, 154–159.

Malabou, Catherine (2008). *What Should We Do with Our Brain?,* trans. Sebastian Rand. New York: Fordham University Press.

Malabou, Catherine (2010). *Plasticity at the Dusk of Writing: Dialectics, Destruction, Deconstruction,* trans. Carolyn Shread. New York: Columbia University Press.

Malabou, Catherine (2023). "Epigenetic Mimesis: Natural Brains and Synaptic Chips," in *Life in the Posthuman Condition: Critical Responses to the Anthropocene,* eds. S. E. Wilmer and Audronė Žukauskaitė. Edinburgh: Edinburgh University Press, 280–288.

Malabou, Catherine, and Hannes Opelz (2022). "L'Avenir de la mimesis: Entretien avec Catherine Malabou." *MLN* 137.4, 801–813.

Nietzsche, Friedrich (1999). "On Truth and Lying in a Non-Moral Sense," trans. Ronald Spiers, in *The Birth of Tragedy and Other Writings,* eds. Raymond Geuss and Ronald Spiers. Cambridge: Cambridge University Press, 139–153.

CHAPTER 7

EROTICISM, GENDER AND THE POSSIBILITY FOR TRANSFORMATION
With and Beyond Merleau-Ponty

Ida Djursaa

In recent years, the field of mimetic studies has staged an impressive reconceptualization of the old concept of mimesis. No longer designating the "bad" copy of an original, this concept has come to refer to a creative process through which the subject forms, reinvents or reinterprets itself through a certain kind of mimicry that is not reducible to a mere copying, and that does not have an absolute point of origin. In this sense, the mimetic conceptualization of the subject, or homo mimeticus, describes the subject as fundamentally open, embodied and malleable, rather than sovereign.[1] As the present volume makes clear, and as we shall see in more detail below, this new notion of mimesis shares an affinity with Catherine Malabou's concept of plasticity, broadly designating the capacity to both give and receive form at the same time (2008, 5).[2] This dual capacity means that the subject thus reconceived is characterized at once by a vulnerability to being shaped, for better or worse, *and* by a certain creativity to shaping oneself in return. How might a phenomenological perspective contribute to this conceptualization of the mimetic/plastic subject? In what follows, I will argue that a certain notion of sensibility which is operative in Merleau-Ponty's phenomenology is productive for further developing the mimetic conceptualization of the human at the level of the body, whilst at the same time providing the ground for understanding the lived dimension of what it means to be a mimetic/plastic body. To show how this is the case, this chapter draws on insights from critical phenomenology,[3] feminist philosophy and mimetic studies to analyze the social and political structuring of the *erotic* dimension of bodily life through the notion of sensibility that is operative in Merleau-Ponty's work.

For although Merleau-Ponty argues in *Phenomenology of Perception* that perception is the primary way in which we come to "know" the world, throughout the book he inadvertently challenges this claim when he points towards a dimension of bodily life that operates prior to perception: "Sensing is this living communication with the world that makes it present to us as the familiar place of our life. The perceived object and the perceiving subject owe their thickness to sensing" (2012, 53). While perception presupposes a tacit distinction between perceived object and perceiving subject, the sensory life of the body operates prior to the differentiation into subject and object.[4] As such, as is increasingly recognized in the literature, a notion of sensibility is operative, even if never explicitly developed, in Merleau-Ponty's work (Al-Saji 2008; Sparrow 2015, 68–109). This notion describes the material and imperceptible interaction of my body with the world insofar as my body is *of* the world.

As we shall see, it is at the level of sensibility that the body is fundamentally vulnerable to the world and others, yet also capable of responding to this world and these others. Here, Malabou's notion of plasticity provides a helpful conceptual framework for understanding the temporality of this dynamic of reception and response. In *What Should We Do with Our Brain?* she defines plasticity as the capacity to at once give and receive form (2008, 5). In the context of the body, this means that the body is not merely a passive receptor for stimuli, yet neither is it a sovereign power. Rather, the notion that the body is plastic means that it is open to being shaped by the world and others, yet also capable of responding to this world and these others, and of shaping itself in the process. To say that the body is plastic is thus to say that it is, in Malabou's words, "modifiable, 'formable,' and formative at the same time" (5). While Malabou conceptualizes the plasticity of the body mainly in relation to the brain, we can extend this concept to describe the ways in which the whole body forms itself through its pre-reflective interaction with the world and others. We know, for instance, that a key part of infant development consists in the pre-conscious imitation of the facial expressions of others.[5] This kind of imitation operates precisely according to a "plastic" logic, where the imitation is not reducible to a passive reception of form, yet neither is it a pure invention *ex nihilo*. This kind of imitation thus breaks with any binary logic of activity/passivity, subject/object. When repeated over time, these imitations sediment into a habitual style, posture, or form of expression, which is itself open to change and transformation.

This plasticity of the body can thus also be described in terms of mimesis, where mimesis should not be conceived as it is commonly understood, as the mere copy of some original or more "proper" thing. Rather, the rethinking of the concept of mimesis as advanced by mimetic studies breaks with the very notion of the "original" insofar as it describes the human subject, or homo mimeticus, as *constitutively* relational, embodied and malleable. The concept of "mimetic pathos" central to mimetic studies helps us analyze this situation at a specifically bodily level. Mimetic pathos broadly designates the way in which the subject/body, far from being a self-contained entity, is constitutively open and drawn to others and the world, and how, as Verkerk explains, this "affective force seduces one towards imitation and, in doing so, is aptly defined as mimetic" (2023, 118). But if the notions of sensibility and mimetic pathos thus have ontological implications for how we think about the body, they also carry ambiguous political implications. On the one hand, the mimetic conceptualization of the body means that it is susceptible to being shaped in restrictive ways through the interaction with oppressive norms and structures. But on the other hand, as we shall see, it is through a certain critical employment of the sensibility of the body itself that transformation might be possible. How, then, might we conceptualize this mimetic malleability of the body in relation to eroticism? How do (human) bodies respond to, imitate or, in Merleau-Ponty's words, "take up" the world in which they are situated, and how does such bodily taking up in turn form the erotic lives of bodies, their capacity for pleasure and abandonment? Finally, given the plastic capacity not only to be shaped but also to shape oneself, how might bodies step into this process of structuring, and perhaps structure it otherwise?

I address these questions in four parts. First, I bring together two chapters from *Phenomenology of Perception*, that on "Sensing" and that on "The Body as a Sexed Being." Reading each chapter through the other, I argue that Merleau-Ponty's analyses of the erotic should be understood to operate at the level of sensibility rather than consciousness or perception.[6] Second, in dialogue with Beauvoir, I argue that an erotic encounter allows for a suspension of gender-normative ways of moving and desiring, and that this suspension harbors a generative potential for transformation. In the third and fourth sections, I draw on the feminist literature and the novel field of social neuroendocrinology to investigate how patriarchal structures of gender- and heteronormativity are taken up by bodies in a mimetic movement of appropriation, and how this taking up, in turn, shapes the degree to which bodies are capable of the kind of abandon required for the erotic encounter to be empowering. Finally, I draw on Malabou's notion of explosive plasticity to suggest how bodies might capitalize on their own malleability in a move towards erotic emancipation.

Sensibility and Eroticism in *Phenomenology of Perception*

What is the specific meaning of sensibility that we find in Merleau-Ponty? Although he does not explicitly develop this concept, it receives its most sustained analysis in the chapter on "Sensing" in *Phenomenology of Perception*. Here, he describes the way in which the body is fundamentally open and sensitive to the world: "In short, my body is not merely one object among all others, not a complex of sensible qualities among others. It is an object sensitive [*sensible*] to all others, which resonates for all sounds, vibrates for all colors" (2012, 245). The notion of sensibility thus describes the way in which the body imitatively responds to, "resonates" with or is solicited by the world prior to any perceptual objectification of this world, such as when we are pre-reflectively drawn towards a certain color, shape or smell.[7] Indeed, whilst perception, as Sparrow writes, "is constantly striving to pull objects out of their ambiguous presence and into workable relief from their background" (2015, 112), the sensory life of the body operates prior to the subject–object distinction. In this sense, the notion of sensibility does not describe the experience *of* something but rather, as Merleau-Ponty notes, "a non-thetic, pre-objective, and preconscious experience" (2012, 252) of *being* a body in the world. What, then, is the relation between this notion of sensibility, on the one hand, and that of eroticism, on the other?

To answer this question, we turn to the chapter on "The Body as a Sexed Being," in which Merleau-Ponty analyzes the sexual and erotic dimensions of bodily life. He rejects both a physiological definition of sexuality that reduces it to anatomical reflexes and a psychological one that reduces it to mental representations. Instead, he formulates a phenomenological notion of sexuality as intrinsically bound up with existence (2012, 179). Indeed, he describes sexuality as "an intentionality that follows the general movement of existence and that weakens along with it" (159). It is an "odor" or an "atmosphere" which is "coextensive with life" (172). Although Merleau-Ponty uses the word "sexuality" to describe this aspect of bodily life, I will argue that it is more properly understood in terms of eroticism. Whilst the term "sexuality" commonly refers to the identification and categorization of sexual identities or orientations, eroticism operates at a pre-reflective level of bodily existence, which is not reducible to sexuality or even the "sexual." Following Audre Lorde, eroticism should be understood as a zest for life, an opening to the world, to oneself and to others, a capacity for joy, for friendship, for the pursuit of knowledge, of pleasure (Lorde 2019). As such, we shall see that there is an eroticism of sensibility itself, and that the notion of sensible eroticism describes an existential structure of the human subject/body, understood as homo mimeticus, insofar as it belongs fundamentally to her to be drawn towards others and the world in different ways.

Merleau-Ponty demonstrates this oscillation of existence and eroticism through the case of Johann Schneider, a war veteran injured by a piece of shrapnel to the occipital region of his brain. Throughout the book, Merleau-Ponty analyzes, through Goldstein and Gelb's psychological examinations of Schneider, the different ways in which his injury has affectively "flattened" almost all aspects of his existence. We hear how he cannot perform abstract movements, such as touching his nose or reaching his arm out, that do not have a concrete aim other than the movement itself. We hear how his attempts to make new friends almost always fail because he has lost the ability to spontaneously interact with others, thus conferring on his movements and engagements a forced deliberateness. In his sexual life, too, he is above all disinterested: he never takes any sexual initiative, he does not kiss and does not find other bodies sexually attractive. In fact, Merleau-Ponty writes, "the very word 'satisfaction' no longer means anything to him" (2012, 159). Merleau-Ponty argues that Schneider's erotic disinterestedness is not the effect of a physiological or psychological defect but is the expression, rather, of an alteration of "the very structure of erotic perception or experience" (158).

Erotic perception differs from objective perception, which turns that which it perceives into an object. Rather than this objectifying function, Merleau-Ponty writes, "erotic perception is not a *cogitatio* that intends a *cogitatum*; through one body it aims at another body, and it is accomplished in the world, not within consciousness" (2012, 159). The objective perception through which we perceive delineated objects, then, is inhabited by an imperceptible erotic rhythm of attraction and repulsion (158). The "abnormality" of the case of Schneider then reveals the "normal" operation of eroticism which we, in the natural attitude, take for granted. For "normal" bodies, erotic perception responds to an erotic "pull" from the world or other bodies prior to any perceptual objectification of this world or these bodies. Erotic perception thus operates at the level of pre-objective sensibility, and Schneider's problem is precisely that he is confined to perceiving other bodies as abstracted from any affective, let alone specifically sexual, "pull."

What determines the desire for engaging in erotic encounters is, for Merleau-Ponty, something like the desire for life itself. Eroticism, he writes, is bound up with "an 'intentional arc' that weakens for the patient and that for the normal subject gives experience its degree of vitality and fecundity" (2012, 160). Erotic life is thus the behavioral expression or dramatization of this life force; it designates the way in which the body takes up the givens of a situation, such as another body, and transforms it into something desirable. In this transformation, however, sexuality "as such" necessarily escapes its own manifestation: "Sexuality hides from itself under a mask of generality, it ceaselessly attempts to escape from the tension and the drama that it institutes" (171). Just as the desire for life expresses itself in the sexual, "sexuality" dissolves into certain behaviors, moods and attitudes that lose their specifically "sexual" sense along the way. Merleau-Ponty's insistence upon the intertwinement of sexuality and existence thus breaks with any notion of a "natural" or fixed essence of sexuality; sexuality cannot be defined once and for all but unfolds and changes in interaction with the existential situation of the body/subject in question.

Yet despite his existentialist conceptualization of sexuality, much feminist literature has critiqued Merleau-Ponty on the basis that he advances a heteronormative conceptualization of desire insofar as he does not address concrete forms of sexual identities that exist.[8] Responding to this critique, Gavin Rae emphasizes the pre-objective structure of erotic perception, which operates prior to, and as generative of, the reflective categorization into sexual identities. Rather than starting from such sexual identities, Rae writes:

> Merleau-Ponty affirms the anonymity of the sexual schema to suspend the conceptual schemas of reflectivity to avoid prejudging the pre-reflective lived body and, indeed, let the latter reveal itself as it is not as how we may wish it to be. (2020, 174)

It is not that eroticism operates at some valueless stage, but rather that the categorization into sexual identities is the result of the reflection upon anonymous, pre-reflective, fluid bodily "schemas" or "rhythms," which draw us towards some bodies and not others. To say that these rhythms are "anonymous" or "pre-personal" does not mean that they are ahistorical, but rather that they operate at a pre-reflective level and thus are not the effectuation of a conscious "I."

As Merleau-Ponty explains in relation to the body schema, but equally applicable to the sexual schemas analyzed here, over time and upon repetition, these rhythms congeal into sedimented habits, identities, or "styles" of moving and desiring (2012, 143–148). These rhythms thus operate at a generative level at which what comes to be defined as a particular sexual identity is continuously *produced*. To say that sexual identities are continuously formed through pre-reflective bodily rhythms or schemas is thus to say that sexual identities, while appearing stable, are themselves open to change and transformation.[9] Further developing Rae's response to the feminist critique, then, we can say that Merleau-Ponty's analysis, when read as operating at the level of sensible eroticism, precisely *allows for* a conceptualization of the continuous becoming of different sexual identities and orientations, even if he does not address specific sexual identities that exist.

Rather than making a universalist claim about desire, then, his phenomenology in fact provides a productive conceptual framework for considering the pre-perceptual, pre-objective level at which eroticism operates. Indeed, insofar as the "visible body" is underpinned by a "secret" sexual schema, Merleau-Ponty implies (2012, 158) that the visual perception of another body does not by itself generate desire: Schneider is perfectly capable of seeing other bodies, but they do not express or mean anything to him. The visible contains, as its own immanent excess, an erotic pull, which is "suggested" to the pre-objective erotic perception of another body, and the "erotic 'comprehension'" (159) at work here transcends any consciousness or perception of it.

Just as Merleau-Ponty, in the chapter on sexuality, argues that "desire comprehends blindly by linking one body to another" (2012, 159), in the chapter on "Sensing" he writes that "the term that [sensation] intends is only recognized blindly through the familiarity of my body with it" (221). The linking of bodies in erotic perception is thus a "blind" process, which implies a strange temporality; in order for my body to have an erotic encounter, it must adopt a specific erotic attitude, which it paradoxically "receives" from another body. This is a mimetic movement of attraction and repulsion which does not have an absolute point of origin but is only maintained in the movement itself. The erotic attitude, then, cannot be willed or forced, for this is precisely what makes sexuality a problem for Schneider. He can *only* will himself to engage in an erotic situation in which he quickly loses interest. While Schneider's case thus helped uncover the notion of a sensible eroticism which belongs to all human bodies, the following section turns to some recent accounts of desire to investigate the transformative potential of, as well as the risk involved in, erotic encounters.

Erotic Encounters: The Need for Abandon

I have argued that eroticism operates at the level of pre-reflective and pre-perceptual sensibility. As such, it describes a *bodily* (rather than conscious) experience. This conceptualization of eroticism thus allows us to understand how an erotic encounter, in Beauvoir's words, "demands total abandon" (2011, 422) to *being* a body if the encounter is to be pleasurable, empowering or transformative. The paradox is that pleasure and empowerment require a certain passivity, a daring to give oneself over to one's desire, to one's body, and to the other. Indeed, it requires precisely a *mimetic pathos* through which one allows oneself to be pulled towards the other without yet merging into one. Turning to some recent autobiographical writings serves to further illuminate what is meant by an erotic encounter proper.

In her recent memoir, the US writer and academic Melissa Febos describes how, after decades of troubling, unpleasurable sexual relations inhibited by anxieties about looking, moving, desiring in too "masculine" a way, she found true pleasure with one partner:

> Our sex does not feel like an exchange of power, but like a natural event that can only occur when both of us stop thinking of ourselves and trust our bodies completely. No one plays the boy, because no one *plays* anything. It can't happen unless we trust that we'll be loved at our most animal. (2021, 127–128)

It was only once Febos shifted the balance from being governed by the culturally mediated perception of her own body as being too "masculine" to a trust in her style of moving, feeling, desiring, that she could give herself over to the erotic relation, trusting that her body and her desire would not be ridiculed, rejected or violated. British writer and academic Katherine Angel writes similarly about her erotic experience with one partner: "I have sunk down into my self, into my desire. I have become a body" (2014, 42). These descriptions thus highlight the erotic encounter as a mimetic play of bodies without any reification into the roles of subject or object, "masculine" or "feminine." As such, they describe the erotic encounter as a bodily response to the other, yet one that is not unilaterally governed by normative categorizations and expectations.

The pleasure described by these authors thus requires that one abandon oneself to *being* a body prior to any reification into subject and object, "masculine" and "feminine."[10] Yet to say that the erotic encounter operates prior to the rigidification into binary categories or identities is not to say that it operates in a utopian realm completely detached from gender. Rather, an erotic encounter operates at a *generative* level of bodily life that has the capacity to momentarily suspend, and thus inadvertently expose, the restrictive force that binary gender norms otherwise impose upon bodies. Through this suspension, the apparent "naturalness" of any rigid categories or norms is revealed *as apparent*. We saw above that the "abnormal" case of Schneider's affective flattening exposes the eroticism that is a basic structure of "normal" bodily life, but which is, in the natural attitude, taken for granted and thus not noticed. Conversely, the erotic encounter suspends the gender norms that are usually taken for granted as "normal" or even "natural" and reveal these as not necessarily "normal" or "natural" at all.[11] The erotic thus describes a *generative* level insofar as this momentary suspension opens the possibility for living out other kinds of desire that do not necessarily conform to the normative prescriptions of how genders ought to desire, move, touch, feel. The freeing up of rigid norms through the abandonment to *being* a body thus opens the possibility for what we might call emancipatory plasticity, which will be explored in more detail in the final section of this chapter.

Whilst the openness of bodies is thus the condition for pleasure to be experienced in giving oneself over to *being* a body, it is precisely this openness that makes bodies at once capable of intimacy and susceptible to violence.[12] Merleau-Ponty points towards this risk of violence at the end of the chapter on sexuality, as he invokes a Sartrean understanding of desire as stuck in the alternative between the objectification of the other and the objectification of oneself (Merleau-Ponty 2012, 170; Sartre 2003, 364–378; 393–412). This understanding of desire as *essentially* objectifying contradicts Merleau-Ponty's previous analyses of the ways in which erotic perception works prior to any objectification. There is, then, an effective ambiguity in "The Body as a Sexed Being" between, on the one hand, an understanding of eroticism as a modality of pre-objective sensibility, and, on the other, an understanding of sexual desire as inherently objectifying. In this latter conception, there would be no possibility for an empowering egalitarian erotic encounter. But whilst Sartre conceives this objectifying relation as essentially descriptive of eroticism, Merleau-Ponty's evocation of Sartre, given its contrast with the rest of the chapter, should be read as emphasizing one potential outcome of the erotic encounter. The ambiguity in the chapter on sexuality thus helps illuminate the ambiguity of the mimetic pathos through which bodies are drawn to one another and the world. As we have seen, this mimetic pathos opens the possibility for pleasure and transformation, yet at the same time, it is this same mimetic pathos which renders the body susceptible to violence. Rather than rejecting Merleau-Ponty's analysis of eroticism because of this ambiguity, then, it should be emphasized to better understand the risk involved in any erotic encounter.

Indeed, bodies abandoning themselves to their sensibility always do so at the risk of the kind of objectification Merleau-Ponty mentions. Given that women in patriarchal society are at higher risk of objectification and violence than men, however, it is not surprising that many women under patriarchy, as we shall see in more detail in the final section, may find it more difficult to give in to their bodies, to their desire. Indeed, the difficulty of finding the balance between *being* a body without being *objectified* is, as Beauvoir writes, not universal in degree: insofar as woman is already Other, "she has to reconquer her dignity as transcendent and free subject while assuming her carnal condition: this is a delicate and risky enterprise that often fails" (2011, 427). As I have argued, an erotic encounter is not unilaterally governed by structures of domination, objectification, or received ideas and norms prescribing how bodies should and should not move, look or feel. However, as we will see in the final section, this is not to say that these norms do not, to a large extent, structure the degree to which bodies are *capable* of the kind of abandonment needed for the erotic encounter to be empowering.[13]

The Taking Up of Existence and the Shaping of Bodies: Merleau-Ponty and Beyond

Before we turn, in the fourth section, to the political structuring of the capacity for abandon required for an erotic encounter, this section employs Merleau-Ponty's formulation of the "taking up" of existence (2012, 173) to analyze the ways in which the plastic/mimetic body shapes itself in interaction with specific social and political contexts. What does it mean to say that the body "takes up" existence? Whilst this term has a moral sense in the existentialist philosophies of Sartre and Beauvoir, Merleau-Ponty employs it in an ontological sense. In the *Phenomenology*, this term describes the process through which the body transforms the givens of its existence into its own meaningful core, its own "essence": "My body is this meaningful core that behaves as a general function and that nevertheless exists and that is susceptible to illness. In the body we learn to recognize this knotting together of essence and existence" (148). As we shall see, the body forms itself through the taking up of existence, yet insofar as the body is anchored in the world, the way in which it forms itself is structured by its material, social and historical situation. This creativity of the body is thus not the activity of a sovereign subject, yet neither is it a passive reception of form. Rather, as we shall see, this shaping operates precisely according to the plastic or mimetic logic described above.

Merleau-Ponty analyzes this bodily taking up of existence through the case of a young girl who, after having been forbidden from seeing her lover, develops aphonia and anorexia. He describes the movement through which her body "translates" the prohibition of her desire into aphonia through an analogy to sleep (2012, 166–167; compare 219). He argues that just as falling asleep is neither a question of willfully "choosing" to sleep nor of being forcefully put to sleep, aphonia is neither a question of choosing not to speak despite being capable of doing so, nor is it explained by purely physiological or mechanical reasons: "the young woman never *stops* speaking; rather, she 'loses' her voice as one loses a memory" (164). The memory and the voice have not been destroyed but lie dormant, just as active consciousness does when we sleep. One is withdrawn into one's body, which is, at the same time, an inescapable anchor to the world.

It is not the case, then, that the girl makes a choice to give up speaking and eating, but that her body takes up the givens of her existence at the time—that of having had her desire denied her—and translates this into the painful meaning it has for her. Ultimately this meaning is that of the refusal of others through the impossibility of speaking and that of life itself through the literal impossibility of eating: "The patient is literally unable 'to swallow' the prohibition that has been imposed upon her" (Merleau-Ponty 2012, 163). Unable to "digest" the world, she retreats into herself, into her body, as when one retreats to sleep to escape an overwhelming sadness. Whilst Merleau-Ponty's description of the ways in which social situations translate into bodily attitudes is phenomenologically orientated, much scientific research spanning the last thirty years supports his analyses. In *The Physiology of Sexist and Racist Oppression*, Shannon Sullivan cites a 1990 study, which found that almost half of all women with chronic gastrointestinal problems have experienced childhood sexual abuse, and that irritable bowel syndrome (IBS) disproportionally affects women in a two-to-one ratio (Drossman et al. 1990; Sullivan 2015, 70). From this, Sullivan concludes:

> [W]omen's guts often have difficulty digesting and absorbing components of a sexist world that tends to be hostile to them, and this difficulty

is as much a biological matter as it is a psychological one. "Digestion" and "absorption" are not metaphors in this claim. (2015, 71–72)

These facts and analyses suggest that the movement through which bodies take up "sexual" elements—such as sexual violence or the prohibition of desire—and translate these into something that has existential significance (IBS, aphonia or anorexia imply a refusal of the world through the refusal of food or a refusal of others through the refusal to speak) happens not only at a cognitive but also at a bodily level. These bodies, then, turn inwards in a protective or defiant posture, a refusal of others and the world so as not to have to suffer the prohibition or the assault again.

This is, then, an attempt to break free from the mimetic pathos which fundamentally links the body to the world and others. But this protective bodily attitude is not only a shield against others; it is at the same time felt as painful or restrictive for the body itself. Insofar as the gut rejects the world through which it is inevitably and continuously constituted, this is a contradictory bodily attitude in which the body is at once, qua body, open to and dependent on its world and others, and at the same time closed off from it. The body's attempt to refuse the mimetic pathos which binds it to the world and others is thus at the same time a refusal or an inhibition of itself, a closing off from itself, too. These cases thus serve to illustrate the plastic logic through which the body at once receives and gives form to itself. Indeed, the body, in these cases, is not unilaterally formed by some external force in the way that a piece of clay may be molded by a human hand, or in the way that a limb may be cut off. Rather, these cases show how the body responds creatively to a situation and shapes itself in the process, even if this shaping does not necessarily further its freedom. However, as we shall see, it is precisely *because* the body is not simply a passive receptor of form but rather creates its own responses, that it might be possible to step into this process of structuring and structure it otherwise. For now, let us note that these movements of bodily translation are cases of the body shaping itself in a protective response to an outside hostility. How, then, does the taking up of existence operate in an appropriative response to historical structures such as patriarchy and heteronormativity?[14]

In *Gender Trouble*, Butler famously argues that gender is performative, that is, that gender norms are reiterated and perpetuated through the ways in which bodies "take up," repeat, or in a certain sense "imitate" these norms in their acts, gestures and styles of moving and desiring.[15] These norms, which do not have existence in themselves outside of their bodily repetition and their discursive institutionalization, sediment in bodily postures and take on the appearance of being "natural" or "substantial" (Butler 2007, 45). The concept of gender performativity thus accounts for the fact that the habits and postures that bodies develop come not only from the actual meetings with other bodies "in the flesh," but also from historical and cultural frameworks. But how, exactly, do normative ideas about how bodies should move come to structure how bodies actually move? We know, of course, that children take on an idiosyncratic style of moving by imitating their parents and close relations. This kind of imitation can explain how children often come to adopt an uncannily similar air of moving to that of their close relations. Yet it does not by itself explain how bodies take on a gender-specific style of moving that transcends concrete relations between bodies and that are not strictly idiosyncratic but are generally shared by bodies of the same gender.

We might then say that the bodies one imitates embody not only an idiosyncratic style of moving but also a historically specific commonality, a certain ideality. In this way, the sensibility through which the mimetic body develops a habitual style or posture is not "merely" material, but contains, as its own immanent excess, a certain ideality that is "embodied" (though not in an exhaustive way). The notion of an embodied ideality explains how normative structures that do not, strictly speaking, have bodily existence, are continuously taken up, imitated and appropriated by bodies, and thus how the material and the symbolic come together in the body itself.[16] This notion of an embodied ideality thus confers a historical and political density onto the mimetic conceptualization of the subject/body, the implications of which we shall investigate more specifically in relation to eroticism in the final section.

The (Un)Freedom of Desire and the Possibility for Transformation

Now that we have established a conceptual framework for understanding how the body shapes itself through the taking up of socially and culturally specific situations and norms, we are able to ask how gender- and heteronormativity impacts, structures or inhibits the *erotic* lives of bodies. I will address this question through a critical investigation into what is widely accepted as the most common sexual "problem" reported by women partnered with men, namely a lack of or a low level of desire to engage in erotic encounters.[17] Contra the common conception in popular and scientific discourse that at once reflects and reinforces the normative idea that female sexual desire is naturally low,[18] I will argue that the ways in which the contexts of patriarchy and heteronormativity are taken up at the level of sensibility come to shape the eroticism of women's bodies in often negative ways. Yet, at the same time, as we shall see, it is through the very structure of sensible eroticism itself that transformation might be possible.

While I am interested in the ways in which desire is lived at the level of the body, I do not rely on the kind of scientific approach which seeks to explain desire through an essentialist conceptualization of the biological body.[19] Continued attempts to "measure" sexual arousal through devices such as vaginal plethysmographs bear witness to a positivism, which considers measurable dimensions of the biological body as one-to-one representations of sexual desire, where such measurements do not necessarily reflect the degree of desire or arousal actually experienced.[20] Furthermore, as Angel argues, the measurement of arousal in a clinical setting removed from the everyday lives of bodies risks neglecting the contextual shaping of physiology itself (2021, 82). But while the body, as Angel argues, "is no arbiter, should be no arbiter" (83), for sexual desire, this does not preclude, as I will argue, a non-essentialist approach to desire such as it is lived at the level of the body. Rather than a positivist approach, I will argue that sexual desire is better investigated through an existential phenomenological approach which, rather than attempting to objectively "determine" or "define" the "causes" for a high or low sexual desire, conceptualizes eroticism in relation to the concrete existential situation and the ways in which bodies *live* desire.

Within a critical phenomenological framework, then, a lack of or a low level of desire should be understood as the bodily closing off from the mimetic pathos involved in erotic encounters, a certain erotic disinterestedness. Whilst low desire is not a problem in itself, and while it may reflect anxieties about pain or an unsatisfactory level of pleasure experienced if sex does happen, might this erotic disinterestedness reflect something more than the context of the relationship? An interdisciplinary team of researchers working in fields spanning neuroscience, gender studies, psychology, public health and gynecology recently argued that "low desire in women partnered with men may not be a problem itself [but] instead reflects one—namely, heteronormativity" (van Anders et al. 2022, 398). The authors list four historically specific areas which prove unconducive to the elicitation of female sexual desire, these being "inequitable gendered divisions of household labor, having to be a partner's mother, the objectification of women, and gender norms surrounding sexual initiation" (398). I will investigate one of these, namely the maternal gender role many women take on in relation to their male partners, focusing ultimately on the ways in which it plays out at a bodily level.

Women have historically invested a disproportionate amount of nonsexual erotic energy into the emotional and physical well-being of others (children, the elderly), resulting in a de-prioritization of their own desire or well-being. This is arguably still true; women in heterosexual relationships still take on a disproportionate amount of childcare, housework and emotional labor, and it often falls on them to remind their partners of social gatherings, resulting in women often taking on a maternal role in relation to their male partners (see van Anders et al. 2022, 400). It is not, of course, that the maternal body is de-eroticized but that the relationship between mother and child is not one of sexual desire. If women take on a parental role in relation to their male partners in their everyday lives, this can translate into their sexual relations, too, reflecting the normative idea that it is women's responsibility to satisfy their male partners' need for sex. In a psychological study into low levels of desire on the part of women in heterosexual relationships, the authors asked the participants why they would sometimes engage in sex despite not desiring it:

> When asked whether she ever said no to her husband's "throwing himself at her," Madge commented that if she did: "we have a sulk and he's tossing and turning all night and y'know, it's not worth it to be honest." (Hayfield and Clarke 2012, 72)

The very way in which Madge talks about having to satisfy her partner's need is suggestive of the way in which a parent would give in to a child to avoid the child kicking up a fuss, which would be worse than giving in to their desires in the first place.

For many women, then, sex becomes an obligation rather than something joyfully engaged in. Caring for one another is essential in a relationship and sometimes involves sacrifice and compromise. But when women engage in sex despite their lack of desire, they do it for the sake of their partners or the relationship, not for the sake of their own pleasure. This, then, takes the form, not of an erotic encounter at all, but of a one-way provision of satisfaction. Whilst women in heterosexual relationships are generally happy to be nonsexually intimate with their partners as they would with their child, sex often becomes another duty women feel obliged to engage in, thus adding to the general stress of being a woman in patriarchal society. How might we comprehend the level at which this resistance to, or disinterest in, erotic sex develops? Is it purely psychological or cognitive or does it also translate at the level of the body?

Whilst an essentialist approach to the biological body cannot, qua essentialist, account for the cultural shaping of the body, the novel field of social neuroendocrinology, which investigates the interaction between hormones and social behavior, can perhaps shed a light on the social malleability of physiology itself. The general situation of being a woman in patriarchal society is often characterized by stress and anxiety about living up to contradictory ideals and having to negotiate the threat of sexual violence and objectification. Whilst stress usually has negative connotations, its clinical definition describes it as "a value-neutral process whereby bodies respond to changes in the internal or external environment" (van Anders et al. 2022, 403). Sexual arousal is an acute stressor, which increases the level of cortisol released from the adrenal gland, and which is usually associated with pleasure. A chronically stressed body, however, means chronically high levels of cortisol, which leads the adrenal glands to shut down from overstimulation. The chronically stressed body, then, no longer responds to acute stressors, of which sexual arousal is one. While chronic stress negatively impacts sexual desire in bodies of all sexes and genders, given that women report disproportionately higher levels of stress and anxiety compared to men (Remes et al. 2016), van Anders et al. suggest that the stress associated with living in patriarchal society might contribute to the low desire many women experience (2022, 404).

While the degree to which bodies are capable of the kind of abandon required for erotic encounters is surely influenced by psychological factors, then, social neuroendocrinology shows that this resistance to abandon also develops at the level of physiology. The closing off from the mimetic pathos involved in erotic encounters, then, is not merely a cognitive or psychic resistance, but arguably also a bodily resistance which is *lived* at the level of sensibility. While I cannot feel my hormones fluctuating, my body nonetheless senses whether it is stressed and wants to be left alone, or whether it is curious and open to being touched and moved by its own or the other's desire. Not unlike Schneider, for whom "tactile stimuli themselves, which the patient adeptly uses elsewhere, have lost their sexual signification [...] because they have, so to speak, ceased speaking to his body" (Merleau-Ponty 2012, 159), the sexual advances by a (male) partner, for many women, no longer speak to their body. Their erotic energy is instead channeled into caring responsibilities or shuts off due to the stress of navigating the contradictory ideals imposed by patriarchal society so that there is little, if any, left for the seeking of sexual pleasure. Consequently, a partner's advance is felt as an intrusion rather than an invitation to mutual pleasure. Recoiling from an otherwise beloved partner's touch, then, is not only a psychical but also a sensible response, a bodily resistance to being moved by the other. As such, it can be described in terms of a patriarchal pathology through which the body attempts to refuse the mimetic pathos which, as we saw previously, implies not simply a susceptibility to violence but also a transformative potential.[21]

If, as Angel writes, "context is everything" (2021, 56) in the elicitation of sexual desire, then, it is not the case that women have a "naturally" lower level of desire, but that the contexts of patriarchy and heteronormativity are generally not conducive to the elicitation of female desire. One of the ways in which women's bodies take up their existential situation thus translates into an erotic indifference similar but not reducible to Schneider's affective flattening, thus casting woman, as Beauvoir teaches us, as "Other," yet not only as other to man but as other to the erotic itself. But if, as I have argued, patriarchal structures are to a certain extent taken up and perpetuated at a bodily level, is there something bodies can do to step into this process of structuring? It is important at this point to note the difference between plasticity and flexibility. Malabou writes that flexibility designates infinite malleability, the capacity to bend in all directions without breaking: "To be flexible is to receive a form or impression, to be able to fold oneself, to take the fold, not to give it. To be docile, to not explode" (2008, 12). In contrast to flexibility, Malabou explains, a plastic body harbors within itself its own resistance to being shaped, ultimately manifested in the capacity to explode, to break the habitual form, and thus to open another future. How might bodies capitalize on this capacity for resistance in a move towards erotic emancipation?

I ask this question not to encourage women to "work" on their desire. Certainly, if it is the case that women are generally more stressed and that this inhibits their sexual desire on a physiological level, "working" to desire more will only add to the stress women already experience, thus only inhibiting desire more. Thus, it seems, women will not desire "more" until gender dynamics and societal structures become more egalitarian (which may, in turn, result in men desiring a bit less). Desiring more is not and should not be an aim in itself, yet the contradictory bodily posture many women unknowingly adopt surely deprives them of a certain enjoyment and pleasure, not only in their sexual relations, but in other areas of their lives. Perhaps it is not so much a case of striving to desire more but of desiring differently; the opening up of other ways of desiring is, perhaps, connected with the desire for and curiosity about life itself. Daring, in other nonsexual areas of life, to be vulnerable, to lose control or to "explode" a little may allow the erotic energy that essentially binds bodies to the world and other bodies to form new, unexpected and non-conforming ways of desiring.[22] This vision of erotic liberation would be compatible, I think, with Malabou's characterization of the clitoris—understood literally and symbolically as the embodiment of feminine pleasure—as an anarchist that *"relates to power* but is not a *power relation"* (2022, 119), and hence her call for a feminism that challenges the a priori status of power and domination. Daring to *be* a body without judgment, a need to control or fear, may elicit new forms of erotic desire and a reopening to others and oneself.

Conclusion

This chapter has developed the notion of a sensible eroticism which, I argued, is operative in Merleau-Ponty's work, even if it is never explicitly developed. Insofar as this notion of a sensible eroticism designates the material openness, malleability and binding of bodies and the world, it strengthens the mimetic conceptualization of the human subject, or homo mimeticus, at the level of the body. But the aim of this chapter was not only to uncover eroticism as an existential structure of the mimetic subject/body, but also to analyze the ways in which the contexts of patriarchy and heteronormativity impact the degree to which this sensible eroticism is enabled to flourish. Reading Merleau-Ponty's notion of the taking up of existence as a mimetic process through which the body forms itself in response to its situation helped us understand the transformability of the body, for better or worse. Contra the popular and scientific presumption that female sexual desire is naturally low, I argued that the ways in which patriarchal structures are taken up, appropriated and in a certain sense imitated at the level of the body often negatively impact the erotic life force, and thus the lived experience of pleasure, of women in both the sexual and the nonsexual domain. Yet at the same time, through a partly prescriptive rather than merely descriptive phenomenology, which draws support from Malabou's notion of explosive plasticity, I argued that one has the possibility to transform oneself through the very structure of sensible eroticism. Unlearning restrictive gender normative ways of moving and desiring demands that one abandon oneself to *being* a body in the world prior to any categorization into subject and object, master and slave. While this abandonment to *being* a body, as we have seen, is easier for some than others, it is precisely by re-engaging this sensible eroticism that one can tune into the possibilities of one's body such as these are apart from social norms and demands. In this way, one creates the possibility for resisting the uncritical imitation of restrictive societal norms and thus for the opening up of new ways of desiring.

Notes

1. For an introduction to the aims and core concepts of mimetic studies, see Lawtoo 2022a and 2022b and Lawtoo and Garcia-Granero 2024. For a feminist development of this field, see Verkerk 2021 and 2023.
2. On the link between the concept of mimesis and that of plasticity, see also Lawtoo 2022a, 129–155.
3. For accounts of the methodology and aims of critical phenomenology, see Salamon 2018; Guenther 2020; Laferté-Coutu 2021.
4. For the difference between perception and sensibility, see also Sparrow 2015, 112. This notion of sensibility pushes the *Phenomenology* towards the later ontology of flesh, thus challenging any strict distinction between Merleau-Ponty's phenomenology and his ontology.
5. See, for example, Gallagher 2006, 65–85.
6. This move from perception to sensibility already takes us "beyond" Merleau-Ponty, and thus my claim is not to discover a notion of eroticism which he sought, but failed, to fully develop. My aim is, rather, to excavate and reappropriate elements of his phenomenology that can help us develop a critical understanding of the ways in which bodies *live* desire prior to perception and reflection. Furthermore, insofar as the bodily experience of erotic desire is not necessarily informed by knowledge of psychoanalytic theory, I do not draw on the psychoanalytic conceptualization of sexuality. This is not to say that a reading that marries phenomenology and psychoanalysis could not prove fruitful for a conceptualization of sexuality and eroticism, yet such a reading would require an investigation that far exceeds the scope of this chapter.
7. For an analysis of the notion of sensibility in Merleau-Ponty in relation to rhythm and resonance, see Al-Saji 2008.
8. See Butler 1989; Grosz 1994, 86–111; Heinämaa 2003, 86–87. For a feminist critical response to this critique, see Foultier 2013.
9. Although not the focus of this chapter, this analysis would also allow us to denaturalize heterosexuality, insofar as any sexual identity is conceived not as pregiven but rather as a becoming, shaped through the ways in which our bodies are "pulled" towards certain others. Important for this denaturalization would be an analysis of how a heteronormative society makes certain bodies available as "legitimate" objects of desire, namely those of the "opposite" sex, whilst excluding others—resulting in what Ahmed calls a "compulsory heterosexuality" (2006, 87). See also Ahmed 2006, 92–107.
10. It is important to note that this abandonment to being a body is not the same as self-objectification, as sensibility operates prior to the subject/object distinction. On this phenomenological account, then, a bodily experience is not the same as the experience of oneself as an object.

11 Indeed, Gail Weiss argues that Merleau-Ponty's discussions of "abnormal" cases such as Schneider's serve to challenge rather than reinforce what is usually taken for granted as normal or accepted as normative. See Weiss 2015.

12 For analyses of this ambiguity of the mimetic subject in relation to Adriana Cavarero's notion of inclination, see Dahms 2023; Verkerk 2023.

13 In *Pleasure Erased: Clitoris Unthought*, Malabou analyzes the figural and literal "erasure" of the clitoris as the symbol and organ for feminine pleasure and sexual autonomy. The figural erasure consists in the fact that the clitoris has received very little attention in scientific discourses and the history of philosophy compared to other sexual organs such as the phallus, the "lips" and the vulva, etc. The literal erasure refers to the material and social excisions and mutilations of the clitoris and clitoral pleasure that are enforced on women throughout the world (2022, 75–89). Malabou notes that the clitoris is the "only organ whose sole function is pleasure" (1). The erasure of the clitoris thus symbolizes the erasure of feminine pleasure as such. Effectively extending this analysis, the rest of this chapter considers the ways in which particular social and cultural contexts might prompt the body to "erase" or distance itself from its *own* eroticism.

14 See e.g. Young 2005 for a paradigmatic analysis of feminine bodily motility under patriarchy. Whilst Young argues that the adoption of a restricted bodily motility by many women under patriarchy can be explained by the fact that women in our society live their bodies as both subject and object, the concept of mimesis can help us understand the modality through which these normative movements and postures are taken up.

15 Interestingly, performativity is itself a mimetic concept, as mimesis comes from mimos, performance.

16 In this sense, my analysis is indebted to Malabou's important break with any dichotomous conceptualization of the symbolic and the material. See, for example, 2008; 2019.

17 See Heiman et al. 2011; Hayfield and Clarke 2012; van Anders et al. 2022, 393. I focus on the example of bodies that live their eroticism in a "heterosexual" way under patriarchy. It would be interesting and important, in another work, to investigate how eroticism expresses itself in bodies that do not live their eroticism "heterosexually."

18 See, for example, the statements by participants in a psychological study into low desire in women partnered with men, which reflect the common presumption that female sexual desire is naturally low, over against male sexual desire, which is presumed to be naturally high (Hayfield and Clarke 2012, 71). See also Rosemary Basson's (2000) "responsive model" of female sexual desire, and Angel's critique of Basson (Angel 2021, 58–66).

19 Essentialist scientific discourses largely assume a linear causality between the level of testosterone and the level of sexual desire, thus proposing a "naturalist" explanation for the phenomenon of low desire in women. Yet according to social neuroendocrinologist Sari M. van Anders (2012), whilst testosterone is complexly linked to desire, the presupposition that there is a linear causality between the two is simplistic and has no empirical evidence. See also Stegenga 2022.

20 Such devices are still widely used in clinical trials to ascertain women's sexual desire. See, for example, Heiman et al. 2011.

21 See Lawtoo 2022b for the notion of mimetic pathologies, on the one hand, and the remedying effect of mimetic pathos, on the other.

22 I reserve for another work the important question of how lesbian and queer eroticism might open up such other possibilities for desire. On this point, see Ahmed 2006.

Bibliography

Ahmed, Sara (2006). *Queer Phenomenology: Orientations, Objects, Others*. Durham, NC: Duke University Press.

Al-Saji, Alia (2008). "'A Past Which Has Never Been Present': Bergsonian Dimensions in Merleau-Ponty's Theory of the Prepersonal." *Research in Phenomenology* 38.1, 41–71.

Angel, Katherine (2014). *Unmastered: A Book on Desire, Most Difficult to Tell*. London: Penguin.

Angel, Katherine (2021). *Tomorrow Sex Will Be Good Again: Women and Desire in the Age of Consent*. London: Verso.

Basson, Rosemary (2000). "The Female Sexual Response: A Different Model." *Journal of Sex and Marital Therapy* 26.1, 51–65.

Beauvoir, Simone de (2011). *The Second Sex*, trans. Constance Borde and Sheila Malovany-Chevallier. London: Vintage Books.

Butler, Judith (1989). "Sexual Ideology and Phenomenological Description: A Feminist Critique of Merleau-Ponty's *Phenomenology of Perception*," in *The Thinking Muse: Feminism and Modern French Philosophy*, eds. Jeffner Allen and Iris Marion Young. Bloomington, IN: Indiana University Press, 85–100.

Butler, Judith (2007). *Gender Trouble: Feminism and the Subversion of Identity*. 2nd ed. New York: Routledge.

Dahms, Isabell (2023). "Maternal Inclinations, Queer Orientations, Common Occupation." *Critical Horizons* 24.2, 147–163.

Drossman, D. A., J. Leserman, G. Nachman, Z. M. Li, H. Gluck, T. C. Toomey and C. M. Mitchell (1990). "Sexual and Physical Abuse in Women with Functional or Organic Gastrointestinal Disorders." *Annals of Internal Medicine* 113.11, 828–833.

Febos, Melissa (2021). *Girlhood*. London: Bloomsbury.

Foultier, Anna (2013). "Language and the Gendered Body: Butler's Early Reading of Merleau-Ponty." *Hypatia* 28.4, 767–783.

Gallagher, Shaun (2006). *How the Body Shapes the Mind*. Oxford: Oxford University Press.

Grosz, Elizabeth (1994). *Volatile Bodies: Toward a Corporeal Feminism*. St Leonards: Allen & Unwin.

Guenther, Lisa (2020). "Critical Phenomenology," in *50 Concepts for a Critical Phenomenology*, eds. Gail Weiss, Ann Murphy and Gayle Salamon. Evanston, IL: Northwestern University Press, 11–16.

Hayfield, Nikki, and Victoria Clarke (2012). "'I'd Be Just as Happy with a Cup of Tea': Women's Accounts of Sex and Affection in Long-Term Heterosexual Relationships." *Women's Studies International Forum* 35.2, 67–74.

Heiman, Julia R., Heather Rupp, Erick Janssen, Sara K. Newhouse, Marieke Brauer and Ellen Laan (2011). "Sexual Desire, Sexual Arousal and Hormonal Differences in Premenopausal US and Dutch Women with and without Low Sexual Desire." *Hormones and Behavior* 59.5, 772–779.

Heinämaa, Sara (2003). *Toward a Phenomenology of Sexual Difference: Husserl, Merleau-Ponty, Beauvoir*. Oxford: Rowman & Littlefield.

Laferté-Coutu, Mérédith (2021). "What is Phenomenological About Critical Phenomenology? Guenther, Al-Saji, and the Husserlian Account of Attitudes." *Puncta: Journal of Critical Phenomenology* 4.2, 89–106.

Lawtoo, Nidesh (ed.) (2022a). *Homo Mimeticus: A New Theory of Imitation*. Leuven: Leuven University Press.
Lawtoo, Nidesh (2022b). "The Mimetic Condition: Theory and Concepts." *CounterText* 8.1, 1–15.
Lawtoo, Nidesh, and Marina Garcia-Granero (eds.) (2024). *Homo Mimeticus II: Re-Turns to Mimesis*. Leuven: Leuven University Press.
Lorde, Audre (2019). "Uses of the Erotic: The Erotic as Power," in *Sister Outsider*. London: Penguin, 43–49.
Malabou, Catherine (2008). *What Should We Do with Our Brain?* trans. Sebastian Rand. New York: Fordham University Press.
Malabou, Catherine (2019). *Morphing Intelligence: From IQ Measurement to Artificial Brains*, trans. Carolyn Shread. New York: Columbia University Press.
Malabou, Catherine (2022). *Pleasure Erased: The Clitoris Unthought*, trans. Carolyn Shread. Cambridge: Polity Press.
Merleau-Ponty, Maurice (1945). *Phénoménologie de la perception*. Paris: Gallimard.
Merleau-Ponty, Maurice (2012). *Phenomenology of Perception*, trans. Donald A. Landes. London: Routledge.
Rae, Gavin (2020). "Merleau-Ponty on the Sexed Body." *Journal of Phenomenological Psychology* 51.2, 162–183.
Salamon, Gayle (2018). "What's Critical about Critical Phenomenology?" *Puncta: Journal of Critical Phenomenology* 1, 8–17.
Sartre, Jean-Paul (2003). *Being and Nothingness: An Essay on Phenomenological Ontology*, trans. Hazel E. Barnes. London: Routledge.
Sparrow, Tom (2015). *Plastic Bodies: Rebuilding Sensation after Phenomenology*. London: Open Humanities Press.
Stegenga, Jacob (2022). "Sex Differences in Sexual Desire." *Philosophy of Science* 89, 1094–1103.
Sullivan, Shannon (2015). *On the Physiology of Sexist and Racist Oppression*. Oxford: Oxford University Press.
van Anders, Sari M. (2012). "Testosterone and Sexual Desire in Healthy Women and Men." *Archives of Sexual Behavior* 41.6, 1471–1484.
van Anders, Sari M., Debby Herbenick, Lori A. Brotto, Emily A. Harris and Sara B. Chadwick (2022). "The Heteronormativity Theory of Low Sexual Desire in Women Partnered with Men." *Archives of Sexual Behavior* 51.1, 391–415.
Verkerk, Willow (2021). "A Feminist Genealogy of the Post-Enlightenment Subject." *Graduate Faculty Philosophy Journal* 42.1, 27–51.
Verkerk, Willow (2023). "A Re-Evaluation of the Androcentric Subject of European Philosophy." *Critical Horizons* 24.2, 115–130.
Weiss, Gail (2015). "The Normal, the Natural, and the Normative: A Merleau-Pontyan Legacy to Feminist Theory, Critical Race Theory, and Disability Studies." *Continental Philosophy Review* 48.1, 77–93.
Young, Iris Marion (2005). "Throwing Like a Girl: A Phenomenology of Feminine Body Comportment, Motility, and Spatiality," in *On Female Bodily Experience: 'Throwing Like a Girl' and Other Essays*. Oxford: Oxford University Press, 27–45.

CHAPTER 8

MIMESIS, RESONANCE AND THE SUBJECT
A Critical Comparison

Mathijs Peters

Introduction: Mimetic and Resonant Creatures

Alluding to Friedrich Nietzsche's *Menschliches, Allzumenschliches*, Nidesh Lawtoo writes in *Homo Mimeticus: A New Theory of Imitation*: "humans remain, for good and ill, all-too-mimetic creatures" (2022, 13). Hartmut Rosa observes in his magnum opus *Resonance: A Sociology of Our Relationship to the World*: "human beings are first and foremost not creatures capable of language, reason, or sensation, but creatures *capable of resonance*" (2019b, 36). Foregrounding the phenomena of mimesis and resonance, these claims indicate that both authors resist the idea(l) of human beings as purely and/or primarily autonomous, rational and linguistic subjects, in control of what they do, think and say, sovereign over themselves as distinct individuals. In short, they problematize what Lawtoo, in his dialogue with Catherine Malabou, included in this volume, describes as the notion of the "volitional, autonomous and free subject" (311).

Both Lawtoo and Rosa suggest that human beings are, to a large extent, driven by processes over which they have only limited control. These are processes that concern the often unconscious imitation of beings around us, from the moment we are born. As Lawtoo writes about mimesis: "it is precisely because the I is, from the very beginning, mimetically entangled with the other, through the other, in a relation of material and affective dependency with the other that our disposition is to remain inclined toward others" (2022, 276). Similarly, Rosa emphasizes that we often unconsciously resonate with others. He observes: "A baby, perhaps even an embryo, experiences and lives in resonances, long before it can say 'I'" (2019b, 449).

To characterize the ways in which processes like these remain unknown to us, Lawtoo frequently refers to Nietzsche's observation that the "largest part of human mental activity" remains "unconscious." Indeed, Nietzsche is a central figure in mimetic studies, since the self-proclaimed "philosopher-physician" observes that, as he states in *The Will to Power*, "one never communicates thoughts: one communicates movements, mimic signs, which we then trace back to thoughts" (qtd. in Lawtoo 2019, 47). Based on claims like these, Lawtoo resists Freudian approaches to the psyche, instead defending the following understanding of the unconscious:

> [U]nconscious in the pre-Freudian, but also post-Freudian realization that actions and reactions are triggered by involuntary habits, automatic reflexes, and mirroring repetitions of gestures that, from birth onward, bridge the gap between self and other via what we have seen him call an imitation or mimicking of gesture. (2022, 115)

Like the idea(l) of the individual, free and rational subject, Freudian understandings of the unconscious are problematized within mimetic studies as well, since these understandings revolve around Oedipal forms of repression "within" an individual entity constituted in a "triangular structure" (36). As this passage indicates, Lawtoo instead embraces "pre-Freudian" and "post-Freudian" anti-Oedipal ideas about the unconscious. These ideas point to mimetic relations of which we are only partly aware, which cannot really be repressed, and which have a material dimension.[1]

Even though both authors foreground similar phenomena, the mimetic turn and the resonant turn have, so far, not yet been compared. Lawtoo writes in the introduction to *Homo Mimeticus II*: "The new relational concept of resonance […] is not only a new conceptual mask of mimesis; it also rests on similar intersubjective, affective and mirroring presuppositions that will have to be explored in the future" (Lawtoo and Garcia-Granero 2024, 20–21).[2] The aim of this chapter is therefore to set such a comparison in motion, providing a stepping-stone to further explorations of the many resonances and mimetic connections between the two theoretical fields. Since both mimetic studies and resonance theory focus on a myriad of phenomena, this chapter will focus on one specific issue as a theoretical and critical lens: the status of the subject. What remains of the subject if we, like scholars within mimetic studies and resonance theory, foreground (unconscious) processes that, to a large extent, are presented as transcending the autonomous, rational and individual self?

I will use this question to critically compare the ways in which mimetic studies and resonance theory refer to and include three interrelated topics: (1) mirror neurons; (2) entwinements of normative and descriptive elements; and (3) self-constitution. This means that I will *first* discuss how Lawtoo and Rosa argue that the discovery of mirror neurons proves their claim that human beings are driven by relational processes over which we have only limited control. *Secondly*, I will show that this claim makes it difficult to distinguish "good" or "healthy" forms of resonant/mimetic subjectivity from "bad" or "pathological" ones. This is the case because Lawtoo and Rosa refer to mimesis and resonance in both normative and descriptive terms without developing a normative yardstick to specifically indicate *when* mimesis or resonance would be "bad" or "good." *Thirdly*, I will argue that a solution to this problem can be developed with the help of Theodor W. Adorno, who distinguishes two forms of mimesis that he characterizes as "primitive" and "aesthetic." Whereas Adorno understands "primitive mimesis" as a state of being in which subjects unconsciously mimic and repeat anything and everything around them, he describes "aesthetic mimesis" as a form of subjectivity that balances cognition with material relationality. The former concerns an uncritical, passive and possibly pathological state of embeddedness, while the latter revolves around a critical form of subjectivity that combines rational (self-)reflection with physical, sensual and resonant ties to others.

To put more flesh on the bones of what Adorno calls "aesthetic mimesis," and to connect it more specifically to forms of subjectivity as they are shaped within mimetic studies and resonance theory, I will turn to Roland Barthes's references to the middle voice. For Barthes, this linguistic "mode" concerns a form of selfhood that is neither completely passive nor completely active. As such, it presents a unique way of describing a subject that is, *to some extent*, rational, self-reflexive and in control as an individual entity, and that is simultaneously, *to some extent*, driven by unconscious processes and mechanisms that transcend the boundaries between individuals. This turn to the middle voice, I will conclude, makes it possible to conceptualize a form of resonant/mimetic subjectivity that is neither completely passive/determined nor completely active/free. Before developing this argument, however, I will first briefly introduce Rosa's theory.

Alienation, Resonance, Mimesis

Hartmut Rosa opens *Resonance* with the claim: "if acceleration is the problem, then resonance may well be the solution" (2019b, 1). To understand what his resonance theory entails, as this statement indicates, it is necessary to first discuss how he, in his earlier work, targets forms of acceleration. In texts such as *Social Acceleration: A New Theory of Modernity*, *Acceleration and Alienation* and *High-Speed Society*, Rosa presents acceleration as the defining characteristic of modernity. In these works, he observes that processes of acceleration take place in three fields. The first concerns "intentional, technical, and above all technological (i.e. machine-based) acceleration of goal-directed processes" (2013b, 71), such as the speeding up of transportation, communication, distribution, production, consumption and more. Secondly, Rosa describes acceleration in the context of social change, discussing, for example, the shortening and multiplying of relationships, marriages and occupations, observing that this "shortening" itself is also accelerating in modern societies.[3]

Thirdly, Rosa focuses on what he calls the "pace of life," and describes the experience of a *scarcity of time*: in contemporary western societies, people do more and more things faster and simultaneously, and have the constant feeling that they have to "use" their time as efficiently as possible. Paradoxically, sociological research indicates that this process leaves them with less time to do the things that they *really* want to do, alienating them from their own goals in life.[4] This results, according to Rosa, in constant feelings of stress and emptiness: the continual idea that one has to "fill" one's life as efficiently as possible leaves less time for the experience of, for example, meaningful moments of connectedness.[5] A helpful example is formed by Rosa's claim that the acceleration of social change results in a "contraction of the present." This points to the idea that the conditions that define the "now," as well as our ideas about past and future, change more and more, resulting in the feeling that we constantly have to redefine our understanding of both and, thereby, in experiences of restlessness and instability.[6] This fragments the bonds we have and corrodes the ability to develop a narrative identity, resulting in what Paul Virilio describes as a "frenetic standstill" (Rosa 2013b, 15, 102). As such, Rosa's critical analysis of acceleration also targets capitalism and neoliberalism. These ideologies are tied, he argues, to a blind and uncritical embrace of the idea that "the" economy needs to grow, resulting in an instrumental and exploitative relationship with, for example, nature.[7]

It is important to stress that Rosa does not categorically reject all forms of acceleration. Instead, he criticizes processes that harm people and undermine their ability to live a meaningful life. In short, he criticizes those processes that generate *alienation*, which he characterizes, referring to Hannah Arendt, Rahel Jaeggi and others as a "relation of relationlessness" (Rosa 2020b, 27, 35). In societies permeated with the adage that everything should accelerate and grow, we become more and more distanced from the world around us, Rosa observes, with "world" referring to anything ranging from other people to nature, artworks, political systems, our own bodies and even time and space.[8] At times, he describes this situation as *pathological* and characterizes acceleration as an "enslaving pressure" and a "totalitarian force" (2013a, 80, 61), linking it to a modernity that is in "crisis" (Reckwitz and Rosa 2023).

This negative "half" of Rosa's theory brings me to its positive counterpart: as mentioned above, the experience of resonance is presented by Rosa as the "solution" to the disconnectedness and alienation caused by the forms of acceleration that permeate modern societies. With the help of a wide variety of authors, ranging from Friedrich Schiller to Max Weber and Samuel Beckett and from Søren Kierkegaard to Karl Marx and Albert Camus, Rosa argues that alienation constitutes a world that does not "listen," that is "mute" and that does not "answer" (2019b, 258–304). It is a silent world that has no meaning and that we, in the modern age, can only approach in an instrumental and exploitative manner. Resonant relationships, on the other hand, revolve around a meaningful and vibrant connection between self and Other.[9] They make us feel at home again in a world that is *responsive*, that "answers."[10] It is here that we can already discern the similarities between the processes foregrounded within resonance theory and mimetic studies, with Lawtoo describing, for example, forms of "vibrant mimesis" that, as foregrounded within the new materialisms, revolve around energetic and pulsating forms of relationality.[11] But let me first briefly discuss Rosa's account of resonance in more detail.

The German sociologist argues that resonant relationships have four characteristics: firstly, they include a process that he describes and writes as "af←fection" (2019b, 172): one is overcome or touched by some "Other" when one undergoes an experience of resonance. This experience, however, is not one-directional: the subject also puts "e→motion" into the experience (2019b, 172). Thirdly, Rosa argues, resonance transforms the subject, which is involved in such an intense matter in this bi-directional experience that it is changed. And fourthly, experiences of resonance cannot be controlled or commodified, Rosa claims: we might go to a tropical paradise to experience resonance, and nothing happens—in fact, the tourist industry and the culture industry both present commodified and therefore false forms of resonance.[12] But we might suddenly hear a song on the radio on our way back from this "paradise," and a motif in the melody spontaneously touches us, we respond to it emotionally, and the song "does" something to and with us that transforms us: we experience resonance.

Rosa continuously emphasizes that one of the key aspects of resonance is a certain *transcendence* of the subject, which comes about because of the *relationality* of this experience: resonance is not an emotional or affective "state" that an individual can be "in," but a "mode of relation" (Rosa 2019b, 168). He therefore emphasizes that, when experiencing resonance, the subject is *given over* to the Other. This is foregrounded by his use of the word "resonance," which comes from the field of acoustics. This suggests that we do not *choose* whether we resonate with something; we do not completely *control* these experiences, and this is precisely what makes them meaningful, according to him.

We can now see more specifically that, and how, Rosa's ideas overlap with claims developed within mimetic studies. As mentioned above, the latter field also revolves around the foregrounding of affective relationships between subjects that destabilize strict binaries between self and other, as well between a rational Cartesian ego and what would then be its "other": irrational bodily matter. Like resonance theory, mimetic studies is rooted in insights developed within philosophy, sociology, psychology, anthropology, literary and film studies, neurobiology and more, and is embedded in a discourse shaped by a wide variety of thinkers, ranging from Friedrich Nietzsche to Georges Bataille, from René Girard to Philippe Lacoue-Labarthe and from Mikkel Borch-Jacobsen to Adriana Cavarero. Based on the ideas developed by these authors, Lawtoo describes how mimetic studies destabilizes notions of the autonomous subject, coming very close to observations made by Rosa:

> [M]imesis blurs the very boundaries of individuation, introducing horizontal continuities between self and others, mind and body, conscious actions and unconscious reactions that take possession of an ego that is not one but double or multiple, generating a phantom ego that is deeply in touch with the materiality of life. (2022, 256–257)

Lawtoo's employment of the Nietzschean notion of the "phantom ego" is especially relevant for this chapter. As he writes in *Homo Mimeticus*: "[T]he subject or ego is not a self-contained, autonomous, and fully rational or intentional subject. On the contrary, it is a phantom ego who is easily possessed by others" (15). Again, the subject here almost disappears into a multitude of tendencies, voices and mimetic moments, "impersonal flows of mesmeric influence that dilate the self or ego to the point of (dis)possession" (Lawtoo 2022, 263).

This emphasis on transcendence and (dis)possession returns in Rosa's rejection of those understandings of relationality that preserve a sense of self that, to some extent, remains disconnected from the other. An example is the Hegelian theory of recognition as developed by Axel Honneth. Rosa writes in an exemplary passage, using love as an example:

> Resonance [...] is always a dynamic event, the expression of a vibrant responsive relationship that can be seen perhaps most splendidly when a person's eyes light up. [...] *I am recognized*, but resonance is something that can only happen *between us*. Love as a resonant experience thus refers not to the fact of loving or being loved, but to the moment or moments of mutual, transformative, fluid, affecting encounter. (2019b, 196–197)

It is therefore, in his view, necessary to let go—at least partially—of the idea of autonomy as tied to a notion of an individual and rational subject, to make space for resonance. Indeed, Rosa writes in *Resonance*: "autonomy, understood as self-determination or self-legislation, lacks any relational character and is thus not a suitable antithesis to alienation, as it overemphasizes the "self" (autos) while at the same time underestimating the transformative aspect of successfully relating to the world" (Rosa 2019b, 474 n. 90).

Again, Lawtoo makes similar observations, writing: "a plurality of assumptions internal to dominant accounts of *Homo sapiens*, including autonomy, free will, and rational presence to selfhood, need to be revisited in light of intersubjective, social, and largely unconscious transformations that take place in relation of communication between self and others, be they human or nonhuman" (2022, 35). We are not disconnected atoms, both Lawtoo and Rosa suggest, but we are fundamentally part of the world, given over to others. Frequently, Rosa therefore refers positively to Merleau-Ponty's phenomenological claim that, as embodied beings, we are *always already* embedded in the world, as well as to Charles Taylor's rejection of political ideologies that revolve around an "atomized" subject.[13] Lawtoo, similarly, rejects what he calls "monadic" understandings of consciousness.[14]

In *The Uncontrollability of the World* ("uncontrollability" being the English translation of the German *Unverfügbarkeit*), Rosa develops this idea further by linking it to a need for *control*. In this book, he argues that one of the ills of modernity is formed by an excessive need to control oneself, others and the environment, in order to increase one's share of the world, often in the name of acceleration processes. Paradoxically, he observes, this frequently results in a loss of control, since the need for control is thwarted by a reality that cannot be completely controlled and is, in fact, experienced as less and less controllable and more and more chaotic, as in *crisis*. Furthermore, this controlling attitude also permeates and corrodes the ways in which we relate to others and ourselves, he claims, as we find ourselves in neoliberal societies in which we seem to have less and less choice over how we want to give our lives meaning.[15] Rosa therefore advocates what he calls a form of "semi-controllability," in between control and loss of control, which opens up spaces for resonance and preserves a form of spontaneity in a world that does not entirely control us, and that we ourselves do not completely control either.[16]

Mirror Neurons

Mimetic studies and resonance theory also share an interest in mirror neurons. Unlike the sociologists who, as Malabou observes in her dialogue with Lawtoo included in this volume, resist theories about mirror neurons because they would result in an uncritical reductionism, Rosa embraces these theories and explores the ways in which they resonate with his own thought. Referring to the "sociologist of emotions" Randall Collins, he observes that mirror neurons prove that human beings are "hard-wired" for social interaction, developing, again, not as disconnected atoms but, fundamentally, as beings who are attuned[17] to each other and only become who they are through forms of relationality, through resonance (Rosa 2019b, 164–167).

Indeed, the "mirroring" that takes place through mirror neurons, Rosa writes, can be understood as a form of resonance. This mirroring not only concerns the *relations* between humans but also plays a crucial role in processes of *perception* and in *movement* or "motor action" (2021, 148–149). He observes:

> Neurobiology, cognitive science, evolutionary biology, developmental psychology, and sociology all seem to converge in the insight that

> the brain does not simply mentally *reproduce* or *represent* the world, and that consciousness or mind is not simply the product of cerebral processes, but rather that *resonant* or *responsive relationships* develop between world (or environment), body, and brain, on the one hand, and between brain and mind, on the other, which relationships first make possible not only human thought and cognition but also learning, communication, and action. The recent rise of empathy research as a key topic in cognitive science doubtlessly provided a starting point for this development, having shown that the capacity for mutual empathy, understanding, and adopting other perspectives is important not just for the development of sociomoral qualities, but for learning, thinking, and acting in general. (2019b, 144)

Touching on various forms of "in-betweenness," Rosa comes close here to Malabou's ideas about "plasticity," an important concept for mimetic studies. The discovery of mirror neurons proves, Rosa observes, that most of the processes that make us into experiencing and thinking creatures concern forms of resonance that transcend dualities between "mind" and "matter" or "inside" and "outside." As material beings, we are *always already* "wired" to respond to each other, relate to each other, and "feel with" each other, and this often happens unconsciously.

It is therefore no surprise that Lawtoo refers to mirror neurons as well, observing in *Homo Mimeticus*:

> [S]ince at least the discovery of mirror neurons in the 1990s, it has become once again clear that humans are imitative animals predisposed to unconsciously mirror the emotions of others. They do so via a form of prelinguistic communication that is not moral and mediated by consciousness but neurological and immediate, opening a different door to the unconscious (2022, 36).

Both Rosa and Lawtoo allude to the "re-discovered" sociologist Gabriel Tarde[18] who, Rosa writes, is "interested in the emergence of affective or emotional 'energy fields' between [...] participants in a given interaction" (2019b, 146). As Lawtoo observes, references to material connections between human beings can already be found in Nietzsche. As briefly mentioned above, the writings of the self-described philosopher with the hammer sketch the contours of a specific form of relationality. This relationality points to an unconscious that, unlike the Oedipal unconscious, does not so much revolve around individual repression but around connected materiality, often on the level of nervous systems. It would therefore be better, Lawtoo observes, to characterize the discovery of mirror neurons as a *re*-discovery, since authors like Nietzsche already described material, unconscious and mimetic processes in the nineteenth century.[19]

Furthermore, both Rosa and Lawtoo describe the "training" of mirror neurons. These descriptions form a critical response to the idea that this physical theory would result in a neurological reductionism that would *only* focus on firing neurons and proclaim everything "above" this physiological level to be a "mere" epiphenomenon. Both can be understood to claim that mirror neurons, as Malabou states in her dialogue with Lawtoo, "are very helpful and indispensable for understanding the functioning of imitation, but if they are not stimulated, shaped, and educated they don't function" (Coda, 311). Rosa makes a similar observation, writing about the two above-mentioned sociologists: "Tarde and Collins of course both make clear that 'social resonances' [...] are not simply processes of mirroring and repetition, but rather *responsive attitudes* that necessarily involve differences and variations" (2019b, 147).

This suggests that resonance, like mimesis, does not come about "automatically," and that cultural and social structures form a thin layer above a more fundamental neurological one. Instead, Rosa writes:

> [M]irror neurons (should they exist) establish a capacity for resonance, but no content. What causes a person (or a macaque) to vibrate in this way is not fixed once and for all. Our "vocabulary" can be (re)programmed; the "interpersonal space of meaning" [...] is evidently dependent on culture (2019b, 150).

Mirror neurons, Lawtoo observes, need to be "trained" and "shaped" within and by social and cultural structures. In his own words: "without the cultural training, a mimetic drive alone is not generative of learning and the strength that potentially ensues" (Coda, 312).

The Normative and the Descriptive

Both Rosa and Lawtoo claim that mirror neurons affirm the idea that we are hard-wired to mimic others and engage in forms of resonance. Nevertheless, both also argue that the drives and tendencies that they describe can, and should be, "trained," "educated" or "(re)programmed." If these "vibrations" can be "educated" or "(re)programmed," this sparks the question of *how* this should be done. Are there good ways of shaping and training them? Are there bad ways of doing this? What happens if they are not "educated"? Does this result in "bad" forms of mimesis or resonance, as opposed to "good" ones? Should they, if not developed "correctly," be "reprogrammed"? And what is the normative yardstick that we can use to distinguish good from bad forms of resonance or mimesis, if this is possible at all? These questions bring me to the second part of my analysis, which concerns entwinements of normative and descriptive elements.

Let us first look at resonance: as discussed above, Rosa not only presents his theory as *explaining* and *describing* what makes human beings "tick" and what they long for in late modernity, but *also* as providing a *solution* to modernity's ills. As such, it results in a *normative* notion that enables him to criticize societies and to indicate how they *should* be structured.[20] In short, it results in a critical social theory driven by a normative ideal. Indeed, Rosa writes in *Acceleration and Alienation*, with reference to Axel Honneth: "the identification of social pathologies is an overriding goal of not just Critical Theory, but of social philosophy in general" (2013a, 51). In fact, we can understand Rosa's notion of resonance as enabling him to indicate *when* the acceleration processes he describes in his earlier works should be criticized: the moment they undermine the ability to experience resonance and, instead, constitute alienation. This results in his defense of a *post-growth* society in which the ideology of acceleration is overcome and the possibility of generating resonance—on various levels—forms a guiding yardstick. According to Rosa, we need to develop spaces in which axes of resonance can be constructed that provide a stable structure for living a meaningful life.[21]

Even though mimetic studies does not present one form of mimesis as a "solution" to societal or political ills, we do find an entwinement of normative and descriptive elements in Lawtoo's writings. He points to this entwinement with the claim that mimesis is "Janus-faced" (2022, 58), characterizing it as "patho(-)logical" (38). Mimesis, this indicates, may function like a *pharmakon* that has a certain material *logic* to it—the "great reason (*logos*) of bodily affect (*pathos*)" (116), but may also become *pathological*. As hinted at by Lawtoo's reading of the phantom ego, the observation that we are mimetic beings makes us highly vulnerable to manipulation, especially because of our tendency to identify with an exemplary other—for which Lawtoo uses Pierre Janet's notion of "socius" (2019, 47). The *pathological* dimension of mimetic relations, for example, explains the rise of new forms of fascism and populism, which rest on processes of mimicking and imitating. As Lawtoo concludes: "mimesis cannot be prescribed only as a cognitive therapy, for it simultaneously works as an irrational pathology" (2019, 50). Returning to my exploration of subjectivity, this means that, for Lawtoo, "'ego' is far from the ideal of a rational, autonomous, and logical Homo sapiens that still informs dominant strands of political theory" (2022, 275). The reference to "cognitive therapy" foregrounds the more positive "face" of mimesis: its *patho-logical* aspects, which can generate relations of a sym-pathetic nature.[22] In a helpful passage, Lawtoo describes these two faces of mimesis as follows:

> The patho(-)logies of mimesis open up complementary possibilities that look simultaneously in opposed directions: namely, both toward social pathologies that trigger violent rivalries, scapegoating, ressentiment, affective contagion, (new) fascism, epidemic contagion and related sicknesses, which, in some cases, can lead to a faith in what is behind the world; and, alternatively, and without contradiction, toward patho-*logies* that strive contra dominant life-negating currents animated by nihilistic forms of ressentiment to promote vital bonds of sympathy, cooperation, public happiness, and joyful inclinations, prompting chameleonlike metamorphoses that aspire to renew our faithfulness to the earth here and now. (2022, 64)

As within resonance theory, these descriptions spark the question of how we can distinguish pathological from patho-logical forms of mimesis. This question especially rises because Lawtoo describes the possibility of turning pathological forms of mimesis into patho-logical ones, a transformation that can perhaps be linked to his references to "educating" mirror neurons and to the idea of mimesis as "cognitive therapy" (273).

Let us return to Rosa's theory again: several authors have argued that this entwinement of descriptive and normative elements renders the concept of resonance problematic. Referring to a phenomenon highlighted by Lawtoo as well, they ask the question: what if a person resonates with a right-wing populist or neofascist leader, feeling embedded in a social and ideological collective? In this situation, this person might be affected and feel emotionally connected, and the

Mimesis, Resonance and the Subject   221

experience might overcome them and even transform them into someone who wants to become part of this political movement. Indeed, *like mimetic studies*, it seems that the theory of resonance provides a fruitful theoretical framework to *understand*, *describe* and *explain* the recent rise/return of forms of populism that make people feel "at home" in the world by presenting them with ideas and figures with whom they experience resonance (or whom they can mimic as a crowd), no matter how false these ideas and figures may be.

However, this idea conflicts with Rosa's own claim that resonance, by definition, is always good, a *solution*. As Simon Susen writes in his review of *Resonance*:

> It is difficult [...] to ignore the fact that there are highly problematic practices that may "resonate" with those performing them. Fascist regimes not only rely on "resonance"-generating techniques and activities, but also provide realms of "resonance" that their supporters experience as "inspiring" and "galvanizing". The same is true of various other reactionary endeavours with which those immersed in them may identify in a resonant fashion. (2019, 17)

In response to critical observations like these, Rosa argues that populist political movements generate "echo chambers" in which people are not confronted with transformative otherness but, instead, only hear their own voice.[23] Since one of the main characteristics of, for example, xenophobic right-wing movements concerns a blocking of otherness, this would mean that it is impossible to resonate with them.

This response, however, conflicts with Rosa's own idea that, like mimesis, resonance is always about a *relationship*, which suggests that people can experience resonance with almost anything. This implies that, to return to the example of neofascism, resonance is not so much about a populist leader or his ideas, but about the *relationality* that might arise when a person sees him speak. Furthermore, this defense might conflict with the idea that resonance arises spontaneously and lies, partly, outside of our control as rational and self-reflective beings. To make this point with reference to mirror neurons, as Lawtoo does extensively in his interview with Vittorio Gallese:[24] what if these neurons start firing when we are part of a neofascist crowd and see a political leader speak? Don't we need a critical yardstick that transcends references to mirror neurons and explores the specific *content* and *meaning* of that which happens at moments like these, critically rejecting or endorsing the ways in which these experiences are socially and politically *mediated*? Shouldn't they, to use Rosa's own word, be "reprogrammed"?[25]

Mimetic and Resonant Self-Constitution

Let me explore this issue further by turning to Rosa again: the discussion of normative and descriptive elements is important for this chapter, since several authors have argued that Rosa's theory needs to include a critical notion of an autonomous subject. This suggestion means that the moment the subject's autonomy is undermined or corroded by experiences of relationality, we should reject this relationality as uncritical. Maeve Cooke describes such a normative notion of autonomous subjectivity as revolving around the ideals of self-efficacy and self-determination, writing in a critical article on resonance theory:

> I see two paths open to Rosa here. One is to metaphorically shrug his shoulders and accept authoritarianism as a prerequisite, at least in certain historical contexts, for providing the material basis necessary for universal resonant self-efficacy. The second is to rearticulate his idea of resonant self-efficacious subjectivity as a mode of agency in which self-determination is an integral element and to use this as the basis for an account of non-authoritarian authority. (Cooke 2020, 380)

Cooke observes here that Rosa must either foreground resonance's *descriptive* dimensions (which, like mimetic studies, enable him to explain the attraction of neofascism and populism) or its *normative* ones (which enable him to reject xenophobic political movements as non-resonant). She concludes that he should choose the latter "path," presenting her own notion of self-efficacy, in which a Foucauldian understanding of "care for the self" is combined with a form of relationality in which the subject preserves its individuality without losing its openness to otherness, as a possible option.[26] This means that if one experiences a form of resonant embeddedness as part of populist crowd, this experience should be criticized with reference to the normative ideal of the individual critical subject. Such a critical subject should be able to formulate and defend rational arguments against certain political ideologies. And it is precisely *because* these ideologies undermine the subject's autonomy—and *therefore* its ability to formulate these kinds of arguments—that they should be rejected.

In *Exploring Hartmut Rosa's Concept of Resonance* (2022), Bareez Majid and I develop an alternative but related suggestion: in light of resonance theory's sometimes problematic entwinement of normative and descriptive elements, we distinguish different forms of resonance that can be positioned on a *spectrum*.

Based on a Deleuzian interpretation of Spinozistic affects, as well as on Hannah Arendt's references to the critical necessity of "unfreezing" fossilized thought structures, we argue that some forms of resonance should be understood as *critical* in nature. These experiences revolve around disruptive moments that force us to think and reflect, triggering us into thought and pulling us out of our comfort zones.[27] Other forms of resonance, we claim in turn, are *affirmationist* in nature. These are experiences that mainly affirm what we *already* believe or feel, nevertheless infusing these beliefs and/or feelings with energy in a way that we describe, with the help of Sergei Eisenstein's analysis of the influence of editing techniques on the spectators of films, as "pulsating."[28] Again, however, to be able to distinguish these forms of resonance, we need an understanding of a critical, reflective subject not purely driven by experiences over which it has little to no control.

To work towards my understanding of a critical mimetic/resonant form of subjectivity, I want to explore the question of whether a similar interpretation can be developed within mimetic studies to more clearly distinguish pathological from patho-logical forms of mimesis. For reasons of space, I offer an essayistic suggestion. The basis of this suggestion is formed by a passage in Adorno's *Aesthetic Theory*, which is also discussed by Hartmut Rosa in *Resonance*. In this passage, Adorno refers to a "shudder" and to "shuddering" (*erschauern*), which point to forms of contact with otherness that manage to break through the reified subject as it comes about, according to Adorno's critical theory, in late capitalist societies. Adorno understands this "shudder" as a form of mimesis, as a sensual and rather ungraspable "touch" that constitutes a material relation between self and world.

What makes these reflections helpful is that Adorno distinguishes two forms of mimesis, which he characterizes as "primitive" and "aesthetic."[29]

He writes in the passage in *Aesthetic Theory* that Rosa quotes as well:

> Ultimately, aesthetic comportment is to be defined as the capacity to shudder, as if goose bumps were the first aesthetic image. What later came to be called subjectivity, freeing itself from the blind anxiety of the shudder, is at the same time the shudder's own development; life in the subject is nothing but what shudders, the reaction to the total spell that transcends the spell. Consciousness without shudder is reified consciousness. That shudder in which subjectivity stirs without yet being subjectivity is the act of being touched by the other. Aesthetic comportment assimilates itself to that other rather than subordinating

> it. Such a constitutive relation of the subject to objectivity in aesthetic comportment joins eros and knowledge. (Adorno 1997, 331; qtd. in Rosa 2019b, 347–348)

Rosa explains this passage with the help of Swen Stein's "Der Begriff der Mimesis in der Ästhetischen Theorie Adornos," writing:

> Adorno distinguishes [...] between *aesthetic mimesis* as an element of successful life that flashes up like a spark and a kind of unconscious *primitive* mimesis in which the subject is so open to and clings so closely to an object that it merges with and loses itself in it. Aesthetic mimesis, by contrast, successfully balances receptive openness with rationality or cognition. It moves between a reifying closedness on the part of the subject, which is no longer capable of perceiving the Other of the object, and the subject's total openness, which would result in a loss of self. (Rosa 2019b, 347)

What makes Adorno's (and Rosa's) references to mimesis helpful is that they hint at a genealogy of subjectivity that includes two moments. *First*, humans do not yet distinguish themselves from their surroundings, responding through resonating and mimetic gestures. At this stage, there are only "shudders": affects, feelings, flows, influx, efflux, mimetic gestures, touches, warmth, cold, "goose bumps," etc. However, it is *then* within and out of this stage that subjectivity comes into being: through the shudder, the self gradually develops awareness, to some extent disconnecting itself from its surroundings as a response to its dependency on forces over which it has no control; a response that Adorno describes as "blind anxiety." It is, thus, out of a "total spell" that, through the shudder, the self *is elevated* but also *elevates itself*, gaining an individual autonomy that is tied to the ability to think and reflect ("cognition"), without completely losing the "shudder" within. The moment this shudder is lost, we have arrived at the closedness that Adorno links to the petrified[30] modern subject that suppresses anything bodily or sensually in the name of complete autonomous self-control, paradoxically turning into its opposite—nature.[31]

What makes Adorno's references helpful as well is that various aspects that he points out in this passage in *Aesthetic Theory* return in mimetic studies. In *Homo Mimeticus*, for example, Lawtoo employs a Nietzschean vocabulary to distinguish what he calls Dionysian from Apollonian forms of mimesis. Whereas the former refers to forms of intoxication and "irrational contagious affects," the latter concerns distance and "rational impersonations of a mirroring role" (2022, 231). The tension between these two forms of mimesis constitutes what Lawtoo characterizes as a Nietzschean *pathos of distance* that should be understood as part of a "hovering vibration between feeling and distance" (2022, 261). Discussing Jane Bennett's[32] understanding of a porous "I" open to external influences, he then writes:

> Since this "I" is embedded in a plurality of human and nonhuman influences the discontinuous efforts at human closure is a legitimate attempt to set up a distance in the continuous flow of impersonal pathos that threatens to overwhelm the subject. It also calls for a negotiation between the contradictory push-pull of a pathos of distance out of which a different, less anthropocentric, and more relational political consciousness, in favorable circumstances, could emerge. (265)

Lawtoo here refers to a "movement" or "gesture" that comes close to Adorno's ideas: in the tension between Dionysian and Apollonian forms of mimesis, a subject comes about that tries to carve out its own position—to generate "human closure"—while continuously being embedded in, and shot through with, material "ebbs" and "flows" that destabilize its autonomy. Like Adorno, furthermore, he suggests that this subject therefore finds a balance between distant rationality and intoxicating relationality.

Self-Constitution and the Middle Voice

In the following, these descriptions of two forms of mimesis will be linked to the role of *language*. This enables me to more specifically describe the peculiar entwinement of passivity and activity that constitutes the above-mentioned subject as simultaneously elevating itself and being elevated by and through the "shudder." Often, Rosa's most passionate descriptions of resonance—like Lawtoo's most captivating discussions of mimesis—revolve around the attempt to put into words in-between positions or experiences that eventually *transcend* the idea of in-betweenness. In these passages, Rosa describes dualisms that liquefy and become a hybrid entwinement of two sides, foregrounding the relationality of resonating experiences, as well as the ways in which selves lose/transcend themselves *and* are lost/transcended "in" resonance.

One of these descriptions can be found in the fourth chapter of *Late Modernity in Crisis*, in which Rosa refers to the middle voice to describe the idea that resonance constitutes a moment in between passivity and activity, and therefore in between total controllability and total uncontrollability. He writes:

> The middle voice no longer exists in modern Western languages (beyond faint vestiges), but it can be found in ancient Greek, Hebrew, Sanskrit, and in many other languages. It makes it possible to express a way of participating or being involved in an event or activity in which the subject is neither the perpetrator nor the victim—in which, in fact, it is not possible to draw a categorical distinction between subject and object. In such situations, people experience themselves as being neither omnipotent nor powerless, but rather as semi-empowered, which means that they take part in and are given a role at the same time (and thus their experience is simultaneously medio-passive and medio-active). The idea of the medio-passive concerns a form of being-in-the-world in which we are both active and passive—or neither active nor passive, but in a state of being beyond this distinction, and perhaps even beyond the distinction between condition and action. (Reckwitz and Rosa 2023, 152–153)

We find echoes here of the notion of *semi-controllability* that Rosa, as mentioned above, presents in *Unverfügbarkeit*. Furthermore, the passage highlights aspects that Lawtoo links to his own notion of "mimesis" and to Malabou's concept of "plasticity," which Lawtoo writes has both a "passive" and "adaptable" side, as well as an "active, productive and creative side generative of new formations, transformations" (Introduction, 12).[33]

Rosa does not really go further into the *grammatical* or *linguistic* aspects of the middle voice, but mainly uses the notion, almost as a metaphor, to characterize the in-betweenness of resonant experiences; to describe a certain form of "semi-controllability." However, in a footnote in *Late Modernity in Crisis* he quotes the following passage from "Différence" in which Jacques Derrida links this elusive concept to the middle voice and the notion of resonance:

> [B]ecause it brings us close to the infinitive and active kernel of différer, différance (with an a) neutralizes what the infinitive denotes as simply active, just as mouvance in our language does not simply mean the fact of moving, of moving oneself or of being moved. No more is

resonance the act of resonating. We must consider that in the usage of our language the ending -ance remains undecided between the active and the passive. And we will see why that which lets itself be designated différance is neither simply active nor simply passive, announcing or rather recalling something like the middle voice, saying an operation that is not an operation, an operation that cannot be conceived either as passion or as the action of a subject on an object. (Derrida 1982, 8–9; qtd in Reckwitz and Rosa 2023, 218 n. 25)

Derrida here describes his notion of *différance* as making meaning possible, as an ungraspable trace or mark that refers to both difference and deference. Meaning is generated within webs of words that are different from each other and also refer to each other, endlessly deferring the arrival of meaning at a foundation or essence. Within this theory, the notion of a stable and autonomous "self" almost disappears, becoming like a trace or ghost that moves and is moved—between activity and passivity—through networks of meaning, constantly producing new ideas and perspectives and itself being the product of this moving as well.

I want to use Rosa's reference to poststructuralism as an invitation to explore another analysis of the middle voice developed after the linguistic turn: more concretely than Derrida, Roland Barthes points out how, in and by this mode, forms of subjectivity are generated within and by grammatical structures. In "To Write: An Intransitive Verb?" Barthes analyzes the verb "writing," linking the middle voice to both modernity and to modernist literature:

> [I]n the middle voice of *to write*, the distance between *scriptor* and language diminishes asymptotically. We could even say that it is the writings of subjectivity, such as romantic writing, which are active, for in them the agent is not interior but *anterior* to the process of writing: here the one who writes does not write for himself, but as if by proxy, for an exterior and antecedent person (even if both bear the same name), while, in the modern verb of middle voice *to write*, the subject is constituted as immediately contemporary with the writing, being effected and affected by it: this is the exemplary case of the Proustian narrator, who exists only by writing, despite the reference to a pseudo-memory. (1986, 19)

The middle voice, Barthes suggests here, indicates that writing is not "done" or "performed" by a subject or self who "exists" before or outside the text. Instead, this self is shaped within and by the text *through* writing, which is therefore neither an active nor a passive phenomenon—instead, the self is enveloped by, and generated within, the linguistic structures of modernist literature.

What I find helpful about Barthes's reflections on the middle voice is that the idea of the subject does not completely disappear; it is not totally determined or undermined by structures and forces outside of it, whether they concern the historical rules and norms as they are—as he observes in *Writing Degree Zero*—sedimented in *language*, or the personal, biological and embodied dimensions of the self as they appear in what Barthes characterizes as one's *style*.[34] The subject *does* have a certain force and therefore a certain semi-autonomy, of which Barthes sketches the contours without having to turn to Kantian understandings of autonomous self-determination; without, in other words, having to rely on that which Lawtoo describes as the notion of a "volitional, autonomous and free subject" (Coda, 311). The subject, as it "comes about" within and through the middle voice, is not completely "free": it is always steered, influenced, touched and affected by structures and dimensions (social, political, historical, economic, biological, physical, personal) that constitute it. It is, therefore, both *because of* and *in spite of* these structures that a self is carved out/carves itself out within, by and through writing, in between language and style and in between autonomy and heteronomy.

Barthes's reflections on the middle voice suggest a way of thinking about subjectivity that helps us put more flesh on the bones of Adorno's distinction between primitive and aesthetic mimesis. Whereas primitive mimesis revolves around an uncritical embeddedness in the world that involves a subject lost in a "total spell," aesthetic mimesis preserves a "shudder"—a spontaneous and rather uncontrollable way of relating to the world—that, at the same time, forms part of a process of individual self-constitution. The latter form of mimesis, Adorno observes, is permeated with cognition, thought and reflection, making it possible for this self to elevate itself out of the "total spell" in which it finds itself thrown, to use an existentialist phrase. Nevertheless, it is not completely disconnected from anything over which it has no control; instead, as mentioned above, this subject is elevated and elevates itself within and through the shudder it experiences.

This approach makes it possible to sketch the contours of a *spectrum of mimesis*, on which pathological forms of mimesis come closer to what Adorno calls "primitive mimesis," and patho-logical ones approach "aesthetic mimesis." On the latter side, the subject carves out its own space through mimetic movements, which at the same time carve out that subject, generating a form of semi-autonomy that is never completely distanced from its "other," not unlike the self that "writes itself" within Barthes's understanding of language. On the other side—that of pathological forms of mimesis—this subject loses its semi-autonomy, its individuality dissolving in the "total spell" of, for example, a neofascist worldview.[35]

In his dialogue with Malabou, Lawtoo indeed describes "automatic mimetic reflexes that sediment into habits and might appear as simply passive yet, through repetition, might also be the condition for the development of a type of strength constitutive of a more active, or productive mimesis" (Coda, 310). Again, referring to the Janus-faced aspects of mimesis, he comes very close here to Rosa's references to the middle voice, as well as to Adorno's genealogy of subjectivity driven by two mimetic "moments" or "gestures." It is therefore no surprise that, in *Homo Mimeticus*, Lawtoo praises Jane Bennett's references to the middle voice, since this mode makes it possible, he writes, to describe a consciousness

> in which the ego experiences itself as both located in the mind and in the body, active and passive, inside and outside, present and absent, conscious and unconscious, in touch with pathos and distant, being mostly herself while being someone else—in short a middle state of pathos of distance that is the defining disposition of homo mimeticus. (2022, 272)

Indeed, it is in this passage that Adorno's references to primitive and aesthetic mimesis resonate strongly with Lawtoo's descriptions of Dionysian and Apollonian mimesis, with the notion of a "pathos of distance" generating a semi-autonomous subject.[36]

Conclusion

This brings me to the conclusion of this chapter, in which I have shown that there are striking similarities between mimetic studies and resonance theory. Both foreground processes that concern forms of relationality that problematize the idea(l) of the autonomous, rational, free and individual subject. Both stress that we are, to a large extent, shaped by connections, gestures, flows and vibrations over which we have limited control, of which we are not completely aware and that often have a material dimension. For Rosa these processes concern experiences of resonance, which he describes as transcending the self because they consist of "af←fective" and "e→motional" relations of uncontrollable and transformative *in-betweenness*. Lawtoo highlights the ways in which we unconsciously imitate others from the moment we come into being. For him, the "unconscious" therefore concerns pre-Freudian and post-Freudian understandings of a self that is always already entangled with others through material forms of relationality. Both Rosa and Lawtoo refer positively to the theory of mirror neurons, which they understand as affirming their ideas about (partly) unconscious ways of resonating with and imitating others.

I have also indicated that both fields struggle with similar problems, which mainly concern entwinements of normative and descriptive elements. Rosa argues that the notion of resonance enables him to both *describe* aspects of modernity *and* to indicate why and how modernity's "pathologies" can and *should* be fixed. For him, resonance is therefore always also a *solution*, and never only a *description* or *explanation*. Lawtoo argues that mimesis is a Janus-faced concept that is "patho(-)logical" in nature. This means that we are vulnerable to pathological forms of mimesis, but also that there are patho-logical manifestations of mimetic relationality, which concern empathy, sympathy, *Mitleid*, communality and more. In fact, he observes that we need to try and transform pathological forms of mimesis into patho-logical ones.

To explain why these entwinements of normative and descriptive elements are problematic, I have discussed the question of subjectivity: to be able to distinguish good from bad forms of resonance/mimesis, we need to develop a notion of subjectivity that can function as a normative yardstick. If this subjectivity is undermined by forms of mimetic/resonant relationality, they should be rejected as pathological. If they strengthen this subjectivity or infuse it with energy, they should be defended. To be able to function as such a normative yardstick, this subjectivity should be understood as strong enough not to be completely overcome or overshadowed by irrational and uncritical forms of anti-individualistic relationality. On the other hand, this understanding of subjectivity should also be able to incorporate the observation, crucial to mimetic studies and resonance theory, that we are never *completely* masters in our own house.

This has resulted in my defense of a *semi-autonomous mimetic/resonant subject* that balances self-critical cognition with material embeddedness. To flesh out this understanding of subjectivity, I have turned to Adorno's distinction between primitive and aesthetic mimesis, as well as to Derrida's and Barthes's references to the middle voice. The latter linguistic mode makes it possible to conceptualize a semi-autonomous form of subjectivity that does not revolve around Cartesian or Kantian understandings of purely rational self-determination. This semi-autonomous subjectivity therefore entails that, *on the one hand*, there are always sensual, affective, desiring, mimetic and resonant elements that flow through the subject—Adorno's "shudder"—over which we have limited control. Without these elements, rational thought would lose its contact with and embeddedness in the world. *On the other hand*, without the rational reflection that Adorno links to "aesthetic mimesis," and therefore without Lawtoo's (and Nietzsche's) "pathos of distance," this contact would remain blind, unable to critically reflect on processes that might overshadow it or that produce pathological social relations. With help of this yardstick of semi-autonomous subjectivity, I conclude, we can position forms of relationality on a *spectrum of resonance* and/or on a *spectrum of mimesis*.

Acknowledgements

This chapter is based on ideas presented at a workshop on mimetic connections, organized in November 2023 at the Leiden University Centre for the Arts in Society. I want to thank Nidesh Lawtoo and Willow Verkerk for their helpful comments on earlier versions of this text. This chapter is also inspired by a 2023 workshop with Hartmut Rosa at the University of Amsterdam. I want to thank Hartmut Rosa for his productive comments on the reflections I presented at this workshop.

Notes

1. See Lawtoo 2022, 116, 264.
2. Whereas Lawtoo characterizes resonance as another mask of mimesis, Rosa would probably understand mimesis as another mask of resonance.
3. Rosa 2013, 17–20.
4. Rosa 2013, 91.
5. Rosa 2013, 97.
6. See Rosa 2013, 76–77.
7. Rosa 2020, 113.
8. Rosa 2019, 195; Cooke 2020, 380 n. 1.
9. Rosa 2019b, 164–174.
10. Rosa 2021, 59.

11 Lawtoo 2022, 255–276.
12 Rosa 2019b, 370–371.
13 Rosa 2019b, 34–35.
14 Lawtoo 2022, 57.
15 Rosa 2021, 110–116.
16 Rosa 2021, 106.
17 The notion of "attunement" plays an important role in Rita Felski's postcritical analysis of the ways in which we respond to works of art. See Felski 2020b, 41–78. Felski has written positively about Rosa's resonance theory. See Felski 2020a.
18 Lawtoo 2022, 291; 2019, 40–41, 44.
19 Lawtoo 2019, 41–42.
20 Rosa 2021, 171.
21 Rosa 2021, 172.
22 Lawtoo 2022, 38–39.
23 See Rosa 2019a, 153–172.
24 See Gallese and Lawtoo 2024.
25 It could be argued that we have brain circuits that often prevent or block forms of full identification. However, this then still raises the question: how are we able to determine whether these preventing circuits are "good" and should be "trained" or "programmed" in specific ways? Where and how, in other words, does the normativity come in?
26 Cooke 2020, 376.
27 Peters and Majid 2022, 34–47.
28 Peters and Majid 2022, 53–54.
29 These two forms of mimesis come close to the Kantian distinction between passive mimesis and creative mimesis, which Malabou discusses in the context of "epigenetic mimesis" (Coda, 325). It should be noted that Adorno's employment of the concept of "primitivity" does raise concerns regarding a cultural bias, since it could resonate with colonialist distinctions between "primitive" and "civilized" societies. In the context of this chapter, however, the distinction is strictly used to describe processes that Lawtoo, as I indicate below, characterizes as "Apollonian" and "Dionysian."
30 Adorno (and Rosa) seem to suggest that, besides a form of uncritical "primitive mimesis," a second pathological form of subjectivity can be discerned, which revolves around a subject that is completely disconnected from others, the world and itself: a reified, fossilized and "mute" subject. This sparks the question whether it would it be possible, within mimetic studies, to conceptualize a non-mimetic subject.
31 Besides Adorno's genealogy of the modern self as it embodies the dialectic of enlightenment, his notion of aesthetic mimesis alludes to his defense of modernist artworks, which, in his view, gain a certain critical autonomy by both mirroring social conditions and turning against them. Arnold Schönberg's compositions, Adorno writes in this context, constitute both a mimetic relation with the reified rationality of late capitalist societies and transcend this rationality through the extreme character of this mirroring. In this way, they paradoxically open up space for brief experiences of otherness—for an aesthetic shudder that might gain a utopian aura (Adorno 1997, 257). Adorno's reference to a "shudder" also resonates with his ideas about the "addendum" (*das Hinzutredende*), a rather ungraspable material "spark" of *Mitleid* with suffering bodies, which again may break through the petrified shell of the modern subject (Peters and Majid 2022, 16–17).

32 A future study could explore the ways in which mimetic studies and resonance theory relate to the new materialisms. See Lawtoo 2022, 259, and Rosa, Henning and Bueno 2021.
33 Jane Bennett links her notion of a "porous I" to the middle voice as well. See Bennett 2020, 112–116.
34 See Barthes 1967, 10–13.
35 It is important to emphasize that Adorno's more vertical Hegelian emphasis on social mediation and negative dialectics, his Kantian defense of rational self-reflection and his Freudian understanding of the enlightened subject, to some extent—but perhaps not in equal measure—might conflict with both Rosa's and Lawtoo's more horizontal descriptions of experiences of transcendence.
36 In *Homo Mimeticus*, Lawtoo extensively discusses Philippe Lacoue-Labarthe's references to positions fluctuating between passivity and activity, which Lacoue-Labarthe takes from ideas on "plasticity" developed by Barthes, Bataille and others. Lacoue-Labarthe's thought is strongly influenced by Derrida and Adorno as well, making him a figure in whom the various traditions discussed in this chapter intersect.

Bibliography

Adorno, Theodor W. (1997). *Aesthetic Theory*, trans. Robert Hullot-Kenter. London: Continuum.

Barthes, Roland (1967). *Writing Degree Zero*, trans. Annette Lavers and Colin Smith. New York: Hill and Wang.

Barthes, Roland (1986). "To Write: An Intransitive Verb?," in *The Rustle of Language*, trans. Richard Howard. New York: Hill and Wang, 11–20.

Bennett, Jane (2020). *Influx & Efflux: Writing Up with Walt Whitman*. Durham, NC: Duke University Press.

Cooke, Maeve (2020). "Self-Efficacious Subjects: Rosa on Alienation and its Antithesis." *Journal of Political Power* 13.3, 366–381.

Derrida, Jacques (1982). "Différance," in *Margins of Philosophy*, trans. Alan Bass. Chicago: The University of Chicago Press, 1–27.

Felski, Rita (2020a). "Good Vibrations." *American Literary History* 32.2, 405–415.

Felski, Rita (2020b). *Hooked: Art and Attachment*. Chicago: The University of Chicago Press.

Gallese, Vittorio, and Nidesh Lawtoo (2024). "Coda: Beyond Brain and Body: A Dialogue with Vittorio Gallese," in *Homo Mimeticus II: Re-Turns to Mimesis*, eds. Nidesh Lawtoo and Marina Garcia-Granero. Leuven: Leuven University Press, 343–375.

Lawtoo, Nidesh (2019). "The Mimetic Unconscious: A Mirror for Genealogical Reflections," in *Imitation, Contagion, Suggestion: On Mimesis and Society*, ed. Christian Borch. London: Routledge, 37–53.

Lawtoo, Nidesh (2022). *Homo Mimeticus: A New Theory of Imitation*. Leuven: Leuven University Press.

Lawtoo, Nidesh, and Marina Garcia-Granero (eds.) (2024). *Homo Mimeticus II: Re-Turns to Mimesis*. Leuven: Leuven University Press.

Nietzsche, Friedrich (2013). "On Truth and Lies in a Nonmoral Sense," in *Philosophy and Truth: Selections from Nietzsche's Notebooks of the Early 1870s*, trans. Daniel Breazeale. New Jersey: Humanity Press, 79–91.

Peters, Mathijs, and Bareez Majid (2022). *Exploring Hartmut Rosa's Notion of Resonance*. London: Palgrave.
Rosa, Hartmut (2009). "Social Acceleration: Ethical and Political Consequences of a Desynchronized High-Speed Society," in *High-Speed Society: Social Acceleration, Power and Modernity*, eds. Hartmut Rosa and William E. Scheuerman. University Park, PA: The Pennsylvania State University Press, 77–112.
Rosa, Hartmut (2013a). *Alienation and Acceleration: Towards a Critical Theory of Late-Modern Temporality*. Aarhus: NSU Press.
Rosa, Hartmut (2013b). *Social Acceleration: A New Theory of Modernity*, trans. Jonathan Trejo-Mathys. New York: Columbia University Press.
Rosa, Hartmut (2019a). "Heimat als anverwandelter Weltausschnitt: Ein resonanztheoretischer Versuch." *Heimat global Modelle, Praxen und Medien der Heimatkonstruktion*, eds. Edoardo Costadura, Klaus Ries and Christiane Wiesenfelldt. Bielefeld: Transcript, 153–172.
Rosa, Hartmut (2019b). *Resonance: A Sociology of Our Relationship to the World*, trans. James C. Wagner. Cambridge: Polity Press.
Rosa, Hartmut (2020a). "Beethoven, the Sailor, the Boy and the Nazi: A Reply to My Critics." *Journal of Political Power* 13.3, 397–414.
Rosa, Hartmut (2020b). *The Uncontrollability of the World*, trans. James C. Wagner. Cambridge: Polity Press.
Rosa, Hartmut, Christoph Henning and Arthur Bueno (2021). *Critical Theory and New Materialisms*. London: Routledge.
Stein, Swen (2008). "Der Begriff der Mimesis in der Ästhetischen Theorie Adornos." *Kunsttexte. de*, January 12.
Susen, Simon (2019). "The Resonance of Resonance: Critical Theory as a Sociology of World-Relations?" *International Journal of Politics, Culture, and Society* 33, 309–334.
Taylor, Charles (1985). "Atomism," in *Philosophical Papers*. Cambridge: Cambridge University Press, 187–210.

PART III

FROM NEUROLITERATURE TO THE MIMETIC SUBCONSCIOUS

CHAPTER 9

SEMIOSIS AND MIMESIS

Sergey Zenkin

The notion of mimesis has changed considerably since the last century. The classical conception of *mimesis-representation* ("imitation of nature") was criticized theoretically in the Romantic epoch, and twentieth-century art definitively rejected it in practice.[1] At the same time, in various disciplines—sociology, psychology, anthropology, philosophy—another form of mimesis attracted a growing interest: *mimesis-communication*, in which there are no longer two objects, an original and a copy, but two or more subjects sharing their emotions, thoughts and movements.[2] To be sure, not all mimetic phenomena are communicational—it is not the case either with representations of non-animated, absent or imaginary objects, nor with mimicry by which a living creature strives to get indistinct from its environment. However, the mobility and plasticity of the "mimetic subject" (Lawtoo 2022, 82) becomes particularly intense when this subject is involved in an energetic communication with others.

In aesthetics, one of the first attempts to describe this phenomenon was undertaken by Leo Tolstoy in his essay *What is Art?* (1897), proposing the idea of "artistic contagion," an affective (and not intellectual) communication between the artist and the public, transmitting intense psychic tensions that Tolstoy associated with hypnotic suggestion.[3] Likewise, the history of aesthetics tends to limit the Greek idea of mimesis to the performing (*musikos*) arts (theater, dance, etc.), transmitting to the public's perception actions and temporal processes, not static objects.[4] The problem of mimesis-communication, with its creative and sometimes destructive effects, has been widely discussed in social sciences, beginning with Tolstoy's contemporaries Gabriel Tarde (1993 [1890]) and Georg Simmel (1905), and up to the influential anthropological theory of René Girard

(1972). In a philosophical way, it is explored by Jacques Derrida (1975), Nidesh Lawtoo (2022) and Valery Podoroga (2006; 2011).

Today, mimetic studies are expanding, considering imitation and plasticity as anthropological conditions of *Homo Mimeticus* and widening more and more the field of application of these notions in intellectual history, social sciences and the humanities.[5] My own project here is complementary to that enterprise: I intend to circumscribe the notion of mimesis by contrasting it to its counterpart. In what follows I will explore, using examples, and in an empirical rather than speculative manner, the limits of mimesis within a larger context of human communication. We tend to consider the latter as an exchange of *signs*, but in fact it combines two different modes: *semiotic* and *mimetic*. An attempt to distinguish them has been made by Timo Maran (2003), but, as his article's title indicates ("Mimesis as a Phenomenon of Semiotic Communication"), he presents mimesis as a particular case of semiosis, and I try to demonstrate their irreducible difference. Moreover, I will attempt to outline some possibilities of their *interplay* within a single social exchange or literary text.

A Pedagogical Example

To make my argument clear, let me first analyze a typical situation having no relation to art but belonging to teaching, a domain where the use of mimesis has the most profound roots, going back to animal practices. Suppose that we want to teach a complex corporeal movement—a gymnastic exercise, say, or a figure of dance. There are several methods to do so: (1) to *tell* the pupil what to do, or (2) to *show* them what to do. The first way is based on classic semiotic communication, operating with verbal and occasionally non-verbal *signs* (words, drawings, etc.). The second way is based on mimetic communication, which is often utilized not only by humans but also by animals when they are educating their young. The movement demonstrated by the instructor does not "signify" or "denote" the movement to be performed by the pupil but actually effectuates it; it is not to be understood like a sign but to be imitated like a model, an example. Understanding a sign implies a certain distance (mental, if not physical) from which the sign is perceived as a clearly distinct object; imitation of models leads to a mental self-identification. I try to exactly reproduce the model in my own actions, even if I see that model in front of me as a visually distinct figure.

This tendency to a close self-identification, mentally abolishing the actual distance between the imitator and the imitated model, is a feature of the "mimetic subject" in communication.

Someone might object that the second mode of teaching (2) is reducible to the first one (1): showing examples might be interpreted as a kind of iconic semiosis, an exchange of analogous signs, so that the instructor's actions are the signified of the sign, and their repetition by the pupil, its signifier. However, there remains an important difference between the two methods, consisting neither in the medium of communication (speech or gestures) nor in the type of transmitted signs (symbolic or iconic, in Charles Peirce's terms) but precisely in the (non-)identity of both elements of the communicational circuit. In the case (2), a fundamental condition of semiosis is not satisfied: an iconic sign, by definition, must be *similar* to the object it denotes, but it cannot be *identical* to the latter. This is an obvious but necessary requirement of semiotic communication, distinguishing it from the mimetic one: there are signs only when the signifier differs from the signified, while the mimetic subject tends to coincide—at least in imagination—with the model. This tendency is predominant in communicational mimesis, while in the representational kind the imitator (for example, an artist) usually maintains a perceptible difference between the model and its reproduction(s).[6]

The difference in question does not depend on the human or nonhuman nature of the material support of signs, which can be represented by separate objects or bodily gestures. Writing on mimesis in art, Willem Jacob Verdenius has remarked that meaning, to which a sign is always oriented, is incompatible with identity: "a thing which means itself is a monstrum, for meaning cannot be defined in terms of self-containment, but always implies a reference to something different from that by which it is meant" (1949, 32). The same is true for corporeal behaviors or linguistic expressions. A stone cannot *mean* a stone, a wave of the hand cannot *mean* a wave of the hand, a written word cannot *mean* its own inscription; even the readers of an absurd (for example surrealist) poem try to guess a phantom of meaning beyond it that they fail to catch. A sign never reproduces exactly what it denotes; it either schematizes its object in the case of iconic signs (a map is an analogous sign of territory, different as to its material, and reduced and simplified as to its form), or replaces it with something completely heterogeneous, in the case of symbolic or indexical signs. A printed character, a symbolic sign par excellence, has nothing to do with the sounds or phonemes it can refer to. Knocking on a door—an example of sign-index, according to Peirce—bears no resemblance to the person wanting to enter and signifying that intention by knocking. On the contrary, a participant in mimetic communication seeks to reproduce the other's aspect or behavior "literally," as accurately as possible; this happens not only in education but also in other social processes, like imitation of a fashionable idol or a movement of panic when people blindly rush in the same direction. This is what Friedrich Balke calls "excessive mimesis" (2018, 194),[7] reaching the point of complete sameness with the imitated one. Excessive mimesis can be applicable to relations between animals as well as between humans, who can recklessly follow one another to the point of giving up any personal difference and personal responsibility. Elsewhere I have called this a "malignant mimesis," proper to the behavior of crowds (including today's disseminated crowds, who are interconnected through social networks) and often leading them to aggressive and/or self-harmful actions (Zenkin 2015).

Roger Caillois describes almost the same phenomenon in his essay "Mimicry and Legendary Psychasthenia," beginning with this epigraph: "Beware: playing the ghost, you become one" (1998, 86).[8] Mimicry, defined in this way, is not exactly a communicative mimesis, for it implies no communication with the imitated (which in this case could be not only a living creature but also inanimate matter: stone, dirt). Here, the imitating animal interacts with an absolutely different being which it does not imitate, for example with a predator that it tries to deceive. Caillois's analysis allows us to consider mimicry as situated at the limit of mimetic communication, which tends to make all social structures dissolve into shapeless masses and in which individuals feel themselves to be mutually equivalent and even become identical, "excessively mimetic."

Let us now return to the two ways of teaching gymnastics or dancing. Looking more closely, we can note that schematizing takes place not only in telling but in showing too: in imitation from a visual distance (case (2) above: "do as I'm doing"), the instructor and the pupil exchange actions which are not absolutely identical (that would be impossible) but only more or less similar to each other: the pupil might take a shorter step, raise an arm not so high, etc. Strictly speaking, they share but an ideal *image* of the gesture being taught, and the image is always an incomplete reproduction, a would-be sign—once repeated and institutionalized, it can become a sign. Schematization also appears in a more complex situation, if a video recording is utilized for teaching. The demo shows how to perform the movements and this kind of communication may be characterized, on the one hand, as mimetic, since the pupil must imitate the person on the screen, but on the other hand, as semiotic, since the image on the screen does not coincide exactly with the real instructor's actions. The image is smaller in size, limited by a framework and does not allow improvisation, whereas a real instructor, showing a movement, can slow down its tempo, divide it into immobile poses, accentuate some of them and so on. Objectively, there is a visual semiosis here, but the participants to communication experience it as a corporeal mimesis. This fact is important: in our case (2), —the imitation of visualized movements—mimesis may be just a part, a moment of semiosis, or more precisely it may appear against the background of semiosis.

Such a limited, or momentary, mimesis might be characterized by another philosophical category, introduced by Nelson Goodman in his *Languages of Art*. Analyzing the situation of the instructor who combines telling and showing, he distinguishes between two symbolic relationships, *denotation* and *exemplification*, whose opposition is similar to that of "labels" and "samples." For instance, in a fabric shop one can see a *label* with information about the textile and its price, as well as a *sample* of the same textile that one may look at and touch. Drawing on these terms, Goodman describes the exchange of words and moves between an instructor and a pupil, in which the latter's corporeal gestures "respond" in the same way to the former's verbal commands (semiosis) or exemplary gestures (mimesis):

> The gymnastics instructor [...] gives samples. His demonstrations exemplify the requisite properties of the actions to be performed by his class, whereas his oral instructions prescribe rather than show what is to be done. The proper response to his knee-bend is a knee-bend; the proper response to his shout "lower" (even if in a high voice) is not to shout "lower" but to bend deeper. Nevertheless, since the demonstrations are part of the instruction, are accompanied by and may be replaced by verbal directions, and have no already established denotation, they may—like any sample not otherwise committed as to denotation—also be taken as denoting what the predicates they exemplify denote, and are then labels exemplifying themselves (1968, 63).

Goodman claims that some gestures "may denote or exemplify or both" (61). They are comparable to certain adjectives which not only signify a quality but also illustrate it: for instance, the English word *short* denotes and exemplifies "shortness," it is a short vocable. Certainly, such a concomitance does not always take place, the command "lower" not always being given in a low voice. Nevertheless, Goodman acknowledges that any gestures, insofar as they are accompanied by words and have "no already established denotation" (a gymnastic movement means nothing by itself, isolated from the educational process), are involved in the field of semiotic communication as specific self-referential signs or "labels exemplifying themselves." The boundary between semiotic (denoting) and mimetic (exemplifying) communication seems to be a permeable one: the elements of the former can belong to the latter as well.

However, until now we have not commented on a third method (3) of physical education, not mentioned by Goodman but often practiced by sports coaches and dance teachers: leading the student by the hand and carrying out the required action with them. Instead of shouting "lower" or performing a knee-bend as a visual demonstration, one can bend one's own knee together with the student. There are two possibilities here: if the pupil cooperates with the instructor (3a), it is still a mimetic communication—not at a distance, but rather in close bodily contact; and without cooperation (3b), it is no longer communication or intentional education, but rather coercion by force, as if in treating a passive material object or even a resisting animal. Both possibilities differ from case (2) by the elimination of distance in space and time between the participants to the mimetic communication: the pupil is in close contact with the instructor, grasps the latter's gestures and reproduces them immediately, without any delay.

Via their differences, these two methods—contact mimesis and coercion—reveal a new parameter of comparison, the ratio of *information* and *energy* in the communication; in the case analyzed here, it is the physical energy of the body in question, which can be economized or not in different manners of teaching. We can now gradually rank all the four pedagogical devices in relation to this parameter, i.e. energy expenditure on the instructor's side. It is minimal in the pure semiotic (telling) method (1), when the instructor can describe a hard and complex exercise, urging the pupil to try hard, but remaining immobile and effortless. In the case of exemplifying (showing) mimesis as a part of semiosis (2), the instructor performs the required actions but still can do so schematically, spending relatively little energy just so that the pupil can see an abstract pattern of the movement: showing is always easier than doing. In contact mimesis (3a), the exercise is performed completely by the instructor and the pupil at the same time, endeavoring a full sameness of their moves, and the energy spent is high. Finally, coercion (3b) takes the most amount of energy from both participants (the instructor must overpower the pupil's resistance, they are physically struggling), while the information transmitted tends to zero (the pupil ultimately learns nothing).

So, we can now make more precise and less permeable the gradual distinction between the two modes of communication, semiotic and mimetic. It is defined on two grounds: (1) semiotic relations are more distant and mimetic relations more close (in the latter case, the messages sent and received are strictly similar, and the participants of communication can physically touch each other in space and sometimes tend to subjectively identify themselves with each other); and (2) the mimetic mode of communication generally expends more physical energy (Zenkin 2022), while the semiotic one conveys more information (like primary and secondary psychic processes, in Freud's theory). The comparative degree of the terms ("more") means that the two modes, without coinciding, can coexist and work together, as in our example situation.

On the Cultural Interplay of Mimesis and Semiosis

There are many culturally institutionalized modes of communication that present a complex combination of mimesis and semiosis. I will focus here on some cases drawn from the literature that can demonstrate the specificity of mimesis-communication. Indeed, a literary text quite often "imitates" people and their speeches, even though in most cases they are imaginary. The writing subject (the author, the narrator) appears to be split into two consecutive instances, a previous and fictional "model" and a present "utterer." These two persons of unequal ontological status can be in communication, conforming to the above-mentioned parameters of mimetic communication, yet different from cases of semiotic communication.

Literature in its "realistic" forms is supposed to aim at a mimetic reflection of reality, at an immediate connection between text and referent, although in fact quite often it obtains, instead of authentic mimesis, only an illusionary "effect of reality" that just *signifies,* or connotes, the notion of reality (Barthes 1989). Some other literary devices, rarely qualified as "realistic," are in fact irreducible to semiotic processes and stand out against them. The example of teaching gymnastics and dancing suggests that the human body often plays a role in such devices. To be sure, not every mention of the body in a text is mimetic: quite often corporeal and even "naturalistic" literary themes are utilized as conventional and codified signs. In the physical aspect of a fictional character, we "read" his or her mental disposition; in openly erotic scenes we identify the author's non-conformist or, on the contrary, commercial project. Not only in texts but also in everyday social life, the human body is an object of semiotization, by means of medicine, fashion, sport, etc. But it can also participate in direct, non-semiotic mimesis, when a text in its unfolding functions as a contagious *gesture,* an energetic impulse without conventional meaning. Like any real facts, gestures often serve as conventional signs (e.g. shaking hands), but they can also produce a direct effect of imitation irreducible to semiosis.

Mimetic and semiotic devices can be variably distributed in a literary text. Let me briefly sketch how they interact, following the traditional division of literature into three "genres," or rather communicative modes: lyric, dramatic and epic (narrative).

In lyric poetry, mimetic devices are often coextensive with the text of the poem, functioning throughout its length, simultaneously with its semiotic meanings, like two parallel levels of communication. The most important such device is the *rhythm*, a generally meaningless perceptive effect, which extends across the whole poetic text and underlies its semantic structures. The Russian poet Vladimir Mayakovsky (1893–1930) in his essay *How to Make Verses?* attempted to describe his process of composition, taking for an example a poem he had written on the suicide in 1925 of another poet, Sergey Esenin. The traumatizing emotion and the need to react to that tragic event produced in Mayakovsky's mind a "hum" or "lowing," an inarticulate sound that he heard in his head prior to giving it a distinct verbal (i.e. semiotic) form (Mayakovsky 1927, 30). So, the instability and mortality of the human body thus revealed transformed into a kind of impersonal noise where the poet's individuality disappeared, like in death. This infra-linguistic "hum" is an imitation—not of the dead Esenin (whose poetry Mayakovsky appreciated, while disliking his personal behavior) but of the author's primary, irreflexive state of mind when he could not yet account for his own experience: "From where comes this fundamental lower-rhythm, it's unknown [...]. I don't know whether the rhythm exists outside or only inside me, most probably inside" (31).

On the first mimetic step of communication, the poet closely "imitates" in his speech his own unarticulated internal sound, almost impersonal (maybe it exists outside him?), obeying a purely energetic rule of rhythm. On the second semiotic step of communication, he will convey this rhythm to his audience through public lectures or to his readers through printed texts. The clear verbal propositions from which they are composed come later, as a secondary semiotic mask for the primary mimetic impulse. In his final verses, Mayakovsky manages to quote, modifying them, the last words of Esenin's poem written before the suicide, thus concluding his rhythmical mimesis with a verbal one (this time, it is really Esenin who is being imitated).

The mimetic devices that extend across the whole text or its long segments, and often resulting from a rhythmic choice, may be defined as *paradigmatic* ones. There are also *syntagmatic* mimetic devices, concentrated and isolated in brief segments of the text. An example, from the dramatic genre, might be the famous speech—in fact, just a few words—of Horace the Father, a character in Pierre Corneille's tragedy *Horace* (1640, Act III, scene 6). Having heard the news (later revealed to be false) that his youngest son has been cowardly and has fled from the outnumbering enemies who are challenging his city, this severe old Roman gives a heroic answer to someone attempting to excuse the young man: he wishes that his son had died in combat.

> *Iulia*:
> What should he against three have done?
> *Horace the Father*:
> Have dy'd...[10]

This short utterance—in French, *Qu'il mourût*—is traditionally pronounced on stage with a loud, solemn voice and divided by a pause from Horace's further speech. It is usually considered to be an example of the classical *sublime*, but it is also a mimetic effect. Separated by the actor's performance from the normal course of the theatrical dialog, containing (in the original text) an estranging verbal tense—the subjunctive imperfect, a bookish form never utilized in oral speech—and referring to a (hypothetical) loss of a close relative of the speaker, that utterance must be perceived by the terrified and admiring spectator or reader as an infra-meaningful energetic strike, a kind of cry, making them intensely live out the exasperated feeling of the father ready to sacrifice his only remaining son: one has to become for a moment his double, to immediately adhere to his experience. So, the corporeal impulse of (hypothetical) death functions as a signal for internal imitation of that primary and self-sufficient affect, which will be only afterwards reintegrated into the system of values, acts and reactions forming a dramatic plot. The theatrical performance alternates "weak" (systemized) and "strong" (isolated) moments, corresponding to semiotic and mimetic modes of communication.

In epic, narrative mode, semiosis also shifts to mimesis in imitation of another person's discourse. Under the classic narrative regime, this imitation could appear only in the characters' direct speech, where diegesis (storytelling) was replaced by mimesis (in the Platonic meaning of the term: direct representation). In modern novelistic prose, the use of the verbal imitation of individual speech is more extensive, also affecting free indirect speech. This mimetic device mostly works only in characteristic passages, standing against the neutral background of the authorial (diegetic) discourse: then the novelistic text tells events and at the same time reproduces someone's particular knowledge, feelings and intentions. In these specific segments, words begin to convey not only messages codified by the common language but also one's personal "tone," the energetic outline of a character's verbal gesture, transmitting their affects and bodily experiences. The reader is supposed to grasp at the same time competing, alternating or simultaneous messages, to experience the narrative text as a space of indetermination.[11]

Here is my last example. At the end of Chapter 2 of the first part of Gustave Flaubert's novel *Madame Bovary* (1856), we find a short paragraph recounting the death of Héloïse Dubuc, the first wife of Charles Bovary, after an altercation with his parents:

> But "the blow had struck home." A week after, as she was hanging up some washing in her yard, she was seized with a spitting of blood, and the next day, while Charles had his back turned to her drawing the window-curtain, she said, "O God!" gave a sigh and fainted. She was dead! What a surprise![12]

In the previous lines, Flaubert has explained the underlying causes of this sudden death: the widow Dubuc, ruined by her notary who has run away, saw herself accused by her parents-in-law of having deceived them by overvaluing her fortune when contracting her second marriage. A family quarrel ensued, which Héloïse's poor husband had to appease as best as he could. These events, reported by verbal means, with the aid of typical narrative (semiotic) devices, constitute a well-structured story and provide a certain knowledge of the novel's characters and of what happens to them. The reader is invited to form a critical idea of the widow Dubuc and her matrimonial fraud, of the parents Bovary and their indignation, and of Charles Bovary, caught between his two families.

But, in the paragraph in question, something unexpected happens too. At several points, instead of neutral narrative information, the reader runs into fragments of direct or indirect speech, loaded with impulses of affective energy. One of them comes from Héloïse herself, and it is almost meaningless: "O God!"; this interjection is as irrational as the sigh that follows it. No clearer is the direct and indirect speech with an unidentified origin. Who says: "but the blow has struck home"? Who is "surprised" at the death of Charles' spouse? These utterances, highlighted in the original French text by italics, quotation marks, or simply by an exclamation mark, refer to an indeterminate "people say," to the opinion of a vague community which surrounds the family Bovary and, like a tragic chorus, comments on their fate.[13] In these segments of text, the mimesis of fictional characters does not serve to "imitate" the words and ideas of someone in particular but constitutes instead an anonymous discharge of psychic energy, transmitted to any reader; that energy is indirectly denoted by the metaphor of "struck" and directly exemplified by the exclamation "What a surprise!" The mimetic figure, breaking away from the story, is explicitly related to the bodily experience of fainting and dying.

Undoubtedly, more examples need to be found, classified and more specifically analyzed. However, my examples demonstrate that communication, including that which is literary and artistic, makes use of semiotic and mimetic devices at once, which contrast with each other as information and energy, as signs and impulses, the latter producing a direct impact on the receiver's corporeal perception. These heterogeneous elements form various configurations, and their ratio varies as well: sometimes mimesis is integrated into semiosis and sometimes, like the primary processes of the unconscious, it comes to the fore and occupies a dominant position in the message. The recurrent theme of death that is present in these literary examples is likely not fortuitous: an instinct of death seems to surface here, contrasting with the stable and well-organized order of semiosis.

At this point, my inquiry might meet Catherine Malabou's idea of *plasticity*. Of course, as I have already remarked, this empirical study, based on the ideas of semiotics and collecting objective facts, can only indirectly correspond to a philosophical reflection departing from a priori data and searching to define the mode of existence of the human subject. However, some hypotheses on mimetic communication, on its interaction and self-identification with the other, have been proposed. The analysis of the mimetic–semiotic interplay in art and literature, using the notion of energy, has a philosophical scope. The energy mobilized in mimesis may be defined, in the most elementary cases, as purely physical (in my examples of teaching gymnastics and dancing); however, in more complex situations, especially in the artistic "contagion" once outlined by Tolstoy, it refers to psychic energy, taking fixed (in semiosis) or fluid (in mimesis) forms. This seems to match Malabou's interpretation of Freud's energetic model of the mind, as applied to the aesthetic activity:

> Binding is an operation which transforms the free traumatic energy into a quiescent energy [...]. The operation of binding is also very close to an artistic practice. It consists in shaping, moulding the scattered energy to unify and gather it. (2022, 285)

In this perspective, the plasticity of the mind, combining its fixed and fluid forms, might be at the origin of the communicational interplay of semiosis and mimesis in art, which sometimes binds and sometimes unbinds psychic energy. While semiosis guarantees the coherence of literary texts and the stability of their recognizable meanings, mimesis overlaps (or underlies) the textual rationality, breaks it up and, at unpredictable points in the text, substitutes energetic blows for articulated meanings. It "unbinds" in turn the aesthetic subject for a risky experience of imitating the impulses the reader receives from the work of art. Standing against the background of semiotic communication, in a position of "insularity," i.e. more or less in isolation, these mimetic effects give the impression of *presence* beyond or before meaning (Gumbrecht 2004, 102). Opposed to the "normal" manner of expression, which is meant to be an exchange of signs, they therefore constitute detached textual *figures* whose exploration, taking over the achievements of the ancient rhetoric, can lead us to a more profound understanding of the dynamics of culture.[14]

Notes

1. On the history and theory of artistic mimesis, see Spariosu 1984 and Gebauer 1995.
2. "La 'vraie' *mimésis*: entre deux sujets producteurs et non entre deux choses produites" (Derrida 1975, 68).
3. See Zenkin's analysis of Tolstoy's theory of mimesis (along with Antonin Artaud's and Gilles Deleuze's) in an article published in Russian (2020). On the importance of hypnotic suggestion in foregrounding a "mimetic unconscious" central to mimetic studies, see Lawtoo 2013 and Malabou's chapter on "Conflicting Subliminalities" in this volume (editors' note).
4. See for example Koller 1954.
5. So do for example the contributors to *Homo Mimeticus II*, exploring mimetic theories from Plato and Nietzsche and mimetic effects from biological imitation to twentieth-century literature and theater.
6. An exception or a limit case is the *serial* (for example, industrial) production of identical items which can be indistinguishable from their model as well as from each other. But I speak here only of mimesis-communication, linking subjects and not objects.
7. Balke founds his idea upon Louis Marin's distinction between *representation* and *simulacrum*, the latter showing to the receiver no longer a substitute of something else but its own literal presence (see Marin 1994).
8. The motto was probably borrowed from Villiers de L'Isle-Adam's novel *L'Ève future* (1886), where it served also as epigraph to Chapter I of the second part, with a reference (not verified): "Precept of the Kabbalah."
9. The connotation of "handcrafting" in this formula referred to similar titles of articles of the Russian Formalists, some of whom were Mayakovsky's close friends: an auxiliary, intertextual mimesis of terms.
10. I quote Corneille's text as it was "englished" by Charles Cotton in 1665: https://quod.lib.umich.edu/e/eebo/A34578.0001.001?rgn=main;view=fulltext.

11 Maurice Blanchot wrote on *indetermination* from the perspective of the author "fascinated" by his own fiction: "Of whoever is fascinated it can be said that he does not perceive any real object, any real figure, for what he sees does not belong to the world of reality, but to the indeterminate milieu of fascination" (1982 [1955], 32). I believe that Blanchot's insight might be reinterpreted as a description of the reader's experience as well, resulting from the complexity and heterogeneity of the literary discourse which is being read.

12 I quote the translation of Eleanor Marx Aveling, available at https://www.gutenberg.org/files/2413/2413-h/2413-h.htm#link2HCH0003, without pagination.

13 It is just a comparison. Friedrich Nietzsche highlighted the importance of the Dionysian pathos, expressed by the Greek chorus, for the aesthetic institutionalization of mimesis, which he claimed to be the origin of semiosis. But my intention here is not to speculate on the genesis nor on the early forms of communication.

14 A considerably shorter version of this article was published in Russian, in *Semiotika v proshlom i nastoyashchtem* [*Semiotics in the Past and in the Present*], eds. I. A. Sedakova, M. V. Zavialova, N. V. Zlydneva and A. B. Ippolitova (Moscow: Institute of Slavic Studies, 2023), 14–27.

Bibliography

Balke, Friedrich (2018). *Mimesis zur Einführung.* Hamburg: Junius Verlag.

Barthes, Roland (1989). "The reality effect" (1968), in *The Rustle of Language*, trans. R. Howard. Berkeley: University of California Press, 141–148.

Blanchot, Maurice (1982 [1955]). *The Space of Literature,* trans. by Ann Smock. Lincoln, NE: University of Nebraska Press.

Caillois, Roger (1998 [1938]). *Le Mythe et l'homme.* Paris: Gallimard.

Derrida, Jacques (1975). "Economimesis," in *Mimésis des articulations* (collectif). Paris: Aubier-Flammarion, 55–94.

Gebauer, Gunter, and Wulf, Christoph (1995 [1992]). *Mimesis: Culture—Art—Society,* trans. Don Reneau. Berkeley: University of California Press.

Girard, René (1972). *La Violence et le sacré.* Paris: Grasset.

Goodman, Nelson (1968). *Languages of Art: An Approach to a Theory of Symbols.* Indianapolis/New York/Kansas City: Bobbs-Merrill.

Gumbrecht, Hans Ulrich (2004). *Production of Presence: What Meaning Cannot Convey,* Stanford: Stanford University Press.

Koller, Hermann (1954). *Die Mimesis in der Antike: Nachamung, Darstellung, Ausdruck.* Bern: A. Francke.

Lawtoo, Nidesh (2013). *The Phantom of the Ego: Modernism and the Mimetic Unconscious.* East Lansing: Michigan State University Press.

Lawtoo, Nidesh (2022). *Homo Mimeticus: A New Theory of Imitation.* Leuven: Leuven University Press.

Malabou, Catherine (2022). *Plasticity: The Promise of Explosion.* Edinburgh: Edinburgh University Press.

Maran, Timo (2003). "Mimesis as a phenomenon of semiotic communication." *Sign Systems Studies* 31.1, 192–205.

Marin, Louis (1994). "Représentation et simulacre," in *De la représentation.* Paris: Seuil, 303–312.

Mayakovsky, Vladimir (1927). *Kak delat' stikhi? [How to Make Verses?].* Moscow: Ogoniok.

Podoroga, Valery (2006, 2011). *Mimesis.* 2 vols. Moscow: Logos, Kulturnaia revolutsia.
Simmel, Georg (1905). "Philosophie der Mode." *Moderne Zeitfragen* 11, 5–41.
Spariosu, Mihai (ed.) (1984). *Mimesis in Contemporary Theory: An Interdisciplinary Approach*, vol. 1-2. Amsterdam: J. Benjamin Publishing Company.
Tarde, Gabriel (1993 [1890]). *Les Lois de l'imitation.* Paris: Kimé.
Tolstoy, Leo (1897). *What is Art?*, trans. Richard Pevear and Larissa Volokhonsky. London: Penguin.
Verdenius, Willem Jacob (1949). *Mimesis: Plato's Doctrine of Artistic Imitation and its Meaning to Us.* Leiden: Brill.
Zenkin, Sergey (2015). "Zlokachestvennyi mimesis" ["A malignant mimesis"]. *Novoe literaturnoe obozrenie* 136, 49–56.
Zenkin, Sergey (2020). "Affektivny mimesis v iskusstve" ["The affective mimesis in art"]. *Mirgorod* 1.15, 137–152.
Zenkin, Sergey (2022). "K energeticheskoy teorii mimesisa" ["Towards an energy theory of mimesis"], in *Energia: transformatsia sily, metamorfoza poniatia,* eds. Ilya Kalinin, Jurij Murašov and Susanne Strätling. Moscow: Novoe literaturnoe obozrenie, 86–100.

CHAPTER 10

NEUROLITERATURE AND THE EXAMPLE

Tyler M. Williams

Introduction

As new materialist movements in critical theory and continental philosophy continue to shift attention from previous orientations in language toward the sciences,[1] Nidesh Lawtoo claims that "the heterogenous field of transdisciplinary humanities" arises from "new generations of critics and theorists attentive to emerging post-literary turns" (2022b, 2). At the forefront of this "new generation" of "post-literary" theorists is Catherine Malabou, whose work on plasticity brings recent developments in neurobiology into conversation with deconstruction to highlight the forms that emerge from their confrontation. Lawtoo rightly points out that critics at times mistake Malabou's materialist, empirical recourse to neural formation to signal a distancing from the symbolic, quasi-transcendental status of literature in post-structuralist philosophy. At least part of the reason for this perceived distancing pertains to the fact that, insofar as "deconstruction is not quite a materialism and should not be confused with it" (Lawtoo 2022a, 147), materialist strides toward the sciences are erroneously taken by some to imply proportional strides away from deconstruction and its interest in literature. However, literature is never absent from Malabou's work and, as Lawtoo shows, the rise of "post-literary" discourse in contemporary continental philosophy is hardly done with literature. Attention to Malabou's elaboration of the neologism "neuroliterature" reveals that Malabou's investment in the plastic frontiers between contemporary scientific discourse and continental philosophy revitalizes the "literary" in our so-called "post-literary" era. Consequently, while critical engagements with Malabou's conceptualization of plasticity understandably focus on its putative *break* from deconstruction, significantly less attention has been paid to the *formation* of literature within Malabou's neuro-materialist turn and its inheritance—to the extent that any inheritance a-teleologically transforms and re-produces the inherited—of a certain deconstructive heritage.

This essay considers the status of the "post-literary" in Malabou's contributions to a new "mimetic studies." Recent renewals of philosophical interest in the concept of mimesis take their cue from thinkers like Derrida and Lacoue-Labarthe, who, each in their own way, deconstruct the metaphysical tradition's relegation of mimesis (as imitation, copy, representation) to a status of derivativeness. In its vulgar sense, mimesis—its work of doubling, difference and reproduction—merely affirms the teleological unity of a stable point of origin. While Derrida and Lacoue-Labarthe both point to a literarity that inscribes the origin—in its originariness—with alterity (an origin that is not one), new strides in mimetic studies "add a materialist supplement […] to broaden the reach" of deconstruction's critical trajectory (Lawtoo 2022a, 148). For her part, Malabou theorizes a formation of the neural subject as always already mimetic, as materially divided against itself and yet produced from this very division. As a result, as the following pages will demonstrate, literature appears in Malabou's work less as an inscription than as a material process of fashioning, a mimesis that metamorphoses, plasticizes the origin in its becoming. Far from sacrificing literature on the altar of science, as some might at first glance mistake Malabou's materialism of doing, plasticity transforms a thinking of "the literary" as philosophy's "outside" for a new era. One of the major contributions that Malabou's thought gives to a revitalization of the concept of mimesis, to a new mimetic studies, or to a mimetic turn in contemporary thought, is her refashioning of the deconstructive potentialities of literature. Beginning with Derrida and then marking Malabou's proximity to, distance from and transformation of his articulation of deconstruction's "constant interest" in literature, what follows attends to the metamorphic shaping of "literature" in its emergence as "neuroliterature," which is to say, as "post-literary."

The Non-Prior Priority of Literature to Philosophy

That literature has no content proper to it, that its appearance disappears behind discourses that are not, properly speaking, literature, allows Derrida to align literature—or, something *about* literature, the *literarity* of literature—with the democratic right to say *anything* and *everything*. Derrida suggests that there "is" no literature precisely because "literature" names the oscillations between inside and outside. Literature has no proper *inside* because nothing resides *outside* its democratic right to such uncircumscribed, unbounded concepts as "anything" and "everything."

Derrida's point, which he develops in a well-known interview with Derek Attridge in 1989, is at once historical and philosophical. Historically, literature as an institution grows in the same soil as Enlightenment institutions of modern democracy and the juridical concept of right. For this reason, Derrida will frequently point out that literary production does not just conveniently coincide with, but is indeed indistinguishable from, a politics of non-censure and free speech. Or, as he succinctly puts it elsewhere: "no democracy without literature; no literature without democracy" (1995, 28).

Philosophically, the fact that the truth of literature is inextricable from its fiction (literature's right to say anything and everything cannot be restricted to the world of nonfiction) means that, on the one hand, absolutely anything and everything resides within literature's reach. In this sense, literature always imagines the world otherwise; it remains uncircumscribed by and thus irresponsible in the face of the empirical objectivity of "the world," since literature names "the very desire that what does not happen should happen" (1992, 35). On the other hand, no philosophical system, no matter how putatively pure or ideal in its self-presence, can absolutely bracket the traces of literary equivocation. Indeed, the very task of deconstruction, which already appears in Derrida's first publications on Husserl, where Derrida shows that Joycean equivocity irrepressibly haunts Husserl's ideal transmission of univocal geometric sense, involves tracing *inside* philosophy this sense of "literature" that, as unassimilable, opens philosophy to the *outside*, to its other, to the other, without which it would never be able to demarcate itself as "philosophy" (or, in Husserl's case, as a phenomenological science) in the first place.

Because Derrida's deconstruction of western metaphysics in part involves exposing a constitutive "literature" at work within the ideality of self-presence, Derrida will remind his readers that his "most constant interest, coming even before [his] philosophical interest [...] if this is possible, is toward literature, toward that writing that is called literary" (2004, 116). Some might take such a remark as proof straight from the horse's mouth that deconstruction more appropriately belongs to "literary theory" than to "philosophy" and that it rightfully deserves its place in the literature departments of Anglo-American universities into which it and other so-called French Theory was corralled in the latter decades of the twentieth century. However, any serious attention to Derrida's remarks cannot fail to notice the precisely *philosophical* stakes of Derrida's expressed interest in "that writing that is called literary."[2] That his interest in literature comes "before" his interest in philosophy, and that Derrida describes literature in this same interview as "the most interesting thing in the world, maybe more interesting than the world" (1992, 47), does not mean that Derrida identifies himself foremost with literature in any traditional, disciplinary sense.

The philosophy of deconstruction does not come after or secondarily to the priority of literature. In fact, deconstruction problematizes this exact logic of prioritization, which hinges upon such a crisp fold between a "before" and an "after." The *originary indistinction* between literature and philosophy reveals their mutual becoming and a-teleological entanglement. Literature "appears before" (in the double sense of being-prior and being-summoned, i.e. both before and after) philosophy as philosophy's outside and without which philosophical discourse could never assert itself as such.[3] In "This Strange Institution Called Literature," Derrida specifies to Attridge that, for him, "literature" is not reducible to novels, poetry, belles-lettres and other generic taxonomies and departmentalizations. Literature is a "strange institution" because the literarity of literature exceeds institutional circumscription; no *there is* will bring literature—its right to say anything and everything—to its fully phenomenal or ontologized presence. Furthermore, Derrida even confesses in *On the Name* that he does not particularly like literature "in general and for its own sake" (1995, 28). He reveals that if he were to "retire to an island," he would not bring with him works of literature. Instead, he would prefer works of history, philosophy, religion or memoirs, "perhaps *to make literature out of them*" (1995, 28; emphasis added). Derrida's point is more serious than this playful hypothetical might imply. The priority of literature to philosophy that Derrida describes here is a philosophical priority. That is, a priority that paradoxically follows what it precedes, a priority that deprioritizes the very logic of prioritization. Or, as Derrida might have put it: a priority without priority. "Literature" signifies for Derrida the originary *différance* that works restlessly inside philosophy: an outside inside, an internal exteriority, an "eccentric center" that opens the inner unity of a system to an equivocal and unbracketable alterity.

Can one go so far as to say that literature is the name of a form of production? That is, a creativity that does not arise teleologically from a concentrated point of origin but instead arises epigenetically, which is to say, from an originary mimesis: a doubling that, as explained above, does not reproduce an original but a doubling—a "*re*-production" (Lawtoo 2022b, 8)—that is itself originary.

Even though Derrida will often generalize "literature" as a synonym for "arche-writing," "arche-trace," "différance," he will also insist on its situatedness within the precise historical context of the European Enlightenment. As both *a part of* and *apart from* this historical circumscription, clearly Derrida does not teleologically ground literature within an archic paradigm. In other words, on the one hand, literature names a historically determined "spacing" at work constitutively yet destructively within the western philosophical tradition's metaphysics of self-presence; but, on the other hand, this historical determination cannot teleologically enclose what Derrida also recognizes as literature's fundamental irresponsibility. Literature appears in (and for) deconstruction as an a-teleological (or an-archic, or mimetic) origin of teleology. Consequently, if deconstruction's interest in literature precedes philosophy, but if this interest in literature remains philosophical, then (even though he does not put it in these terms) Derrida exchanges a linearly teleological structure of genesis for an a-teleological epigenesis.

This epigenetic formation of literature draws upon a materialism already at work quietly within Derrida's elaboration of deconstruction's priority (without priority) of literature to philosophy. Of Derrida's "followers" (i.e. those who come after but also recast, and thus stand before, deconstruction), Malabou goes furthest in bringing to light these materialist stakes, which for her ultimately signal the "dusk" of deconstruction's commitments to "symbolic" registers of language.[4] According to Malabou, current advancements in the biological sciences—specifically in neuroscience—have ushered in a new epoch in which long-held borders between the sciences and humanities no longer hold and in which, consequently, material biological processes (neuroplasticity, for example) enact what philosophy previously consigned to this quasi-transcendental status of the symbolic. In short, Malabou contends that conceptual fixtures of deconstruction—like trace, writing, spacing, text, literature and so on—themselves undergo transformation or re-formation in this new era in which transformability (i.e. plasticity) operates as a "motor scheme" (2010b, 15).

Plasticity, derived from the Greek *plassein* (to give and receive form), describes the ability of form to undergo transformation. Whether plasticity describes the adaptability of the brain's neural pathways to environmental input or the sculpture's emergence from a mass of clay, plasticity's biological and aesthetic metamorphoses highlight the *non-anteriority* of meaning: the symbolic emerges in the process of form's material, a-teleological becoming. The reason is because Malabou defines "materialism" as "the absence of any outside of the process of formation. Matter's self-formation and self-information is then systematically non-transcendental" (2022, 204). As a result, Malabou sees in plasticity evidence that form includes its own deconstruction at work materially *within* its formation: an outside at work inside the materiality of formation itself. But, if plasticity mimetically *re*-produces deconstruction for a new era, if plasticity indeed dawns at the "dusk of writing," then what exactly remains of literature?

It would appear as though Malabou's philosophical recourse to neuroplasticity, cellular epigenesis and other areas of the biological sciences displaces or dismisses deconstruction's taste for literature. Even though Malabou never explicitly articulates an entire concept of "literature," and even though plasticity often resides at the vanguard of a "post-literary" new materialism that sometimes appears to have relinquished deconstruction's investment in language, a form of literature pervades her work and remains inscribed, as it were, in its material becomings. On this point, Malabou explains in a 2022 interview that literature hardly plays a secondary or tangential role in her thought. Rather, it operates integrally with plasticity:

> The problem of plasticity, ontologically speaking, is that it is a movement that defines itself as a priority of fashioning over being. Plasticity has to invent itself and never depends on pre-set or pre-defined principles. It has to become the forms that it creates, as it creates itself through these forms. This is where literature intervenes for me. The kind of literary examples I use are all about the emergence of forms. Be it Kafka's metamorphoses or Duras's transformations, I always refer to the moment of the emergence of a form as an event. I think that plasticity and literature share this common destiny: they invent the form that they are. [...] It is from this space [of literature] that the forming of an invention and the invention of a form can emerge. (2022, 315)

Literature thus appears as both a form and the process of formation. If the "post-literary" announces a new formation of literature, then the shape this "literature" takes still requires elaboration lest the "post-" of "post-literary" be taken to imply the total abandonment of literature altogether. In fact, although Malabou's theorization of plasticity—the giving, receiving and negation of form—most famously stages a confrontation between continental *philosophy* and neuroscience, among the most radical contributions of her thought is its plasticization of the border between science and *literature*.[5]

Again, this insistence on the priority of literature does not make Malabou a literary theorist (in the traditional sense) any more than it does Derrida. But, for this reason, the plasticity of literature requires an elaboration of the metamorphic re-shaping of the relation between literature and philosophy for a "post-literary" era now under the lens of "mimetic studies."

Directions

To elaborate how plasticity presents a post-literary understanding of literature, what follows will trace the intersections of three moments across Malabou's work in which a discourse on literature begins to take shape. First, Malabou's understanding of disaffection at the heart of cerebral trauma, which, in the name of destructive plasticity, she argues highlights a *neutrality* at work within the cerebral subject. Second, Malabou's turn to show that this neutrality articulated—or at least bolstered—by neuroscientific research realigns the long history of philosophy's relation to literature, which has traditionally posited literature, Malabou shows via Foucault, as a thought from *outside*. "Neuroliterature" is the name Malabou gives to the metamorphic encounter between literature, philosophy and neuroscience around the configuration of this outside and its neutrality. Third, an elaboration of exactly how literature *works* in Malabou's work on plasticity, particularly regarding the question of literature's exemplarity within Malabou's articulation of plasticity and its "post-literary" movement.

While the purpose of this itinerary seeks to justify the continued relevance of literature to the future of new materialist studies, it also draws attention to inherent philosophical limits of traditional neuroaesthetic readings of the relationship between neuroscience and literature. As a result, for a body of work as attuned to the plasticity of disciplinary borders as Malabou's, to such an extent that Ian James will point out that "plasticity" entails as much the *conceptual passage* between discourses as plastic materiality itself,[6] the plastic transformation of "literature" as "post-literary" entails a metamorphosis of the entire constellation of frontiers between philosophy, the humanities and the sciences.

Material and Theoretical Woundings

In her book *The New Wounded: From Neurosis to Brain Damage,* Malabou elaborates a new concept of cerebral trauma that, distinct from the psycho-sexual structure of trauma germane to psychoanalysis, does not gain its traumatic force from, and does not shape its subject in relation to, prior, sedimented, causal, affective conflict within the subject. In this sense, Malabou shares recent strides in "mimetic studies" to think beyond the Oedipal unconscious by engaging materialist concepts of trauma elaborated in neurobiology.[7] The accidents that produce what Malabou calls the "new wounded" are cerebral accidents. These accidents can occur either in the form of quick and unforeseeable brain traumas or in the form of slow-moving neurodegenerative diseases. The reason Malabou assimilates these various sources and speeds of accident into a single category is because, despite their obvious differences, they share a common feature: the rupture of "everything that attaches the subject to himself and to others" (2012a, 9).

Examples of this detachment of the subject from "himself" abound in the clinical literature, particularly since neuroscientists typically study the neural integration of affect and subjectivity by examining patients whose cerebral lesions cause disintegration and disaffection. Whether caused by a sudden rupture, a slow-moving neurodegenerative disease like Alzheimer's or Parkinson's, traumas of war and terrorism, or prolonged exposure to the indignities of social exclusion, this irruption in the continuity of the self produces a new subject, "a form born of the accident, born by accident," a form whose "identity does not reflect itself, does not live its own transformation, does not subjectivize its change" (Malabou 2012b, 2, 11).

By far the most famous case comes from Vermont in 1848. A railroad worker named Phineas Gage suffered catastrophic damage to his prefrontal cortex when an explosion blasted a tamping iron diagonally through his left lower cheek, behind his left eye socket and out the frontal bone at the top of his skull. After miraculously recovering from his injuries, Gage underwent a personality transformation that included a disaffected inability to process emotions. A well-known refrain summarizes Gage's condition: Gage "was no longer Gage."[8] From this case Malabou concludes the following:

> Coolness, neutrality, absence and the state of being emotionally "flat" are the basic indexes of the meaninglessness of wounds that have the power to cause a metamorphosis which destroys individual history, that cannot be reintegrated into the normal course of a life or a destiny, and that, therefore, must be recognized as such even though it is impossible to categorize them as neurosis, psychosis, or, more vaguely, "madness." (2012a, 53)

In short, these brain injuries are not traumas that amplify or metastasize a pre-existent, latent history within the subject. They are accidents that, insofar as they sever the subject from themselves, constitute what Malabou calls a "wound without hermeneutic feature," an event "blind to the hermeneutic dimension" (8, 9). This is why Malabou will so often refer to this type of trauma as a "desert" or a "desertification" within the subject.

As Xavier Emmanuelli and Malabou both contend in their co-authored book *La Grande exclusion*, a major feature of cerebral trauma is the surprising indifference and disaffection of the wounded victim to their own suffering. Malabou contends that, among the "uniformity of neurological reaction" to trauma, the most devastating symptom "is the affective and emotional indifference of the patients" (14). At the same time, insofar as this trauma does not spark from a prior, narratable psychical history, the hermeneutic dimension of this form of trauma is not only lost on its victim but is also lost on the analytic ability to relate to it or make narratable sense of it. As Malabou puts it in *Self and Emotional Life*, "[b]rain damage is also a theoretical accident" (2013, 58).

Precisely insofar as the brain wound transforms the subject at the moment of their *material* wounding, this form of what Malabou repeatedly calls "destructive plasticity" (i.e. an annihilation that is not sublated into a more productive creation) also wounds the *symbolic* ground upon which any hermeneutic would take place. These material wounds are theoretical wounds because the new wounded are "new figures of the void or of identitarian abandonment who elude most therapies, especially psychoanalysis" (2012b, 12). Furthermore, insofar as these accidents are "simultaneously logical and biological," they escape therapeutic and interpretive terrain because they follow "a law that does not allow us to anticipate its instances." Or, in other words, they follow "a law that is surprised by its own instances" (2012b, 30).

When Malabou includes victims of social exclusion among these new wounded, when Emmanuelli claims (for this same reason) that social emergency is really a medical condition rather than a sociopolitical one, what sense are we to make—particularly in the absence of an adequate hermeneutic—of this disaffected absence of a sense of emergency? What care to provide to the "great excluded," and how to see, across the opacity of this indifferent void, the urgency of this care?[9] As Malabou asks, is it not precisely this absence of sense that constitutes the emergency?[10]

Literature is Outside (Philosophy) Because the Brain is Outside (Me)

The fact that this type of disaffected neutrality evades psychotherapeutic hermeneutics is related to what Paul Ricoeur identifies as a wider hermeneutic problem of *any* phenomenological access to the brain, wounded or otherwise. In his conversation with Jean-Pierre Changeux, published in English as *What Makes Us Think?*, Ricoeur argues that one cannot reflexively take one's own brain as a philosophical object because, unlike the hands and the eyes, the cortex does not have a distinct bodily experience. Ricoeur points out that there is no "parallelism" between the statements "I grasp with my hands," "I see with my eyes," and "I think with my brain," because "the 'with' does not function in the same way when I see with my eyes and when I think with my cortex" (2000, 49). Articulating what he sees as an inherent rift between the object of neuroscience and the object of philosophical hermeneutics, Ricoeur argues that one's brain, despite being the material site of consciousness, "will never belong to the experience of one's own body" (52). I think from my brain but I never really reflect on it. My brain is, in a sense, *outside* of "me."

Ricoeur uses this position to identify what he believes to be a philosophical limit of neurobiology. He argues that neuroscience remains unable to account for a phenomenology of bodily experience precisely because the brain resides outside the interiority of hermeneutics. But this limit also signals Malabou's divergence from Ricoeur. While Ricoeur argues that our brains *do not* hermeneutically factor into a phenomenology of bodily experience, Malabou adjusts Ricoeur's dismissal by arguing that we *do* and *can* think our brains, but we do so *as works of fiction*.

For Malabou, neural experience happens *as if* such impossible reflexivity is indeed possible, thus plasticizing the passage between the possible and impossible.[11] As Malabou puts it: "A brain can be thus characterized as a mechanism that creates its own fiction, that creates itself as a fiction for want of consciousness, reflexivity, and appropriate language" (2016a, 81). Or, restating this point in her essay, "You Are (Not) Your Synapses," Malabou writes: "If subjectivity does not exist, because it doesn't exist, we have to invent it" (2016b, 28–29). Is this not a new, material encounter with literature's right to say anything and everything?

Literature here takes shape as the mimetic emergence of a form, an invention. And this literary emergence occurs because "subjectivity never precedes its own invention" (Malabou 2016b, 30). Because "I" never purely coincides with "my brain," the necessity of subjectivity ("we *have to* invent it") entails an irrepressible literature within neural consciousness. Consciousness happens as a necessary fiction, as what Damasio calls a *representation*. Immediately, though, this use of the term "representation" requires clarification because for Damasio "representation" describes a kind of production rather than its typical connotations as a secondary copying of a prior original:

> The problem with the term representation is not its ambiguity, since everyone can guess what it means, but the implication that, somehow, the mental image or the neural pattern *represents*, in mind and in brain, with some degree of fidelity, the object to which the representation refers, as if the structure of the object were replicated in the representation. When I use the term representation, I make no such suggestion. I do not have any idea about how faithful neural patterns and mental images are, relative to the objects to which they refer. Moreover, whatever the fidelity may be, neural patterns and their corresponding mental images are as much creations of the brain as they are products of the external reality that prompts their creation. When you and I look at an object outside ourselves, we form comparable images in our respective brains. We know this well because you and I can describe the object in very similar ways, down to fine details. But that does not mean that the image we see is the copy of whatever the object outside is like. Whatever it is like, in absolute terms, we do not know. [...] Thus the images you and I see in our minds are not facsimiles of the particular object, but rather images of the interactions between each of us and an object which engaged our organisms, constructed in neural pattern form according to the organism's design. (1999, 320–321)

Damasio here describes the mimetic production of the self as an image. Since my brain "has no subjective site," since it remains outside of "me" and thus "challenges the phenomenological concept of the proper," I reflect on "my brain" as what Damasio calls an "image" or "proto-self," or as what Malabou calls a work of fiction. Even the first-person perspective of "conscious instantaneousness" appears as a "temporal fiction," as a kind of invention, an originary mimesis, since the immediacy of consciousness is "not an origin or a foundation but the result of a series of many progressive biological processes" (Malabou 2016b, 83). No longer understood according to its conventional sense as a copy of a stably preset original, representation here describes the "original" presentation of the self as precisely a re-presentation.

The claim that subjectivity results a-teleologically from pre-subjective biological processes to which consciousness remains blind, to such an extent that the proto-self is already itself a self-representation, a representation of the self to itself, and that there "is" no "self" outside this economy, describes a neuro-mental phenomenon known as *transparency*. In his book *The Ego Tunnel*, Thomas Metzinger argues that "there is no such thing as a self" because what we take for granted as a "self" is actually a "phenomenal self-model" responsible for "creating a unified and dynamic inner portrait of reality," that is, "a world-simulation so perfect that we do not recognize it as an image in our minds" (2009, 1, 6–7). Because the phenomenal self-model and world-simulation are representations produced by the brain, our subjectivity remains blind to the biological processes that make this representation of a proto-self possible. Consequently, the mimetic originariness of consciousness includes—indeed, produces—a phenomenological blindness to this very mimesis. As Metzinger explains, "we are unable to experience and introspectively recognize our self-models *as* models" (2009, 7).

Transparency describes this phenomenological opacity: "We do not see the window but only the bird flying by. We do not see neurons firing away in our brain but only what they represent for us. A conscious world-model active in the brain is transparent if the brain has no chance of discovering that it is a model—we look right through it, directly onto the world, as it were" (Metzinger 2009, 7). Consciousness is an illusory and convenient, yet nonetheless convincing, framework enabled precisely by this transparency, which erases its mimetic formation in the process of its emergence. Malabou uses a similar refrain to demonstrate this point throughout *What Should We Do With Our Brain?*: "The brain is a work, and we do not know it" (2008, 1). In this sense, "representation" is not a representation *of* something more real; reality is always already representative; it is originally mimetic. At the heart of conscious experience, Metzinger argues, resides a kind of "self-less" desert (2009, 63).

Returning to Ricoeur, Malabou clearly shares Ricoeur's positioning of the brain "outside" the intimately phenomenological coherence of the subject. However, she—like Damasio and Metzinger—denies the absolute priority of "the subject" and challenges Ricoeur's philosophical exclusion of the cortex. Against Ricoeur's claim that the brain cannot be an object of philosophical scrutiny, Malabou argues that "neural experience develops itself *as literature*" (2016b, 81; emphasis added).

The brain can be a philosophical object *as literature* because, Malabou argues, neuroscience today demonstrates the alignment of neural experience with what philosophy traditionally calls literature's outside. This is a way of saying that "literature" operates materially in the brain as the brain's self-deconstruction, as the possible-impossibility of neural consciousness to reflect upon itself, as the non-coincidence of the conscious subject with their brain. Malabou's claim that the subject's auto-affection is a kind of "literature" thus posits the subject as mimetic formation, as a priority without priority, a "delusion of the first person" (2016a, 84).[12] "Between 'my' brain and myself there is a sort of opaque wall, an absence of mirror, even as it is the most intimate part of myself, the 'me' who thinks and feels within 'me'" (Malabou 2012a, 140). As literature, the first person (re)presents itself to itself and, in doing so, mimetically produces for itself the delusion of a priority without which there would be no phenomenology of neural experience in the first place.

Literature takes the shape of an impossible hermeneutics, or, more specifically, the shape of the impossibility of a certain phenomenological hermeneutic of the brain. Significantly, though, it is from this impossibility that the subject emerges: consciousness produces itself *as literature*. And "literature" can be the name for this task (even though Malabou does not put it this way) insofar as literature retains the right to everything and anything. Importantly, whereas Derrida's elaboration of literature's *tout dire* remains within a quasi-transcendental paradigm of inscription, particularly regarding literature's symbolic excesses traced within philosophical systematization, for Malabou literature operates materially as the mimetic invention of a form.

Literature appears in Malabou's work as a plastic formation rather than as an incidental duplication of a prior, more real, original. Accordingly, Malabou's work explodes traditional connotations of the terms "literature," "mimesis," and "representation." These terms have conventionally coincided since Plato to describe the secondary process of "realist" duplication, but here, as with the ongoing emergence of "new mimetic studies," they account for the a-teleological process by which a form takes shape. A representation beyond representation; priority without priority. In *The New Wounded*, Malabou calls attention to this sense of literature as soon as she articulates psychoanalysis's inability to access the wounded brain. "One does not fantasize a brain injury," she argues, in the sense that brain injuries cannot be assimilated into the sense-making of an analytical space. She adds further that "one cannot even *represent* it" (2012a, 9; emphasis added). Even as a possible impossibility, the fiction literature mobilizes to think the brain transforms the traditional sense of mimesis as a "realist" representation into a kind of originary re-presentation. Rather than confine literature to secondariness, to a mimesis that belatedly duplicates the real, which is to say, to a kind of literary realism, literature here appears as an integral part of plasticity's priority of becoming over being.

Representation and Example

There are several moments in *The New Wounded* and *Ontology of the Accident*, among others, where Malabou introduces literature—Kafka, Bernhard, Duras, Proust, Mann—as a viable basis for reconciling the abyss that severs the new wounded from a possible analysis. Not in the sense that literature resides within the analytic gap she has just identified, as if literature will somehow take the place of psychoanalysis, nor in the sense that literature will simply reproduce psychoanalysis in the traditional sense of a mimetic copy, but in the sense that literature appears to be particularly attuned to the very presence of this gap in the first place.

In this sense, the work of literature and the work of neuroscience appear to be in closer conversation than continental philosophers and literary critics have so far acknowledged.[13] Typically, the close conversation between literature and neuroscience takes the form of what Patrick Colm Hogan calls "correlational criticism" (2014, 293). As Hogan explains, "in correlational criticism, the critic takes some theory—whether deconstruction or neuroscience—and finds parallels for its elements in principles of literature" (293).[14]

A well-known instance of this correlational criticism is Jonah Lehrer's *Proust Was a Neuroscientist* (2007), which praises works by Proust, Stein, Whitman, Woolf and others for their ability to "anticipate the discoveries of neuroscience" (vii). Lehrer's readings of these novels and poems reduce them to passive representations of neurobiological consensus, as if to suggest that *In Search of Lost Time, Tender Buttons, Leaves of Grass* or *Mrs. Dalloway* deserve their status as nineteenth- and twentieth-century literary masterpieces because they convincingly represent elements of neural experience consistent with and confirmable by the twenty-first-century neuroscientific field. The argumentative thrust of Lehrer's book relies, on the one hand, on a remarkably conventional understanding of literature as imitative representation and, on the other hand, as a secondary subordinate to the primacy of science. Lehrer's readings reduce literary merit to "accuracy" (ix) and deputize "modern neuroscience" to "[confirm] these artistic intuitions" (x).

Instances of this correlation might point to the presence of neurobiological conditions in works of literature, even works of literature that predate modern neuroscience, such as Melville's account of Ahab's phantom limb in *Moby Dick*. Others might biographically point to the interest that certain novelists and poets took in the science of their time, such as Whitman's complicated relation to nineteenth-century phrenology, which influenced his poetics of emotional embodiment, or his own observations of phantom limbs while serving as a volunteer nurse during the American Civil War. Others still might point to particular syndromes narrated in or exhibited by works of literature (even if these syndromes are never specifically named) that later gain scientific confirmation and their authors commendation for their "accurate" representation, like the aphasia that characterizes Beckett's stark prose or like Proust's articulation of voluntary and involuntary memory.[15] But, despite the relevant excitement that neuroscientific applause for literary innovation might produce in so-called "neuroaesthetic" literary studies, this applause rigidifies an impassable gap. First, this correlationism disregards the *literarity* of literature and, second, its reductionism hardens the border between literature and science by granting to neuroscience a position of original authenticity against which it then authorizes itself to judge the quality of literature's belated representation of it.

Malabou's interest in literature, her priority (without priority) of literature to philosophy, operates according to an entirely different form of mimetic representation than is typical of correlational criticism. A privileged example by Malabou (but also by Damasio) of this figure of the "new wounded" is Samuel Beckett's character Winnie in his play *Happy Days*. Winnie displays all the telltale signs of cerebral disaffection, indifferent as she is to the extent of her own suffering, detached as she is from the recognition of her past as an integral aspect of herself, eager to start each day de-contextually anew, repeating the same tasks, narrating herself in a desert, and so on.

While Beckett's play appears in this context to serve simply as a literary example of an otherwise neuroscientific phenomenon, Malabou explains at length in a recent interview that literary texts in her work are not *merely* examples that reiterate scientific conclusions. Literature is exemplary for Malabou rather than simply demonstrative, since literature shares in the same processes of formation and destruction; indeed it is calibrated to address precisely this desertified sense of trauma, which she aligns with destructive plasticity. In the face of what Malabou identifies as the hermeneutic constraints of philosophy and psychoanalysis, literature's right to say anything and everything grants it the irresponsible position of a perpetual in-between, a neutral and indifferent non-allegiance, which, on the one hand, places literature, as Derrida says, simultaneously outside and inside philosophical systematization and, on the other hand, as Malabou says, in an a-teleological economy of plastic self-fashioning, of re-presentation, independent of "pre-set or pre-defined principles" (2022, 315).[16] The point being: if destructive plasticity's desertified neutrality cannot be conceived from within a positive analytic hermeneutic, then literature is for Malabou the space of this neutrality. Accordingly, *plasticity materializes what in deconstruction goes by the name of literature.*

Returning to Beckett, *Happy Days* is not an example of destructive plasticity simply because it artfully represents a phenomenon available for neuroscientific confirmation, philosophic systematization and other forms of correlation. Rather, Malabou treats *Happy Days* as an "example" because Winnie's disaffection also mimetically re-presents the literarity of Beckett's work and vice versa.[17]

It is in this vein that Malabou coins the term "neuroliterature" *not* to identify a new discipline but rather to highlight that access to this desertified "outside," which has traditionally been accorded (by Foucault, for example) uniquely to the work of "modern literature," now finds its radical "post-literary" expression in neuroscience. Neuroliterature therefore names the a-teleological encounter—and thus the mutual transformation of the plastic border—between deconstruction and neuroscience as discourses of the outside. As discussed above, recent neuroscientific attention to what Malabou calls "destructive plasticity" reveals that the subject is materially absent to itself and that first-person auto-affection remains predicated not only on a *logical* structure of hetero-affection (as elaborated by Derrida) but on a *biological* hetero-affection, neutrality, desertification at the heart of neural transparency. Insofar as this transparency can never be experienced as such, this absolute outside of the subject emerges in the disaffection and transformation of the new wounded. Hence the clinical interest neurobiologists have shown in the effects of brain lesions on the emotional arrangement of the proto-self. Yet whereas philosophers like Derrida and Foucault posit "literature" as language's irresponsible exteriorization of the interiority of philosophical signification (for Derrida, the priority of equivocation to the univocality of sense, or for Foucault, modern literature as a non-subjective and non-representational reflection of language back upon itself), Malabou asks whether these ontologies of literature "prevent literature from becoming what it was attempting to become, that is, precisely a neutral and consequently inauthentic space" (2016a, 80).

If "modern literature" enacts, as Foucault argues in *The Thought from Outside*, the doubling of language back upon itself, to such an extent that literature has no object other than the abyssal formation of language itself, and if literature's experience of the outside thus undermines the coherence and solidity of the discourses it touches and inhabits (like philosophy), then, Malabou argues, *literature is also, in a sense, neural*. Even further, Malabou argues that Derrida's and Foucault's thinking of literature can, today, be radicalized beyond its traditional ontological registers. Neuroliterature, the "post-literary" encounter between deconstruction's literature and neuroscience's materiality, is the form of this radicalization.

Neuroliterature

"Neuroliterature" does not inaugurate "a new discipline" because, in Malabou's words, neuroliterature does not entail the analytical appropriation of "biological neural processes" for a "new foundation for literature" (2016a, 78). And, further, "literature" in this sense does not present itself as an exteriorly convenient example, one among others, in Malabou's work. Instead, Malabou's coinage of the term "neuroliterature" describes how innovations in neurobiology transform the deconstructive role "literature" conceptually plays in philosophy.[18] *Neuroliterature takes shape at the moment of philosophy's encounter with the outside.*

Neuroliterature thus entails neither a scientification of literature, nor a literaturing of science, nor a specifically literary subsection of neuroaesthetics. Neuroliterature is not a literary subgenre that describes the presence of brains in novels, and neither is it a subdiscipline within cognitive literary studies that marshals neuroscience to confirm or refute the accuracy of literary representation of neural experience. Furthermore, it does not describe that unique genre of science writing, the "neurological novel," which, popularized by A. R. Luria, Oliver Sacks and others, uses narrative to popularize interest in scientific studies of the brain. Neuroliterature names an *encounter*, an occurrence. It takes place, it happens, the moment continental philosophy's "common faith in literature" encounters neurobiology's materialist "deconstruction" of subjectivity, and vice versa (2016a, 78, 87). From this encounter, literature and neurobiology reveal themselves to share strides toward a decentering of self-consciousness, and the encounter itself—its occurrence—transforms the boundaries of *the literary* and *the neural* as such.

Unlike applicative approaches to literary studies, which treat scientific discourse as a tool for literary analysis, or that reduce works of literature to representative examples of neuroscientific phenomena, neuroliterature names this encounter at the plastic border between the sciences and the humanities and announces their co-transformations. The mimetic work of "literature" in neuroliterature is productive rather than simply passive and receptive. Consequently, if neuroliterature comprises Malabou's contribution to the "post-literary" turn in new materialism, then what we are "post" in post-literary materialism is clearly not "the literary" as such. As Nidesh Lawtoo (2022b) argues, the post-literary turn moves beyond ("post-") the representational status traditionally accorded to "realist" literature in favor of a rejuvenated sense of literary production. The post-literary plastically exchanges (or, ex-changes) one form of mimetic production for another. Furthermore, as Hannes Opelz notes, Malabou's elaboration of neuroliterature does not construct a simple *comparison* between the "de(con)struction of the cerebral subject" and that of the "literary subject" but rather uses the arrival of the former to announce the plastic *transformation* of the latter (Opelz 2022, 665).

At stake is a reactivation, or at least an expansion or re-presentation, of mimesis beyond its classical register. Post-literary literature does not produce a representation of a more authentic "original." Rather, it produces a concept of mimesis that is itself originary: a priority without priority. This is its truth. And, as Gebauer and Wulf put it: "Mimesis resembles truth insofar as truth never resembles itself, can never resemble itself, and never ceases retreating and donning masks" (1992, 306). Malabou describes this originary mimesis as "a priority of fashioning over being, a priority of transformation over what is to be transformed" (2010a, 12), which is to say, a process of formation within which the teleology of priority no longer holds sway. And she shows that this fashioning re-fashions the symbolic motricity of literature in deconstruction for a new "post-literary" era. Literature, as plasticity, as neuroliterature, becomes the form it creates.

Notes

1. For a succinct summary of this migration, see, for example, Barad 2007, 132.
2. For one of the earliest, and still one of the best, articulations of the intrinsically *philosophical* project of deconstruction, including deconstruction's interventions in "literature," see Gasché 1986.
3. I pursue this topic of the plastic boundaries between philosophy and the "literature" of its "outside" in Williams 2023.
4. This placement of plasticity vis-à-vis the "graphic" elements of deconstruction appears in the majority of Malabou's writings, but perhaps most explicitly in *Plasticity at the Dusk of Writing* (2010b) and in her chapter "Plasticity and Grammatology" in *Changing Difference* (2011). For a defense of Derrida's graphism against Malabou's charge that it remains limited in its transformability by its predication on "writing," see ch. 5 of Goldgaber's *Speculative Grammatology* (2021).
5. See Malabou 2022, 314–315.

6   See James's introduction to Malabou's *Plasticity: The Promise of Explosion* (2022).
7   Indicative texts of this turn in mimetic studies are three recent books published by Nidesh Lawtoo: *The Phantom of the Ego* (2013), *Violence and the Oedipal Unconscious* (2023a), and *Violence and the Mimetic Unconscious* (2023b).
8   For instance, see Damasio 1994, 7. On the nature of Gage's personality transformations and what these transformations indicate about the neurological processes that regulate emotion, see Damasio 1994, 56.
9   The French phrase *la grande exclusion* contains an idiomatic usage not captured by the English "great exclusion." For example, French policy will address *la lutte contre la grande exclusion,* as in the June 2022 signing of the *Pacte parisien de lutte contre l'exclusion*, which is itself an extension of the initial form of this pact signed in 2015, designed to provide city-wide resources to address the precarity of some of the city's most vulnerable residents. More generally, Emmanuelli describes *la grande exclusion* as the encounter between social exclusion and self-exclusion (Malabou and Emmanueli 2009, 68).
10   On this question, see Malabou and Emmanueli 2009, 106 and Malabou 2012a, 155.
11   For a fuller elaboration of the boundaries and oscillations between the possible and impossible in Malabou's thought, see Williams 2019.
12   Although "literature" never *explicitly* appears in her analysis, see Malabou's contribution to *Self and Emotional Life* (2013) for a detailed exposition of how this neurobiological concept of transparency transforms deconstruction's argument for an originary hetero-affection at the heart of the subject's auto-affection.
13   Demonstrating the proximity between the sciences and the humanities, despite the reluctance of the latter to acknowledge the stakes of reconciling itself to the former, comprises the main objective of Malabou's essay "The Future of the Humanities" (2010a).
14   For a critique of this correlational criticism in the reception of Malabou, see Williams 2019.
15   See Oppenheim 2008 for an example of this type of neuroaesthetic reading of Beckett. Oppenheim seeks to show that "Beckett's work reveals a preoccupation with neuro-psychiatric disorders uncanny in the accuracy of their representation" (188). Of particular interest to Oppenheim is Beckett's representation of hysteria and asomatognosia in his play *Not I* (194). An interesting example of reading Beckett as distinguished in his ability to represent, and at times predict, neurobiological and neuropsychiatric disorders is the "Beckett and Brain Science" project by Barry, Maude and Salisbury (2016).
16   Along these same lines, Blanchot describes "literature" in *The Book to Come* as being, on the one hand, "opposed to the order of essences" and thus, on the other hand, an "impersonal neutrality" (2003, 200).
17   For another instance of this kind of "exemplary" positioning of literature, see Lawtoo 2016.
18   This point marks a gentle disagreement with Martell 2021, who takes this epigenetic self-shaping—form giving form to itself, a structure produced in simultaneity with what it structures—as an indication that plasticity "goes beyond" rather than re-produces deconstruction.

Bibliography

Barad, Karen (2007). *Meeting the Universe Halfway: Quantum Physics and the Entanglement of Matter and Meaning*. Durham, NC: Duke University Press.

Barry, Elizabeth, Ulrika Maude and Laura Salisbury (2016). "Introduction—Beckett, Medicine and the Brain." *Journal of Medical Humanities* 37, 127–135.

Blanchot, Maurice (2003). *The Book to Come*, trans. Charlotte Mandell. Stanford: Stanford University Press.

Changeux, Jean-Pierre, and Paul Ricoeur (2000). *What Makes Us Think? A Neuroscientist and a Philosopher Argue About Ethics, Human Nature, and the Brain*, trans. M. B. DeBoise. Princeton: Princeton University Press.

Damasio, Antonio (1994). *Descartes' Error: Emotion, Reason, and the Human Brain*. New York: Putnam.

Damasio, Antonio (1999). *The Feeling of What Happens: Body and Emotion in the Making of Consciousness*. New York: Harvest.

Derrida, Jacques (1992). "This Strange Institution Called Literature," trans. Geoffrey Bennington and Rachel Bowlby, in *Acts of Literature*, ed. Derek Attridge. New York: Routledge.

Derrida, Jacques (1995). *On the Name*, ed. Thomas Dutoit, trans. David Wood, John P. Leavey, Jr. and Ian MacLeod. Stanford: Stanford University Press.

Derrida, Jacques (2004). *Eyes of the University: Right to Philosophy 2*, trans. Jan Plug et al. Stanford: Stanford University Press.

Gasché, Rodolphe (1986). *The Tain of the Mirror: Derrida and the Philosophy of Reflection*. Cambridge: Harvard University Press.

Gebauer, Gunter, and Christoph Wulf (1992). *Mimesis: Culture, Art, Society*, trans. Don Reneau. Berkeley: University of California Press.

Goldgaber, Deborah (2021). *Speculative Grammatology: Deconstruction and the New Materialism*. Edinburgh: Edinburgh University Press.

Lawtoo, Nidesh (2013). *The Phantom of the Ego: Modernism and the Mimetic Unconscious*. East Lansing: Michigan State University Press.

Lawtoo, Nidesh (2016). "Conrad's Neuroplasticity." *Modernism/modernity* 23.4, 771–788.

Lawtoo, Nidesh (2022a). *Homo Mimeticus: A New Theory of Imitation*. Leuven: Leuven University Press.

Lawtoo, Nidesh (2022b). "The Mimetic Condition: Theory and Concepts." *CounterText* 8.1, 1–22.

Lawtoo, Nidesh (2023a). *Violence and the Oedipal Unconscious. Volume 1: The Catharsis Hypothesis*. East Lansing: Michigan State University Press.

Lawtoo, Nidesh (2023b). *Violence and the Mimetic Unconscious. Volume 2: The Affective Hypothesis*. East Lansing: Michigan State University Press.

Lehrer, Jonah (2007). *Proust Was a Neuroscientist*. New York: Houghton Mifflin.

Malabou, Catherine (2008). *What Should We Do With Our Brain?*, trans. Sebastian Rand. New York: Fordham University Press.

Malabou, Catherine (2010a). "The Future of the Humanities." *theory@buffalo* 14, 8–16.

Malabou, Catherine (2010b). *Plasticity at the Dusk of Writing: Dialectic, Destruction, Deconstruction*, trans. Carolyn Shread. New York: Columbia University Press.

Malabou, Catherine (2012a). *The New Wounded: From Neurosis to Brain Damage*, trans. Steven Miller. New York: Fordham University Press.

Malabou, Catherine (2012b). *Ontology of the Accident*, trans. Carolyn Shread. Malden: Polity.
Malabou, Catherine (2013). "Go Wonder: Subjectivity and Affects in Neurobiological Times," in Catherine Malabou and Adrian Johnston, *Self and Emotional Life: Philosophy, Psychoanalysis, and Neuroscience*. New York: Columbia University Press, 1–71.
Malabou, Catherine (2016a). "What is Neuro-Literature?" *SubStance* 45.2, 78–87.
Malabou, Catherine (2016b). "'You Are (Not) Your Synapses': Toward a Critical Approach to Neuroscience," in *Plasticity and Pathology: On the Formation of the Neural Subject*, eds. David Bates and Nima Bassiri. New York: Fordham University Press, 20–34.
Malabou, Catherine (2022). *Plasticity: The Promise of Explosion*, ed. Tyler M. Williams. Edinburgh: Edinburgh University Press.
Malabou, Catherine, and Xavier Emmanuelli (2009). *La Grande exclusion. L'urgence sociale, symptômes et thérapeutique*. Paris: Bayard.
Martell, James (2021). "Malabouian Plasticity Beyond Surfaces." *Mosaic* 54.1, 93–112.
Metzinger, Thomas (2009). *The Ego Tunnel: The Science of the Mind and the Myth of the Self*. New York: Basic Books.
Opelz, Hannes (2022). "Plasticité du dehors." *MLN* 137.4, 657–672.
Oppenheim, Lois (2008). "A Twenty-First Century Perspective on a Play by Samuel Beckett." *Journal of Beckett Studies* 17.1–2, 187–198.
Williams, Tyler M. (2013). "Plasticity, in Retrospect: Changing the Future of the Humanities." *Diacritics* 41.1, 6–27.
Williams, Tyler M. (2019). "Following Catherine Malabou." *boundary2 online*. https://www.boundary2.org/2019/03/tyler-m-williams-following-catherine-malabou-review-of-brenna-bhandar-and-jonathan-goldberg-hillers-plastic-materialities-politics-legality-and-metamorphosis-in-the-work-of-c/
Williams, Tyler M. (2023). "Outside and Outside: Plastic Passages—Of Philosophy and Literature." *philoSOPHIA* 13, 99–123.

CHAPTER 11

PROUST, REALISM AND THE PLASTICITY OF NATURAL SIGNS

Ian James

It may, at first sight, seem odd or counterintuitive to bring Proust together with contemporary biological theory, and with Malabou's philosophical engagement with biology, let alone with dominant accounts of mimesis restricted to realism. Proust, of course, and throughout his career, famously opposed the literary naturalism of his day and rejected its alignment of aesthetic practice with science and with the scientist thinking that permeated the intellectual environment of the French Third Republic in the last decades of the nineteenth century.[1] His own aesthetic practice, such as it unfolded across his youthful and mature writing, and such as it evolved across the years during which the long drafting of *À la Recherche du temps perdu* took place, consistently set itself in opposition to that of literary naturalism and realism and what Proust's narrator dubs their "miserable abstract of lines and surfaces" (RTP IV, 463; SLT VI, 284).[2]

It is precisely Proust's anti-naturalism and his antipathy towards naturalist realism that motivate bringing him together with the contemporary theory of biosemiotics and with Malabou's thinking of the plasticity of biological forms. They also motivate this bringing together in the context of the mimetic turn or return that is the concern of this volume. For if, broadly speaking, mimetic studies has its origins in modernist aesthetics and its opposition to mimetic realism, then Proust will always have been from the outset an ally of any contemporary attempt to rethink mimesis today.[3] The argument that follows pursues this possibility in an exploration of Proustian transformations. The presence and operation of transformation in the *Recherche* suggest a model of literary realism, and with that of literary mimesis, that is distinctly *not* one of an imitation or copying of the manifest "real" world as per the nineteenth-century naturalism that the novel and the Proustian oeuvre more generally rejects. The specifics and internal working of the specific modality of transformation at stake here can be usefully illuminated via Malabou's concept of plasticity and its alignment with Peircean semiotics and biosemiotics. For, as will become clear, if Malabou's plasticity refers to the giving and receiving of form but also to the way in which forms are both liable to, but also resist, transformation, then Peircean semiosis, as assimilated by contemporary biosemiotics, finds itself in close proximity with Malabou's metamorphic thinking. This should not, in fact, be surprising given the beginnings of her philosophy in the interpretation of Hegel in her doctoral thesis and first published work, and Peirce's own acknowledged debt to, and transformation of, Hegelian thought.[4] The proximity between the two opens the way for a thinking of a fully materialist, naturalized and novel mimetic account of the relation between the forms of biological lived life and the forms of human thought and symbolic culture understood now as so many different layers or levels of semiotic organization and life which are successively scaffolded by, and built upon, each other. In this context one can once again speak of the realism of aesthetic forms (those of human literature, art, film and so on). One can once again talk of aesthetic mimesis as a realist (but also naturalist) cultural production.

Yet, as indicated above, this is possible not so much because one form *imitates* another but rather because one form transformatively or metamorphically *generates* another. The novelty of this naturalism and realism therefore lies in its eschewal of representation in the traditional sense of the term, that is to say the notion that the work or art "re-presents," in all its manifest detail, a knowable world. Rather this is a realism in which the world of lived existence finds itself transformed or metamorphosed into the space of the literary, and in which mimesis obeys a logic of metamorphic transformation rather than one of copying or imitation. So, in this context, figures of transformation and metamorphosis in Proust are read alongside biosemiotics and in terms of the plasticity of natural signs in order to discern a new way of understanding the relation of aesthetic forms to the real of natural life. In this light, aesthetic form should be understood as emerging from the dimension of natural, biological life within which they are embedded. This is less a gesture of reading Proust anachronistically *through* the conceptual lens of biosemiotics and plasticity "à la Malabou" than it is an attempt to find resonances between the three. Proust's late nineteenth-century turn towards a kind of semiotic materialism finds its echo in the twenty-first-century attempt to uncover sense and meaning within organic life processes. For all three—Proust, biosemiotic theory and Malabou alike—it is a question of an affirmation of sense in life and natural processes, thought in the wake, and in the eclipse, of idealism.[5] This will be the key claim of this chapter, one which resonates with this volume as a whole and with the wider ambition of mimetic studies according to which mimetic transformation occurs, not as imitation, but as material, immanent transformation in the *absence* of any originary instance or model.

Proust and Nature

Despite his anti-naturalism, Proust is, in his early work, his literary essays and the *Recherche*, nevertheless, and famously, invested in nature and in the natural world. The young narrator of *Jean Santeuil* is charmed by lilac blossoms, a tree in flower and, in a prototype of the later celebrated episode of the *Recherche*, a pink hawthorn. He encounters in these the "Genius of Nature" and the "Glory of the Spring" (Proust 1955, 131–133). The poet invoked in the short essay "Poetry or mysterious laws" contemplates the blossoms of a double cherry tree to discern some kind of unconscious thought or design that inhabits its natural form (Proust 1971, 418; 1988, 147). The narrator of the *Recherche* tries, almost always in vain, to divine the sense or meaning proposed by, amongst other natural phenomena, hawthorn blossoms, trees and skyscapes. Towards the end of the *Recherche* he even notes that it is nature itself that has taught him the art of metaphor, that figural practice so fundamental to the writing of Proust's novel itself (RTP IV, 468; SLT VI, 290).

In his early work, his literary essays, and in the *Recherche*, then, Proust is profoundly preoccupied with what might be called "natural signs" and with the possibility that sense and meaning inhere within the world of nonhuman living entities just as they do within human historical and social worlds. This preoccupation is not on the face of it an indicator of any concealed leanings that might run against the explicit antipathy he has for naturalism.[6] Rather it indicates the presence within his early work—and the traces of that presence within the late—of the legacy of German Romanticism and its idealist philosophy of nature, principally that of Schelling. In this context nature is viewed as a manifestation of a divine script or writing that reflects an organization of *Geist*, that is to say, an inscription of idealized meaning within matter. This reflects a hermeneutic view of the natural world that permeates idealist *Naturphilosophie*. This is a legacy that Proust inherited via a number of different routes: the spiritualist and neo-Kantian tradition of nineteenth-century French philosophy that runs from Félix Ravaisson to Jules Lachelier and then to his teachers, Émile Boutroux and Alphonse Darlu; the influence of Anglophone writers and thinkers working in the wake of German Romanticism, and perhaps even that of the lesser known French aesthetician, Gabrielle Séailles.[7] This broad legacy of German Romanticism and its resurgent influence in France in the second half of the nineteenth century has been dubbed by Anne Henry as "*naturisme*," an idealist philosophical and aesthetic rival to the naturalism of the day, which formed Proust's intellectual horizons in his youth (Henry 1981, 79, 81).[8]

In the last decades of the twentieth and the first two decades of the twenty-first century a view, if not a consensus, has emerged that Proust gradually sloughed off his youthful idealist influences, embraced more and more a materialist inclination and, in effect, ceased to believe.[9] Yet, as Deleuze's important book, *Proust et les signes*, clearly demonstrates, the final version of the *Recherche* remains fully invested in the reading and interpretation of signs, both natural and human, and this to the extent that the whole work can plausibly be characterized a kind of semiotic apprenticeship (Deleuze 2014, 10–11). That Deleuze can read Proust's novel (albeit with some philosophical forcing of the kind he does so well) in the terms of the Nietzschean-naturalist theory of signs that he developed in the early 1960s, suggests in turn that it might not be so odd or counterintuitive to read Proust today in terms of biological theory or philosophy, provided, that is, that such theory and philosophy places sense, meaning and semiotic processes at the center of the organic life and the activity of the living.[10] If Proust's investment in signs really does shift from an early affirmation of a Schellingian divine script permeating the natural world to a late orientation towards materialism in which the life of signs nevertheless remains central, it might just make perfect sense to read his mature aesthetic practice alongside contemporary scientific and philosophical approaches that place sense, meaning and semiotics at the heart of biological life.[11]

This is just what the contemporary science of biosemiotics does. It is also what Catherine Malabou has done in her recent work on Kant and epigenetics in which she poses the question of whether epigenesis and epigenetic processes can be understood in terms of a naturalized transcendental that gives a "hermeneutic latitude, the power of *sense*, opened in the heart of the biological?" (2014, 153; 2016, 89). It is here, in this notion of nature as semiotic and of life as the action of natural signs that the bringing together of Proust, Malabou and biosemiotics is confirmed as a decisive move in the context of the recasting of materialist/plastic mimesis within the context of the contemporary mimetic turn or re-turn.

The Plasticity of Natural Signs

John Deely has defined biosemiotics simply and ambitiously as "the thesis that semiosis is coextensive with life" (Deely 2015, 345). It has also, variably, been defined as "the theoretical apparatus for the description of biological phenomena in all levels of organization of life" and as "the *study of qualitative diversity found in and by living systems*" (Emmeche and Kull 2011, 4, 72). On the basis of these definitions, it can be said that a) biosemiotics treats all living processes in terms of sign activity; b) that this activity inheres within and supports physiological processes to inform the organization and production of biological forms; and c) that sign activity therefore also informs the qualitative functioning of organisms and their environmental interactions in a manner which is systemic and productive of further organizational levels of increasing complexity and scale. Biosemiotics is, like Malabou's thinking, concerned with the production and transformation of form and with the sense, meaning or interpretative activity that inheres within the processes of production and transformation.

As a theory it borrows from, and is underpinned by, the account of the sign offered by the nineteenth-century American pragmatist philosopher Charles Sanders Peirce. Peirce gives a fairly straightforward definition of a sign as follows: "A sign, or *reprasentamen*, is something that stands to somebody for something in some respect or capacity" (Peirce 1955, 99). Peirce's sign differs in a decisive manner from the dyadic structure of the Saussurian sign and in a way which has far reaching philosophical consequences. Where, of course, Saussure defines the sign as a dyadic relation between signifier and signified, elements that take on their value from a synchronic system of relations that are made up of pure differences "with no positive terms," the Peircean sign is always constituted in a threefold relation of an "object" to a "sign-vehicle" (otherwise known as the "representamen") to an "interpretant." Sometimes, as in the quotation above, Peirce uses the word "sign" to designate the representamen or sign-vehicle but the essential point is that a sign only functions when all three elements are related together in the triad "object-representamen-interpretant." This threefold relation gives the basic structure of what becomes a very complex and theoretically developed account of sign action in its different forms, aspects and modalities. What is important to note in this context is that this triadic relation allows for the formation of semiotic chains and networks, according to which the interpretant of one sign can then function as the object of another in a signifying sequence that is potentially without limit. In the same way signifying chains and networks can form the building blocks of further structural levels of chains and networks which can in turn scaffold "higher" structural levels in a manner which is also potentially without limit. In this way Peircean biosemiotics in principle offers a nonreductive conceptual framework which allows human sign-activity, cultural, symbolic and linguistic to be thought as semiotic processes that are continuous with, and arise out of, natural and biological semiotic processes.[12] In contradistinction to the Saussurian dyadic understanding of signifier-signified, the Peircean sign is constituted in a singularity of triadic relation that is always intrinsically plural, complex and evolutive (see Gangle 2020, 127) yielding a production of quantitatively determinable physical *and* qualitative non-physical forms according to a specific mode of what might be called semiotic causality.

The exact status of the causality that inheres within biosemiosis is much debated within the literature of biosemiotics itself. Peirce gives some indication of the manner in which the different elements of the triadic sign causally determine each other:

> As a *medium* the Sign is essentially in a triadic relation, to its Object, which determines it, and to its Interpretant which it determines. In its relation to the Object, the Sign is *passive*, that is to say, its correspondence to the Object is brought about by an effect upon the Sign, the Object remaining unaffected. On the other hand, in its relation to the Interpretant, the Sign is *active*, determining the Interpretant without being itself thereby affected (1998, 544)

What is decisive in this formulation is, I would argue, the *unilateral* direction of determination within the triadicity of the sign and the manner in which one term is passive with regard to that which precedes it and active with regard to the term which follows it. Within any given sign relation, then, it can be said that a logic of unilateral determination pertains, one which could be schematically described as follows:

OBJECT ➔ SIGN(-VEHICLE) ➔ INTERPTRETANT

The arrows here indicate a one-way causality which precludes any possibility of the sign-vehicle or representamen *retroactively affecting* the object or of the interpretant *acting back* upon the sign-vehicle. This logic of unilateral determination, or operation of one-way causality, necessarily implies a temporality internal to semiotic triadicity. Eliseo Fernandez, one of the most acute and perceptive readers of Peirce with regard to the status of biosemiotic causality, clearly foregrounds this temporal structure of the sign noting: "Peirce correlates the three relata in semiosis to the three time "dimensions": present time with the representamen, past with the object and future with the interpretant. A sign does not exist at any particular instant [...] semiosis is radically temporal" (2010, 154). The temporality of the Peircean sign is decisive for the overall argument advanced here since, if mimesis is to be a process of transformation rather than of copying or imitation such a process needs to obey a temporality that is specific to it, what might be called the time of transformation, one that is distinct from the re-presentation (by way of copying) of a past moment in a present of writing. The time of Proust's novel is one of multiple lived temporalities and the possibility of the signs of life being transformed *in time* into the signs of art which will themselves be read and interpreted *in time*.

The causation that inheres in semiosis concerns *organization*. It concerns the organization of processes and the interaction of biological processes with the maintenance of both the physiological form of the organism and of its meaningful and survival-oriented activity in a surrounding environment. It is not a question of any directedness towards a wider metaphysical goal of harmony and unity within the realm of the living or the wider cosmos. Rather "everything fundamentally consists of *process organization*, in which causality is a characteristic of such process organization" (Hoffmeyer 2008a, 46), or as he also puts it, the final causality of biosemiosis concerns its status as a "controlling agency," that is to say. "bringing things about under the guidance of interpretation in a local context" (Hoffmeyer 2008b, 171). The emphasis on "process organization" here also means that (bio)semiotic causality, insofar as it operates in relation to the construction of physiological form, needs also to be understood as a mode of *formal* causation. Again, this can be discerned in Peirce's original definitions as when, for instance, he underlines that a sign is not necessarily a function of consciousness: "a Sign may be defined as the Medium for the communication of a *Form*. It is not necessary that anything possessing consciousness [...] should be concerned" (Peirce 1998, 544; emphasis added).

So, according to the triadic structure of the Peircean sign, the interpretant is always affected and thereby unilaterally modified by the form of the terms that precede it. It, in turn, affects and modifies the terms of the sign(s) which follow. In this way the semiotic process itself is necessarily one of ongoing metamorphosis and transformation. This allows Peircean semiosis to be recast in terms that resonate with Malabou's thinking such that one might now be able to speak of the *plasticity* of natural signs in the manner that was noted in the introduction.

So, we see that the bringing together of Peirce, Proust and Malabou under the rubric of "natural signs" takes place within a wider field of shared historical context and intellectual genealogy. The influence of German idealism on Proust (via Schelling, the Anglophone reception of Naturphilosophie, Ravaisson, and late nineteenth-century French spiritualist thought) runs in parallel with the influence of Hegel on Peirce and Malabou. This wider shared trajectory also sits within the context of a more general emergence of sign theory, semiology or semiotics within the nineteenth and twentieth centuries. It has been argued elsewhere that the legacy of German idealism in Proust, and the specific manner in which he takes this up, shows that aspects of the *Recherche* in fact prefigure the works of Russian formalism and structuralism (Henry 1981, 81, 91). At the same time, aspects of Russian formalism (notably Lotman's concept of the "semiosphere") go on to influence twentieth-century and contemporary Peircean biosemiotics and, of course, structuralism has its vast and complex presence in France that can be traced through to poststructuralism, deconstruction and then to Malabou. In this way, the readings of Proust's transformations and of mimesis given here through the lens of Peircean biosemiotics and Malabou's plasticity are as much a work of restoring the intellectual-historical context that brings them together as it is a work of placing literature into dialogue with theory or philosophy.

Proust's Transformations

For a television program on Proust that was broadcast in 1971, and commissioned by his friend Michel Butor, Pierre Klossowski wrote a text that was published much later in print form in 2019 (Klossowski 2019). Like his friend Gilles Deleuze, Klossowski aligns Proust's conception of art and literature with the decoding of signs and with a materialist, immanentist orientation:

> [W]hat Proust calls art [...] does not refer to being gifted at writing—rather it refers to the art of deciphering the signs of one's own existence: Proust proposes to reveal to each and within each of his readers that region in which real life moves (the life of the self)—or even better: that region that our individual person and its conditions [...] never cease to occlude and make inaccessible to us. (Klossowski 2019, 75–76)

Yet here, for Klossowski, the emphasis is less, as it arguably is for Deleuze in *Proust et les signes*, on a philosophical theory of signs, and far more on the possibility that Proust the author is decoding the signs of his own life and world and that the novel we read may be understood as the result of this decoding, as a transformation of a lived, immanent semiotics into an imaginary, literary-fictional semiotics. The act of reading would then in turn provoke a similar act of decoding and a similar transformation on the part of the reader. In this way, for Klossowski, Proust's work returns us, via transformational semiotic chains and interpretative acts, to the immanence of material life itself in all its opacity and inaccessibility and not to a philosophical or conceptual theory or *representation* of that immanence.

Proust's treatment of the doctrine of metempsychosis, or the transmigration of souls, is directly relevant in this context. This doctrine is used metaphorically by Proust in both *Contre Sainte Beuve* and the *Recherche* to describe the operation of memory, the workings of inner experience and the transition from impersonal to personal life. It describes the transformational and metamorphic passage of meaning and memory through time from the self to objects and from objects to self. It is associated with the loss and recovery of self in deep sleep and refers also to the way in which impersonal memory can migrate through nonhuman and human "immanent life," deep history and more recent historical experience. Most importantly perhaps, it describes the way in which both personal and impersonal memory are retained and passed on through the work of art in "poetic resurrection" (Proust 1971, 213; Proust 1988, 5). Proust has taken an ancient metaphysical doctrine and adapted it to a psychological account of memory and to an understanding of how individual and collective reminiscence operate in relation to aesthetic experience. Yet his figural or metaphorical use of the term transmigration still appears to engage a cosmological register insofar as it retains that nonhuman dimension which describes the transmission of impersonal but also natural and zoological memory from an opaque and archaic zone of origin into which, the *Recherche* often tells us, deep sleep is a descent.

The component parts of the word "transmigration" are, of course, both spatial. In its original sense as a prefix, "trans-" is appended to loanwords from Latin and gives the sense of "across," "beyond," or "through," while "migration" indicates movement from one region or place to another. According to the original doctrine of metempsychosis, however, the transmigration of souls, being not of this world, can only obscurely or indeterminately be spatial, the passage of a soul after death into another body implying a unidirectional and irreversible temporality in a dimension of time which is not exactly of the worldly time that attaches to spatial locations or situated differences between living bodies. Transmigration, understood either as the literal passage of a soul from one body to another, or more figuratively as reminiscence, implies a past, an anteriority and the possibility of a futurity, or posteriority. It implies a successive chain of transitions and transmutations of souls or of forms, figures, instances of sense, of signs and meaning in a chain which is, Proust's narrator argues in key points in the *Recherche*, immersed in a field of forgetting or oblivion. To switch the metaphor from that of a "chain," it could also be said that transmigration, when used as a figure for memory or reminiscence, indicates an "overlayering" of strata of past experiences, with each layer or stratum accruing in time over preceding strata, thereby forming the medium through which memory and its attached meanings can be said to transmigrate in an unceasingly transformative or metamorphic movement. It thus indicates the possibility of a penetration of past or anterior layers of experience into the layer which forms the present as such. In this context, its sense refers far more to a temporal migration than it does to a spatial displacement.

This structure of the overlayering of anterior instances in a deep sedimented formation is described by Proust using the figure of superimposition, "superposition." In one of the many meditations on sleep and waking in the *Recherche*, Proust's narrator associates superimposition with a mode of perception experienced in sleep: "In the world of sleep, our perceptions are so overloaded, each of them blanketed by a superimposed counterpart which doubles its bulk and blinds it to no purpose, that we are unable even to distinguish what is happening in the bewilderment of awakening" (RTP III, 629; SLT V, 155). In a much longer meditation, this structure of superimposition is framed as a regression through sedimented layers of first personal, and then impersonal, immanent life, both human and nonhuman.

> Suddenly I fell asleep, plunged into that deep slumber in which vistas are opened to us of a return to childhood, the recapture of past years, and forgotten feelings, of disincarnation, the transmigration of souls, the evoking of the dead, the illusions of madness, retrogression towards the most elementary realms of nature [...] all those mysteries which we imagine ourselves not to know and into which we are in reality initiated almost every night, as into the other great mystery of extinction and resurrection. (RTP II, 176–177; SLT II, 545; trans. modified)

If sleep and dream are a regression through these anterior layers of self and back further into impersonal and anonymous layers of human, animal and natural existence, then the experience of waking life can be said to be the exposed surface of an outer layer which is in no less of a relation to these regressive anterior layers encountered in oneiric experience. This outer layer is a surface superimposed over the immediately past layers of the personal self, which would themselves be layered over the infinitely regressing layers that constitute the deep well of immanent life and its field or zone of impersonal memory.[13] Yet what is clear here is that this layering of sedimentary strata, for all that it involves forgetting and oblivion, does not preclude the possibility of hidden layers rising and penetrating into this outer layer of the self. The importance for the novel as a whole of this layered model of experience can be discerned in the proliferation of the figure of superimposition over the pages of the *Recherche*, occurring as it does in its different variants ("superposition," "superposable," "superposer," "superpose") no less than fifty-five times during the course of its narration.[14]

Superimposition in Proust's novel is as much related to historical or impersonal elements as it is to individual and subjective perception. Personal impressions can be layered over previous impressions of art and of aesthetic experience, but they are subjected to transformations from the natural and nonhuman to the human, the impersonal to the personal and then again from the personal to the impersonal realm of the aesthetic. For instance, in *La Prisonnière*, the narrator views Albertine playing the pianola and superimposes this image over that of a magic lantern:

> [T]he pianola was to us at times like a scientific magic lantern (historical and geographical), and on the walls of the room in Paris, supplied with inventions more modern than my room at Combray, I would see extending before me, according to whether Albertine played me Rameau or Borodin, now an eighteenth-century tapestry sprinkled with cupids and roses, now the Eastern steppe in which sounds are muffled by the boundless distances and the soft carpet of snow. (RTP III, 883–884; SLT V, 514)

Here the image of the desired other, merged with strains of music, morphs at first into that of an eighteenth-century tapestry personifying Love against a background of flowers and then into an image of natural landscape where all sonority is dissipated in a vastness without limit. There is a temporal migration and transformation here from individual affect, back to cultural artefact, historical artefact, and from there to natural, geographical expanse that speaks of a regression through dimensions of human experience and culture to their attenuation and dissipation in a blankness or indistinction of nature.

A brief sample of Proust's incorporations from his biographical experience may give some indication of the degrees of transformation, and therefore of fictionality, at play in the *Recherche* as a whole and the way in which the facts of biographical experience transformatively migrate into its literary and fictional space. Jean-Yves Tadié has noted that "Proust made use of everything he experienced or thought about during his life" (Tadié 2000, xxii). The key point to be made in this context is that the apparent or "surface" content of Proust's novel, and therefore of Marcel the narrator's "*récit*," has taken material from the author's life and transformed it in one way or another for the purposes of demonstrating a "truth" which is not that of biographical facts but rather that of real, lived immanence. The truth in question would be "generic" in the sense of being general or non-specific and not copying or imitating the field of manifest appearance or biographical experience in a representational manner. It would be the truth of an immanent, "semiotic" real which would gain its generic character insofar as the novel presents the general structure of relations that articulate it as such and not the specific worldly manifestation of that structure. The truth of life presented in Proust's demonstration may not be one that has manifested itself in the surface phenomena of a shared historical world. Yet, as the underlying truth of *that world*, it is no less real for all that.

A most obvious example of biographical incorporation and transformation would, of course, be the character of Albertine and Proust's relationship with Alfred Agostinelli. This relationship is often taken as the model for that of Marcel and Albertine. In his biography, Tadié has noted that Proust may have begun to use the name of Albertine in May 1913 (as a substitute for the character hitherto named Maria). This month coincides with the time in which Proust hired Agostinelli as his secretary and gave him a room in his house. If, Tadié muses, the life and the novel had previously evolved along parallel lines at this point: "those lines were at right angles, and the life began to cut across the book" (2000, 605). So, while, as has been noted, there may have been a progressive removal of biographical elements from Proust's writing between the period of *Jean Santeuil* and that of the composition of the *Recherche*, this may not mean that biographical material did not continue, and perhaps increasingly, to be used in some form or another. This is clear, for instance, in the very close correspondence or mirroring between events relating to Agostinelli and moments in the novel relating to Albertine. So, for instance, Proust attempted to bestow on Agostinelli the gift of an aeroplane costing 27,000 francs and also a Rolls-Royce at a similar price (Tadié 2000, 615). In the novel, Marcel promises to buy Albertine a yacht and again a Rolls-Royce and indicates in his correspondence to her that he has already ordered them (RTP IV, 38–39; SLT V, 613–614).[15] This might confirm something like a "key" relation between Agostinelli and Albertine. Yet at the very same time one can note that Proust's relationship with Agostinelli was clearly not the only one that found its way into the Marcel–Albertine story. Henri Rochat, for instance, lived in Proust's apartment and in a state of dependency on his employer for much longer than did Agostinelli and is far more likely to have been the model for the "captive" Albertine of *La Prisonnière* (Tadié 2000, 680). Clearly, Albertine has many models and the warning not to seek the "truth" of the *Recherche* in one-to-one correspondences is born out in the proliferation of models one can fall upon if one is ever inclined to go down such a path (606).

Perhaps, then, the degree of fictionality that attaches to any of Proust's biographical incorporations can be judged by the extent to which they have undergone metamorphic transformation, displacement or condensation with other diverse elements that have been included. Rather than corresponding to real-life figures, Proust himself suggested that "each of his characters corresponded to a tendency within himself and to a need he had to express" (Tadié 2000, 748). This might clearly confirm that Proust the author, like Marcel the future author, is a reader of his own "inner book of unknown signs" (RTP IV, 458; SLT VI, 274). Yet the reading of this interior book of unknown signs, the descent into inwardness and immanence must also be understood as a passage to a limit-point which opens onto the anonymous real that has dictated the inner signs in question. In this perspective, Proust's inner tendencies would be deeply entangled and immersed within an immanent semiotic reality in which there is no clear separation between the subjective and the objective, the personal and the impersonal or anonymous. The signs that are written in the book of Proust's inner tendencies would be dictated by that anonymous reality. His inner tendencies would be written, as the narrator puts it, in a book "whose hieroglyphs are patterns not traced by us," and the interpretation of this immanent semiotic field would be the act of creation from which the *Recherche* as a novel emerges (RTP, IV, 458; SLT VI, 275).

If we do assume that both author and narrator will have imagined their respective works (the real one we are reading by Proust and the imaginary one yet to be written by the narrator Marcel) out of a difficult decipherment or decoding of a lived "inner book of unknown signs," then the idea of a one-to-one correspondence of fictional to real characters is again confirmed as deeply misleading. For rather than reading the *Recherche* and its extensive biographical incorporations according to a simple translation of the signs of Proust's manifest biography into the signs of his novel (Albertine=Agostinelli), the interpreter of signs will perhaps only decipher the book they have to read and attain to its "truth" by attending to the complex relations *between* the signs that make up the textual weave of each given book. Whether it is a question of Proust deciphering of his own "inner life" in order to create the *Recherche*, or Marcel reading his book of inner signs in order to imagine his future "oeuvre," or, indeed, whether it be us as readers of the *Recherche* interpreting Proust's novel, the book that is read has its "truth" not in any direct referential correspondence or identity between the surface signs of manifest biographical life and those of the literary text. The "truth" does not lie in any representational operation of signs as they can be said to correspond to a manifest field appearance. Rather it would *inhere* in the *complex* of signs that, taken in their relations to each other, constitute an imaginary and transformational semiotic *diagram* of lived immanence. Such a diagram would be able to formally map and thereby interpret the anterior semiotic relations in which it, qua diagram, participates. A point of convergence between Proust, Peirce and Malabou is arrived at here. According to this interpretation, the organization of Proustian signs in the *Recherche* is constituted in a *metamorphic and plastic transformation* (understood in Malabou's terms) of the *signs of life* (understood in Peircean terms) into the narrative and symbolic structure of the novel understood as a diagram.[16]

There is a return here to the layered structure of superimposed forms and anterior instances discussed above. The semiotic universe which can be imagined here is one in which natural or biological life constitutes successive layers of an increasingly complex set of structures and meaning relations upon which the layers of human symbolic activity and life are formed. In this way the immanent semiotic of Proust's "inner book of unknown signs" would be, as it were, the final, uppermost sedimentation of a layered immanent life in which Proust the author and historical subject was immersed. This would be a book that interprets or models the immanent semiotic relations that underpinned Proust's lived experience in the historical world and aesthetic culture of the French Third Republic and all its social, familial, political and economic relations. But these relations would themselves, of course, be layered or superimposed over prior historical and cultural worlds, deep history and the nonhuman natural and biological world, participating in them all, immanent to them all. In this way something like a resolutely materialist and, in an entirely novel sense, realist, naturalist and mimetic Proust can be discerned in structures of regression, anteriority, impersonality and superimposition in *Recherche*. The immanent semiotic real of Proust's lived historical experience is superimposed upon the anterior layers of historical, zoological and biological existence. In the context of his lived experience, however, the operations of regression through anterior layers of personal and impersonal experience are supplemented by a transformational decoding and mapping, or what might be called a non-representational modeling of the relations and sense structures that underlie shared social, historical and cultural-historical experience.

Realism Transformed

Proust's transformations suggest a model of literary realism, and with that of literary mimesis, that is not one of an imitation or copying of the manifest "real" world as per the nineteenth-century naturalism that is so firmly rejected in both the *Recherche* and elsewhere in the Proustian corpus. It is not, or not simply, a recreation of human action or of events or a portrayal of objects. Rather, as an imaginative and aesthetic presentation or as a literary space and construct, the *Recherche* should be understood as a "heteropoietic" creation. It is produced out of a relation to a field of semiotic anteriority and alterity and as a metamorphic transformation of that field. So "heteropoiesis" here would designate the act of creation or production out of a field of alterity that precedes that which is created, that is to say, the anterior real of (bio)semiotic life.[17] This "real" is material and immanent, cultural and biological. It is constituted in the superimposed, temporal layering of strata, each of which is a transformation or metamorphosis of preceding or anterior layers. Yet this is a metamorphosis *in* semiosis. Or rather, it is metamorphosis *as* semiosis according to the plasticity of natural signs, a generative transformation of life and art, of life into art and of art into life, each immanently and successively superimposed, or indeed superposed, upon the other.

The term superposition here is drawn from geology and not, as one might perhaps at first expect, from quantum theory. It refers to the order in which sedimentary strata are ordered one above the other. As was shown earlier in the discussion, the plasticity of natural signs, understood as such in a reading which brings biosemiotics and Malabou's thought together, allows for semiotic chains, networks and scaffolded levels or layers of chains and networks, to be viewed in terms of metamorphic and transformational processes that construct living forms and are therefore constitutive of life as such. The plasticity of natural signs also allows us to understand the way in which the *internal* organization of living organisms can, along with their interactions with their *external* environments, be understood in qualitative terms as so many transmissions of sense and meaning that are productive of forms. These forms may be organismal, physiological, behavioral, communicative and, in the case of humans, symbolic, cultural and linguistic. The decisive point to note in the model of naturalist realism that emerges here is that the latter (symbolic, cultural, linguistic) find themselves layered over, or superposed upon, the former according to the logic of metamorphic transformation that informs the plasticity of natural signs. In this regard, one might talk of a "superpositional" realism that is not predicated on reference, on a system of (Saussurian, dyadic) signs referring to a lived world and mimetically re-presenting it. Rather the model of superpositional realism always understands symbolic spaces in a metamorphic continuity with the semiotic layers of life that precede them and of whose relations of sense and meaning they are therefore a transformative continuation.

The reading of Proust's transformations, and of the relationship between art and life that can be discerned in the *Recherche*, does not rely on the conceptual framework of biosemiotics or on that of Malabou's plasticity in order to make its case and to confer upon it theoretical and philosophical authority. Arguably it can stand alone based on an interpretation of the work of signs in the novel and of the way the narrative creates a vision of a temporally layered semiotic worlds. This is a narrative vision in which the personal and the impersonal, the present and the past, the social and the historical, the cultural and the natural all find themselves as so many layers each super(im)posed upon the other, each transforming itself into the other. According to such a vision, the transformation of life into art is one final, and distinctively privileged, transformation and metamorphic layer. Similarly, the Peircean conceptual framework of biosemiotics and that of Malabou's plasticity do not need each other to gain whatever epistemological or philosophical authority they may have. Bringing all three together in a relation of resonance or parallelism does, however, allow for the abstraction or the modeling of a transformed realism. This superpositional realism is more relational than representational. In this way such a realism is fully in line with the re-turn to the metamorphic, relational and plastic mimesis considered in this volume. Signs bear the meanings of the anterior semiotic chains and networks that precede them rather than presenting within an imaginary frame a reality that would be external to that frame. According to this model, the relations that works of art and literature maintain with the real from which they are engendered need to be understood not as relations of reference, but as relations of retrogression towards a field of immanent anteriority and alterity. They are, like sleep and dreaming in the *Recherche*, born of a "retrogression towards the most elementary realms of nature".

Notes

1. Proust's antipathy towards naturalism is exemplified in *Contre Sainte Beuve* itself and his references to Hippolyte Taine. He notes, for instance, that Taine's "intellectual conception of reality allowed of no truth except the scientific" (Proust 1971, 220; 1988, 11).
2. All references to Proust's *Recherche* will be to the editions listed in the bibliography and given in the English. The original French is referred to with the abbreviation RTP followed by the volume and page number. The English translation is referred to with the abbreviation SLT, again followed by volume and page number.
3. On the origins of mimetic studies in "literary and philosophical modernism" see Lawtoo 2013 and the *MLN* special issue on the "mimetic turn" (Lawtoo 2023) and the essays collected in the *Homo Mimeticus* trilogy.
4. As Peirce himself put it: "My philosophy resuscitates Hegel, though in a strange costume" (Peirce 1931, 18).
5. It is notable that Malabou's thinking of plasticity and epigenetics arises out of deconstructive readings of Hegel and Kant. Biosemiotics, which affirms itself as a thoroughly materialist science, nevertheless has idealist roots, as reflected in the neo-Kantian orientations of its key intellectual and scientific forerunners such as Jakob von Uexküll, Thomas Sebeok and Gregory Bateson. There is arguably a determinable intellectual-historical parallel to be drawn between these contexts and Proust's self-divestment of neo-Kantian, spiritualist idealism in the wake of Lachelier and Boutroux.
6. In the French context, naturalism, associated with prominent literary figures of the late nineteenth century such as Émile Zola or the Goncourt brothers, has a distinctively scientistic flavor, strongly influenced by Taine (see n. 1 above) and his scientific and sociological positivism. It is this latter that distinguishes French literary naturalism from the realism of earlier in the century, associated with figures such as Balzac and Stendhal.
7. Anne Henry places great emphasis on the influence exerted over Proust by Gabriel Séailles and the signal importance played by him in imbuing the Proustian aesthetic with a Schellingian orientation; see in particular Henry 1981, 81–82, 86–97. Jean-Yves Tadié, for his part, suggests that, although the young Marcel attended lectures by Séailles, "his influence on Proust, who only refers to him once [...], has probably been exaggerated" (2000, 206).
8. Interesting connections suggest themselves here between the hinterland of Proustian influences and the key thinkers of the mimetic turn, since, of course, Nancy and Lacoue-Labarthe begin their careers with a sustained engagement with German Romanticism in *The Literary Absolute*. See Nancy and Lacoue-Labarthe 1988.
9. As Erika Fülöp pointed out in her 2012 work *Proust, the One, and the Many*, since Vincent Descombes' seminal *Marcel Proust: Philosophie du roman* (Descombes 1987), it "has become paradigmatic of the subsequent studies concerned with the novel's philosophy" that "the narrator's views as expounded in the text [of the *Recherche*] do not correspond to the reality of the novel's actual practice" (Fülöp 2012, 1). This suggests that the distinctive idealism that characterizes so much of the narrators' headline aesthetic theorizing is not reflected in the aesthetic practice of the *Recherche* itself.
10. On Deleuze's relation to naturalism see Patton 2017.
11. Of course, this important shift from Romanticism/idealism towards materialism is perfectly in line with the mimetic turn in general and the mimetic studies turn to Deleuzian figures like Bennett and Connolly, as well as Malabou. For a more extended development of these

arguments relating to Proust's gradual turn towards materialism and the possibility this opens up for reading the *Recherche* in semiotic and naturalist terms, see James 2025. Some of the material included in this chapter is reproduced from this book, *Rethinking Literary Naturalism: Proust and Quignard After Life*, and I am very grateful to Liverpool University Press for permission to so reproduce it.

12 Terence Deacon uses Peircean sign theory in his account of the development of the human capacity for symbolization in *The Symbolic Species* (Deacon 1997). For pioneering theoretical and critical work appealing to biosemiotics and building conceptual bridges between biological and cultural theory, see Wheeler 2016.

13 Breeur also highlights the manner in which, for Proust, superimposition is a fundamental structure of the self and places an emphasis on a fragmentation or fissuring that prevents it from fusing into a unity or whole (2000, 169).

14 Thomas Baldwin in his masterful reading of Proust alongside Barthes has noted that geological metaphors and the figure of superimposition in Proust represent for Barthes aspects of the structural economy of the "erotic text": "Geological metaphors and images of superimposition abound in Barthes's attempts to describe the drifting intermittences of the erotic text" (Baldwin 2019, 49). In this context, then, superimposition as a structural feature of the *Recherche* would relate less to the regression into immanence and more to the play of *signifiance* within the novel. Tadié, in his biography, has also identified the preeminent role played by superimposition in the *Recherche*, identifying it not simply with the structuring of self or logic of temporality in the novel, but with Proust's method of writing and composition over its long period of creation. Referring to the "substance" of color evoked by the narrator in relation to paintings described in the novel, Tadié remarks: "The secret of the 'substance' lies in the superimposition of 'several layers of colour'. This is something that cannot be overstated: the precious character of *À la recherche* derives from the superimposition of these successive stages" (Tadié 2000, 762).

15 A useful editor's note in the Pléiade edition indicates, as does Tadié in his biography, that the matching of the aeroplane promised to Agostinelli, the yacht to Albertine and the Rolls-Royce to both was discovered by Philippe Kolb, who had access to the only surviving letter from Proust to Agostinelli. Kolb also established that the cost of the aeroplane, 27,000 francs, would also have been that of a Rolls-Royce in the same period; see RTP IV, 1054–1055, n. 1.

16 This evokes Rocco Gangle's thinking such as it is elaborated in his book on Spinoza, Peirce, Deleuze and category theory, in which the concepts of the diagrammatic sign and of semiotic immanence have a central place. See Gangle 2020.

17 On this see James 2022.

Bibliography

Baldwin, Thomas (2019). *Roland Barthes: The Proust Variations*. Liverpool: Liverpool University Press.
Breeur, Roland (2000). *Singularité et sujet*. Grenoble: J. Million.
Deacon, Terence (1997). *The Symbolic Species*. London: Allen Lane.
Deely, John (2015). "Building a Scaffold: Semiosis in Nature and Culture." *Biosemiotics* 8, 341–360.
Deleuze, Gilles (2014 [1964]). *Proust et les signes*. 5th ed. Paris: Presses Universitaires de France.
Descombes, Vincent (1987). *Marcel Proust: Philosophie du roman*. Paris: Minuit.
Emmeche, Claude, and Kalevi Kull (2011). *Towards a Semiotic Biology: Life is the Action of Signs*. London: Imperial College Press.
Fernandez, Elisio (2010). "Taking the Relational Turn: Biosemiotics and Some New Trends in Biology." *Biosemiotics* 3, 147–156.
Fülöp, Erika (2012). *Proust, the One, and the Many: Identity and Difference in À la recherche du temps perdu*. Oxford: Legenda.
Gangle, Rocco (2020). *Diagrammatic Immanence: Category Theory and Philosophy*. Edinburgh: Edinburgh University Press.
Henry, Anne (1981). *Marcel Proust: Théories pour une esthétique*. Paris: Klincksieck.
Hoffmeyer, Jesper (2008a). *Biosemiotics: An Examination into the Signs of Life and the Life of Signs*. Scranton: Scranton University Press.
Hoffmeyer, Jesper (2008b). "The Semiotic Body." *Biosemiotics*, 1, 169–190.
Lawtoo, Nidesh (2013). *The Phantom of the Ego: Modernism and the Mimetic Unconscious*. East Lansing: Michigan State University Press.
Lawtoo, Nidesh, (ed.) (2023). *The Mimetic Turn. MLN* 138.5.
James, Ian (2022). "Narrative, Heteropoiesis, and the Outside," in *Perspectives on the Self-Reflexivity in the Humanities*, eds. Tereza Matejckova and Vojtech Kolman. Berlin: De Gruyter.
James, Ian (2025). *Rethinking Literary Naturalism: Proust and Quignard After Life*. Liverpool: Liverpool University Press.
Klossowski, Pierre (2019). *Sur Proust*. Paris: Serge Safran.
Malabou, Catherine (2014). *Avant demain: Épigenèse et rationalité*. Paris: Presses Universitaires de France.
Malabou, Catherine (2016). *Before Tomorrow: Epigenesis and Rationality*, trans. Carolyn Shread. Cambridge: Polity.
Nancy, J.-L., and P. Lacoue-Labarthe (2002). *The Literary Absolute*, trans. Philip Barnard and Cheryl Lester. Albany: State University of New York Press.
Patton, Paul (2017). *Deleuze and Naturalism*. London: Routledge.
Peirce, Charles Sanders (1931). *Collected Papers*, vol. I. Cambridge, MA: Harvard University Press.
Peirce, Charles Sanders (1955). *Philosophical Writings of Peirce*, ed. Justus Buchler. New York: Dover.
Peirce, Charles Sanders (1998). *The Essential Peirce: Selected Philosophical Writings (1893–1913)*, vol. II. Bloomington, IN: Indiana University Press.
Proust, Marcel (1955). *Jean Santeuil*, trans. Gerard Hopkins. London: Weidenfeld and Nicholson.

Proust, Marcel (1971). *Contre Sainte Beuve* précédé de *Pastiches et Mélanges* et suivi de *Essais et articles*. Bibliothèque de la Pléiade. Paris: Gallimard.
Proust, Marcel (1987). *À la Recherche du temps perdu*, ed. Jean-Yves Tadié. 4 vols. Bibliothèque de la Pléiade. Paris: Gallimard.
Proust, Marcel (1988). *Against Sainte Beuve and Other Essays*, trans. John Sturrock. Harmondsworth: Penguin.
Proust, Marcel (1992). *In Search of Lost Time*. 6 vols, trans. C. K. Scott Montcrieff and Terence Kilmartin. London: Chatto and Windus.
Tadié, Jean-Yves (2000). *Marcel Proust: A Life*. Harmondsworth: Penguin.
Wheeler, Wendy (2016). *Expecting the Earth: Life, Culture, Biosemiotics*. London: Lawrence and Wishart.

CHAPTER 12

CONFLICTING SUBLIMINALITIES

The Other Ancestors of Mimesis

Catherine Malabou

We all agree that the concept of mimesis, as reframed by mimetic studies, cannot be confused with its traditional meaning of imitation and reproduction of a model. We know, at the same time, that this original/copy structure is not easy to dismiss. It still commands many representations and artistic practices. The task, then, is to understand and analyze how this traditional notion of mimesis can coexist with more recent accounts of mimesis sensitive to the interplay of sameness and difference, and to conceptually grasp this very difference.

Among many precursors of mimetic studies convoked in the *Homo Mimeticus* trilogy and elsewhere, in *The Location of Culture* Homi Bhabha thematizes what he calls the "moment of transit" in which Western culture finds itself caught and, perhaps, swept away. In such a moment, at once political, theoretical and cultural, "space and time cross to produce complex figures of difference and identity," like those inherent to "race/class/gender" (Bhabha 2004, 2). This "transit," or displacement, of the traditional Western paradigms profoundly disrupts the understandings of "mimesis": both the traditional one—reproduction of a model—and the deconstructive ones—the explosion of the very notion of model.

The new figures of difference and identity are no doubt embedded in specific forms of mimicry, but they do not entail any vertical relationships between the original and its reproduction. The concept of dissemination does not exhaust them either. The new mimetic dynamics operate horizontally, in places that deconstruction never really explored: that is, in the in-between spaces opened up by the differences between sex and gender, Black and white, colonizer and colonized, and natural and artificial intelligence. Bhabha claims that such spaces are spaces of hybrid resemblances, characterized as "almost the same but not quite" (2004, 127). Bhabha then concludes on the need to consider mimesis in terms of borders or, more precisely, "liminalities." The term "liminality," as we know, comes from the Latin *limen,* meaning "threshold."[1] Mimesis is now liminal.

While reading Bhabha, and in total agreement with his argument, it appeared to me that "subliminality" was perhaps even more helpful a determination than "liminalities" to describe the new situation of *mimesis*. Subliminality is coined from the term "subliminal," which is synonymous with subconscious and designates a space that lies below the threshold of consciousness. Why this choice? Why the addition of that prefix "sub-" to liminality or liminalities? How helpful is it for exploring contemporaneous occurrences of mimesis? The purpose of the present text is to answer these questions.

Before returning to Bhabha, I will start with a definition of the term "subliminal," then move toward the concept of subliminality to shed light on the relationships I see at work between this concept and mimesis. Secondly, I will confront "white" and "Black" visions of subliminal mimesis thus defined. First, the French surrealist poet André Breton's conception of "subliminal imitation." Second Franz Fanon's, Sylvia Wynter's, and the Yoruba African writer Amos Tutuola's understandings of the same phenomenon. In conclusion, I will attempt to bring light to the political stakes of this confrontation, arguing that surrealist subliminalities, however dismissive of the reproductive understanding of mimesis, are still trapped within it.

First, a few definitions. "Subliminal" is synonymous with "subconscious." The "subliminal" and the "subconscious," frequently used interchangeably, are important terms in psychology. They both literally mean "below the threshold" of awareness, thus designating the regions of the brain where images, thoughts and impressions are formed prior to conscious processes. The terms "subconscious" and "subliminal" come from two main sources. The first one is to be found in the French psychologist Pierre Janet's work, notably in his important book *Psychological Automatism* (1889). Janet posits two contrasting forms of mental activity, automatism and synthesis. The former corresponds to the primal and archaic zones of the psyche; the latter, to creativity and higher levels of consciousness. The subconscious belongs to the former as it appears as the site of automatic mental behaviors like reflexes and routines, but also to hysteria and sleepwalking in line with what Nidesh Lawtoo, also drawing on Janet, calls the "mimetic unconscious" (2013, 266–276). Based on experimental work with hysterics, Janet demonstrated that in morbid states, due to a diminished field of consciousness, automatism took precedence over the activity of synthesis. In volume 2 of *Psychological Automatisms*, Janet lists the following topics in the table of contents: "the divinatory wand, the explorer pendulum, the reading of thoughts, Historical summary of spiritualism, Spiritualism Assumptions, Spiritism and Psychological Disintegration, Comparison of mediums and somnambulists, Cerebral duality as an explanation of spiritualism, impulsive madness, fixed ideas, etc" (1898).

The second source is provided by the theory of the "subliminal self," elaborated by the British poet, philologist and psychologist Frederic Myers, the cousin of William James. The theory of the subliminal self is developed mainly in the book *Human Personality and Its Survival of Bodily Death* (1903). The question whether, and to what extent, the dead can be considered to speak in us, through us, became Myer's main preoccupation.[2] Myers intends to *rigorously* explore phenomena that go beyond the vigilant consciousness, such as telepathy, transmission of thought, visions of the future or the past, and out-of-body experiences. Anything that brings success to magnetizers deserve to become objects of rigorous scientific study. A scientific field then appears, "metapsychics," which takes a new look at the paranormal. Survival is central to this approach: to what extent can the spirit be said to survive the disappearance of the body? A strong link is made between two sources: between the subliminal understood as the reservation of automatisms (Janet), and the subliminal understood as the psychic reservation of ghosts (Myers). I will return to this link later.

As I was reading different psychological and neurological accounts of the subliminal, it suddenly occurred to me that it was perhaps nothing other than the biological and psychological site for mimesis. Its bodily inscription. And there is more: the subliminal constitutes a point of articulation between two kinds of mimesis: the reproductive one (model/copy) and the creative one, the imitative one and the liminal one, thus acting as a lynchpin between different histories.

Let us start with the reproductive mimesis. If we follow Janet's and Meyers's aforementioned definitions, we see that the subliminal appears to be the most influenceable part of the psyche—what Janet calls its "suggestible" part. The subliminal is the psychological and neurological site for imitation. We can think of the so-called subliminal techniques used by public media in advertisements of all sorts, or in political propaganda. These techniques aim at manipulating attitudes and behaviors in such a way that individuals are unaware of the source of influence or even the fact they are being influenced. This is also the case of messages embedded in a song, words and images briefly flashing in between frames of film, usually for only one tenth of a second, drawings or photos that contain hidden or subtle images, etc.

A subliminal message imprints a certain content onto the reader or viewer's mind without it being immediately noticeable, but enduring over a period of time. A significant example of this can be found John Carpenter's 1988 film *They Live*: the protagonist finds a pair of glasses that allows him to see the real intent behind advertising messages, such as money, billboards and magazines, and discovers that a secret society of aliens is planning on brainwashing the population by impersonating high-level authority figures.[3] We must also mention the even more famous film *The Exorcist* (1973), which (initially) contained a subliminal image of the devil.[4] These examples presuppose that there exists a part of the brain and the psyche that is ready to form automatisms if influenced. Once imprinted, the images or words automatically recur and determine repetitive behaviors, using the mimetic logic of habit.

Let us turn now to creative mimesis. The creative potential of the subliminal has been powerfully brought to light by surrealist poets, André Breton in particular. In his book *Surrealism and Painting*, Breton contrasts what he calls imitation of an "external" model and imitation of an "internal" model.

> The very narrow conception of imitation which art has been given as its aim is at the bottom of the serious misunderstanding that we see continuing right up to the present. In the belief that they are only capable of reproducing more or less fortunately the image of that which moves them, painters have been far too easy-going in their choice of models. The mistake lies in thinking that the model can only be taken from the exterior world, or even simply that it can be taken at all. [...] There lies the inexcusable abdication. It is in any case impossible, under the present conditions of thought, when above all the exterior world appears more and more suspect, still to consent to such a sacrifice. The plastic work of art, in order to respond to the undisputed necessity of thoroughly revising all real values, will either refer to a purely interior model or cease to exist. (Breton 1936, 405)

It remains for us to determine what is meant by the term "interior model." This interior model, Breton says, is not "conscious" but subliminal. In the *Manifesto of Surrealism* from 1924, he equates surrealism with automatism, defining the word surrealism as "psychic automatism in its pure state" based on the "actual function in thought [...] in the absence of any control exercised by reason," or consciousness (1992, 87–88). He confirms this assertion nine years later in "The Automatic Message" (1933), where he affirms that mediumism and surrealism might actually be very similar (2007, 33–35).

A problem immediately arises: how can an automatism be creative? Breton explains that most of the time, mediums—and a great majority of people who say they keep hearing voices—believe that the "spirits" they are in contact with come from outside, or from other people, beyond the grave, even other planets (2007, 33–35). It is on the contrary vital, for Breton, to understand that these ghosts, even if they seem to come from outside, are first of all present in us, in our subconscious, not as persons but as signs, ciphers, that need to be interpreted. That is, in reality, *(re)created*. Suggestion is also very important in automatic writing practices, and there is an obvious relationship between automatism and haunting. However, and once again, the model is interior, the ghost is the outside of the inside, and it is the task of poetry to give them a form.

We are touching here on the plasticity of subliminal mimesis. The two mimetic trends, reproductive and creative, operate at the same site, the automatism, thus being "almost the same but not quite" (Bhabha 2004, 127). The subconscious and the subliminal have been undervalued and dismissed by psychoanalysis, which caused their disappearance as major concepts for a long time. There has been a recent and strong rebirth of these terms in current neurobiology as well as in mimetic studies.[5] Inside the brain, the subconscious is located in the basal ganglia, a set of subcortical nuclei. Basal ganglia are not only involved in motor automaticity, but also in the functioning of intellectual and affective faculties. In an article called "Conscious, preconscious, and subliminal processing: a testable taxonomy," a group of French neurologists declare:

> We define subliminal processing (etymologically "below the threshold") as a condition of information inaccessibility where bottom-up activation is insufficient to trigger a large-scale reverberating state in a global network of neurons with long range axons. [...] Note that, under our hypothesis, subliminal processing is not confined to a passive spreading of activation, independent of the subject's attention and strategies, [...]. On the contrary, [...] it can orient and amplify the processing of a conscious stimulus, even if its bottom-up strength remains insufficient for global ignition. (Dehaene et al. 2006, 206)

In other words, the subliminal is not only passive; it can initiate a creative conscious dynamism. This remark echoes what the great mathematician Henri Poincaré used to say about mathematical invention:

> What happens then? Among the great numbers of combinations blindly formed by the subliminal self, almost all are without interest and without utility; but just for that reason they are also without effect upon the esthetic sensibility. Consciousness will never know them; only certain ones are harmonious, and, consequently, at once useful and beautiful. They will be capable of touching this special sensibility of the geometer of which I have just spoken, and which, once aroused, will call our attention to them, and thus give them occasion to become conscious. [This is only a hypothesis, and yet here is an observation which may confirm it]: when a sudden illumination seizes upon the mind of the mathematician, it usually happens that it does not deceive him, [it always] gratifies [the] natural feeling for mathematical elegance. (Poincaré 1948, 55)

Mathematical creation then has a subliminal origin, and we see that successful mathematical ideas are, most of the time, the most poetic ones. Now, is it not the case that poetic invention, or mathematical invention, as defined by Breton or Poincaré, have become in turn genuine models imposing themselves as universal upon non-western minds, thus dispossessing them of their own ghosts? There is subliminal and subliminal, subconscious and subconscious. Mimesis and mimesis. But also ghosts and ghosts. Internal models and internal models.

Sylvia Wynter shows this very powerfully when she analyzes Fanon's concept of "sociogeny" that appears in *Black Skin, White Masks*. Fanon writes: "Beside phylogeny and ontogeny stands sociogeny" (1986, 4). Wynter affirms that "sociogeny," in opposition to Western psychoanalysis and psychology, relies on a split between Black and white subliminalities (2001). She interprets this split as being another version of what Du Bois in *The Soul of Black Folks* famously calls "double consciousness" (Wynter 2001, 31). Double consciousness designates the fracture between the Black person's two selves: one that identifies with the normative white self, and the other who knows itself to be dominated. The subliminal is the neural site where the fragmentation of the self, due to the contradiction with that dominant position, is inscribed and elaborated. The first self is reproductive; the second is creative, generated from the ground of its own domination.

Wynter reinterprets the phenomenon of double consciousness by relating it to neurobiology. She declares: "Fanon's new conception of the human, one generated from the ground of his own, as well as [...], that of his fellow French Caribbean subjects' lived experience of what it is like to be black, also opens a frontier onto the solution to the problem defined by David Chalmers as that of the 'puzzle of conscious experience'" (2001, 31). For Wynter, the "puzzle of conscious experience" here pertains to the subliminal split that sustains Black consciousness.

The economy brought to light by Breton between reproductive and creative mimesis finds itself redoubled here. When Du Bois declares that Black consciousness mimics the white one, Wynter adds that this mimicry is a mimic of a mimic. Or even a mimic of two mimics. The Black has to interiorize the ways in which white (sub)consciousness is reproductive (mimic 1), but it also has to interiorize the ways in which white subconsciousness is creative (2). The Black subconscious has to imitate and mimetically recreate the ways in which the white subconscious imitates and creates. We might think of all Black artists who have been led to "invent" works that remained assimilable by white culture. There exists a Black mimetic version of white reproduction and a Black mimetic version of white creativity. In that sense, double consciousness (which in reality is a double subconscious) appears as multilayered, going beyond the form of the dyad. It shelters a series of chiasmatic subliminalities.

What about Black mimesis, then, Black-specific reproductive mimesis and Black-specific creative mimesis? Wynter argues that both pertain to the voices of the ancestors, which will never be assimilated with white ghosts. The ancestral voices are requesting to be repeated, transmitted through generations. However, these voices have been forever erased and must be invented. The model is not even interior; it is absent, born dead from dispossession.

In a beautiful book devoted to the difficult problem of the translation of African languages, *Le Sable de Babel* (*The Sand of Babel*), the French anthropologist Alain Ricard comments on the fact that many African writers do not write, as we know, in their mother tongues but in European languages, mostly English or French (2011, 317; my trans.). For Ricard, it is a case of what he calls "subliminal translation." A subliminal translation is the restitution, by the writer, of an original text written in an African language, like Yoruba for instance, in a European or foreign language, except that there is no original text. The writer translates themselves from their native tongue into the colonizing one, except that the native tongue is not a written one. The subliminal translation "does not operate from a text in one language to a text in another language, but from one language to another in the same text. Such texts are palimpsests because under the scriptural authority of the target European text, the obliterated vestiges of the African source are still [supposedly] visible" (Ricard 2011, 380). Further, he specifies: "obscured translations are read as translations, but there are no originals. They 'mimic' an original language, which the author does not or no longer write. I consider this practice to be an original variety of translation, 'subliminal' translation: that which 'has difficulty reaching consciousness'" (381). Ricard takes the example of the Nigerian writer Amos Tutuola, who is regarded as the founder of English-speaking Nigerian novel. The breathing of his text aligns strongly with the rhythms of Yoruba speech. The English is imperfect, very close to oral colloquial language, one that can be heard in the streets of the Yoruba city of Ibadan and thus very far away from the European models imposed on African writers. This English is supposed to be a translation from Yoruba. We might think of *The Palm-Wine Drinkard* (1952), *My Life in the Bush of Ghosts* (1954), *Simbi and the Satyr of the Dark Jungle* (1955) and *The Feather Woman of the Jungle* (1962). The Yoruba/English in which they are written is a poetic construction. As Ricard states, the texts are "translated from a subliminal Yoruba" (2011, 383). He adds:

> In his own way, when the first book appeared, and let us remember that it was, in 1952, the first Nigerian and English novel, [Tutuola] was a traitor: he did not translate tales but invented them, furthermore in English! This first novelist, who ignores grammar, dishonors his country, humiliates the Nigerian intelligentsia, and it will take some time for him to be rid of his stigmata. In the colonial world, only those who have the money and the authorizations publish locally, those who appeal to Paris or London for their linguistic mastery, are recognized as writers. [...] There is no literary field in the colony. (386–387)

Nevertheless, Tutuola's subliminal translations not only survived, but were in their turn translated into several languages.

Where are we at the end of a journey that took us from the inner model of the surrealists to the absence of a model for colonized thinkers and writers? Such a journey has retraced a trajectory that symbolizes, in my view, one of the most important political and artistic paradigm shifts of our time: the shift from the sublime to the subliminal. Both words are of course very similar (the word "sublime" is often understood as above the threshold, but it can also mean below), but their use and their political consequences are dramatically different. As we know, the sublime became, at the end of the twentieth century (it started around the 1980s), a major artistic and political category. Taken from Kant's aesthetics and powerfully reinterpreted by Jean-François Lyotard, it was understood as the "unpresentable" character of political traumas (1994, sections 23–29).

For Kant, the sublime is the name given to the conflict between reason and imagination when they encounter a magnitude that surpasses all measure. Imagination speaks the language of forms; reason speaks a language of the without-form, of infinity. The conflict between them is insoluble. Lyotard describes it as a "differend." What cannot be presented consequently cannot be imitated. The sublime is another name for the ban on the reproductive type of mimesis. That is why Lyotard declares that the sublime can only give way to abstract art or, in the domain of philosophy, to testimony. In a certain sense, the sublime is comparable to the recreation of an absent mother tongue. In a certain sense, a testimony, or an abstract painting, is comparable to a subliminal translation, but in a certain sense only, and the comparison stops there.

My journey has precisely and secretly followed the path of a gradual distancing from the sublime. Even if for surrealists, art has nothing to do with imagination and reason, but with the pre-conscious zones of the mind, surrealism still belongs to the sublime paradigm. Surrealist creative mimesis is still sublime. In *L'Amour fou*, Breton talks about this "sublime point" from which he creates. I situate, he says, "my sublime point in the mountain" (1937, 171; my trans.). The sublime is not reproductive, and this is the reason why it can be said to be free. For Kant, the sublime opens a perspective to the absolute of freedom. And it is clear that creative mimesis, in the West, is said to be free.

Subliminal translation, on the contrary, is a mimesis of loss, of the missing narrative, of dispossession, colonization and slavery. There is no point from which this scenery can be overlooked. Its mimetic fabric is made, as Bhabha says, of "overlapping and displacement of domains of difference" (2004, 1–2) that never end up in something like freedom. In Lyotard's view, the sublime is a disruptive event that challenges authoritative and institutionalized modes of power and authority. Subliminal translation for its part calls into question this ideal suspension of authority.

Subliminal translation is never done with power; it sits in its gaps, plays with it, but is constantly under the threat of crushed by it. Decolonial mimesis is contemporaneous with its repression. Therefore, its poetic work has nothing to do with a work of freedom. Today's great cultural and political shift, the great "transit," coincides with the movement of a subliminal that does not sublimate oppression. These, for the time being, will be my last words about mimesis, of what it has become: a subliminal force without any sublimating power.

Notes

1. Bhabha defines liminalities as "intersticial passages between fixed identifications that open [...] up the possibilities of a cultural hybridity that entertains difference without an assumed or imposed hierarchy" (2004, 4). For a prior engagement with Bhabha's theory of mimicry in mimetic studies see Lawtoo 2016, 198–2017 (editors' note).
2. Cf. Myers' speech delivered on May 28, 1913, on taking possession of the presidential seat of the Society for Psychical Research in London. Cf. also Bergson, "Phantasms of the Livings" in *Mind-Energy*, 1920, 75–104.
3. Carpenter's *They Live* was based on the 1963 short story "Eight o'clock in the morning" by Ray Nekson. Psychologists and scientists have not yet come to a full consensus about whether subliminal messages are actually effective at convincing people to do or want things that they would otherwise not want. While some people are convinced that subliminal messages do indeed work wonders, it seems that when they do make a change, it is down to the placebo effect.
4. On the deleted subliminal image in the film, see Kermode 1997.
5. For a dialogue that foregrounds the links between suggestion, subconscious mechanisms and hypnosis in relation to the neurosciences, see also Gallese and Lawtoo 2023, 346–355.

Bibliography

Bergson, Henri (1920). *Mind-Energy: Lectures and Essays (L'Energie spirituelle*, 1913), trans. H. Wildon Carr. New York: Henry Holt and Company.
Bhabha, Homi K. (2004). *The Location of Culture*. New York: Routledge.
Breton, André (1936). *Surrealism in Painting*, trans. David Gascoyne. London: Faber and Faber.
Breton, André (1937). *L'Amour fou*. Paris: Gallimard.
Breton, André (1992). *First Manifesto of Surrealism in Art in Theory 1900–1990: An Anthology of Changing Ideas*, eds. Charles Harrison and Paul Wood. Oxford: Blackwell Publishers.
Breton, André (2007). "The Automatic Message," in *The Message. Art and Occultism*, eds. Claudia Dichter, Hans Günter Golinski, Michael Krajewski and Susanne Zander. Cologne: Walther König.
Dehaene, Stanislas, Jean-Pierre Changeux, Lionel Naccache, Jérôme Sackur and Claire Sergent (2006). "Conscious, preconscious, and subliminal processing: a testable taxonomy." *Trends in Cognitive Science* 10.5, 204–211.
Du Bois, W. E. B. (1903). *The Souls of Black Folks*. Chicago: A. C. Mc Clurg and Co.
Fanon, Franz (1986). *Black Skin, White Masks*, trans. Charles Lam Markmann. London: Pluto Press.
Janet, Pierre (1898). *L'Automatisme psyhologique, Essai de psychologie expérimentale sur les formes inférieures de l'activité humaine*, 2 vols. 4th ed., version électronique.
Janet, Pierre, and Giuseppe Craparo (2021). *Psychological Automatism, 2 Volumes: Total Automatism and Partial Automatism*, ed. Onno van den Hart. New York: Routledge.
Kermode, Mark (1997). *The Exorcist*. London: The British Film Institute.
Lawtoo, Nidesh (2013). *The Phantom of the Ego*. East Lansing: Michigan State University Press.
Lyotard, Jean-François (1994). *Lessons on the Analytic of the Sublime: Kant's Critique of Judgment*, trans. Elisabeth Rottenberg. Stanford: Stanford University Press.

Myers, Frederic W. H. (2011). *Human Personality and Its Survival of Bodily Death*, ed. Leopold Hamilton Myers. Whitefish: Kessinger Publishing.
Poincaré, Henri (1948). "Mathematical Creation" (1910). *Scientific American* 179, 54–57.
Ricard, Alain (2011). *Le Sable de Babel. Traduction et apartheid: esquisse d'une anthropologie de la textualité*. Paris, CNRS éditions.
Wynter, Sylvia (2001). "Towards the Sociogenic Principle: Fanon, Identity, the Puzzle of Consciousness, and What It is Like to Be "Black," in *National Identities and Socio-Political Changes in Latin America Experience*, eds. Antonio Gomez-Moriana and Mercedes Duran-Cogan. New York: Routledge, 30–66.

CODA

THE THREE METAMORPHOSES OF MIMESIS
Thinking with Catherine Malabou

Catherine Malabou and Nidesh Lawtoo

As the chapters assembled in this volume suggest, and the original title of our dialogue confirms,[1] there seems to be a disconcerting mirroring relation between plasticity and mimesis. This also means that when plasticity and mimesis face each other, in a dialogic interplay, they have the potential to generate metamorphoses that cut across old-fashioned mind/body, nature/culture dualisms, including those which are patriarchal. The performative powers of mimesis/plasticity also operate in subliminal ways that are not under full agentic or conscious control and are in this sense *un*-conscious or subconscious. In the process of dramatization, plastic-mimetic subjects trouble the very essence of foundational concepts in western thought, like the subject, freedom, intelligence, consciousness, anarchism, automatism, pleasure, the unconscious—including, of course, plasticity and mimesis.

Furthering a first foray into the plasticity of mimesis that is constitutive of the genealogy of homo mimeticus,[2] the dialogue that follows takes stock of Catherine Malabou's recent engagements with the problematic of mimesis—whether behind the conceptual masks of "simulation," "mimicry," "repetition," "mirroring" or "epigenetic mimesis," among other emerging concepts that are currently contributing to the field of mimetic studies.[3] Our assumption is that if the subject is indeed plastic, mimetic and constitutively relational, then philosophers and theorists will benefit from dialogic practices of thinking together—or sym-philosophizing—that not only represent but actually perform the mimetic turn. To that end, we draw on a genealogical practice of dialogic encounters with influential thinkers currently broadening the reach of mimetic studies across disciplines.[4] I am thus honored to add Catherine Malabou as an ally to this emerging field. In the company of Isabell Dahms and Giulia Rignano, who join the conversation for an intermezzo on gendered mimesis, Malabou is engaged dialogically in the metamorphoses of mimesis to reveal a transformation of her understanding of plasticity as well.

Catherine Malabou: I have to thank you Nidesh, for in reality mimesis was not one of my fields of interest and you made me aware of the importance of this concept. In the past, like most philosophers, I have touched on mimesis, but I never really focused on it and discovered how important it actually was—so thank you for that. I'm very curious to see how we can join plasticity and mimesis in productive ways, while transforming them in the process.

Nidesh Lawtoo: Yes, you are known for your influential concept of plasticity, which serves as a red thread, or *fil conducteur*, in your protean oeuvre. It is true that until recently, you haven't explicitly examined the *concept* of mimesis itself. And yet, the *problematic* of mimesis has been making increasingly frequent appearances in your most recent books, often under different conceptual masks such as "mirroring" or "simulation," for instance. The notion of the "mask" itself that you often convoke to speak about plasticity is, of course, also a mimetic concept. It recalls the origins of mimesis (from *mîmos*, actor or performance) in theatrical spectacles where the figure of the mimos wears a mask, from which our notion of personality also comes (from *persona*, theatrical mask). And now your more recent focus on "epigenetic mimesis" indicates that this problematic is becoming explicitly central to your concerns. If my work was in any way helpful for this mimetic turn of yours, I am of course honored.

To begin with, I was wondering if you could specify the underlying philosophical reasons that led to your recent interest in mimesis, a mimesis that is not simply a passive copy or representation of nature but entails a creative and productive dimension on the part of a plastic subject?

CM: There are many possible reasons I could advance to answer your question. The first one would be my reflections on artificial intelligence (AI) and technology, on which you have also written a beautiful text.[5] Given the developments in AI, at the moment, it has become inevitable to reflect on simulation and to create or elaborate a new concept of mimesis that definitely goes beyond

ChatGPT; many technophobes said that this AI chatbot was not to be taken seriously because this system was only mimetic in the pejorative sense and that it was unable to create anything. For me this kind of discourse is to be eliminated from the philosophical realm because it doesn't grasp the very troubling power of simulating or imitating... what? Is it imitating the human, really? I don't know, but AI uses the power of simulation to create a new world. So, I think my interest in mimesis comes from my reflection on technology.

NL: Yes, your wonderful book, *Morphing Intelligence*, published in French under the title *Métamorphoses de l'intelligence,* is in many ways a correction or critique of your previous book titled *What Should We Do with Our Brain?*

CM: Yes, it was an incredible discovery for me. When I read in an article that IBM was creating synaptic chips that were "miming" the function of the brain, my previous distinction between the natural brain, let's say, and the machine was becoming obsolete. If a machine is able to function as a natural brain, if there exist such things as synaptic chips, then the difference between a human brain and a technological one might become difficult to tell.

NL: We'll come back to the troubling question of AI simulations and the posthuman later on, but let us first step back to the embodied and material aspect of imitation on the part of the human subject. For me, the first and most direct connection between plasticity and mimesis stems from their shared genealogy and the shift of emphasis they have triggered in recent years: both plasticity and mimesis are traditionally confined to aesthetic preoccupations with artistic representations or formations, be it in sculpture or in painting, for instance; and yet, from different perspectives—you by focusing on plasticity's double capacity to give and receive form via your reading of Hegel, I by focusing on the pathological and patho-*logical* manifestations of mimesis I saw at play in Nietzsche—we brought these traditional aesthetic concepts back in touch with the problematic of subject formation and transformation, thereby transforming their meanings in the process as well. Although you are most known for your materialist reading of Hegel's dialectics, for your defense of the transcendental in Kant as an epigenetic category, and for your agonistic supplement to Derrida's logic of the trace, I also find your sensitivity to the materiality of the brain, including its epigenetic plasticity prone to metamorphoses that cut across the biological and the symbolic, to be very Nietzschean in spirit.

For instance, I was pleased to read in *Morphing Intelligence* that you enlist Nietzsche as a "great thinker of the brain" (Malabou 2017, 176); you also call attention to his interests in "physiology" and physio-psychology in order to affirm that "life cannot be divided" (176) according to dualistic binaries like mind/body, culture/nature, physiology/psychology, original/copy, male/female, among others. As you speak of the "three metamorphoses of intelligence" in your detailed genealogy of AI simulations—which goes from nineteenth-century genetics to epigenetics in the Blue Brain project to automatisms internal to AI—I thus propose a little dialogic experiment. Let us take Nietzsche's "Three Metamorphoses of the Spirit" that opens *Thus Spoke Zarathustra* as a provisional starting point. I discuss it briefly in the Prologue at the start of this volume, and since you were perhaps implicitly also alluding to this text to structure your three metamorphoses of intelligence, it might be a good way to bring *Homo Mimeticus III* to an end. The goal would not be to close the discussion but rather to establish new genealogical bridges between plasticity and mimesis and favor new metamorphoses of both mirroring concepts.

As you recall, in the "Three Metamorphoses of the Spirit" Nietzsche uses animal figures to account for the plastic and metamorphic powers of an immanent, embodied and material spirit prone to protean transformations that might help us join plasticity and mimesis. For this operation it is important not to restrict mimesis to the dominant metaphysical definition that reduces it to a debased copy of nature. Instead, let us focus on a mimetic pathos, or power, that drives the biological evolution of the spirit itself in ways that transgress the frontiers between the biological and the symbolic. As is well known, Nietzsche's parable of the *Verwandlungen* of the spirit describes "how the spirit becomes a camel, and the camel a lion, and the lion at last a child" (2005, 23). It's a parable dealing with the transformation of the spirit that remains rooted in the animality of the body in ways that entangle symbolic, spiritual and biological perspectives that are central to both mimesis and plasticity. And since in your work you often point to the biological specificity of certain animals—the salamander that regrows its tail, for instance, generating a second tail that both supplements the missing one while differing from it—we could do the same with the mimetic, anti-mimetic and hypermimetic animals Nietzsche convokes.

First Metamorphosis: Cultural Load/Biological Heritage

NL: The first symbolic figure, or animal, is the one of the camel that passively submits to the weighty values of tradition Nietzsche generally critiques: namely, moral values the spirit is supposed to bow down to and carry on its back. It's the phase of learning and submission characteristic of the first step in education, whose passivity, for Nietzsche, is inscribed in the animal's bodily submission. Mimesis seems to play a role in this submission. In fact, the camel, not unlike the cow, is a herd animal. In this biological but also sociocultural sense it is a mimetic animal that is driven by a type of mimicry that, for Nietzsche, is not only animal but all too human. It's a first step that is often dismissed as simply passive and submissive. And yet, precisely, as a first step, it also suggests that a biological mimetic drive is present in all humans, while the symbolic focus on the load of education indicates that the mimetic experience of learning also plays a major role in forming and transforming subjectivity. Could you articulate this interplay between the innate and the acquired, the biological and the symbolic, in this first metamorphosis of the spirit rooted in a mimetic animal?

CM: It is strange that for Nietzsche the weight of biology and the weight of culture ends up being one and the same weight. The camel is the animal that carries something on its back, I remember that metaphor. What the camel carries and what they obey is a mixture between the sedimentation of cultural tradition and biology. There is a point of indistinction between the two in Nietzsche. And I think this indistinction is at the core of what he calls memory. The child is the ultimate form of metamorphosis because the child is forgetful. So, memory in Nietzsche is this mixture between genetically inherited weight and all the cultural traditions that are taught and infused by education.

NL: Yes, in this bio-cultural inheritance the following paradox struck me. In this complex interplay between what is given and what is acquired, biology and culture, that is central to the plastic formation of a mimetic animal, the line dividing activity from passivity, consciousness and the unconscious, does not seem clear-cut. After all, Nietzsche, who is arguably thinking about his own education in philology as well, tells us: "the heavy and the hardest [load] is what the camel's strength desires" (2005, 23). This seems to indicate a correlation between the weight of cultural training or mimetic submission to tradition on the one hand, and the plastic development of a type of mimetic strength that might be creative and productive in nature, on the other. Could you comment on this form of imitation based on automatic mimetic reflexes that sediment into habits and might appear as simply passive, yet, through repetition, might also be the condition for the development of a type of strength constitutive of a more active, or productive, mimesis?

CM: Yes, I don't think Nietzsche only criticizes the camel and the mimetic drives it embodies. It's part of a process that leads to the next two metamorphoses. Of course, there is an evolution and transformation, but Nietzsche does not eliminate the camel, and thus the mimetic animal because, as you say, the camel is not only passive; it is also a figure of obedience. And in a certain sense, for Nietzsche, obedience is necessary. It drives the vital form of resentment. He is not entirely against resentment. Resentment is necessary as a form of reaction against aggression, or any form of threat. The camel is desiring to carry the weight in order to defend itself and protect itself, which also entails an active side. In this sense, mimesis functions as a protection. So, it's not as negative a first step as it's often taken to be, even though it's not the ultimate form of liberation, of course.

NL: It's interesting that by reading the metaphor of the animal literally and taking the mimetic drive that defines the camel as a starting point for a metamorphosis of the "spirit" we immediately trouble, or deconstruct, the symbolic/biological but also active/passive binaries that do not capture the Janus-faced properties of both mimesis and plasticity. As your focus on brain plasticity and epigenetics suggests, you are one of the few continental philosophers who engages with the neurosciences in order to establish productive dialogues across the two-cultures divide. When I started working on a theory of the mimetic subject via Nietzsche and other modernist authors around twenty years ago, I noted they were drawing on little-discussed philosophical physicians like Hippolyte Bernheim, Gabriel Tarde, Pierre Janet and other late nineteenth-century psychologists who were attentive to the physio-psychology of mirroring mechanisms they posited in the brain. I then realized that they were anticipating, by over a century, the so-called discovery of "mirror neurons," which, as you know, were discovered first in monkeys in the 1990s and were then confirmed in humans as well in the form of a network or system—thereby confirming the ancient idea that we are mimetic animals, or homo mimeticus.

It is in this context that I also came across your work on plasticity and the engagement with the neurosciences. I thus started thinking about the ways in which these two concepts could complement each other. What I find interesting, for instance, is that mirror neurons stress the relational orientation of the brain and point to automatic mechanisms that blur the line between consciousness and the unconscious; they also complicate the dominant picture of a volitional, autonomous and free subject in favor of relationality, embodiment and intersubjectivity. So, I was wondering: what is your take on mirror neurons? While far from providing the only key to intersubjective phenomena like empathy, mind reading and imitation, could they complement brain plasticity by stressing the relational orientation of human brains that are impressed by models while having formative powers of their own?

CM: The theory of mirror neurons has raised an immense resistance, at least in France, from sociologists, who argued that the origins of society have nothing to do with something biological, and that the mimetic relations between people are based on mutual constructions that are never given as such. They posit that in living beings there is no automatic sense of imitation and that everything is constructed and so is mimesis. And so, as you say, mirror neuron theory was interpreted as a form of reduction of the unmotivated character of human society defended by figures like Durkheim and other classical sociologists. In reality, mirror neurons don't explain everything; this is what the sociologists didn't understand. Mirror neurons are implied in all activities in which I'm not actively face to face with someone. For example, when I read a book which describes a situation I'm not myself in, it is because of my mirror neurons that I can represent such a situation, I can fiction myself as part of this scenario. But they don't explain everything. For autistic children, for example, their mirror neurons do not work, so they don't function automatically. Even in "normal" brains they need to be educated. If one doesn't read, doesn't watch films, is not in interaction with others, mirror neurons are just unhelpful. Look for instance at what happens to abandoned orphans in Romania who were left alone and uneducated: they couldn't speak, for their mirror neurons were left unemployed. This is what sociologists haven't really understood: that mirror neurons were not a threat to their theory. Of course, they are very helpful and indispensable for understanding the functioning of imitation, but if they are not stimulated, shaped and educated, they don't function.

NL: This is very interesting and helpful for two reasons. First, what you say reminds me that a figure I consider a precursor of mirror neuron theory was a sociologist, albeit one marginalized precisely by Durkheim: namely, Gabriel Tarde in *The Laws of Imitation* (1890), where he argues that "there is in the brain an innate tendency to imitation [*une tendance innée à l'imitation*]" (2001, 148; my trans.). And second, what you say confirms Nietzsche's parable of the camel: without the load, without the cultural training, a mimetic drive alone is not generative of learning and the strength that potentially ensues. Would you then speak of a plasticity of the mirror neuron system, shaped by life experience?

CM: Yes, exactly.

NL: Now that we have complicated what appeared to be a simply passive form of imitation, we can perhaps move on to the second metamorphosis, which does not seem to be mimetic at all; instead, it requires a plastic and quite explosive transformation of the spirit.

Second Metamorphosis: The Paradox of Mimetic Agonism

NL: Building on its mimetic strength, the camel turns into a lion, who seems to be totally anti-mimetic. No longer submissive to the values of the past, the lion is a proud, independent and sovereign animal, who, Nietzsche tells us, will "seize freedom for itself and become lord of its own desert" (2005, 23). An activity of negation is needed for this free affirmation to emerge. Thus, the lion stands in opposition to the religious and metaphysical values of the past embodied by the dragon "thou shalt" in view of seizing its freedom. This is an important moment of rupture in the metamorphosis of the spirit, especially philosophical spirits like Nietzsche, who do not want to remain passive disciples in—let's admit it—a weighty discipline like philosophy.

CM: Yes, I see it. Also, for me, "The Three Metamorphoses" is a metaphor of the personal trajectory to philosophy via education. I think there is a moment in which the young philosopher is trying to invent their own concepts. This is necessary but Nietzsche is also ironic when it comes to that.

NL: If we transpose this confessional element to your own work, I also find a strong and healthy *anti*-mimetic dimension in your books. This is especially vital when confronted with powerful intellectual models like Jacques Derrida, who once told you that you don't need a master but, rather, a "counter-master" (*contre-maître*). This anti-mimetic dimension is central to our theory of homo mimeticus as well and to the critique of herd behavior it entails. It also appears repeatedly in your work, often in conjunction with plasticity and the explosions it generates. At times, it leads you, in early works, to set up an opposition between plasticity and mimesis that might not be clear-cut. For instance, in *What Should We Do with Our Brain* you speak of plasticity's "refusal to submit to a model" (2007, 6). Could you comment on the anti-mimetic drive in your development as a philosopher in general and a woman philosopher in particular?

CM: Of course, we are all the same: at some point we want to develop our own concepts and ideas in a non-mimetic way. Paradoxically, this is perhaps the moment when we are most mimetic. There is a beautiful text by Proust about "pastiche" and he says: we are never closer to pastiching than when we think we are not; when we think we are independent, and creating our own style like the figure of the lion, thinking "I'm the sovereign, I don't imitate anyone, etc.," this is the moment when we are perhaps totally embedded in imitation. You cannot say "I'm free," "I'm not imitating," without having in mind your model. That is the paradox of sovereignty: sovereignty is the arche-model. When you're denying imitation, in reality you are trying to get as close as possible to that model of the sovereign. So, I think the lion is a very ambiguous figure: on the one hand, it's admirable, beautiful and sovereign; on the other hand, it's a victim of its own independence.

NL: I asked this question for two reasons. First because, as Nietzsche says, there is often a "confessional" element in philosophical thought that is important to acknowledge. And second, because the affect or pathos of mimesis informs and transforms philosophical logos over time. The time of your anti-mimetic rupture—you'll tell me if the term is too strong—with Derrida was marked in books written over a decade ago, books like *Changing Difference, What Should We Do With Our Brain*, and even more clearly in *Plasticity at the Dusk of Writing,* a book that marks your distance from your former mentor by proposing plasticity as a "motor scheme" that replaces writing. The focus on "form" in particular is a key distancing anti-mimetic move from the deconstructive emphasis on formlessness and so is your focus on the neurosciences, which proved to be very productive.

Intermezzo: Gendered Mimesis

NL: A gendered perspective that Nietzsche does not develop also seems constitutive of this anti-mimetic move of distance in your thought. In *Changing Difference,* for instance, you make clear that this break with models, or this refusal of imitation, is more important if one is a "woman philosopher" in a patriarchal world in which she is often confined to what you call the "miming of male mastery" (2011, 106). An anti-mimetic drive central to all creative thinkers in general is thus redoubled in the case of women thinkers given that in the patriarchal tradition women have been reduced to a bad copy or imitation of men. For feminist philosophers working still in a predominantly patriarchal context (this is certainly still the case in France and Belgium but also elsewhere), it is thus vital to take critical distance from mimesis, or develop subversive strategies of mimicry, as Luce Irigaray would say, to develop their own thought.

CM: Irigaray is precisely trying to get rid of the dominant notion of mimesis understood as just the imitation of masculine thinking by developing strategies of mimicry. So, I don't think we can get rid of mimesis at all. We have to use it against itself, so to speak. That is why in her beautiful reading of the *Timaeus,* she identifies with *chora* and says that women should mime the *chora,* mime plasticity in order to subvert the very image of passivity, the mother, and the receptacle, and again, use mimesis against itself. I totally agree with that. I don't believe in the total freedom of the lion. At the same time, when it comes to women philosophers in France, it has been a catastrophe. These women philosophers we are talking about, like Irigaray and others, have never been studied and been part of any curriculum. Even at this international conference that provides the context for our dialogue, there are no French students. There is a kind of split between the French academic structure and all kind of independent research, particularly feminine research.

NL: Indeed. I discovered Irigaray in the United States.

CM: Yes, of course. It's the same for Monique Witting; Julia Kristeva a bit less, but she is more a psychoanalyst than a philosopher; and even Simone de Beauvoir is not that read in the philosophical academic realm. They are not part of the traditional curriculum. For example, when you have to go through the *agrégation de philosophie,* the exam one needs to pass to become a teacher, these women philosophers have never been part of the curriculum.

NL: Patriarchal structures are hard to change. Yet, these figures are very important to both the homo mimeticus and gendered mimesis projects. We recently benefited from an encounter with the feminist philosopher and political theorist Adriana Cavarero, and her relational notion of inclinations in particular, which also overlaps with mimesis; the work of Judith Butler on the performative dimensions of gender is equally important.[6] To broaden connections with this feminist and post-feminist genealogical traditions, Isabelle Dahms and Giulia Rignano, who are part of the Gendered Mimesis team, have some questions for you as well.

Isabelle Dahms: Yes, indeed. You say that philosophy also shapes bodies, and I was wondering if you could say a bit more about this process of shaping.

CM: Yes, philosophy also shapes bodies. This is something that is very rarely said in philosophy, which is more concerned with shaping minds and spirits. I know that Foucault wrote about how philosophy is a kind of *dressage*. It's a discipline in the bad sense of the term. But there are very few developments on how philosophy entails a training which is not only mental, but also physical, bodily, and it's in that sense I meant that phrase. It's about the distribution of zones, bodily zones of pleasure, because clearly, and Plato was the first to say it, philosophy and love are very close to each other. I totally agree with Plato that philosophy is impossible without love and consequently also physical desire. But this is where Plato stops, because he says that this passionate relationship that philosophy is in fact, shapes only the soul, and when it comes to the body, it's not really philosophical. It is a step lower. I don't agree with that. A woman, man or any kind of gender has a distributed type of body in which different nuances of pleasure are expressed, so to speak, and they are born out of the different reactions we have to texts for instance. I think that we are not equal. We are not equally sensitive, philosophically speaking, to all authors. For example, there are authors that I do not feel attracted to. For example, I always had problems with Leibniz or Husserl. For some reason, these philosophers don't have a direct effect on my body. I know this is strange, but Hegel for me is instead "excitable speech," as Butler would say, and creates a distribution of erotic zones.

ID: Following up on this, how would you explain the relationship between performativity and plasticity: that is, Butler's thinking and your own.

CM: Performativity is, of course, very important. I totally understand why Butler could make such use of it in, for example, in *Gender Trouble*; it was a way for them to declare that gender had no pre-existing basis and that a gendered identity formed itself only through repetition, performative iteration, etc., and that there was nothing behind that. Okay. But at the same time, because we talk so much about essence today, this seems to me to erase a little bit too quickly the problem of essence. In the notion of performativity, you have something like an idea of non-conservation; for example, a work of art that is just a performance cannot be kept. And this lack of constitution of an archive is a problem for me. I think this is what is perhaps missing, if I may say so, in Butler's work. Where is the archive? Where is the archive of identity? If gender identity is only performative, where does this repetition, this performativity, inscribe itself and constitute an essence in the good sense of the term? That would be my answer. Plasticity is perhaps more open to both, of course, repetition, iteration, etc., and at the same time, to the question of form. This was also the topic of our discussion with Butler in the book *You Be My Body for Me*. What do you do with form? Where does form enter the picture in your performative system?

Giulia Rignano: I was wondering if you could point out what is the major difference between the kind of mimesis at play in Luce Irigaray's subversive repetition and Paul Preciado's intake of testosterone. Could this comparison add something to the continuation of a subversive mimesis, or do you see an incompatible difference?

CM: The obvious answer is that Preciado does not believe at all in sexual difference. This is the reproach he addresses to Irigaray: to be still too dependent on the woman/man, feminine/masculine distinction. So, the first point concerns the nonbinary schema that Preciado is definitely adopting and trying to substitute for the sexual difference one. It is indeed true that Irigaray, because of her time, is still very attached to sexual difference. Now the question about testosterone and hormones points toward transgenderism, which is also something that is quite alien to Irigaray, because she has never tried to change her gender. Of course, Irigaray wrote a lot about the transformability of femininity; she presented the woman as a plastic essence, but she never envisaged overcoming the fact of being a woman and engaging in something like transgenderism. Testosterone is instead a way to act upon the biology of one's own gender in order to pass into another gender. So, I wouldn't see many connections between the two.

GR: I see some similarity in Irigaray's subversive repetition, which, of course, comes from another period. But in a way she speaks to a carnality and a zone of indifferentiation that she wants to play with to actually go beyond the male and female binary. Preciado today uses his own body, actually not through a subversive repetition of discourse, but through hormones. It's almost as if he's enacting this subversive repetition through the assumption of a substance that changes his body first and then allows for a different representation. So, I see a connection, but it is as if they are starting from two different points.

CM: Yes, I think the notion of dysphoria developed in Preciado's last book *Dysphoria Mundi* is very important in this respect. He's talking about this dysphoric zone of the world, a kind of extra space, almost an outer space from which he talks, seeing the world from another space. Maybe we could find something like that in Irigaray; I'd have to think about it.

GR: It's maybe also related to the change in our conception of matter, because sexual difference was very important to give materiality a space in discourse. And now queer theory is actually amplifying sexual difference and the power of materiality that they opened up. I see a continuity between sexual difference and queer theories, even though this continuity came after seeing all the discontinuities. But now it's as if the body is so much rooted in materiality, and I was thinking how mimesis actually occupies a place both on a discursive side and on a material side.

CM: You're right. I was also surprised to see that Carla Lonzi, for instance, was just translated in French this year, in 2023. *Let's Spit on Hegel* was translated a month ago, but there is still nothing about *Clitoridean Woman*. Because she was the one to invent the term clitoridean in order to insist on the fact that the material and the symbolic were working hand in hand. It was thus important to insist on the clitoris to affirm that it symbolized women, women's independence. It was not only an organ but also an agent of autonomy. So, I totally agree on this double value of materiality and the symbolic.

NL: In different forms, mimesis seems indeed at the center of the complex articulation of the symbolic and materiality. From Luce Irigaray's destabilizing notion of mimicry central to the materialist tradition of sexual difference of which Carla Lonzi is an important precursor to Judith Butler's theory of performativity tied to forms of mimetic iteration that are perhaps still rooted in a linguistic/deconstructive ontology but are also receiving a materialist supplement from transgender theorists like Preciado, it seems that mimesis could help us articulate different and often competing traditions in feminist philosophy. There should thus be work for the Gendered Mimesis team!

Mimetic Agonism, Pathos and Style

NL: In order to further our understanding of the ontologies of difference informing gendered difference as well, let us pick up the thread of the metamorphoses of the spirit. I am happy to hear you also endorse an agonistic conception of mimesis that is neither passively mimetic nor reducible to parodic mimicry but is based on what I would call mimetic agonism. Broadly speaking, mimetic agonism is driven by a strong *anti*-mimetic or agonistic drive in the sense that the model is opposed or supplemented, but in this movement of supplementation a creative mimesis is at play that draws selectively on the model, paradoxically, in order to push with-and-against him, her, them. I found traces of this mimetic agonism, which is again not simply passive nor does it lead to mimetic rivalry, but is productive in nature in major figures that tend to be simply opposed: Plato contra Homer, Aristotle contra Plato, Nietzsche contra Plato, Freud contra Nietzsche, Girard contra Freud, and now Malabou contra Derrida. My sense is that these thinkers benefit from being read as part of an agonistic and creative mimetic relation. This would entail that a creative mimesis is still internal to the anti-mimetic lion and that the sovereign subject retains epigenetic traces of the strength of the mimetic camel. Do you think this strategy of mimetic agonism can be creatively adopted by feminist or feminine philosophers more generally as a strategy for thinking with and against the tradition?

CM: Yes, somebody at the conference asked, "What would be a feminist, or rather feminine philosophy?" It is true that this is a possible trap to say that something like a feminine philosophy might exist because it would be an essentialization in the bad sense of the term—and I don't think that such a thing exists. At the same time, what is specifically feminine in this agonistic mimesis is that precisely "the woman" has been denied any kind of essence. That's the reason I was interested in this concept of "essence," to rebuild it from a feminist point of view, because we women are the subjects of this erasure. Clearly there is no essence of the woman for philosophers. If we have an essence, it is the masculine one. We are a kind of "appendix" to the masculine. At the same time, this absence of essence is a very productive basis for a reconstruction that necessarily borrows from the traditional definition of essence. The "I" has to be mimetic in some sense; we have to do with what we have. But then, once we have something like a model, we can transform it and subvert it. That would be what I would call a strategy for feminine philosophy: to play with this absence of essence; rebuild an essence; and then subvert it.

NL: Your understanding of essence complicates, subverts or deconstructs the dominant understanding of essence rooted in a static and universal conception of being. You remind us that the etymology of essence (*eidos*) points to the very opposite: namely, a movement of becoming. The movement that I often find at play in the concept of mimetic agon is a double movement of attraction and repulsion that I group under the Nietzschean rubric of "pathos of distance," in which the distance or detachment internal to an agonistic critique at the level of thought or logos is nonetheless driven by a mimetic pathos of attraction in which emotions, or pathos, play a role.

CM: You are totally right to stress pathos because in plasticity there is a type of passivity in the sense of *pathein* in Greek, which is suffering, and at the same time I don't like the term affect. It's a term I don't use very much, only when I speak about Deleuze because he uses it frequently, particularly in his reading of Spinoza. I'm a bit suspicious of affect because you cannot have affect without auto-affection, for all affects proceed from auto-affection, from a source which entails the relation of the self to itself. It thus presupposes a notion of a totally constituted subject able to talk, exchange, dialogue with itself, etc. and all forms of particular affects derive from auto-affection. This is something that Derrida has totally deconstructed, and I fully agree with him. I thus prefer terms like drives or passions, even feelings or emotions. Even Deleuze, in his reading of Spinoza, originates affects in auto-affection because for Spinoza the essence of God affects itself. So, you cannot easily get rid of this theory of auto-affection, which remains in fact very linked with the sovereign theory of the subject. This is of course not what Deleuze wants to do but there is nevertheless something of a trace of that in the sovereignty of the auto-affected subject in his thinking.

NL: This is indeed the reason I prefer the notion of pathos to affect because it stresses the relational dimension of mimetic drives. Somewhere in a fragment in Nietzsche's *Nachlass* he describes the will to power as "not a being, not a becoming but a pathos," an emotional force that comes from the outside and takes possession of the ego, dispossessing even sovereign subjects of their presence to selfhood and generating what he calls a "phantom of the ego."

Independently of how we call this drive, force or pathos, my sense is that it has the power to generate a movement of thought in mimetic thinkers, or thinkers of mimesis, in which both logos and pathos are at play. This double movement seems to me to be constitutive of your philosophical style. There is a strength in your style that is obviously driven by your admirable conceptual rigor and clarity of logical argumentation but is also doubled by a pathos that gives your voice a distinctive tonality and timbre needed to confront the oppressive thou shalts of traditional philosophical imperatives. Did I hear correctly? And does what I called mimetic agonism inform not only what you say, your *logos*, but also how you say it, or philosophical *lexis*?

CM: It's very difficult for me to answer because I have no clear idea of it. I'll answer briefly by saying that I never write anything without an interpellation. It is always as if someone was asking me something. It's an address. I never write in another form than address. I hear something like a question, a solicitation or a voice, and I would situate my writing as answers, always. This is what Heidegger says about language: that the first words of children are always an answer; that the child starts speaking by answering someone or something, and I think this is totally right. For Heidegger it is language answering itself, for the first solicitation comes from language itself and is totally rigorous. He says: "*Die Sprache spricht*" (language speaks), which means language is calling itself and answering itself. Even if the question does not exist, then, we answer. The first word is an answer, and this is how I write. For that reason, the writing is necessarily *patho*-logical, in the sense of pathos. Because when you write while addressing someone, emotions and autobiographical elements necessarily enter into the picture.

NL: Yes, the relational dimension of your thinking resonates with the relationality of mimesis; it also rendered the mimetic genre of the dialogue based on question and answer doubly appropriate for our chosen topic. Before we come to the figure of the child, I have a last question for the lion. It concerns the problematic of the unconscious and the science that supposedly discovered it, which casts a long shadow over contemporary theory, including feminist philosophy. Both at the level of the camel and the lion, the plastic and mimetic metamorphoses that ensue involved affects that are not under the control of consciousness, are engrained in habits and automatic reflexes, and are in this sense un-conscious. The discovery of the unconscious is often still synonymous with psychoanalysis, though historians of psychoanalysis from Henry Ellenberger's *The Discovery of the Unconscious* to more recent historians like Mikkel Borch-Jacobsen's and Sonu Shamdasani's *The Freud Files* demonstrate, convincingly in my view, that this discovery is part of a "Freudian Legend" (Ellenberger 1970, 547). It is a legend for it tells the story of a solitary anti-mimetic hero who discovers the unconscious in genial isolation in theory, while in practice he erases important philosophical physicians, precursors and competitors, from Pierre Janet to

Alfred Binet, Hippolyte Bernheim to Auguste Forel, among others. Given the limits of Freudian, Lacanian and other Oedipal approaches to the psyche, with their focus on familial triangles, normative views of sexuality, symbolic focus on the phallus, sexist and racist concepts like "penis envy," "dark continent," etc., among other problematic aspects that have come massively to the fore in recent years, you often take psychoanalysis to task on issues such as "the new wounded" or "pleasure erased," to mention two of your book titles. The discontent with psychoanalysis is palpable on many fronts, and their inability to engage with trans-identities has been made clear by transgender figures like Paul Preciado. I wonder if rather than trying to reform a system that is obviously resistant to reform, a step back to pre-psychoanalytical theories of the unconscious, attentive to what Nietzsche called "genuine physio-psychology," might not serve as an alternative strategy?

I ask this question because it seems to me you are already pursuing it. In addition to being critical of psychoanalysis, in your recent work on intelligence you have engaged with forgotten figures like Alfred Binet, who was, amongst the psychologists interested in automatism, movement and emotions. In a book co-authored with Charles Féré, Binet argued that movement seen generates a reflex to move, thereby anticipating mirror neurons by over a century. Nietzsche was an avid reader of that physio-psychological literature and it's via them that I came across this pre-Freudian but also post-Freudian genealogy of what Marcel Gauchet calls the "cerebral unconscious." I called it the "mimetic unconscious," to stress its mimetic but also plastic, relational and embodied character. Given these philosophical physicians' attention to what we now call the brain, could figures like Binet or Janet not be more directly aligned with contemporary neurologists like Changeux than Freud and Lacan?

CM: I don't want to give too much away about my talk because the "subconscious" and its relation to the synonymous concept of the "subliminal" will be my topic and I will come back precisely to Janet and the pre-Freudian theories you mention.[7] As you know, Freud has eliminated the concept of the "subconscious." In the beginning Freud was identifying the pre-conscious with the subconscious. And then, in time he moved away from the subconscious because it is too biologically determined, and he was referring to Janet. He got rid of that vocabulary and elaborated on the theory of the pre-conscious, the conscious and the unconscious. Clearly there is a move in psychoanalysis that tends to eliminate any kind of biologically anchored vision of the unconscious. Even if Freud starts with the brain in the "Project for a Scientific Psychology," he clearly and very quickly gets rid of it. Lacan also radicalizes this abandonment of biology. I think that you are totally right that today there is a movement of coming back to the "cerebral unconscious" with figures like Pierre Janet, Alfred Binet, with the sociology of Gabriel Tarde, and Pierre Changeux can be inscribed in this genealogy. I will explain in my talk why this notion of the subconscious remains interesting.

Third Metamorphosis: Overmimesis

NL. After passing through the mimetic camel, the (anti-)mimetic lion, and having addressed questions of gender, affective life and style, the spirit is ready for the third and last metamorphosis. In a circular movement, this last transformation brings us back to the plastic and mimetic sphere of becoming that has been driving us all along—albeit with a difference. The spirit, in fact, turns into a figure of pure affirmation, play and innocence that can create new values: as Nietzsche puts it, "innocence the child is and forgetting, a beginning anew, a play, a self-propelling weel, a first movement, a sacred Yea-saying" (2005, 24). An embodiment of the innocence of becoming, the child is both a plastic and a mimetic creature. Even at the neurological level, it is in childhood that both brain plasticity and the mimetic faculty are at its highest. Could it be that the much-misunderstood *Übermensch* is given power, or will to power, by the over-mimetic and over-plastic properties of childhood? That the will to power is entangled with plastic and mimetic powers? Interestingly, the child, *das Kind*, as Nietzsche understands it, is a figure of metamorphosis par excellence that goes beyond male and female binaries, is open to affirmative transformations oriented toward the future, and operates more as a "bridge" or a "wheel" than a stable point of arrival.

Now, to come back to the future-oriented question of AI with which we started, I find it interesting that in recent years the Nietzschean figure of the Overhuman, has been read as a prefiguration of posthumanism and transhumanism as well. While I seriously doubt Nietzsche would have been invested in transhumanist dreams of immortality in imaginary technological *Hinterwelten*, he would probably have taken the posthuman problematic of AI as seriously as you do. Since at least *Metamorphoses of Intelligence*, you have been addressing AI simulations that challenge the distinction between the human brain and artificial intelligence you had set up in *What Shall We Do with Our Brain?* Synaptic chips now have the power to imitate or simulate the human brain in ways that are not only passive and mechanical but productive and plastically creative and are contributing to the current revolution in AI. I'm thinking of generative AI created by OpenAI like ChatGPT that can write poetry, answer questions and even simulate falling in love, apparently... It's interesting we both found Spike Jonze's film *Her* inspiring to think about this mimetic, or as I call it, hypermimetic revolution in this respect.

Here is my question: The logical and therapeutic advantages of the recent leap forward in AI are very promising indeed, especially when it comes to the developments of cures for neurodegenerative disorders or reducing experiments on animals, for instance. At the same time, in a mirroring inversion of perspectives, AI simulations also cast a long pathological shadow, particularly the power of simulations to affect and infect the hypermimetic brain of homo mimeticus 2.0 with disinformation, conspiracies and other contagious pathologies that can dispossess the ego along the lines dramatized by *Her*. Without falling into the trap of technophobia, I worry that posthumans, all-too-human subjects, have made much technological progress on AI simulations, but still have a long way to go to offer diagnostic evaluations simultaneously attentive to both the therapeutic and pathological effects of the metamorphoses of mimesis. Since you stressed the productive or patho-*logical* side of AI, could you comment on its dangerous, pathological side?

CM: I think the pathological side of technology comes from capitalism and from the ways these new technologies are used to normalize, to flatten and reduce all kinds of creativity, intelligence and singularity. Technology per se is neither good nor bad; what is dangerous is the use that is made of it. Speakers from Finland at the conference spoke about how neuroliberality was becoming a discipline taught in Finnish universities, for example, and there are numerous ways in which neuroliberalism puts technology to use to develop pathologies of subjectivation. I hope we can resist the way technology is becoming neuroliberal and neurocapitalist, because the positive aspects are numerous.

A friend of mine who is very involved in the development of AI refuses to call it "artificial intelligence" and calls it rather "artificial imagination." He told me that AI systems are working in concert with humans. It's similar to mirror neurons: in themselves they have no power; their power comes from what you do with them. For example, ChatGPT is often used like Google; people ask, "please remind me of this or that." But it's not the way it functions. ChatGPT is a creative tool, so I can ask it to write something, for example, in Malabou's style, it will give you an answer; and then you can correct it and give it more specific directions, like "I'd like it in a romantic style"; and then gradually you start a dialogue, and you create something. So, I can only hope that this creative dimension of technology, which relies on interactions, will have breathing room and it won't only be used, for example, to generate bad-quality translations, or create bad scripts or books. In the end, it really depends on the use.

NL: Yes, like all *pharmaka,* AI simulations can be put to pathological and patho-*logical* uses and require new diagnostic evaluations. Given the sedimented layers of mimesis that drive the plastic metamorphoses of the spirit in its evolutionary development from the camel to the lion to the child, I recognize the logical and creative potential of AI for the future—if not for all, at least for the free, playful spirits that went through the different metamorphoses of the spirit Nietzsche outlines. On the other side, for the relational, mirroring and emotional pathos rooted in the evolutionary biology of a herd animal living increasingly digitized lives, and often deprived of the heavy load of education and the solid philological training Nietzsche was implicitly alluding to in his confessional parable, the dangers might also be high. AI simulations can generate conspiracy theories that render humans and posthumans alike very vulnerable to all kinds of manipulations that operate subliminally on the mimetic unconscious generating phantom egos that are not mere copies or reproductions of other egos but are dispossessed by subliminal forms of passive imitation constitutive of the *vita mimetica.*

To close the circle and return to the point with which we started, namely your recent turn to mimesis to account for the innovative power of AI simulations, here is my last question. You recently wrote that "we lack an updated notion of mimesis that would adequately characterize the imitating powers of artificial epigenetic systems" and you propose the concept of "epigenetic mimesis" (Malabou 2023, 185) as a step in this direction. In line with the mimetic turn you also stressed the need to go beyond definitions of mimesis as a realistic copy of nature, for synaptic chips do not simply copy the brain—though a productive mimesis seems to be at play. Do you see continuities between "epigenetic mimesis" and the Kantian distinction between passive mimesis and creative mimesis, *nachmachen* and *nachahmen,* and the Janus-faced sides of the patho(-)logies of mimesis we have been discussing via the three metamorphoses of the spirit? And why do you think a mimetic turn, or re-turn, remains important for the present and future?

CM: When I wrote on epigenetic mimesis via Kant I started from the dominant notion of art imitating nature, but in the creative sense. And the goal of that for Kant is that nature acquires something like a self through art—nature mirroring itself through art. It's not a passive imitation, which Kant also condemned. Mimesis is a way for nature to acquire something like a self, as if nature was able to reflect on itself. And my question was: could we apply the same type of reflection to technology. Could we say that a certain use of technology might be able to give technology the possibility of a self? That is, technology mirroring itself, as if an AI was able in the end to have something like a self, to self-reflect.

So yes, the genealogy we traced via Nietzsche's account of metamorphoses could be usefully aligned with this productive notion of mimesis as well. As you know, Nietzsche has a very strong critique of the notion of the subject. At the same time, he thinks that creativity has to incarnate itself in forms like *Zarathustra*. These incarnations are not subjects; they are more like theatrical actors, and I think they proceed from the same logic as the one I was describing: imitation in a creative sense is a way to confer a self to something or someone that is not a subject but is an actor or mimos, as you remind us, that at the same time incarnates something. So yes, I think this embodied, emotional and creative rethinking of mimesis is very important.

Notes

1. Originally titled "Plastic Mimesis / Mimetic Plasticity," this oral dialogue concluded the first day of the "Metamorphoses of Mimesis: Plasticity, Subjectivity and Transformation with Catherine Malabou" conference organized by the Gendered Mimesis project at KU Leuven on February 23–24, 2023. It has been revised and expanded for the present written version.
2. See Lawtoo 2022, 129–156. A version of this chapter arguing for the shared genealogy of plasticity and mimesis in its double powers to receive/give form appeared in *MLN* 132.5 (2017).
3. See Malabou 2021; 2022. See also *MLN* 137.4 (2022) for a dialogue with Malabou on "L'avenir de la mimèsis" that explicitly furthers mimetic studies and its dialogic tradition.
4. For dialogues on imitation including disciplines as diverse as literary theory (J. Hillis Miller), philosophy (Jean-Luc Nancy), sociology (Edgar Morin), posthuman studies (Katherine Hayles), feminist philosophy (Adriana Cavarero), neuroscience (Vittorio Gallese) and gender studies (Judith Butler), among others, see HOM Videos, https://www.youtube.com/@homvideosercprojecthomomim971.
5. See Lawtoo 2020.
6. For a special issue on gendered mimesis and Cavarero see the essays collected in Lawtoo and Verkek 2023; for a dialogue with Butler on "Troubling Mimesis" see https://www.youtube.com/watch?v=u38wLSRrg1Q&t=499s.
7. See Malabou's chapter on "Conflicting Subliminalities" in this volume.

Bibliography

Ellenberger, Henry (1970). *The Discovery of the Unconscious: The History and Evolution of Dynamic Psychiatry*. New York: Basic Books.

Lawtoo, Nidesh (2020). "'This Is No Simulation!': Hypermimesis from *Being John Malkovich* to *Her*." *Quarterly Review of Film and Television* 37.2, 116–144.

Lawtoo, Nidesh, and Willow Verkerk (eds.) (2023). *Mimetic Inclinations with Adriana Cavarero*. *Critical Horizons* 24.2.

Malabou, Catherine (2011). *Changing Difference: The Feminine and the Question of Philosophy*, trans. Carolyn Shread. Cambridge: Polity.

Malabou, Catherine (2017). *Métamorphoses de l'intelligence: Que faire de leur cerveau bleu?* Paris: Presses Universitaires de France.

Malabou, Catherine (2022). *Morphing Intelligence: From IQ Measurement to Artificial Brains*, trans. Carolyn Schread. New York: Columbia University Press.

Malabou, Catherine (2023). "Epigenetic Mimesis: Natural Brains and Synaptic Chips," in *Life in the Posthuman Condition: Critical Responses to the Anthropocene*, eds. S. E. Wilmer and Audronė Žukauskaitė. Edinburgh: Edinburgh University Press, 280–288.

Nietzsche, Friedrich (2005). *Thus Spoke Zarathustra*, trans. Graham Parkes. Oxford: Oxford University Press.

Tarde, Gabriel (2011). *Les Lois de l'imitation*. Paris: Seuil.

NOTES ON CONTRIBUTORS

Catherine Malabou is Professor of Philosophy in the departments of Comparative Literature and European Languages and Studies at UC Irvine. Her last books include *Before Tomorrow: Epigenesis and Rationality* (Cambridge: Polity Press, 2016), *Morphing Intelligence, From IQ to IA*, (New York: Columbia University Press, 2018), *Pleasure Erased, The Clitoris Unthought* (Cambridge: Polity Press, 2022), *Stop Thief! Anarchism and Philosophy* (Cambridge: Polity Press, 2024), and *There Was No Revolution*, forthcoming with Polity Press, 2026.

Nidesh Lawtoo is Professor of Modern European Literature and Culture at Leiden University and PI of the *Homo Mimeticus* project. Located at the juncture of philosophy, literature, and political theory his work opens up the field of mimetic studies via *The Phantom of the Ego* (2013), *Conrad's Shadow* (2016, Adam Gillon Award), *(New) Fascism* (2019), *Homo Mimeticus* (2022), and a diptych on *Violence and the Unconscious* (2023). He recently edited *Mimetic Posthumanism* (2024) and is currently co-editing a mini-series on *Homo Mimeticus* for Leuven University Press.

Willow Verkerk is Lecturer in Continental Philosophy and Social Philosophy at the University of British Columbia. Her research has been published in academic journals such as *Philosophy and Literature*, *Nietzsche-Studien*, *Symposium*, *Graduate Faculty Philosophy Journal* and *Critical Horizons* as well as in *Rethinking Political Thinkers* (Oxford University Press, 2023). She is the author of *Nietzsche and Friendship* (Bloomsbury, 2019).

Tom Boland is Senior Lecturer in Sociology at University College Cork. His main areas of research are in Social Theory, particularly the sociology of critique and studies of the welfare state and unemployment. He is the author of *The Spectacle of Critique* (2019), and, with Ray Griffin, *The Sociology of Unemployment* (2015) and *The Reformation of Welfare* (2021). He is an interdisciplinary scholar, with interests in anthropology, cultural studies, literature, philosophy and politics.

Ida Djursaa is Lecturer in Continental Philosophy at Newcastle University, UK. Her research investigates the social and political structuring of bodily existence and experience from the perspectives of classical and critical phenomenology, new materialisms, and feminist philosophy. She is particularly interested in questions of sensibility, intercorporeality, and desire in and beyond the works of Husserl, Levinas and Merleau-Ponty. Her work has appeared most recently in *Hypatia: A Journal of Feminist Philosophy* (2025), under the title: "Having Been Born: Sensibility and Intercorporeality beyond Levinas's *Otherwise than Being*."

Alice Iacobone is Postdoctoral Researcher at Universität St. Gallen. She received her PhD in Philosophy from the University of Eastern Piedmont, with a dissertation on plasticity and sculpture. Her research unfolds at the intersection between Continental Philosophy, Art History and the Environmental Humanities, and she is currently working on a project on the speculative aesthetics and material politics of plastics. She is the editor of the journal issue "Plasticity. Lives and Forms of an Aesthetic Concept" (*Philosophy Kitchen*, 2025) and the author of a monograph on the aesthetics and poetics of Giuseppe Penone (Quodlibet, 2023).

Ian James is a Fellow of King's College and Professor of Modern French Philosophy and Literature in the Faculty of Modern and Medieval Languages and Linguistics at the University of Cambridge. He is the author of *Pierre Klossowski: The Persistence of a Name* (Oxford: Legenda, 2000), *The Fragmentary Demand: An Introduction to the Philosophy of Jean-Luc Nancy* (Stanford: Stanford University Press, 2006), *Paul Virilio* (London: Routledge, 2007), *The New French Philosophy* (Cambridge: Polity, 2012), *The Technique of Thought: Nancy, Laruelle, Malabou and Stiegler after Naturalism* (Minneapolis: Minnesota University Press, 2019), and *Rethinking Literary Naturalism: Proust and Quignard After Life* (Liverpool: Liverpool University Press, 2025).

Alex Obrigewitsch received his PhD in Philosophy from the University of Sussex in 2024, with a thesis on rethinking the relation between philosophy and literature with Maurice Blanchot and Philippe Lacoue-Labarthe. His most recent publications include "Intimations of a Lyricism *sans* Subject: On the Poetics of Philippe Lacoue-Labarthe" in the *Croatian Journal of Philosophy* 24.70 (2024), as well as a forthcoming article in the special issue of the *Oxford Literary Review* (2025) devoted to Blanchot and ecological thought, and a chapter in the forthcoming *Palgrave Handbook for Phenomenology and Literature* (2026).

Mathijs Peters is Assistant Professor at the Leiden University Center for the Arts in Society. His research focuses on the interactions between philosophy and (popular) culture. He published on the moral thinking of Theodor W. Adorno and Arthur Schopenhauer (*Schopenhauer and Adorno on Bodily Suffering: A Comparative Analysis*, 2014), the critical dimensions of popular music (*Popular Music, Critique and Manic Street Preachers*, 2020) and the resonance theory of Hartmut Rosa (*Exploring Hartmut Rosa's Concept of Resonance*, together with Bareez Majid, 2022). His current research concerns self-constitution and the genre of autography (autobiographical comics and graphic novels).

Kristian Schaeferling is a PhD candidate in Philosophy at the University of Dundee and Goethe-Universität Frankfurt. His thesis (working title: *The Concept of the Real Subject in Post-Hegelian Discourse*) examines theoretical links between German Idealist conceptions of subjectivity and theorems of Freudian and Lacanian psychoanalysis, underlying contemporary, political-philosophical rereadings of Hegel. Recent articles include: "Meillassoux's Reinterpretation of Kant's *Transcendental Dialectic*", in: *Open Philosophy*, 5,1, 2022; and "Kritik des Rechtssubjekts als absolutes Verhältnis des Tragischen zum Komischen: Zum Zusammenhang von Staat, Geschichte und Religion bei Rosenzweig und Hegel", in: *Utopie einer neuen normativen Ordnung*. Stuttgart, 2025.

Gabriel Wartinger holds PhDs from University College London and the European Graduate School. His research, situated at the critical juncture of philosophy and political thought, has appeared or is forthcoming in *Parrhesia* and *Philosophy Today*, alongside contributions to a range of lesser-known venues. Wartinger's work interrogates post-phenomenological thought, political emergence, and the ontological structures of relationality, engaging with thinkers such as Schmitt, Heidegger, Benjamin, Bataille, Derrida, Nancy, and Malabou.

Tyler M. Williams is Associate Professor of English, Humanities, and Philosophy at Midwestern State University. He is editor of Catherine Malabou's *Plasticity: The Promise of Explosion* (Edinburgh University Press, 2022). He is also co-editor and co-translator of a collection of Malabou's early writings entitled *Formations* (Fordham University Press, forthcoming). His other recent work has appeared in such journals as *philoSOPHIA, CR: The New Centennial Review, College Literature* and *Política Común*.

Sergey Zenkin is Professor of Literature and Intellectual History at two Russian universities, in Moscow and Saint Petersburg, a member of Academia Europaea. His field of research includes literary theory, history of twentieth-century theoretical ideas, history of French literature. He published, in Russia and France, books and articles on French Romanticism, on Structuralism and Russian Formalism in literature, on modern theories of the sacred, on the visual representations functioning in literary and cinematographic narratives. He is also a Russian translator of French philosophy and literary theory (Bataille, Caillois, Barthes, Deleuze et Guattari, Baudrillard, and others).

www.ingramcontent.com/pod-product-compliance
Lightning Source LLC
Chambersburg PA
CBHW061706300426
44115CB00014B/2582